The First Christian Theol

The Great Theologians

A comprehensive series devoted to highlighting the major theologians of different periods. Each theologian is presented by a world-renowned scholar.

Published

The Modern Theologians
An Introduction to Christian Theology in the Twentieth Century
David Ford

The Medieval Theologians
An Introduction to Theology in the Medieval Period
G. R. Evans

The Reformation Theologians
An Introduction to Theology in the Early Modern Period
Carter Lindberg

The First Christian Theologians
An Introduction to Theology in the Early Church
G. R. Evans

Forthcoming

The Pietist Theologians
Carter Lindberg

The First Christian Theologians

An Introduction to Theology in the Early Church

Edited by

G. R. Evans

Blackwell
Publishing

BLACKWELL PUBLISHING
350 Main Street, Malden, MA 02148-5020, USA
9600 Garsington Road, Oxford OX4 2DQ, UK
550 Swanston Street, Carlton, Victoria 3053, Australia

First published 2004 by Blackwell Publishing Ltd

4   2007

Library of Congress Cataloging-in-Publication Data

The first Christian theologians : an introduction to theology in the early
church / edited by G. R. Evans.
      p. cm. — (The great theologians)
Includes bibliographical references and index.
      ISBN 0-631-23188-9 (alk. paper) — ISBN 0-631-23187-0 (pbk. : alk. paper)
      1. Theology—History—Early church, ca. 30–600. 2. Theology, Doctrinal—
History—Early church, ca. 30–600 3. Fathers of the church. I. Evans, G. R.
(Gillian Rosemary) II. Series.

BT25.F57 2004
230'.11—dc22

2003022141

ISBN-13: 978-0-631-23188-2 (alk. paper) — ISBN-13: 978-0-631-23187-5 (pbk. : alk. paper)

A catalogue record for this title is available from the British Library.

Set in 10/12.5 pt Galliard
by Graphicraft Ltd, Hong Kong
Printed and bound in India
by Gopsons Papers Ltd, Noida

For further information on
Blackwell Publishing, visit our website:
www.blackwellpublishing.com

Contents

Preface

Christianity began with a person, known to history as Jesus Christ. His teaching and example, his death by crucifixion, his disciples' confidence that he had been resurrected, and their perseverance in "spreading the Gospel" he had taught them, had an impact so immense that it gave birth to a "world religion" which has survived two thousand years. If his followers were right in believing that Jesus was the Son of God, that is scarcely surprising. This volume cannot address itself to that great question. It is concerned more modestly with the processes by which Christianity survived the end of Jesus' life on earth, formed itself into a coherent body of beliefs, and spread throughout the ancient world. It seeks to tell a story remarkable enough in itself and with incalculable long-term consequences for the history of the world.

The first Christians were not consciously theologians. They were disciples, following Jesus. Some of them became apostles, missionaries. The "faith" they were preaching was first and foremost an act of trust and commitment to a person. Nevertheless, making that act of faith soon came to involve adherence to a set of propositions. Those who came to be baptized affirmed their faith in words. For this purpose a baptismal "creed" was used, which was probably the ancestor of what we now know as the Apostles' Creed. This was on the face of it a short and simple list of points, but it did not long remain a simple matter to know what it meant, for people began to ask questions. That can already be seen to be happening in the Acts of the Apostles, and throughout the Epistles of the New Testament.

The earliest of our authors are as conscious as the later ones that they are working within a body of thought and belief which has been handed to them, and that they in their turn are handing it on. Continuity in, and faithfulness to, "tradition" in this literal sense of "handing on" is a concern of all the early councils of the Church. Again and again the bishops meeting express their unanimous agreement with the decrees of previous councils.

It is from the "questions" that a written Christian theology evolved. Every Christian writer in these pages was addressing matters which threatened to become controversial, or required clarification so that there might be no stumbling blocks to the faithful. The individual "journey of the soul to God" might or might not include engagement with that debate, for we do not hear from the vast majority of ordinary Christians of these early centuries. But those we do hear from were busily arguing, and it is their contribution which forms the matter for this book.

This first volume in a series about the Christian theologians has to negotiate a passage through the most crucial period of this tentative early development of Christian thought. What is "early Christian"? What authors among the vast throng who wrote on themes of concern to Christians is it appropriate to include in a book on "early Christian theologians"?

The notion that there could be a body of especially weighty Christian writing lay behind the Church's gradual acceptance and "approval" of the books which came to make up the Bible. The use of the label "patristic" to denote other writings of the early Christian centuries came much later. The word "Fathers" was used at first almost exclusively to refer to a quite different body of authoritative figures, the patriarchs of the Old Testament. Then it came to be used for bishops who met in council. Thus the formula of the council of Chalcedon in 451 was said to be "in agreement with the Holy Fathers." Only slowly did "Father" come to seem an appropriate term for the early author who may or may not be a bishop, but whose writings are recognized to constitute an important contribution to Christian understanding. Augustine (d. 430) speaks of Jerome (d. 420) as a "father" in this sense.

Jerome himself was instrumental in encouraging the habit of thinking of certain writers as the "fathers." He wrote a book "On Famous Men" (*De viris illustribus*), listing Christian authors who could be trusted and respected. Gennadius of Marseilles continued Jerome's work late in the fifth century, adding about a hundred names, mainly writers of the fifth century, and drawn from both the East and the West. Gelasius I, Pope from 492 to 496, issued a *decretum* "On books to be received and books which should not be received." He begins with the books of the Old and New Testaments "on which the catholic Church was founded" (*fundata est*) by the grace of God. There is a list of those whose writings are approved or merely not prohibited. There is a list of those writings which should be avoided because they contain teachings which are heretical. This is an extensive catalogue, including, once more, Eastern as well as Western writers. The papal approval of these names by Gelasius lent the names on the list added authority. A series of writers became "Fathers" in this way. The last of the line in the West was perhaps Bede; the chronological boundary is not so easy to draw in the East, and wherever we attempt to set the dividing line it will include authors who are covered not in this volume but in the next in the series, *The Medieval Theologians*.[1] There are to be found Augustine of Hippo, Gregory the Great, and Bede himself.

This is a book about the earliest individual Christian theologians and those who entered into dialogue with them. It is also about the complexity of the process by which a "Christian theology" came into existence. The reader will notice that several names have a place in more than one context. The formation of the system of thought which was to give articulation to the "faith in a person" with which it all began, proved to be the work of centuries and of many, many minds. It became bound into the intellectual, social, and political life of the age, and eventually decisively formed it. Our authors were taking part in the great European and Middle Eastern colloquy which ultimately made the ancient world into the modern world.

GRE

Note

1   *The Medieval Theologians*, ed. G. R. Evans (Blackwell, 2001).

Notes on Contributors

G. R. Evans is Professor of Medieval Theology and Intellectual History at the University of Cambridge. She is the author of numerous books in the fields of patristic, medieval, and ecumenical history and theology, including *Augustine on Evil* (1983), *Anselm* (1989), *Problems of Authority in the Reformation Debates* (1992), *The Church and the Churches* (1994), *Law and Theology in the Middle Ages* (2002), and *Philosophy and Theology in the Middle Ages* (repr. 2003). Published by Blackwell, G. R. Evans is also the author of *A Brief History of Heresy* (2003), and the editor of *The Medieval Theologians* (2001) and *The First Christian Theologians* (2004).

Paula Fredriksen is the William Goodwin Aurelio Professor of Scripture in the Department of Religion, Boston University. Educated at Oxford University in theology (1974) and at Princeton University in ancient Mediterranean religions (1979), she has published *Augustine on Romans* (1982), *From Jesus to Christ* (1988; 2000), *Jesus of Nazareth, King of the Jews* (1999), and, together with Professor Adele Reinhartz, *Jesus, Judaism, and Christian Anti-Judaism: Reading the New Testament after the Holocaust* (2002). Her most recent study, *Augustine and the Jews*, will be published in 2004.

Clarence Gallagher, SJ was lecturer in canon law at Heythrop College, London and at the Gregorian University, Rome, subsequently Dean of the Canon Law Faculty, and then Rector of the Pontifical Oriental Institute, Rome. He is at present tutor in canon law at Campion Hall, Oxford University and lecturer in canon law in London. His publications include *Canon Law and the Christian Community: The Role of Law in the Church According to the* Summa Aurea *of Cardinal Hostiensis* (1978), and *Church Law and Church Order in Rome and Byzantium: A Comparative Study* (2002), as well as a series of articles on canon law and ecclesiology.

Stuart G. Hall graduated in Classics and Theology at Oxford and entered the priesthood in the Church of England. Academic service in Birmingham and Nottingham culminated in the Chair of Ecclesiastical History at King's College London from 1978 to 1990. After retirement he served as priest in the Scottish Episcopal Church from 1990 to 1998 and is an Honorary Professor of Divinity in the University of St. Andrews. Among his publications are an edition of *Melito of Sardis* (1979), and *Doctrine and Practice in the Early Church* (1991).

Judith Lieu is Professor of New Testament Studies at King's College London. She has also previously taught at Macquarrie University, Sydney. She was educated at the Universities of Durham, Oxford, and Birmingham. Her publications include *The Second and Third Epistles of John* (1986), *The Theology of the Johannine Epistles* (1991), *Image and Reality: The Jews in the World of the Christians in the 2nd Century* (1996), and *Neither Jew nor Greek: Constructing Early Christianity* (2002).

Morwenna Ludlow is the A. G. Leventis Departmental Lecturer in Patristics at Oxford University. She has a special interest in Gregory of Nyssa and his interpretation by later theologians and has also written on patristic and modern eschatology.

Eric Osborn is Honorary Professor at La Trobe University and Professorial Fellow at the University of Melbourne. He was educated at Melbourne and Cambridge (Ph.D. 1954, D.D. 1977); he has taught at Queen's College, University of Melbourne (1958–87) and briefly at the universities of Strasbourg, Göttingen, and Rome and at Pittsburgh Theological Seminary. His books include *Ethical Patterns in Early Christian Thought* (1976), *The Beginning of Christian Philosophy* (1981), *The Emergence of Christian Theology* (1993), *Tertullian: First Theologian of the West* (1997), and *Irenaeus of Lyons* (2001). Some of these have been translated into French or German. His chief interest is the interaction of biblical and philosophical ideas in early Christian thought.

Boniface Ramsey received his doctorate in theology at the Institut Catholique, Paris. Most recently he was a full professor at Seton Hall University, New Jersey. He is the editor of the series *The Works of Saint Augustine: A Translation for the 21st Century*, for which he is also translating a volume. Among his publications are *Beginning to Read the Fathers* (1985), as well as annotated translations of the sermons of Maximus of Turin, *The Institutes* and *The Conferences* of John Cassian, and a selection of works of Ambrose of Milan.

John M. Rist is Professor Emeritus of Classics and Philosophy at the University of Toronto and currently Visiting Professor at the Institutum Patristicum Augustinianum, Rome. He was educated at Trinity College Cambridge and was Regius Professor of Classics in Aberdeen from 1980 to 1983 and Visiting Professor at the Hebrew University of Jerusalem in 1995. His publications (mostly on ancient philosophy, patristics, and ethics) include *Eros and Psyche* (1964), *Plotinus: The Road to Reality* (1967), *Human Value* (1982), *The Mind of Aristotle* (1989), *Augustine: Ancient Thought Baptized* (1994), and *Real Ethics* (2001).

John W. Rogerson is Emeritus Professor of Biblical Studies, University of Sheffield. He studied in Manchester, Oxford, and Jerusalem before teaching in Durham, and in Sheffield where he was Head of Department from 1979 to 1995. He has published extensively in the fields of history and theory of biblical interpretation, and the history, geography, sociology, and ethics of the Old Testament. His latest publications include *An Introduction to the Bible* and *Chronicle of the Old Testament Kings* (both 1999) and *The Oxford Illustrated History of the Bible* (edited, 2001).

David T. Runia is Master of Queen's College, University of Melbourne. He studied in Melbourne and Amsterdam, obtaining his doctorate in 1983 with his study *Philo of Alexandria and the* Timaeus *of Plato* (1986). Before returning to Australia he was Professor of Ancient and Medieval Philosophy at the University of Leiden. He has published extensively on both Philo of Alexandria and ancient philosophy. Recent publications are *Philo in Early Christian Thought* (1993), *Aëtiana: The Method and Intellectual Context of a Doxographer* (1997, together with J. Mansfeld), and *Philo of Alexandria On the Creation of the Cosmos According to Moses: Translation and Commentary* (2001).

David G. K. Taylor is University Lecturer in Aramaic and Syriac at the Oriental Institute, University of Oxford. Recent publications include *The Syriac Versions of the De Spiritu Sancto by Basil of Caesarea* (1999) and, with S. P. Brock, *The Hidden Pearl: The Syrian Orthodox Church and its Ancient Aramaic Heritage* (2001). He is currently editing the great sixth-century Psalm Commentary of Daniel of Salah, the earliest and largest commentary on the psalter to be produced in Syriac.

Janet P. Williams is Lecturer in Humanities at Cirencester College, and has lectured in Theology, Religious Studies, and Philosophy at King Alfred's College, Winchester, Oxford Brookes University, and Temple University, Tokyo. She has previously published *Denying Divinity* (2000) and a range of articles on patristic and apophatic theology.

Rowan Williams, Archbishop of Canterbury, was Lady Margaret Professor of Theology at Oxford University until he was enthroned as Bishop of Monmouth in 1992, Archbishop of Wales in 2000 and, most recently, Archbishop of Canterbury in 2003. Dr. Williams has written a number of books on the history of theology and spirituality and published collections of articles and sermons – as well as two books of poetry. He has been involved in various commissions on theology and theological education. He was a member of the Church Schools Review Group led by Lord Dearing and chaired the group that produced the report *Wales: A Moral Society?*

Frances Young has been the Edward Cadbury Professor of Theology in the University of Birmingham since 1986, having taught there since 1971. She was educated at Bedford College, University of London, where she read Classics, and then read Theology at the University of Cambridge, where she also obtained her doctorate. Her publications include *From Nicaea to Chalcedon* (1991), *The Art of Performance* (1990, published in the USA as *Virtuoso Theology*), *The Making of the Creeds* (1991), and *Biblical Exegesis and the Formation of Christian Culture* (1997).

Abbreviations

1 Apol.	*Justin Martyr, First apology*
2 Apol.	*Justin Martyr, Second apology*
ACW	Ancient Christian Writers
An.	Tertullian, *On the soul* (*De anima*)
ANCL	Ante-Nicene Christian Library
Ant. Jud.	*Antiquitates Judaicae*
Ap.	Tertullian, *Apology* (*Apologeticum*)
Bapt.	Tertullian, *On baptism* (*De baptismo*)
Carn.	Tertullian, *On the flesh of Christ* (*De carne Christi*)
CCCM	*Corpus Christianorum Continuatio Medievalis*
CCSL	*Corpus Christianorum Series Latina*
C. Diat.	*Commentary on the Diatessaron*: L. Leloir, *Saint Ephrem: Commentaire de l'Evangile Concordant* (Dublin, 1963)
Comm. in Mt. ser.	*Commentariorum in Mattheum series*
CQ	*Classical Quarterly*
CRINT	*Compendia rerum Iudaicarum ad Novum Testamentum*
CSCO	[Syr.] *Corpus Scriptorum Christianorum Orientalium*
CSEL	*Corpus Scriptorum Ecclesiasticorum Latinorum*
CSSL	*Corpus Scriptorum Series Latina*
CT	*Codex Theodosianus*, ed. T. Mommsen and P. M. Meyer (Berlin, 1954)
Dem.	*Irenaeus, The Demonstration of the Apostolic Preaching*
Dial.	*Justin Martyr, Dialogue with Trypho*
ET	English translation
GCS	*Die griechischen christlichen Schriftsteller der ersten drei Jahrhunderte* (Leipzig and Berlin, 1897–1941)
Haer.	Irenaeus, *Against Heresies*
Hist. ecc.	*Eusebius, The History of the Church*, trans. G. A. Williamson, rev. and ed. with a new intro. by Andrew Louth (London, 1989)

Iei.	Tertullian, *On fasting (De ieiunio)*
JJS	*Journal of Jewish Studies*
LCL	Loeb Classical Library
LM	*Le Muséon*
Marc.	Tertullian, *Against Marcion (Adversus Marcionem)*
Mart.	*Justin Martyr, Martyrdom of Justin*
Mon.	Tertullian, *On sole marriage (De monogamia)*
NPNF	Nicene and Post-Nicene Fathers
OCA	*Orientalia Christiana Analecta*
OCP	*Orientalia Christiana Periodica*
OLA	*Orientalia Lovaniensia Analecta*
Orat.	Tertullian, *On prayer (De oratione)*
Paed.	*Clement of Alexandria, Instructor (Paedagogus)*
Pall.	Tertullian, *On the philosopher's cloak (De pallio)*
Pat.	Tertullian, *On patience (De patientia)*
PG	*Patrologia Graeca*
PL	*Patrologia Latina*
Praescr.	Tertullian, *On prescription of heretics (De praescriptione haereticorum)*
Prax.	Tertullian, *Against Praxeas (Adversus Praxean)*
Prot.	*Clement of Alexandria, Exhortation to the Greeks (Protrepticus)*
Res.	Tertullian, *On the resurrection (De resurrectione)*
Str.	*Clement of Alexandria, Miscellanies (Stromateis)*
Test.	Tertullian, *On the testimony of the soul (De testimonio animae)*
Ux.	Tertullian, *To his wife (Ad uxorem)*
ZDMG	*Zeitschrift der deutschen morgenländischen Gesellschaft*

Introduction

G. R. Evans

Jesus sent his disciples out to preach the Gospel and proclaim the Kingdom of God (Luke 9:60). The importance and urgency of its sense of mission has been a defining feature of the Christian community from the beginning, and much of this book is concerned with what happened when the mission reached the articulate, the argumentative, the writers and opinion-formers, as they formed and articulated the faith in a detail not yet thought through by the first generations.

Many of the very first Christians were the poor, or even slaves. The first Christians were intent on something quite practical, and simple enough in its essence for unlettered men and women to describe successfully to other unlettered men and women. There were social and intellectual barriers to be overcome before the better-off and better-educated could be won over. So the success of Christian "mission" is not easy to evaluate in any but sociological and political and economic terms, except through the writings of exceptional individuals who left a record of their intellectual and spiritual struggles in written accounts.

They are the people we hear from. There is a question which should not be sidestepped about the relation of what they had to say to the faith of the ordinary majority of Christians. It is often alleged that after the emperor Constantine became a Christian in the early fourth century, and with him the Roman Empire itself, there was a sudden rise in Church membership. Jerome (d. 420) gives examples of pagans of recent times who have turned to Christ: "Now the Egyptian Serapis is made a Christian." "We receive crowds of monks every day from India, Persia, Ethiopia." "Huns learn the Psalter and the icy regions of Scythia burn with the heat of faith."[1] We cannot be sure how many of these additional Christians had experienced a real alteration of attitude and commitment. The mission which succeeds in achieving the support and "conversion" of political leaders can of course win numerous "converts" in whom there has not necessarily been any real change of heart (*metanoia*), or any understanding in depth of the beliefs to which they "turn." Gregory the Great sent Augustine of Canterbury on the mission to the Anglo-Saxons from Rome in 597. Bede's *Ecclesiastical History*[2] makes plain the relatively limited character of the inward change involved as the rulers of the day debated whether they were Roman or Celtic Christians.

We can really know very little in detail of what the majority of these individuals, now making up the body of "official" or "open" Christians, understood of the particulars of their new faith. Yet a *consensus fidelium* was forming, a "general acceptance of points of belief by the faithful as a community." In every age that has balanced and tested the "official" pronouncements of leaders of the Church and the views expressed by those who wrote as individuals, like most of those in these pages. The evolution of this pattern of checks and balances was one of the most important achievements of the centuries with which this book is concerned.

By the end of the period covered by this book something approaching a "systematic theology" had been brought into existence. It had not yet been set out in the order which was settled on during the Middle Ages and there were areas not yet touched on by active controversy which the eye of a later age would see as a gap. Nevertheless, the elements were there.

Finally, the enlargement of the conspectus of topics on which the Church had pronounced encouraged the detailed work which was eventually to lead to the creation of the systematic theology already sketched. Irenaeus, suggests Eric Osborn, was one of the first to attempt a comprehensive picture. But while Christian theology was thus in process of being brought into order, there were shifts of fashion and emphasis.

There was a need to identify and pose the questions which needed to be answered if the Christian faithful were to be kept secure in the true faith. Eric Osborn provides one map, of four areas: questions concerning God's intellectual being (divine intellect); his plan of salvation (the divine economy or operation of providence); the summing up of all things in Christ (recapitulation); the sharing of the believer in God's salvation (participation). But the scene never finally settled down, and the map had constantly to be redrawn. Pseudo-Dionysius was writing with reference to the very latest Platonisms of his own day. Irenaeus, as Eric Osborn points out, placed an emphasis on man's ascent to God. For Augustine, the greater concern is the Fall and its consequences. There continued to be gaps. Some topics of high importance in later controversies – such as justification by faith – had little if any place in the early debates and others which did – for example the doctrines of the Church and sacraments – left only the slightest of markers in the creeds, with much remaining to be debated in the medieval millennium.

There had been comprehensive discussions of the existence and nature of God; the doctrine of the Trinity had been formulated in both Greek and Latin; the doctrine of the Incarnation was particularly well-trodden ground and with it the theology of redemption and the history of salvation; the idea of the Church was well-developed, though not so well-developed as it was to become during the millennium which followed; there was a nascent theology of the sacraments,[3] particularly baptism and penance, and a eucharistic theology, though as yet untouched by the later subtleties of debate about transubstantiation, real presence, and sacrifice; there was a theology of ministry,[4] but without the themes developed in the fierce controversies of the late Middle Ages and the Reformation about sacerdotal power and whether bishops should be allowed at all; there had been a great deal of thought given to the "last things," death, judgement, resurrection, and eternity.

The first Christian centuries were an age of great intellectual sophistication, the last phase of the high culture of the ancient world. As the educated began to join in the debate with Christians, a literature emerged which made Christianity the battle-ground of controversies attracting the best minds of the day. It may be that we cannot use the term "theology" appropriately at the beginning of it all, when the fishermen were called to be "fishers of men" (Mark 1:17) and Jesus sent them out to preach the Gospel. But it was not many generations before there was, by any definition of the term, a Christian theology.

Reason and revelation

What, then, was the "theological project" of these first Christian centuries? When Rowan Williams describes *theologia* as "the study of the nature of God as the philosophers and poets had described it," he is referring to the time of Origen (c.185–254), when there was already an active engagement with contemporary philosophy. David Runia attaches a different sense to "theologian" when he calls the Jewish author Philo of Alexandria (c.20BC–AD20) "the first theologian," but he, too, emphasizes the importance of the degree to which Philo was hellenized, and writing in the categories of secular Greek thought. Paula Fredriksen and Judith Lieu see "theology" differently again, in the context of the comparison between the (Christian) system of thought and belief and the (Jewish) pattern of "social and religious activities."

Theologia, as defined by Boethius in the sixth century,[5] is essentially "speculation." It is the area of thought in which the human mind reaches beyond what it can know from sense-experience and seeks to use reasoning to explore the supernatural or divine. A large area of well-established ancient philosophical interest could be reached and explored by this method: the existence and nature of God or the gods; the origin of human beings and the way they should live their lives; the very purpose of human life. Among the topics already in play and being hotly debated, as noted by John Rist, were free will, and whether the world was created from nothing or formed from some pre-existent matter; what was the nature of the transcendental realm; and whether ethical behaviour ought to conform with rigorous and fixed principles of good conduct.

The only aspects of special concern to Christians which could not be addressed in this way were those which required the "revelation" of an account of the actual events of Christ's life in the Scriptures. The writing and acceptance by the Church of the books which make up what we now recognise as the Scriptures was a long-drawn-out business, as John Rogerson shows, and the "study of Holy Scripture" was an element in the "theological project" for the earliest Christian theologians in ways which are sometimes hard to pin down while the content and authority of the text were still being settled.

That process in itself raised huge questions: Did the Scriptures constitute a "sacred text"? Did that mean that they were divinely inspired, and, if so, was every word "dictated" by the Holy Spirit, and how? What was the role of the human authors of Scripture? Its translators, according to Jerome, the author of the Latin

Vulgate which became the standard Latin text from the late fourth century for more than a millennium, were not inspired. At least, he was sure that he himself was not. But that did not stop students of his text consistently treating it as though it had been.

Early Christian theology was much preoccupied with interpretation of this text. Early exegesis is the subject of Frances Young's chapter. In the earlier "theologians," as we shall see, there are many modes of reference to the emerging biblical text and many ways of relying on it, interpreting it, using it to illustrate a point. The Jewish tradition had its own exegetical habits, as Paula Fredriksen and Judith Lieu explain.

A number of the Christian "theologians" of the first centuries were bishops, whose duties included the teaching of the faith. They did some of their "public" theological thinking in lengthy series of sermons in which they would work their way through a book of the Bible, both "lecturing" on it, and giving pastoral guidance. Such sermons could easily last an hour or two, and the huge congregation would often applaud if it was pleased and felt edified.

One preacher could become an authority for another later homilist. To take some of the best-known examples of the end of the period covered in this book and the beginning of *The Medieval Theologians*, Ambrose's sermons on Genesis were instrumental in the conversion of Augustine of Hippo. Augustine's own sermons on the Psalms and on John in their turn influenced Gregory the Great. Gregory preached on Ezekiel and Kings. He took the book of Job as the focus of an immense series of dialogues with members of a monastic community, the *Moralia in Job*.[6]

In the chapters which follow, this duality of method, interpretation of a text and philosophically-informed reasoning, can be seen in their earliest and most experimental relationship in the work of these "first Christian theologians."

The first "orthodoxies" which saw themselves as challenged were those of the philosophers themselves. The second-century pagan philosopher Celsus was one of the first on record to mount a full-scale attack on Christian ideas. Origen wrote a wide-ranging response, in his book *Contra Celsum*. John Rist asks "why they thought [the philosophers] even needed to reply" to the teaching and writing of Christian theologians. The fact that they did, and that an adversarial debate began, is of huge importance to the history of Christian theology itself, and also, ironically, to the reshaping of the philosophers' own priorities. As John Rist points out,[7] the Middle Platonist period was a period of complex and changing synthesis of the thought of Plato, Aristotle, the Stoics, the Sceptics, the Pythagoreans. The addition of an increasingly articulate and challenging Christian apologetic to that mix affected the philosophers themselves as well as the Christian thinkers with whom this volume is principally concerned.

There is nothing like extended disputation for clarifying and hardening the positions of the combatants, and it is a nice irony that Origen himself appeared to later ages to have said some very unorthodox things in his defence of the Christian faith. John Rist makes the point in his paper in this volume that it was only as various possible positions and beliefs were defined as heresy that they were denied to the Christians faithful, who might inadvertently have held them previously without undue concern that they might not be the true faith. For example, Marcion (d. c.160) could write of the "inferior" creator of the world and the "higher" God of love. The notion of

Plotinus (c.205–70) that the Trinity is One, Mind and Soul, was untenable by an orthodox Christian after the council of Nicaea of 325. Victorinus, one of the principal sources of Latin discussion of late Greek Platonism to which Augustine of Hippo had access in his period of exploration of the contemporary world of thought, made direct use of the work of the late Platonist Porphyry (c.232–303) in his writing on the Trinity.[8]

Statements of faith were already evolving in the form of the baptismal creeds long before the issuing of the Niceno-Constantinopolitan Creed (that is, the Nicene Creed of 325, with its revision at the council of Constantinople in 381). But this kind of thing sharpened the realization that there was going to be a need to avoid any danger of Christianity becoming another philosophical element in the complex and continuously changing late antique mix. Blurring of boundaries, inculturation taken to the point where anyone could hold any view, mingling Christian and philosophical as if from an à la carte menu, could lead to uncertainty as to who was "with" and who "against" Christ (Matt. 12:30). If philosophers could define their positions, so could Christians and indeed Christians must, for much would turn on the ability of the Christian to give account of his faith in such a way that he could not be confused with a philosopher. It was very important; the salvation of the individual was at stake.

The task of spreading the Gospel thus became inseparable from the debates about what was to be borrowed from the philosophers or how far, on the contrary, the philosophers and all their opinions were to be rejected. Origen addresses this aspect of the "missionary" question at the beginning of his *Contra Celsum*. Jesus was silent in the face of his accusers (Matt. 26:59–63; Mark 14:55–61). He was confident that there was refutation enough in his life and works (Preface, para. 1). Origen is forced to wonder whether if he himself attempts to write an *apologia* for the faith he would not weaken rather than strengthen that unassailable teaching which lies open for all to see in the very life of Jesus (Preface, para. 3). On the other hand, the philosophers are plausible. The general public may easily accept their lies as truth. Origen points out that St. Paul himself saw that Greek philosophy contains reasons which are by no means negligible (Col. 2:8) (Preface, para. 5).

Many of the chapters in this book describe the struggle of early Christian authors to find a working position on aspects of the enormous problem of the relationship which was to be struck between the pagan and the Christian traditions, where the pagan tradition owned all the most respected arguments at the outset, and there was a continuing discourse between the two. The intellectual interests of educated people entered into every equation. Christians could not speak of God's plans for the universe, for example, without the cluster of familiar questions about fate, fortune, and providence coming into view. Augustine devotes several chapters of Book VIII of his *City of God* to the supernatural beings whose numinous presence as *daemones* is so troublesome to mankind. He refers the reader to Apuleius' *De deo Socratis*.[9] Jerome says that it is the way of the Stoics to make no difference between sins and to consider a wickedness and a mistake to be the same.[10] He urges vigilance about every act, every word, every thought, so that the mind is always armed against sin.[11]

These encounters, personal and intellectual, were by no means all adversarial. Sidonius Apollinaris, senior administrator turned Christian, was a conscious imitator of Cicero and Pliny in his earlier correspondence. When he became a bishop in 470, he explains, he thought it appropriate to alter his letter style (*Letter* 4.10.2).[12] He found this difficult to keep up, however, and late in life he reverted to some of his old literary habits. In the early fourth century the Spanish author Iuvencus, described by Jerome as a priest who came from an upper-class family, tried the experiment of turning the Gospels into Virgilian hexameters, which could be expected to make them more palatable to upper-class readers. Prudentius, the hymnographer and author of the much-read epic on the battle between vice and virtue (*Psychomachia*)[13] and another writer from Spain in the second half of the fourth century, offered the idea that the shrines of the martyrs could be regarded in much the same light as those of the old pagan protectors of cities.[14] His *Apotheosis* and *Hamartigenia* set forth the truth and refute false doctrine for Christian readers in a spirit of modest compromise.

As time went on, philosophically-informed reasoning tended to set the agenda for those early theologians who did not see themselves as "defending" the faith, but as exploring it, and they would make reference to Scripture, as appropriate, to test and support their views. There was, however, another category of theological activity, in which the *defense* of the faith was the leading concern. For these were also the centuries in which the exploration of the faith repeatedly threw up interpretations and understandings which, on reflection, appeared to challenge orthodoxy. The process was complicated by the fact that the very idea of "orthodoxy" had to be conceived, and then it had to be established by trial and error what was orthodox and what was not.

This was the period when the concept of heresy emerged. The term *haeresis* itself did not at first necessarily carry any pejorative sense. It could mean just a party or sect. It is there in Acts 5:17 to describe the Sadducees. In 1 Corinthians 11:19, however, it is definitely a term of opprobrium, for Paul is saying that it was fitting that there should be those who dissented so that it might be clear who the truly faithful were. Ignatius and after him other patristic authors clearly have it in a condemnatory sense.

A heretic was not simply someone who had fallen into error. That was no real fault if he turned from his error as soon as it was pointed out to him, or as soon as the Church, having given the matter some thought, determined in a council or by some official pronouncement where the truth lay. A heretic was someone who persisted in error, who made a serious "choice" (*haeresis*) in the "wrong" direction. A cluster of such "false directions" in the centuries we are concerned with concentrated chiefly on the person of Christ. There were Docetists, who held that Christ only seemed to be a man; Subordinationists, who said that he was less than the Father and had an origin which some how made him subsequent or less; Arians, Monophysites, and others, discussed in Morwenna Ludlow's chapter on the Cappadocians and elsewhere in this book. These, and the Trinitarian heresies of which they form a subset, were by far the most important heresies of our period and so intimately entangled are they with the views which gradually emerged as "orthodox" that to give them chapters to themselves would mean loss of clarity and excessive overlap.[15] A glance back at the list of topics just given in the sketch of the emergence of a "systematic theology" will show how similar the preoccupations were.

It was one thing for Christians to insist on Christian distinctiveness and to refuse to be drawn into the syncretistic patterns of the Roman world; it was quite another for them to be able to prevent others claiming to be Christian while spreading what they saw as distorted versions of the Gospel. For the Christians were not the only evangelizing sect in the late Roman Empire. Gnostic groups could be sufficiently persuasive for several early Christian authors, such as Irenaeus and Tertullian, to make active attempts to rebut their insidious teachings. As Paula Fredriksen and Judith Lieu make clear, Jewish thinkers had their own encounters with dualists and had to reach their own accommodation with this strong and pervasive "tradition." The Manichees, too, were active in spreading belief falling broadly within the same dualist tradition. Mani was born into a Christian community. He himself claimed to be an apostle of Jesus Christ called by an angel or God and preaching a divine relevation; and his followers took him to be the Paraclete Jesus had promised, the very Holy Spirit.[16] Yet Manicheeism was dualist, and therefore incompatible with orthodox Christian teaching, and it was tainted with magical practices and sorcery. Diocletian suspected the Manichees of being a positive fifth column of the Persian authorities. His edict against the Manichees of 297, addressed to the proconsul of Africa, evinces a fierce hostility. In an imperial rescript of 302, in the year before his edict encouraging the persecution of the Christians, he orders that Manichees be executed.[17] These active condemnations proceeded from the expectation that if they were not curbed, they would win converts. Conversely, as we shall see throughout this book, Christian apologists themselves were involved in all sorts of "encounters" with non-Christians or wavering Christians or apostatizing, lapsing, and returning Christians.

The Church: Faith and Order

The development of the first "self-consciousness" of the Church is a significant element in the story this book has to tell. The debates about the faith run alongside debates about "order." It was very early understood to be important that there should be one faith and one baptism, but there was considerable scope for variability in the detail of the rites each church used in worship. The difficulty lay in determining where a proper diversity of practice ended and divergence in things which really mattered began, and with it the danger of dividing the Church. The notes or marks of the Church as "one, holy, catholic, and apostolic" were all of a piece; its "unity" was quickly recognised to be of its essence. The council of Constantinople in 381, in the series of conciliar "credal staging-posts" beginning with the council of Nicaea in 325, already found it natural to speak of this "one" Church as *sancta, catholica*, and *apostolica*, and in the next generation in the West, Augustine's battle with the Donatist schismatics turned partly on his concern that they were setting themselves apart from the universal Church, the *ecclesia catholica*. Unless it had a way of making its decisions and expressing its "mind" it could not know itself to be "one."

Order is a concept of some profundity in the theology of the Church. It is far more than an institutionalized structure, and at its deepest level it includes within it the understanding that the way the Church conducts itself is an expression of the will of God, through the Holy Spirit who dwells within the Church, as its teacher and leader. The emergence of the *consensus fidelium* and its infinitely subtle interaction with the making of official approved statements exemplifies the complexity of this deeper orderliness, this "right order" (*rectus ordo*).

A settled "structure," a regular way of doing things, was, from the earliest days, often set over against "charism," the direct moving of the Holy Spirit, as though the one challenged the other. This sense of an antithesis between the two was independent of the presumption that the Church yet had any fixed institutional pattern. The perceived antithesis was between charism and order, not between charism and any particular form of order. Acts records a number of moments when the disciples spoke as the Spirit prompted them (Acts 2:4) or could not resist the Spirit (Acts 6:10). Indeed, this last example, when Stephen, full of grace and power (Acts 6:8), was doing miracles, prompted one of the first serious confrontations between the institutional order of the Jewish authorities who presided over the Temple, and the free movement of the Spirit working directly in and through individuals. Stephen was dragged before the high priest and the council, and stoned to death (Acts 7). The Spirit carried on working through individuals. The next chapter of Acts has Philip instructed by an angel to go south from Jerusalem to Gaza, and then to convert and baptize the official of the queen of Ethiopia whom he encountered (Acts 8:26–39). Chapters 10 and 11 of Acts describe the process by which the disciples, collectively, were brought to recognize and respect the right of the Gentiles to be included in their mission. By Chapter 13 the disciples were responding to the Holy Spirit's call to Barnabas and Saul to set out on special missionary work, by sending them off with the community's blessing, with fasting and prayer and the laying-on of hands for the purpose. In Chapter 15, some of the brethren were causing scandal by preaching that those who had not been circumcized could not be saved. The community responded by calling a first "council" and making a determination of the matter so that there would be a more or less official "Church position." These examples illustrate graphically enough the kind of problem which was bound to continue to arise as individuals, believing themselves to be Spirit-led, acted independently and sometimes as a consequence challenged the institutional order of the Church.

The preoccupation with the importance of unity in the faith is visible in the pronouncements of the Church's councils at which bishops met, as one by one they reaffirm the decrees of the bishops of the council before them, and all earlier councils. It is there at the heart of the Donatist controversy in the fourth century[18] and in the complexion of the Easter Controversy a couple of centuries later.[19] Once there is an expectation that a true Christian will hold the true faith, as it has been formally defined, it becomes possible to think in terms of the outlawing of certain positions as heretical and of the condemnation of those who hold them. Heresy and orthodoxy emerged by reference to one another, and not always with finality.

In both the achieving of a degree of certainty and clarity in the progressive statement and restatement of the faith and in the whole process of setting up a pastoral, sacramental, and teaching "ministry," the early Church was "doing theology," as Stuart Hall shows in his chapter. The theology of ministry was not, in these early centuries, hung about with quite the same concerns as led to controversy in later centuries. This was not a period when sacerdotalism was debated and there was outrage at the idea that the priest who celebrated the eucharist was making a sacrifice in imitation of Christ or presuming to try to supplement his sacrifice on the Cross, or when it was widely suggested that there should be no such things as bishops. The phrase *in persona Christi* (2 Cor. 2:10) is certainly found in early Christian theologians but not in such contexts of debate. These were the worries of a much later age.

There were the beginnings of rites, or liturgical order, in the earliest Christian churches. Jesus' words at the Last Supper became the words of consecration as his disciples obeyed his instructions and repeated what he had done, in his memory.[20] The imposition of hands and the invocation of the Holy Spirit too are there in the early record, as we have just seen in Acts 13. But things developed far beyond these early elements and even the original basics need not occur in the same place in the rite, or indeed, always have the same significance or the same effect. The bishop might lay his hands on the baptized in confirmation or upon the ordinand he was making a priest, but the effect was different depending on the intention.

The two sacraments which have New Testament authority were there at the heart of worship from the beginning. The early Christians practiced baptism in imitation of the example Jesus himself had set, but using a Trinitarian formula which became essential to the validity of the sacrament. The neophyte to be baptized was asked whether he or she believed in God the Father, in God the Son, in God the Holy Spirit. There followed a further series of questions covering the points in the baptismal creed from which in due course emerged the form now known as the Apostles' Creed. 1 Peter 3:21 mentions such an interrogation. The profession of faith was therefore quite detailed and went beyond the Trinitarian essentials, and of course it was of its essence that it should be a profession of the true faith. Similarly, with the celebration of the eucharist, or thanksgiving (the term used in the *Didachê* and by Ignatius and Justin), sacrifice or gifts formed an "offering" (1 Clement and Ignatius). These examples hint at the degree to which the Church at worship, the community at prayer, was also, as time went on, expressing its faith, and doing so in quite sophisticated theological terms. There was, naturally, room for further theological reflection about what this meant.

The early councils repeatedly make allowance for variety of liturgical usage. This is striking, as it has since become a commonplace that liturgy carries a theology within it, and differences in patterns of worship could in principle allow for divergences of faith to develop. The Ambrosian Rite (which may have no real connection with Ambrose, the bishop of Milan[21] in the late fourth century) represents a useful example of the way in which rites could vary from place to place without any sense that the Church was thereby divided. Various theories have been put forward: one is that the rite in use at Milan may simply have been a development of the Roman rite; another is that it was a survival of a period before the Roman rite took its characteristic form; another is that it was brought from the East by one of Ambrose's predecessors and amended by Ambrose for local use. Whichever is correct, the survival of this distinctive rite underlines the freedom all local churches enjoyed to worship, within limits, as they chose or as their local bishops permitted.

It was in baptism (and in consequence in penance) that the theologically most load-bearing aspects of the liturgical life of the Church were concentrated. For these were the centuries in which it was settled that the individual could be baptized only once, that baptism availed for the remission of both original and actual sin, that there was a serious question whether the person who was baptized and who fell into serious sin afterwards could ever be restored to the community. There was also a debate about membership, whether all those who were baptized were members of the body of Christ in the eyes of God, and whether some who were not baptized might be recognised by him. These were the centuries in which there were the beginnings of a move to private penance, from the older public penance, in which the lapsed were kept visibly separated from the congregation and readmitted to communion with them (if at all) only by a public act of the bishop.

These questions take us full circle, back to the great task of these early centuries, the unfolding of the first simple faith in Jesus and the working out of its implications, for they remind us that this was never a merely intellectual assent. It was a way of life, and above all the way of life of a community.

Christian worship is predicated upon a number of assumptions which – with qualifications explored in the chapters on Judaism – separate the Christian faith from the other religions among which it had to find its place in the late Roman Empire in which it took its origin. Christians understood themselves to be a community, the united body of Christ, one with their Lord (1 Cor. 10:17; Col. 3:15; Eph. 2:16). Jesus' own words at the Last Supper when he broke bread were "This is my body which is given for you," and he instructed his disciples to do what he had just done in memory of him. So the community from the first formed the custom of meeting to break bread and to give thanks and praise the Lord (Acts 16:25). This was an activity which foreshadowed the life of the community of heaven (Rev. 19:5). It was a celebration and an adoration.

Prayer, whether personal or liturgical, has, however, another purpose, and that is to ask for benefits. This was a familiar activity in the lowlier forms of polytheistic paganism, where it was often accompanied by the bringing of gifts to please the gods. Christian intercession raised a number of theological questions for those who believed that God foreordains all things for good and cannot be mistaken about what he foresees will happen.[22] Where that is so, how can prayer make any difference to what is to become of the Christian who makes his supplications? The Church kept an open mind on this important question.

It was that very "community" character, the ubiquitous presence of "Church," that made the debate which is Christian theology so rich and took it so far, for it brought Christian people together in teaching and learning and worship and it also divided them in dispute.

Notes

1 *Letter* 107.ii, CSEL, 55, p. 292.
2 Ed. B. Colgrave and R. A. B. Mynors (Oxford, 1969).
3 On marriage see ch. 5.
4 See ch. 3.
5 Boethius, *De Trinitate*, II. For Boethius, see *Medieval Theologians*.
6 Ed. M. Adraian, CCSL, 143 (1979).

7 See pp. 105–14.

8 See P. Hadot, *Porphyre et Victorinus, Études augustiniennes* (Paris, 1968), 2 vols.

9 Ed. C. Moreschini (Leipzig, 1991).

10 Letter 148, 6, CSEL 56, p. 334.

11 Ibid., 148, 15 and 18, CSEL 56, pp. 341 and 345.

12 Ed. W. B. Anderson (London and Cambridge, MA, 1936), 2 vols., Vol. 1.

13 Details of these and other works can be found in *Works*, ed. H. J. Thomson (Loeb, 1949–53, 2 vols.).

14 Letter 148, 15 and 18, CSEL 56, pp. 341 and 345.

15 G. R. Evans, *A Short History of Heresy* (Oxford, 2002) attempts a brief survey of the issues.

16 Cyril of Jerusalem, *Catecheses*, VI.35, ed. C. Reischl (Monaco, 1848), and see S. N. C. Lieu, *Manicheism* (Cambridge, 1985), p. 93.

17 Lieu, *Manicheism*, p. 91.

18 See *Medieval Theologians*, pp. 14, 20, 33, 273–4.

19 See ibid., pp. 57–64.

20 B. J. Van der Veken, "De primordiis liturgiae paschalis," *Sacris Eruditi*, 13 (1962), pp. 461–501.

21 See pp. 225–34.

22 Eric Segelberg, "Prayer among the Gnostics? The Evidence of some Nag Hammadi Documents," *Gnosis and Gnosticism*, ed. Martin Krause (Leiden, 1977), pp. 55–69.

Bibliography

F. E. Brightman, *Liturgies Eastern and Western* (Oxford, 1895).

Henry Chadwick, *The Church in Ancient Society* (Oxford, 2001).

E. Dekkers, "Autour de l'oeuvre liturgique de S. Léon le Grand," *Sacris erudiri*, 10 (1958), pp. 363–98.

E. R. Dodds, *Pagan and Christian in an Age of Anxiety* (Oxford, 1965).

W. H. C. Frend, *The Early Church: From the Beginnings to 461* (London, 3rd edn., 1991).

J. H. W. G. Liebeschuetz, *Continuity and Change in Roman Religion* (Oxford, 1979).

S. N. C. Lieu, *Manicheism* (Cambridge, 1985).

A. Momigliani, ed., *The Conflict between Paganism and Christianity in the Fourth Century* (London, 1963).

B. Poschmann, *Penance and the Anointing of the Sick* (Freiburg, 1964).

The Bible

The First Christian Writings

John W. Rogerson

Why were some writings accepted as Holy Scripture by the Jewish and Christian faith communities, and why were other books not accorded this status? The history of the formation of the canon of scripture is complicated, and at first sight it has little to do with the beginnings of Christian theology. However, it was precisely as the early Church struggled with the question of which particular books should be regarded as Scripture and why, that it began to "do theology." This was a two-way process. Most of the books familiar to us from our Bibles were recognized to contain an inherent authority. Once this authority was accepted, these writings shaped theology and set the limits within which it could be creatively developed.

In the Babylonian Talmud, Baba Bathra 14b, a Jewish tradition dating probably from the late third century CE gives the order of the books of the Hebrew Bible as follows:

> The order of the Prophets: Joshua and Judges, Samuel and Kings, Jeremiah and Ezekiel, Isaiah and the Twelve [a discussion follows about the order of the Twelve minor prophets].

> The order of the Writings: Ruth and the book of Psalms, and Job and Proverbs, Ecclesiastes, Song of Songs and Lamentations, Daniel and the Scroll of Esther, Ezra and Chronicles.

There is no discussion of the order of the Law (i.e. Genesis to Deuteronomy) as this was not a matter of dispute. However, there is some discussion of why Ruth heads the writings.

Canon 47 of the Christian third council of Carthage held in 397 CE (the canons represent decisions made in Carthage on several occasions) lists as divine and canonical scripture:

> Genesis, Exodus, Leviticus, Numbers, Deuteronomy, Joshua, Judges, Ruth; Kings, four books (i.e. Samuel and Kings); Chronicles, two books; Job, the Davidic Psalter; Solomon, five books (i.e. Proverbs, Ecclesiastes, Song of Songs, Wisdom,

Ecclesiasticus(!)), Isaiah, Jeremiah (i.e. Jeremiah, Lamentations, Baruch and the Letter of Jeremiah), Ezekiel, Daniel (i.e. Daniel and additions), Tobit, Judith, Esther (i.e. Greek Esther); Esdras, two books (i.e. Ezra and Nehemiah); Maccabees, two books.

The New Testament: four books of the Gospels; Acts of the Apostles, one book; thirteen epistles of the apostle Paul, and one by him to the Hebrews, two of the apostle Peter, three of the apostle John, one each of the apostles Jude and James; the Apocalypse of John, one book.[1]

A comparison of these lists reveals the obvious difference that the Jewish tradition does not mention the New Testament. An examination of the books of the Hebrew Bible/Old Testament indicates subtle differences of content and of arrangement. Regarding content, the Christian list is longer, and adds to the Jewish list Wisdom and Ecclesiasticus, Baruch and the Letter of Jeremiah, additions to Daniel and Esther; and Judith, Tobit and 1 and 2 Maccabees. On the matter of order, the rigid distinction in the Jewish list between Prophets and Writings has been broken down in the Christian list. Ruth, for example, precedes Kings, while Daniel follows Ezekiel. Chronicles, Job, Psalms, and the five books of Solomon follow the books of Kings.

These two traditions, which indicate that the "fixed" order of books of the Hebrew and Christian Bibles, with which modern readers are familiar, had not yet been finally reached, come from a time when the Jewish and Christian communities had parted company over the issue of the extent of the Scriptures. This was not simply a matter of the acceptance of the New Testament in the Christian Church. Equally significant were the differences regarding the Hebrew Bible/Old Testament. Indeed these differences are summed up in the terms Hebrew Bible and Old Testament, because for the Christian Church the books listed in the first part of Canon 47 of the Council of Carthage were *Christian* Scripture, which could only be properly understood in the light of the life, death, and resurrection of Jesus. How did the Hebrew Bible become Scripture, become the Old Testament for the Christian Church, and how did this shape Christian theology?

It is generally agreed that, by the beginning of the Common Era, Jews (with the exception of the Sadducees) accepted that the following books were sacred Scripture: in the Law, Genesis to Deuteronomy; in the Prophets, Joshua to 2 Kings (minus Ruth), Isaiah, Jeremiah, Ezekiel, and the Twelve "minor prophets". In addition, the book of Psalms was recognised as Scripture. The earliest datable reference to this situation comes in the New Testament in Luke 24:44: "everything written about me in the law of Moses and the prophets and the psalms must be fulfilled." Whether these books should be described as "canonical" is a matter of debate. The idea of "canon" can be understood in several different ways, and in using the term in connection with early periods there is always the danger that later theological issues will be read back into the past. It is often preferable to use terms such as "Scripture" or "authoritative texts."

If, at the beginning of the Common Era, most Jews accepted that the Law, the Prophets and the Psalms were sacred Scripture, there was less agreement among them about according this status to other books. Of books written in Hebrew, there were debates among the Rabbis of the early second century CE as to whether the Song of Songs "defiled the hands", that is, possessed a degree of holiness that required users to wash their hands after handling the scrolls on which they were written. There were also books that were regarded as Scripture by the Greek-speaking Jewish communities, especially that in Alexandria. These included the Wisdom of Solomon, the Wisdom of Jesus ben Sirach (Ecclesiasticus), Tobit, Judith, and 1 and 2 Maccabees. It has sometimes been customary to speak of these books as belonging to an "Alexandrian canon," but such a designation obscures the fact that these books were also known and valued by Jewish communities other than those who read the Bible in Greek. What is important for the present essay is the fact that, for the writers of the New Testament, the "Scriptures" were the Bible in Greek, the translation known as the Septuagint (so named because it was believed to have been made by 70 or 72 translators), which had been begun in the third century BCE.[2] The Greek Bible had come to include books such as the Wisdom of Solomon, and although the Jewish community ultimately never accepted them as sacred Scripture, they were regarded as such by the early Church, as in Canon 47 of the third council of Carthage. Of less importance than the precise extent of Scripture was the issue of the meaning of the Scriptures, which issue must now be addressed.

If we imagine a late first-century, Greek-speaking city in the Roman Empire which contained both a Jewish and a Christian community, it is likely that they will have read the same Bible, bearing in mind that the Bible was a collection of scrolls and not yet a book or codex. However, they will have read this Bible in radically different ways, the crucial difference being that the Christian community will have understood it in the light of the life, death, and resurrection of Jesus, will have believed that the coming of Jesus was foretold in the Scriptures and that this coming had somehow "fulfilled" them. Further, the Christian community will have used the Scriptures to articulate Christian doctrine, or theology. Examples of this will now be given from the New Testament.

The Letter to the Hebrews begins with the statement that the God who spoke of old through the prophets has spoken in the latter days through a Son (i.e. Jesus). The writer then goes on to claim that this Son was the means by which God created the world, that he reflects the glory of God, and that he bears the stamp of the divine nature (Hebr. 1:2–3). There then follows a series of quotations from the Bible to prove that the name granted to the Son following his sacrificial death and exaltation is more excellent than that of the angels. Of these quotations, that from Psalm 102:25–7 is especially striking, as it interprets as an address to the Son what is in the psalm an address to God. This use of the psalm enables the claim to be made that the Son (Jesus) is the creator of the universe.

Thou Lord, didst found the earth in the beginning,
And the heavens are the work of thy hands;
They will perish, but thou remainest;
They will all grow old like a garment,
Like a mantle thou will roll them up,
And they will be changed.
But thou art the same, and thy years will never end. [Hebr. 1:10–12]

Another informative example comes in Hebrews 2:6–8, where the author quotes from Psalm 8:5–7 (Greek numbering). The normal English translation of the Hebrew of verse 6 (verse 5 in English) is "Thou hast made him little less than God," the reference being to humankind. The Greek Bible translated the word for "God" as "angels" in accordance with Jewish interpretation of the Hebrew word for God in various passages of the Bible. The Hebrew for "little" was rendered in the Greek by a word that could mean both "slightly" and "temporarily." The writer of Hebrews fastened on the meaning "temporarily" and was thus able to understand the quotation not in terms of humankind, but in terms of Christ. As quoted in Hebrews 2:7–8 the passage reads

> Thou didst make him for a little while lower than the angels,
> thou hast crowned him with glory and honour,
> putting everything in subjection under his feet.

In this interpretation the psalm describes the temporary subordination of Jesus to the angels in his Incarnation and passion, as the prelude to his exaltation and the promise that all things will be put in subjection under his feet. Throughout the letter to the Hebrews we see a Christian writer "doing theology" by interpreting the Bible, that is, the Bible in Greek.

Hebrews concentrates particularly on the person and status of Christ. Another theological issue of importance in the New Testament period was that of the admission to the Christian Church of non-Jews, or Gentiles. This was a situation that was foreseen in the Bible, as read by the first Christians. In Romans 15:9–12 passages from the psalms, Deuteronomy and Isaiah are quoted in order to prove that the Gentiles were destined to "glorify God for his mercy". The Hebrew of one of the passages, Isaiah 11:10, says that the root of Jesse will be a sign or ensign of, or to, the peoples, and that the nations will seek him. The Greek Bible uses one word for the two Hebrew words rendered as "peoples" and "nations," a word that can be understood in Greek to mean "Gentiles." There are two other differences. The Greek Bible, which Romans 15:12 follows, has "to rule" instead of "sign" or "ensign," and "hope" instead of "seek." Romans 15:12 cites Isaiah 11:10 as follows:

> The root of Jesse shall come,
> he who rises to rule the Gentiles;
> in him shall the Gentiles hope.

How the differences between the Hebrew and the Greek came about is less important than the fact that the Greek Bible provided evidence for the early Church that the root of Jesse (i.e. Christ) would become the hope and ruler of the Gentiles.

The Greek Bible also played a part in shaping the New Testament passion narrative. The importance of Psalm 22 was secured by the tradition that Jesus had quoted its opening verses on the cross (Matt. 27:46). The Greek Bible contained a version of verse 16 (Psalm 21:17 in the Greek numbering and 22:17 in the Hebrew) that strikingly confirmed the crucifixion. The Hebrew is usually described as corrupt and is variously translated: "My hands and my feet have shrivelled" is given by the New Revised Standard Version. The Greek has "they pierced my hands and feet." Although this verse is not explicitly quoted in the New Testament, it is implied in the tradition about the risen Christ showing his hands and his feet to the disciples (Luke 24:39; John 20:24–7). Other verses from the psalms that are alluded to in the passion narrative include Psalm 22:18 (English numbering): "they divide my garments among them . . ." (see Matt. 27:35; Mark 15:24; Luke 23:34 and explicitly John 19:24). John refers the word from the Cross "I thirst" (John 19:28) to Psalm 69:21 (English numbering) "for my thirst they gave me vinegar to drink." The reference to this passage is also implicit in the other three gospels.

For the Church in the New Testament period the Greek Bible was authoritative because it was believed to foretell the Incarnation, the sacrificial death, and the exaltation of Christ. It also contained material that dealt with the question of the admission of the Gentiles, and which enabled a high Christology to be expressed, as in the letter to the Hebrews. But there are also one or two surprises. The letter of Jude contains an explicit reference to Enoch 1:9 in verses 14–15, although the quotation does not correspond exactly to any surviving edition of Enoch. Enoch was certainly regarded as Scripture by several early Christian writers and is so regarded today by the Ethiopic Church.[3] Jude also alludes to The Assumption of Moses in verse 9, where it speaks of the archangel Michael contending with the devil for the body of Moses. In what has survived of this text, which was probably written in Hebrew around the beginning of the Common Era, the incident alluded to in Jude 9 does not appear, but several early Christian writers understood Jude 9 to be referring to The Assumption of Moses.[4]

The implication that in some early Christian circles Enoch and The Assumption of Moses were regarded as Scripture is an important reminder that it is not appropriate to use the word "canon" in this connection. While there was agreement among Jews and Christians that the Law, Prophets, and Psalms were authoritative, and while these books formed the backbone of what would later be called a canon, there was still a certain amount of freedom of view about which books were authoritative, that is, contained divine revelation. And it must not be forgotten that the way in which the Jewish and Christian communities interpreted the books that were regarded as authoritative was significantly different.

When we move from the New Testament to the so-called Apostolic Fathers, we find that the Scriptures (the Bible in Greek) are used not only to affirm Christian doctrine but to emphasize differences between Jews and Christians. The *Letter of Barnabas*,[5] a work composed around 130CE, is best known for its allegorical interpretation of the Old Testament, of which the most famous is probably that in *Barnabas* 9.8 in which the figure of 318 trained men used by Abraham to rescue Lot in Genesis 14:14 is seen to refer to Jesus and the cross. Less fanciful is the use made of the Bible by *Barnabas* to argue that the prophets had condemned the sacrificial system of the Jerusalem temple, and that neither these sacrifices nor fasting were ways of attaining salvation. Long quotations, from Isaiah 1:11–13 against sacrifices, and Isaiah 58:4–10 against fasting, appear in *Barnabas* 2.5 and 3.1–4. Indeed, there are quotations from well over a hundred passages from the Old Testament in *Barnabas*, including one possibly from Enoch 91:13 at Barnabas 16:6.

The First Letter of Clement of Rome,[6] written about 96 CE, does not make such extensive use of the Old Testament as *Barnabas*, but there are nonetheless significant quotations. Formal confession of sins is commended on the grounds of Isaiah

1:16–20 in *1 Clement* 8.4. In chapter 53 Clement refers to the story of the Golden Calf made during the sojourn of Moses upon Mount Sinai, to the divine anger that this provoked and the intercession that Moses made for the sparing of the people (*1 Clement* 53.1–4 referring to Exodus 32:7, 10, 31; Deuteronomy 9:12–13).

So far, attention has been drawn only to quotations from Old Testament books later usually regarded as protocanonical, as opposed to the deuterocanonical books of the so-called Apocrypha. However given that early Christian writers used the Greek Bible as Scripture, it is not surprising that references to what were later called deuterocanonical or apocryphal books are to be found. The clearest reference is in *1 Clement* 55.5, where the story of Judith is mentioned, and how God delivered Holofernes into the hands of a woman. *1 Clement* 3.4 cites Wisdom 2:24: "death came into the world" and *1 Clement* 7.5 cites Wisdom 12:10: "he gave them a place (or opportunity – Greek *topos*) of repentance." Other references to "apocryphal" books are found in the *Didachê* (c.100 CE) 4:8, which quotes Sirach (Ecclesiasticus) 4:5: "do not reject the supplication of the afflicted", while it has been maintained that the letters of Ignatius of Antioch (martyred before 117 CE) show the influence of 4 Maccabees.[7]

Writing in 397 CE, Augustine of Hippo indicated that there were still some differences of opinion in the churches about the exact extent of the canon, and advised readers to prefer only those books that were received by all the Catholic churches. In the case of books not received by all of the churches, a rule to be followed was to prefer books that were received either by the greater number of churches, or by the churches of greatest authority.[8] Augustine's comments on the books of the canon, which follow, are worth quoting at length given some of their observations, which vary from the position of modern scholarship:

> Now the whole canon of Scripture on which we say this judgement is to be exercised, is contained in the following books: – Five books of Moses, that is, Genesis, Exodus, Leviticus, Numbers, Deuteronomy; one book of Joshua the son of Nun; one of Judges; one short book called Ruth, which seems rather to belong to the beginning of Kings; next, four books of Kings, and two of Chronicles – these last not following one another, but running parallel, so to speak, and going over the same ground. The books now mentioned are history, which contains a connected narrative of the times, and follows the order of the events. There are other books which seem to follow no regular order, and are connected neither with the order of the preceding books nor with one another, such as Job, and Tobias, and Esther, and Judith, and the two books of Maccabees, and the two of Ezra, which last look more like a sequel to the continuous regular history which terminates with the books of Kings and Chronicles. Next are the Prophets, in which there is one book of the Psalms of David; and three books of Solomon, viz., Proverbs, Song of Songs, and Ecclesiastes. For two books, one called Wisdom and the other Ecclesiasticus, are ascribed to Solomon from a certain resemblance of style, but the most likely opinion is that they were written by Jesus the son of Sirach. Still they are to be reckoned among the prophetical books, since they have attained recognition as being authoritative. The remainder are the books which are strictly called the Prophets: twelve separate books of the prophets which are connected with one another, and having never been disjoined, are reckoned as one book; the names of these prophets are as follows: – Hosea, Joel, Amos, Obadiah, Jonah, Micah, Nahum, Habakkuk, Zephaniah, Haggai, Zechariah, Malachi; then there are the four

greater prophets, Isaiah, Jeremiah, Daniel, Ezekiel. The authority of the Old Testament is contained within the limits of these forty-four books.[9]

Several observations are in order. First, if Augustine is listing the books in the order in which they were arranged in copies known to him, the two books of Ezra (i.e. Ezra and Nehemiah) did not follow Chronicles, as they do in modern Bibles. Secondly, it is noteworthy that books such as the psalms and the writings ascribed to Solomon are described as prophets. This is perhaps because the psalms, in particular, were believed to foretell Christ's suffering and exaltation. In his *Retractiones*, written in 427 CE, Augustine revised his opinion that Wisdom had been written by Jesus ben Sirach, and noted that the Apostle (Paul) used the term "Old Testament" to refer only to the law given to Moses at Sinai.[10]

The canon of the New Testament, or how the writings that are called the New Testament were accepted as authoritative, can be dealt with more briefly. There are three lines of approach to the problem: the use of New Testament texts by early Christian writers; official lists of canonical books; and the evidence of manuscripts. The first category is made difficult by the fact that early writers, such as those discussed with reference to the Old Testament, often seem to allude to New Testament texts, but do not quote them in such a way that it is possible to conclude with absolute certainty that they regard these texts as Scripture. The evidence is surveyed exhaustively by Metzger,[11] and of the so-called Apostolic Fathers (e.g. *1 Clement*, *Barnabas*, the *Didachê*) he concludes that while there is no idea of a duty to quote exactly from books that are regarded as canonical, there is a sense that certain books that would later appear in the New Testament possess authority, even if this is not embodied in a theory of canonicity.[12] It is not until the end of the second century CE that anything like a sense of an authoritative canon can be found. Metzger writes of Clement of Alexandria (c.150–215) that he regarded the four Gospels, 14 letters of Paul (including Hebrews) and Acts, 1 Peter, 1 John, and Revelation as authoritative Scripture.[13]

The evidence of manuscripts is that in the third century, books that would later appear in the New Testament were being collected together. The Chester Beatty papyrus **P** 45 contains the four Gospels and the Acts of the Apostles, while **P** 4, which may have contained Matthew, Luke, and another gospel, dates from no later than 200CE.[14] The Chester Beatty papyrus **P** 46 dating around 200CE contains portions of the Pauline letters (Romans to 1 Thessalonians) including Hebrews. Such collections indicate the workings of what might be called a "canonical process." As Elliott puts it: "There are no manuscripts that contain say Matthew, Luke and [the Gospel of] Peter, or John, Mark and [the Gospel of] Thomas. Only the Gospels of Matthew, Mark, Luke and John were considered as scriptural and then as canonical."[15]

Elliott regards the adoption of the codex (i.e. pages bound together at one end, as in a modern book) by the Church as an important factor in the canonical process. While the adoption of the codex did not in itself create authoritative books, decisions about which books should be bound together obviously concentrated minds upon the question of what to include and what not to include. In this connection it is interesting that the fourth-century Codex Sinaiticus included the *Letter of Barnabas* and part of The Shepherd of Hermas, while the fifth-century Codex Alexandrinus contains 1 and 2 Clement. These facts are reminders that, at these dates, the canon of the New Testament was still uncertain round the edges. The users of Sinaiticus and Alexandrinus must have regarded these extra books as equally authoritative as the other writings with which they were bound up.[16]

The earliest list defining which books belong to the New Testament is usually held to be the Muratorian Canon (named after its discoverer, L. A. Muratori). Thought to have been written in Rome in the latter part of the second century, it mentions, as books accepted universally, the four Gospels, Acts, 13 letters of Paul, the letter of Jude, two (or, perhaps, three) letters of John, the Wisdom of Solomon(!), and Revelation. The Apocalypse of Peter is mentioned as a disputed book, while The Shepherd of Hermas is commended for private study, although it is not regarded as authoritative.[17]

It has often been suggested that the Church was encouraged to formulate a canon of the New Testament in order to counteract the minimalizing activity of Marcion on the one hand, and the maximalizing activity of Gnostics on the other. Marcion (c.85–c.160), who originated from Sinope on the Black Sea, and who was condemned as a heretic in 144CE, went on to found his own church. He rejected the Old Testament because he believed its God to be inferior to the God proclaimed by Jesus, and he favoured a New Testament that apparently consisted of Luke's gospel and the following Pauline letters: Galatians, Corinthians, Romans, Thessalonians, Ephesians, Colossians, Philippians, and Philemon.[18] According to Harnack, Marcion placed Galatians first because it was the Magna Carta of his faith. The other books followed in order of length, beginning with the longest. Gnostic forms of Christianity as represented by Basilides of Alexandria (active during the reigns of Hadrian (117–38) and Antoninus Pius (138–61)), Valentinus (active in Rome and the West c.140–c.165) and the Nag Hammadi library discovered in Egypt in 1945, supplemented apostolic Christianity with esoteric teachings contained in writings such as The Gospel of Truth. Attempts by the Church to establish a canon of the New Testament can therefore partly be seen as a need to acknowledge more books than Marcion did, and to exclude additional Gnostic-type writings.

The question is often raised as to whether the Church regarded books as authoritative because they were declared to be canonical, or whether they were declared to be canonical because the Church recognized their authority. The answer surely is that both statements are true. Initially, books were regarded as authoritative because their intrinsic value was recognized. In the case of the Old Testament this was because the Greek Bible could be interpreted as bearing witness to the Incarnation, suffering, and exaltation of Jesus, the divine Son through whom all things had been created, and whom all nations would acknowledge. In the case of the New Testament writings, the Gospels contained the teachings of Jesus, while the letters contained the authoritative interpretation of the meaning of Jesus' suffering and exaltation. The recognition of the intrinsic value of these writings led to their being collected together, a process no doubt affected by the need to exclude the teachings of Marcion and the Gnostics, and later assisted by the adoption of the codex, and the need for decisions about which books should be bound up together. The official lists defining the canon never achieved universal acceptance. However, they were sufficiently in agreement to establish norms that then conferred the status of Scripture upon certain writings, and guaranteed their authority. Yet even within the canon as defined, texts such as Genesis, Psalms, Isaiah, the Gospels, and Romans have attracted the lion's share of attention from interpreters down the ages because of their content, and every church, if it is honest, will admit that it operates in practice with a "canon within the canon," that is, that it concentrates on some books more than others. This is a reminder that theology has always been shaped by certain books of the Bible. Study of the earliest stages of the "canonical process" affords valuable insights into the way in which the recognition that certain texts contained divine revelation affected and shaped the way in which the earliest Christian theologians "did theology."

Notes

1   E. J. Jonkers (ed.), *Acta et symbola conciliorum quae saeculo quarto habita sunt* (Textus Minores XIX), Leiden, 1954, p. 136. An English version is also found in Metzger, 1987, p. 315.

2   See especially Müller, 1996; Hans Hübner, "Vetus Testamentum und Vetus Testamentum in Novo receptum. Die Frage nach dem Kanon des Alten Testaments aus neutestamentlicher Sicht" in P. D. Hanson et al. (eds.), *Zum Problem des biblischen Kanons* (Jahrbuch für Biblische Theologie 3 (1988), pp. 147–62.

3   See Kelly, 1969, p. 277.

4   Ibid., p. 265.

5   Klaus Wengst, *Didache (Apostellehre), Barnabasbrief, Zweiter Klemensbrief, Schrift an Diognet*, Schriften des Urchristentums, zweiter Teil (Darmstadt, 1984), pp. 103–202.

6   Joseph H. Fischer, *Die Apostolischen Väter*, Schriften des Urchristentums, erster Teil (Darmstadt, 1993), pp. 1–107.

7   Fischer, *Apostolischen Väter*, p. 123.

8   Augustine, *De doctrina Christiana* II, viii, 12, CCSL, vol. XXXII, pp. 38–9, ET *On Christian Doctrine* (The Nicene and Post-Nicene Fathers of the Christian Church, 1st ser., vol. II), p. 538.

9   Augustine, *De doctrina Christiana* II, viii, 13, CCSL, vol. XXXII, pp. 39–40, ET pp. 538–9.

10   Augustine, *Retractiones* II, iv, 2–3, CCSL, vol. LVII, p. 93.

11   Metzger, 1987.

12   Ibid., pp. 72–3.

13   Ibid., p. 135.

14   K. Elliott, "Manuscripts, the Codex and the Canon", *Journal for the Study of the New Testament* 63 (1996), p. 107.

15   Ibid., p. 107.

16   Ibid., p. 111.

17   See Metzger, 1987, pp. 191–9.

18   See A. von Harnack, *Marcion. Das Evangelium vom fremden Gott*, Darmstadt (repr. 1996), p. 168*.

Bibliography

J. N. D. Kelly, *The Epistles of Peter and of Jude* (Black's New Testament Commentaries) (London, 1969) .

B. M. Metzger, *The Canon of the New Testament. Its Origin, Development and Significance* (Oxford, 1987).

Mogens Müller, *The First Bible of the Church. A Plea for the Septuagint* (*Journal for the Study of the Old Testament* Supplement Series 206), (Sheffield, 1996).

The Interpretation
of Scripture

Frances Young

From the beginning Christians were interpreters of the Jewish Scriptures. The first Christians were Jews, soon to be joined by Gentile God-fearers, people already attracted to Jewish synagogues. All alike would have accepted without question the fundamental significance of the Law and the Prophets, the Psalms, and other Jewish literature, and converts would subsequently have been enculturated into this perspective. The earliest Christian exegesis has left its traces in the writings now collected together in the New Testament. However, it was only when these texts became part of the Christian canon that a systematic biblical theology emerged or scholarly methods of exegesis developed. So we will begin our exploration at that stage, and discuss the biblical interpretation of the first Christian theologians by focusing on particular individuals and particular developments in the course of the second to fourth centuries.

Irenaeus and the Rule of Faith

Irenaeus was bishop of Lyons toward the end of the second century. His interpretation of Scripture is displayed in his massive compendium of books, *Against the Heresies*. The smaller guide to Christian belief called *The Demonstration of the Apostolic Preaching* crystallizes his approach. Both are important: the one shows how his position was honed in controversy; the other how it summed up coherently assumptions and traditions that go back far earlier. Irenaeus did not wish to be original, though he has often been regarded among modern scholars as the first systematic theologian. His writings testify to an emerging scriptural canon which is roughly the same as that accepted by the Church in the longer term. His theological perspective is determined by a commitment to the unity and narrative integrity of the whole Bible. The one God, who created and redeemed the world through his Word and Spirit, is for Irenaeus the consistent subject of the biblical story. God's providential ordering of all things is demonstrated by the fact that the prophecies have been fulfilled. The Law foreshadows the Gospel. Adam is "recapitulated" in Christ, who restores humankind to communion with God.

Several issues preoccupy Irenaeus in his controversial work. The first is the way heretics selectively use books that he accepts as biblical, and/or treat as Scripture writings he regards as apocryphal and spurious. The second is the way they distort Scripture to support their crazy ideas. The most notorious of those pursuing the first policy was Marcion, who suggested that the Jewish Scriptures came from a God of wrath and justice, totally incompatible with the God of love revealed by Jesus Christ; so the only Scriptures Christians should use were the Pauline Epistles, which set Gospel and Law against each other, and a version of Luke's Gospel which excised references to those misguided older Scriptures. Both tendencies were found among various sects seeking "knowledge [gnosis] falsely so-called," known to modern scholars as Gnostics. It was characteristic of these groups to consider the creation of the material world a dreadful mistake, and to regard salvation as escape from it through the revelation of a saviour who came from the spiritual world, often but not exclusively identified with Christ. The twentieth-century discovery of certain Gnostic texts, notably the find at Nag Hammadi in Egypt, has revealed how some exploited Genesis, regarding the serpent as the embodiment of saving wisdom and knowledge, and identifying the Creator God of the Bible as the fallen Demiurge (or Craftsman–Creator) who trapped sparks of the spiritual world in his material creation. Gnostic texts demonstrate their propensity to attribute revelation to the period after the resurrection, disregarding the earthly life of Jesus more or less entirely. Already well-known from anti-Gnostic texts was their Docetic outlook – in other words, how they devalued the humanity of Jesus, either treating the life and ministry of Christ as a kind of mirage or regarding the spiritual Christ as having lodged temporarily in Jesus of Nazareth, arriving at the baptism and leaving before the crucifixion.

It is against this background that we see Irenaeus seeking to establish the unity of the Bible, the books to be treated as Scripture, the criteria of interpretation, and a theology of redemption which really did reflect the overarching biblical narrative. We will assume the question of the canon has already been treated in the previous chapter, and turn to the other issues.

The problem with the heretics was that, in their wild speculations, they had lost the plot. In the eyes of Irenaeus, they twisted scriptural texts to suit their myths and genealogies:

> Such then is their system, which the prophets did not announce, the Lord did not teach, and the Apostles did not hand down; but which they boastfully declare that they understand better than others . . . As the saying is, they attempt to make ropes of sand in applying the parables of the Lord, or prophetic utterances, or apostolic statements to their plausible scheme, in order that they may have foundation for it. But they alter the scriptural context and connection, and dismember the truth as much as they can . . . It is just as if there was a beautiful representation of a king made in a mosaic by a skilled artist, and one altered the arrangement of the pieces of stone into the shape of a dog or a fox, and then should assert that this was the original representation of a king. In much the same way they stitch together old wives' tales, and wresting sayings and parables, however they may, from the context, attempt to fit the oracles of God into their myths. [*Against the Heresies* 1.8.1]

To uphold, in the face of these distortions, the unity and narrative coherence of all the Scriptures (the Gospel and the books of the Old Covenant), Irenaeus appeals to the "Canon of Truth," sometimes called the "Rule of Faith." Guaranteed by a tradition which was public and open, this "Rule" provides the story-line, the overarching sense of Scripture, and so the framework for interpretation:

> The Church, although scattered over the whole world even to its extremities, received from the Apostles and their disciples the faith in one God, the Father Almighty, Maker of heaven and earth . . . and in one Christ Jesus, the Son of God, who became incarnate for our salvation; and in the Holy Spirit, who by the prophets proclaimed the dispensations, the advents, the virgin birth, the passion and resurrection from the dead, the bodily ascension of the well-beloved Christ Jesus our Lord into heaven, and his Parousia from the heavens in the glory of the Father to gather all things up in Himself . . . Christ Jesus our Lord and God, our Saviour and King. [*Against the Heresies* 1.10.1]

Summaries of this kind appear time and again in the works of Irenaeus, always threefold, but in various different forms. What is interesting about this particular version is the way features of Christ's life and death do not appear in the second clause, but are attributed to the prophetic Holy Spirit. The argument from prophecy is, for Irenaeus as for the Apologist, Justin Martyr, before him, the key proof of the Gospel. It matters that it all happened and so the prophetic predictions were vindicated; conversely the fulfilled prophecies prove it all happened according to God's providence. This is made clear in his other work, the *Demonstration of the Apostolic Preaching*, which not only tells the biblical story from creation and fall, through Noah, Abraham, Moses, the Exodus, and the Prophets in a way that constantly prepares for the denouement, but also tells the story of Jesus Christ and his redemption through the words of the prophets. In practice, his interpretation of Scripture gives priority to the validity of prophecy, over against the cosmological speculations of his opponents, almost to the point where this is set up as another criterion of right interpretation.

In the *Demonstration* (6) Irenaeus links the threefold "Rule of Faith" with baptism, and insists on the importance it has for "our regeneration." He details the second article as follows: "The Word of God, the Son of God, Christ Jesus our Lord, who was revealed by the prophets . . . and who, in the last times, to recapitulate all things, became a man amongst men, visible and palpable, in order to abolish death, to demonstrate life, and to effect communion between God and man." And when he comes to the third article, he speaks of the Holy Spirit, "who, in the last times, was poured out in a new fashion upon the human race renewing man . . . to God."

Renewal and regeneration are key concepts, and they are achieved through "recapitulation." What Christ did was again to go over the ground trod by Adam, reversing his disobedience with obedience. Since all humanity is implicated in the Fall, so in Christ all humanity is potentially involved in the Redemption. Details of the correspondence and reversal are pressed: Adam was made through God's will and wisdom, from the virgin earth, so the Word, "summing up Adam in himself, duly received from Mary, still a virgin, the birth of that nature in which Adam was summed up" (*Against the Heresies* 3.21.10; cf. *Demonstration* 32). Mary's obedience in response to the angelic announcement reverses Eve's disobedience when seduced by the devil (*Against the Heresies* 3.22.3; 5.19.1; *Demonstration* 33). The transgression which occurred through a tree was undone by the obedience when Christ was nailed to the tree and hung from it (*Against the Heresies* 5.19.1; *Demonstration* 33–4). Thus Irenaeus develops the typology of Adam and Christ found first in St. Paul's Epistle to the Romans, and briefly redeployed by Justin Martyr before him.

It is tempting to think that Irenaeus recast, if not invented, this notion of Fall and Redemption in the face of Gnostic ideas. Earlier Christianity seems to have worked more often with the notion of a re-played Exodus, Christ overcoming the tyranny of the devil (Pharoah) so that people could walk free (from Egypt) in expectation of the "Promised Land," or the coming Kingdom of God. Faced with Gnostic mis-reading of Genesis, Irenaeus seems to have advanced a contrary reading, determined to undermine a cosmological approach that turned the story on its head and made it impossible to see creation and redemption as the gracious act of the one God of all. The Gospel recapitulates Genesis. For the material creation is good, the eucharist is a thank-offering of the first-fruits of creation, and the Resurrection involved a restoration of the human creature, physical and spiritual, to its intended wholeness.

Thus Irenaeus developed a soteriology that exploited the over-arching plot summed up in the "Canon of Truth." The story of the old covenant prepared the way for the new. Prophecy and event foreshadowed the future. The Word to be incarnate was present already in the words of Scripture, its narratives and its prophecies. Inevitably this Christocentric reading of the whole unified Scripture involved symbolic reading of details. Irenaeus saw "types and shadows" of the future in texts about the past, inevitably resorting to allegory at times. Yet he opposed the allegorical readings of the Gnostics. For him such readings were arbitrary because they had no grasp of the whole. In this approach, as we shall see, Irenaeus anticipated the position both of Athanasius in the face of the Arian appeal to Scripture and of the anti-allegorists of the fourth century.

Origen and the Advent of Scholarship

Those fourth-century anti-allegorists had one figure in mind in all their polemic, and that was Origen. Eventually Origen would be condemned, not only for his allegorical approach to Scripture but on other counts. Yet no account of the first Christian theologians can ignore this towering figure of third-century Alexandria. His influence was profound, not least because, as the first intellectual committed to the Church and opposed to Gnosticism, he created Christian scholarship.

Books and their interpretation shaped the culture and education of antiquity, even though quite a small proportion of society as a whole would have been literate. In school pupils learned to read, construe, understand, and appropriately imitate the classics, whether Greek or Latin. Rhetoric and persuasive oratory were the goal – for public speech brought honour and glory. But the means to that end were linguistic analysis and exegesis. Most subjects in the curriculum were subservient to this. Alexandria was the Harvard of the Roman world. There Origen is said to have founded a catechetical school, but the evidence suggests that the programme he offered was far from a beginners' class. He set out to provide a Christian version of the Hellenistic educational programme, substituting the Scriptures for the classics.

To do this he had to be able to justify the adoption of a canon of "barbarian" and linguistically unsophisticated literature. Allegory was one way of dealing with some of its crudities. The anthropomorphic God of Scripture was for him the same kind of problem as the Homeric gods were for the philosophers. Origen was a prolific writer. The bulk of what has come down to us consists of homilies or commentaries on Scripture. A great deal has only survived in Latin translation, or in fragmentary form – after all, his works were proscribed after his condemnation. Yet there is plenty enough to observe his use of the techniques employed in the grammatical, rhetorical, and philosophical schools.

In school the most significant things have always happened orally in the undocumented interactions between teacher and pupil, but from the rhetorical guides produced in both Greek and Latin over the course of several centuries, we can glean something of what went on. One of the clearest accounts is that of Quintilian (especially *Institutio oratoria* I. iv–ix). Quintilian notes that correct reading has to precede interpretation. To appreciate that, we have to imagine what reading was like prior to the development of many familiar conventions. There being no word division or punctuation, the very act of reading aloud presupposed interpretation, since ambiguities could arise about where a word or sentence ended, whether a particular sentence was a statement or a question, or where the stress was to fall. Origen frequently discusses problems of construal in his commentaries. Furthermore, a class might be faced with a number of hand-written copies which did not exactly correspond in their wording. Establishing the correct reading would be necessary. Spurious material would need to be rejected, omissions made up. In his *Commentary on Matthew* XV.14, Origen tells us how he adopted standard scholarly practices with regard to textual divergences, recognizing that scribal copyists had not for various reasons produced the same text. He also explains how he handled the particular difficulties of the Old Testament, where he was dealing with the Greek version of a Hebrew original. The Septuagint (hereafter the LXX, the translation reputedly made by 70 scholars for Ptolemy's library in Alexandria and by now used as standard among Christians) was not the only Greek version in circulation. He claims that he always employed versions other than the LXX for comparison. He marked words not occurring in the Hebrew with an obelus; others, missing from the LXX but in the Hebrew, he inserted from other versions, marking them with an asterisk. This sounds like the production of a critical edition.

Some, however, have thought that in this passage Origen was referring to his work known as the *Hexapla* (or "sixfold"). According to Eusebius of Caesarea (the first historian of the Church), this was a tome in which the Hebrew was set out with a transliteration beside it, and four different Greek versions (the LXX with Aquila, Symmachus, and Theodotion). The *Hexapla* has long since disappeared – it is doubtful whether the original can ever have been copied, though it was probably in the library at Caesarea in Palestine, where Origen spent the latter part of his life. Exactly what it was like is intriguing; in the case of the Psalms, Eusebius speaks of Origen adding not merely a fifth, but even a sixth and seventh translation, one of which was found in a jar at Jericho. Whatever the answer, there can be no doubt that Origen concerned himself with text-critical matters and wished to get the wording of the scriptural text accurately established.

The next issue discussed in school reading of texts was the language and vocabulary. Much classical literature contained archaic and unfamiliar words and forms. Parts of speech, etymologies, stylistic devices, meter, ornamentation, figures of speech such as metaphor, simile, hyperbole, irony, etc. – such linguistic features had to be identified, discussed, and classified. A range of examples would be used to establish the particular meaning and usage of words in an author such as Homer, and problems in Homer would be elucidated by reference to other Homeric passages. All such comment contributed to analysis at the level of the "letter," and together with textual criticism and construal constituted *to methodikon*. Again, Origen's commentaries display his skill in these techniques. He would draw up huge collections of texts to demonstrate the biblical meaning of a particular word or phrase, and he would refer to other passages in Scripture to elucidate problems he faced with particular texts. He was constantly fascinated by etymology and figures of speech, often using the identification of metaphor or hyperbole as a reason for pointing out that the words of Scripture could not be taken literally – for that just produced impossibilities. These figures of speech were placed there by the Holy Spirit to stimulate people into looking for the spiritual meaning.

From *to methodikon*, the student would proceed to *to historikon*. We should not jump to the conclusion that this was principally concerned with history in our sense. It involved elucidating all the references to unexplained stories and characters, background features, and so on. In the case of the classical literature this often meant sorting out allusions to myths and legends, gods and heroes; it was here that the erudite drew on their knowledge of all kinds of subjects, from geography to astronomy, from mathematics to natural history. Origen loves to do this too. One typical example is his discussion of pearls in the *Commentary on Matthew* X. 7–10. Commenting on the merchant's search for the pearl of great price becomes an excuse for a long disquisition on the nature of the pearl, drawn from the compendia of those who have written on stones. We learn that the best come from the Red Sea, and the next best from Britain. They come from seashells, and Origen tells us how they are collected, how long it takes for a pearl to form, and what natural phenomena enhance or damage the formation.

To historikon, then, was the research that produced as much information as possible as explanatory comment. But the budding orator was also trained to challenge the narratives advanced by their opponents in court. So a kind of narrative criticism developed for assessing the plausibility of the stories told in texts. Three types of narrative were identified: true history (or an accurate account of real events); fiction (or what could have happened but did not); and myth (what could not have taken place, or a false account portraying truth). Origen can be observed practicing these techniques, particularly when refuting Celsus' hostile account of Christian stories, but also in his commentaries. One example concerns his assessment of the various versions of the Cleansing of the Temple. The difference in timing between John and the Synoptics leads him to comment that it is impossible "for those who admit nothing more than the history in their interpretation" to find a way of harmonizing the different accounts. He proceeds to use narrative criticism to demonstrate first the implausibility of the Johannine account and then the difficulties of the Matthean account. He concludes that it is not the history that is important but the deeper intent of each evangelist. This is but the latest example of how Origen utilizes the methods of the schools to urge the necessity of moving from a "literal" to a "spiritual" reading. He appears to revel in interpretative problems, simply because they necessitate the move to a deeper approach – an allegorical interpretation. Allegory, of course, is what he became notorious for, and he justified this in a formal account of his hermeneutics in Book IV of the work known as *De principiis,* that is, *On First Principles.* To that we now turn.

Origen begins with the presumption of the divine inspiration of Scripture and the fulfillment of prophecy in Jesus Christ, yet notes there are difficulties in interpretation. On the one hand, there are those who do not accept the fulfilment of the prophecies because they imagine they were to be visibly accomplished, and since the wolf does not lie down with the lamb, or the lion eat straw like the ox, the advent cannot have happened. On the other hand, there are those who reject the words of the Old Testament on the grounds that they came from an imperfect and wrathful Deity, not the God of Jesus Christ. He considers that these problems arise from failure to understand the Scriptures according to their spiritual meaning.

Oracles, he suggests, have always been in the form of enigmas and dark sayings. He finds the clue in Proverbs 22:20–1: a threefold way of reading Scripture – the "fleshly" or obvious sense, a sense related to the "soul" (sometimes identified as the "moral" sense), and the perfect way which is the hidden wisdom that St. Paul speaks of in 1 Corinthians 2:6–7. If you take this spiritual sense seriously, you soon find that there are certain passages of Scripture which do not have a "corporeal" sense at all – indeed God has arranged certain stumbling blocks and impossibilities, in the midst of the law and history, in order to ensure that we move on from the "letter." This applies not only to the Scriptures which were composed prior to the advent of Christ, but also to the Evangelists and the Apostles, for the same Spirit inspired all of Scripture. What really matters for Origen are the truths which the Spirit communicates through the mysteries and enigmas of Scripture. The particularities of the text or the history are merely the vehicle of these truths. Nevertheless he clearly thinks that much of Scripture is to be taken at face value – commands, like "Honour your father and mother," are meant to be obeyed. To search the Scriptures is to distinguish how far the literal meaning is true and how far impossible.

The truths Origen so cared about we would describe as moral and doctrinal. Even here Origen follows the trends of the surrounding culture. Rhetorical schools had long assumed that classical texts conveyed moral truths, and authors like Plutarch had written essays on how to read the classics with moral profit. Philosophical schools had allegorized ancient literature, regarding the stories as figurative representations of the physical or moral truths of their own system. The argument as to whether Origen was primarily a Platonic philosopher or a biblical scholar misses the profound interpenetration of his schooling, with all its intellectual influences, and his sincere adoption of a "barbarian" literary canon. Committed to the Christian "Rule of Faith," influenced also by contacts with Jewish scholars, he sought a hermeneutic which could deliver a unified understanding of a diverse, and sometimes even contradictory, collection of texts, just as he tried in his theology to resolve the tension between the One and the Many, God and the multiplicity of creation. For him Scripture had one author, the Holy Spirit, and one intent: as in the incarnation of the Word, so in the words of the Bible, God accommodated the divine self to the human level so as graciously to communicate with his finite creatures and win them back to contemplation of the divine reality.

The Fourth-Century Reaction against Allegory

Reaction against Origen's allegorical interpretation of Scripture became explicit among the so-called Antiochenes. This group is also known for affirming two natures in Christ in opposition to the Alexandrians, and includes Diodore of Tarsus and Theodore of Mopsuestia, whose works remain only in fragments because they were retrospectively condemned as a result of the Christological controversy, together with John Chrysostom, whose exegetical homilies earned him the title "Golden-mouth", and Theodoret of Cyrus, a participant in the council of Chalcedon. Many twentieth-century scholars have claimed the Antiochenes as theologians concerned like themselves with the literal meaning of Scripture and the historicity of the human life of Jesus. Closer attention to the surviving texts, however, surely disabuses us of this anachronism. Antiochene commentaries are as full of moral and dogmatic deductions as ever allegorists produced. They were generally as committed to the notion of prophetic fulfillment, and as sophisticated in their acceptance of the metaphoricity of language. We must look elsewhere for what drove their opposition to allegory.

A little non-polemical handbook on interpretation by one Adrianos shows that the philological methods observed in Origen's exegesis were applied just as much by the Antiochenes. Analysis of the particular idioms of Hebrew texts is required, but proper attention must also be paid to the "mind" of Scripture: in other words, the wording and the sense need distinguishing. The idioms discussed include the way in which Scripture represents God's "energies" or activities by human attributes – no more than Origen does Adrianos take literally references to God's eyes, mouth, hands, feet, anger, or passions, nor indeed to God sitting, walking, or being clothed. Metaphors, parables, types, and symbols have their place in Antiochene interpretation, and this handbook largely consists of listing and exemplifying a wide range of figures of speech. Much is similar, so where is the difference?

Adrianos does include allegory among figures of speech, but discusses it very briefly and is far from treating it as a description of a whole interpretative approach. Other Antiochenes, like Chrysostom, affirmed that allegory should only be identified where the text makes it clear that that figure is being used, and all of the main Antiochene commentators provide extended discussion when commenting on Galatians 4:24 where St. Paul uses the term. So that is one methodological difference. The other lies in the overall approach to the text.

For Adrianos meaning is grounded in the "sequence." He uses the analogy of a steersman – the interpreter is blown about if not fixed on the goal. The "mind" of the words must be earthed in the order found in the body of the text, and the "spiritual insight" (or *theoria*, the term used instead of allegory by the Antiochenes) grounded in the shape of that body, the limbs and their synthesis thus being discerned properly. In other words the straightforward meaning in context shapes even the spiritual interpretation. What the Antiochenes objected to was the indiscriminate subverting of the text by ignoring its sequence and treating it as a code in which each word was a kind of token signifying something other than the obvious meaning. An example is provided by the earliest essay which explicitly adopted an anti-allegorical stance, namely, the treatise of Eustathius, *On the Witch of Endor and against Origen*. At one point Origen is accused of paying too much attention to the "letter" and drawing false conclusions by not attending to the narrative logic of the whole: the story surely does not imply that Samuel actually came up from Hades – rather the witch played upon the mad mind of Saul so that he seemed to see Samuel. One must look at the thrust of the narrative, which clearly indicates that the witch was *engastrimythos* – generating myths within.

There was a methodological issue, then, but methodology rarely generates passion. Much more important to the controversialists, I suggest, was their fear that the excessive spiritualizing implicit in Origen's allegory undermined the overarching narrative of the "Rule of Faith." Eustathius betrays this – for he protests against Origen literalizing Samuel's ascent from Hades while allegorizing creation and paradise, the resurrection of the body and the Kingdom of God. The same point is made by Epiphanius and Jerome, and in the classic discussions of allegory in the extant works of Diodore, Theodore, Theodoret, and Chrysostom. In other words, their theological concern was much the same as the kind of anxiety voiced by Irenaeus when faced with the way Gnostic interpretation had lost the plot. It was not at all the same as modern concerns about historicity – indeed, they wanted to retain as history the Beginning and the End, precisely the features that many modern exegetes find problematic, as Origen did before them. Even Diodore is bothered by the talking, scheming serpent in the Garden of Eden, but he insists that the "serpent" points "by an enigma" to the Devil. His successor, Theodore, was determined to rescue a sequence of salvation-history made up of reliable stories, not mere parables:

> Those people turn it all to the contrary, as if the entire *historia* of divine scripture differed in no way from dreams in the night. When they start expounding divine scripture "spiritually" – spiritual interpretation is the name they give to their folly – they claim that Adam is not Adam, paradise is not paradise, the serpent not the serpent. I should like to tell them this: If they make *historia* serve their own ends, they will have no *historia* left. (Swete, *Theodore on the Minor Epistles*, vol. I (Cambridge, 1880), p. 79; E. T. Froehlich, *Biblical Interpretation*, pp. 99–100)

The providential activity of the one God who creates and recreates could not be reduced to a charade whose real meaning lay elsewhere.

The Bible and Doctrine

It was not just allegory that could undermine the "mind" of Scripture. Certain key texts of Scripture lay at the heart of the fourth-century Arian controversy, the most serious debate about the nature of Christ to take place in the history of the Church. Here it would seem that too great a literalism produced heresy. Some controversial texts came from the Gospels, but the most significant was Proverbs 8:22ff.

From the second century on, this passage appears among those texts which were taken to refer to the pre-existent Word or Wisdom of God, through whom God created everything. The biblical passage depicts Wisdom making the following claims:

> The Lord created me at the beginning of his work, the first of his acts of long ago. Ages ago I was set up at the first, before the beginning of the earth. When there were no depths I was brought forth, when there were no springs abounding with water. Before the mountains were shaped, before the hills, I was brought forth . . . [W]hen he marked out the foundations of the earth, then I was beside him, like a master worker; and I was daily his delight. [Proverbs 8:22–5, 30, NRSV]

That modern English translation does not capture some of the way in which the text was read in the Greek of the Septuagint: the opening sentence was usually construed as having a double object so that the sense was "The Lord made [in the sense of 'appointed'] me [the/a] beginning of his work"; and the Greek avoided the obscurity of the Hebrew represented by "like a master worker" (otherwise understood as "little child"), instead expressing the closeness of the relationship between God and his Wisdom, a relationship which the Fathers saw as captured elsewhere in the baptismal voice: "This is my beloved Son," or in the Johannine Prologue where the Word is pictured as the Son in the Father's bosom. The passage as a whole, then, was taken to refer to the Son of God who became incarnate in Jesus Christ. This reference was long established, and went unquestioned in the Arian controversy.

Up to the time of the controversy, no clear distinction was drawn between "brought forth" or "begotten" (v. 25) and "created" (v. 22). Arius, however, insisted that the pre-existent Word, through whom God created everything else, was himself a creature – maybe the first and greatest of the creatures, but still a creature rather than the offspring of the one uncreated God. It was for this reason that this text lay at the very heart of the controversy. By taking this text literally, and then cross-referencing texts in the Gospels which attributed creaturely weaknesses to Jesus Christ, including the Johannine statement, "My Father is greater than I," Arius built up a biblical case for seeing the Father alone as truly God. His heresy was countered by the Nicene confession that the Son of God was of one substance (*homoousios*) with the Father.

That confession was controversial from the time of the council in 325, and in the course of his lifelong struggle to defend the Nicene formula, Athanasius was confronted with the charge that *homoousios* was a non-scriptural word, besides needing to rescue the Arian proof texts from the literalizing interpretation so damaging to what he saw as the Church's traditional confession of Christ. In his *De decretis Nicaenae synodi*, Athanasius' fundamental argument concerns the need to discern the mind of Scripture, to distinguish the "wording" and the "sense." This meant identifying its underlying coherence, its unitive testimony to the one true Son of God.

Observation of Athanasius' use of scriptural texts reveals a deductive process whereby texts are assembled, and the normal or "earthly" meaning of words is respected while elevating their sense appropriately for their theological context. His discussion of what Scripture means by "son" is a case in point: (1) anyone obedient to God's commandments is a son of God; and (2) Scripture speaks of natural sons, like Isaac being the son of Abraham. It is inadequate to regard the only-begotten Word of God as Son of God in the first sense, and the second sense is problematic if you take it as an exact analogy. One must avoid conceiving of God in a human way. Crude literalism will not do. That God is incomposite and incorporeal, that the divine Being is incomprehensible – such concepts are grounded in God's mysterious name revealed to Moses at the Burning Bush. Yet they betray the extra-biblical theological presuppositions which determine the reading of the text.

The exegesis of Proverbs 8:22ff. necessarily has a high profile in Athanasius' anti-Arian works – the bulk of *Contra Arianos* II is devoted to it. Athanasius notes the genre: proverbs. That means the sense must be unfolded and sought as something hidden. This is done by attending to scriptural usage. "Create" has two scriptural senses, one concerning origin, the other renewal, as in the text "Create in me a new heart." So the proverb in question is to be understood as referring not to the Word's generation, but rather to regeneration – so not to the essence but to the humanity of the Word. He notes that in verse 25, as elsewhere in Scripture, the "begetting" is stated absolutely, whereas "created" in verse 22 is relative – "for his works." It is relative to the created order and the Incarnation as an expression of God's providential plan.

This distinction between speaking absolutely of the Son's Being and speaking of him relative to the created order (or the "Economy") is crucial for Athanasius' discernment of the mind of Scripture. Such an overarching perspective, coupled with intertextual references, enables further elaboration of the interpretation in terms of renewal or re-creation: "We are his workmanship, created in Jesus Christ," he suggests, using Ephesians 2:10 among many other passages. Thus he arrives at a classic distinction which he regards as fundamental to Scripture: God's offspring was begotten then made, made flesh for our salvation in the Economy, whereas creatures were made and then begotten through Christ, becoming sons by grace.

Athanasius thus proves that the same theological principle was at work in doctrinal argument as in our previous examples, Irenaeus, Origen, and the Anti-allegorists: the reading of particular texts had to be subservient to the overarching sense of Scripture as whole.

Figural Reading of Scripture

The unity of the Bible was fundamental. So was resistance to a merely literal or "material" reading. The Bible was about God and the divine providential plan for creation. Its diversity pointed beyond itself to a single meaning intended by the Holy Spirit. Yet this did not exclude the notion of multiple senses.

Origen, as we have seen, theoretically identified a threefold sense; in practice he often produced more than one "moral" or "spiritual" sense of any given passage. The Anti-allegorists were just as interested in moral and doctrinal readings, yet the outcome was different. This may be exemplified by comparing the way in which Christ's feeding of the multitude is treated by Origen and John Chrysostom. On the one hand, Origen (*Commentary on Matthew* XI) treats it as symbolic of spiritual feeding: the desert place represents the desert condition of the masses without the Law and the Word of God, and the disciples are given power to nourish the crowds with rational food. The five loaves and two fishes symbolize Scripture and the Word. Thus the items in the story become tokens, the text a code to be cracked. On the other hand, the great "Golden-mouthed" preacher, John (*Homilies on Matthew* XLIX), turns the story into proofs of dogma and moral lessons for his congregation: Christ looked up to heaven to prove he is of the Father, and he used the loaves and fish, rather than creating out of nothing, to stop the mouths of dualist heretics like Marcion and Manichaeus. He let the crowds become hungry and gave them only loaves and fish, equally distributed, to teach the crowd humility, temperance, and charity, and to have all things in common. He wanted to be sure they did not become slaves to the belly. Thus deductive techniques facilitate the drawing of morals, or a move from the surface of the text to a more doctrinal or spiritual meaning.

Moral meanings, however, were more often drawn through "types" or exemplars of particular virtues. Job became the embodiment of patience, while biblical characters became models for contemporary bishops or celebrated saints and martyrs. This exploited the normal usage of the Greek word *typos*, and the usual rhetorical practice of *syncrisis*, or comparison between the person being honoured in a speech and the well-known heroes of classical literature. The oratory of the great Cappadocian Fathers provides evidence of how Christian preaching was assimilated to the culture and rhetoric of the time, as do the homilies of John Chrysostom. But such use of "types" was married with another long-standing typological practice, one that enabled the allegorical tradition to develop a kind of parallel universe of discourse which consistently understood biblical terms in a spiritual sense: e.g. Jerusalem = the Church; Joshua = Jesus. To understand this we need to return to the earliest period.

Again we may take as an example the feeding stories in the Gospels. Built into them is a back-reference to the giving of manna in the wilderness during the Israelites' exodus from Egypt. The term "typology" is most frequently used to describe the tendency, already noticeable within the Hebrew Bible, to shape one story in terms of another, so that layers of association and meaning are built into the narrative. Such typology became prophetic, as expectations of the Eschaton were shaped according to earlier saving narratives. This kind of typology was exploited, alongside other symbolical readings of the Jewish Scriptures, in the earliest Christian endeavours to show how the prophets predicted everything about Christ, including the Passion. While Moses held up his arms, the Israelites prevailed against the Amalekites; so when Christ holds his arms out on the cross, Christians prevail against the forces of evil. Such models of redemption etched, as it were, into the stories of the past became traditional. In the Old Testament the future was set out in "types and shadows," to be fully discerned in the future. The classic example of a fully-worked typology occurs in the paschal homilies, where the Passover becomes the precursor of the Passion and Easter. The rediscovered *Peri Pascha* of Melito of Sardis (ed. S. G. Hall, Oxford, 1979) from the mid-second century, reveals his concern to explain to a Hellenistic audience this strange kind of prophecy whereby a prophetic "model" of what was to come is displayed in advance. Scripture provides a "parable," a "designer's sketch" or prefiguration, which is temporary and becomes obsolete when the reality is revealed. A "type" is a sign that points beyond itself.

The most important thing about this "figural" approach to Scripture was the way it enabled the discernment of Christ, the Church, and the Eschaton in the whole of Scripture, from Beginning to End. Already in the New Testament (1 Cor. 10:4) Christ is present as the spiritual Rock in the wilderness from which "our ancestors" drank. Rapidly the Crossing of the Red Sea became a prefiguration of baptism. The Christological reading of key Old Testament texts became traditional, and was largely untouched by the reaction against allegory. From Irenaeus through Origen to Augustine, this way of reading the whole Bible as referring to the Christian dispensation lay at the heart of exegesis. Whatever the debate about allegory, traditional "types" ensured the continuing figural reading of Scripture.

Augustine's *De doctrina Christiana* sums up the legacy of the first Christian theologians to the Middle Ages. Augustine sets out to discuss what the Christian teacher needs (*doctrina* simply means "teaching"), producing a Christianized *Institutio oratoria*, or rhetorical handbook, with the Bible replacing the classics as the core curriculum. Like so many other early Christian exegetes, Augustine distinguishes between the wording and the content, or, as he puts it, the "thing" and the "signs." So the first book sets out the essential subject matter of Scripture, or the "Rule of Faith," Augustine reflecting the approach of Irenaeus and Athanasius as he seeks to distil the "mind" of Scripture as a whole, discussing doctrine in the more usual English sense – the Trinity and the Incarnation.

Books II and III turn to the "signs" by which Scripture signifies these things. He discusses the "sign" character of writing and of language itself, recognizing the problem of human discord which necessitates translation from one language to another. His hermeneutical principle is to try and ascertain the thought and will of those who wrote the Scriptures, and through this to find the will of God. But he recognizes that the signs are not all transparent, and there are many obscurities in Scripture. He thinks, a bit like Origen, that this is to prevent pride and to stimulate the intellectual appetite. The qualities that the interpreter needs include fear of the Lord, piety, knowledge, strength and resolution, purity of vision, and wisdom. It is in this spirit that he then deals with all the issues of interpretation we have already noted. The range of knowledge required for interpreting the "signs" includes some skill in Hebrew and Greek, etymology and numerology, music and the liberal arts, together with dialectic and logic. Then there are the "grammatical" issues of punctuation, pronunciation, and correct construal. The rule is that whatever in the Word of God, when taken literally, cannot be referred to purity of life or soundness of doctrine, must be treated as figurative, and figures of speech are listed, such as allegory, enigma, parable, metaphor, irony.

Augustine then reviews the *Rules of Tychonius*. This work had just been produced, and purported to provide keys to open the secrets of Scripture. At first sight the seven rules listed hardly seem to us to be rules: "On the Lord and his body"; "On the Lord's twofold Body"; "On the promises and the law"; "On species and genus"; "On measurements of time"; "On recapitulation"; "On the devil and his body." The discussion shows that Tychonius assumes the Christological reference of the whole of Scripture, and is concerned to systematize the reference of figurative texts within the Christian dispensation. An example from discussion of the first rule should give some sense of what this is all about: Daniel calls the Lord "the stone hewn from the mountain," but when "the stone became a mountain and filled the whole earth," he is speaking of the Lord's body. "Becoming a mountain" cannot apply to Christ since he "had this glory before the world was made" (John 17:5). On the other hand, "we grow up in all things into him who is the head, Christ, from whom the whole body . . . derives its increase" (Eph. 4:15–16). Deductive argument and biblical cross-reference establishes the distinction. According to Augustine, consideration of these rules is helpful in penetrating the obscure parts of the divine writings, but actually they do not cover every eventuality. The important thing is that they state that one thing is to be understood by another. To have the right wisdom and insight for this, in Augustine's view, requires not just reason but holiness.

For a long time the biblical exegesis of the earliest Christian theologians has been discussed in terms of the categories "literal," "typological", and "allegorical." This chapter has not been shaped in that way, though it certainly provides commentary upon that approach, which would seem to have arisen from the tendency to read back into the ancient world the medieval "senses" of Scripture. The suggestion here is that greater understanding is possible if we examine early exegesis within the cultural parameters of the period, and observe what they do as much as what they say. Theologically speaking, what has emerged is the crucial importance of reading Scripture as a whole, to discern the overarching narrative from the Beginning to the End, and to gain insight into the "mind" of Scripture. This contrasts with modern analytical and historical approaches. Scholars did not overlook the necessity for sophisticated philological discussion. All the notes in a typical commentary have their precedents in the work of ancient exegetes. Yet the theological mind of the Church's scholars led to a universal tendency to find the text referring to eternal realities through the material and physical "signs" and contents of the text. The categories "literal" and "allegorical" are simply not sophisticated enough for analyzing the differences between exegetes, all of whom expected to find the text pointing beyond itself, and being in some sense symbolic of moral and spiritual realities beyond human linguistic expression. Scripture was theology, and theological doctrine was all to be found in the Bible.

Bibliography

Much of this chapter draws on my previously published work, especially *Biblical Exegesis and the Formation of Christian Culture* (Cambridge, 1997); and "The Fourth Century Reaction against Allegory," *Studia Patristica* xxx (1997), pp. 120–5.

For parts of the discussion I am indebted to Elizabeth A. Clark, *The Origenist Controversy. The Construction of an Early Christian Debate* (Princeton, 1992); and R. M. Grant, *The Earliest Lives of Jesus* (London, 1961).

For access to key extracts from the Fathers, particularly the Anti-allegorists, see K. Froehlich, *Biblical Interpretation in the Early Church*, Sources of Early Christian Thought, Philadelphia, PA, 1984. Adrianos' little treatise, *Isagoge ad sacras scripturas*, can be found in Migne, PG 98.1273–1312.

Harry Y. Gamble, *Books and Readers in the Early Church* (New Haven, CT and London, 1995).

R. M. Grant, with David Tracy, *A Short History of the Interpretation of the Bible*, 2nd edn, revised and enlarged (London, 1984).

R. P. C. Hanson, *Allegory and Event. A Study of the Sources and Significance of Origen's Inter-* *pretation of Scripture,* with an Introduction by Joseph W. Trigg (Louisville and London, 2002).

M. Simonetti, *Biblical Interpretation in the Early Church: An Historical Introduction to Patristic Exegesis.* ET by John A. Hughes, with Anders Bergquist and Markus Bockmuehl as editors, and William Horbury as Consultant Editor (Edinburgh, 1994).

The Church

The Early Idea of the Church

Stuart G. Hall

The earliest Christians believed that God was creating a new people for himself: he had inaugurated the Last Times, when by the Spirit he raised Jesus from the dead, and sent his Apostles first to Israel, and then to the Gentiles, to call out what moderns describe as "the eschatological community of salvation".[1] This was "God's assembly". The word ἐκκλησία, transliterated into Latin as *ecclesia*, and usually translated as "Church," originates as a Greek political term for a civic or similar assembly. It is often used in the Septuagint (the Greek version of the Old Testament books) for the assembly of the Lord's people; it was an alternative to συναγωγή ("synagogue" or "gathering"). It is probably to be understood always as "the Church *of God*," even when it is called merely "the Church." In Paul and Acts, where it is frequent, it is usually localized: "The church of God which is in Corinth" (1 Cor. 1:2), "the church throughout Judaea" (Acts 9:31); it can therefore be plural: "the churches of Galatia" (Gal. 1:2). But there was always only one divinely-generated community, apparent in each locality, and in the later Pauline tradition this is explicit: Christ is the Head of the body, which is the Church (Col. 1:18); it makes him known to the world (Eph. 2:10), and there is only one such body (Eph. 4:4).[2] In the canonical Gospels the word occurs only in two passages, both originating in the disciplinary arrangements of the later ecclesial community rather than in the teaching of Jesus (Matt. 16:18; 18:17). In the former, Jesus names Simon "the Rock" (Peter), on whom he will build his Church, and Peter is to determine whose sins shall be forgiven and whose retained, so the Church controls the gates of Hades. This passage was later used, especially by Cyprian, to authorize the role of the bishop in each locality to determine disciplinary questions, and that may in fact already have been the meaning when Matthew wrote. It reflects the fact that from the start the Church was held to be pure, as being the community created by the Spirit of God for his incoming Kingdom, but it consisted of human beings who sometimes defaulted and needed moral correction.

We have a record of the beginning of the Church in The Acts of the Apostles, written about AD90. It belongs to the "third generation" of Christian leaders, following Jesus and his immediate apostolic successors. It is a continuation of The

Gospel according to Luke, and shares its characteristics. Luke (we use that name, though the author's identity is uncertain) has positive historical and literary purposes. Some of these affect his idea of the Church. Plümacher identifies three: (1) the "age of the Church" displaces belief in an immediate consummation in the coming of Christ; (2) the Church becomes a phenomenon in world history; (3) the Church has a history of its own.[3]

1 Many among the first generation of believers expected the return of Christ (the *Parousia*) and the end of the world in their own lifetime. Contrary indications in the New Testament are the result of efforts by writers to correct this widespread tendency. A surge of expectation that the world would soon be ending apparently followed the deaths of leading Apostles (James the Just, Peter, and Paul, about AD62–4), a savage persecution in Rome (AD64) and the sufferings culminating in the fall of Jerusalem (AD70), which might encourage the hope that the Lord would come before the last of the Apostles' generation died (cf. Mark 9:1; John 21:22–3; 2 Peter 3:3–10). Luke minimizes this hope of an imminent end; the Kingdom of God does not come "with observation", it is "within you" or "among you" (Luke 17:20–1).

2 Both Jesus and the Church become for Luke part of world history. The first followers saw the authorities as alien, a persecuting, sinful, and adulterous generation (Mark 8:34–8; 13:8–9); their own life was distinct, "hidden with Christ in God" (Col. 3:3). Luke now argues, "This thing was not done in a corner" (Acts 26:26). Events are related to datable public history (Luke 2:1–2; 3:1–2; Acts 11:27–8; 18:2), traditional mysterious prophecies become direct forecasts of historical events (Luke 21:20–4), and political allegations and manipulations are part of the story (Luke 23:1–12). Agrippa's persecution and its consequences are related to public policy (Acts 12:1–4; 20–3); public process and officials are often involved (Luke 23:1–12; Acts 13:7–12; 24:24; 25:22–6, 28). Asiarchs appear at Ephesus (Acts 19:31) and members of the Areopagus in Athens (Acts 17:18–34), where Paul discusses public religion and quotes pagan literature (Acts 17:23 and 28). Persecution comes not from the Empire, but from the Jews, in Jerusalem (Acts 5:17–18; 6:8–15; 21:27–8) and in the cities of Paul's missionary travels (Acts 13:50; 14:2; 17:5). Paul exercises his birthright as a Roman citizen (cf. Acts 22:24–9; 25:9–11). The function of the Church is to fulfill the true destiny of Israel, which is to bring light to all nations, and that means the Roman Empire. This calling was offered time and again to the Jews, both by Jesus in the Gospel and by the Apostles in Acts. The Jews repudiated the calling, though a faithful remnant have taken the message to the heart of Empire. In the final scene of Acts, anticipated earlier in the work, the Jews in Rome itself are offered the calling, but, as Isaiah had predicted, rejected it (Acts 28:23–7). In the end Paul says, "Be it known therefore that this salvation of God is sent to the nations: they will surely listen" (Acts 28:28).

3 For Luke the Church has a history and a role of its own. The other Gospel-writers all know a church originating in Galilee after Jesus' resurrection. In Matthew and Mark it is exclusively so (Mark 16:7; Matt. 28:16–20); Matthew already describes a huge following of the Jesus movement in the north (all Syria, Galilee, and Decapolis, as well as Judea, Jerusalem, and Trans-Jordan (Matthew 4:24–5)). In John the risen

Jesus bestows the Spirit on the Apostles in Jerusalem (20:19–29) but, as the Gospel stands, they went back to Galilee for the commissioning of Peter (John 21). By contrast, Luke puts all the Resurrection appearances in or about Jerusalem, and the Apostles are sent "to all nations, beginning from Jerusalem" (Luke 24:47), programmatically, "Jerusalem, all Judea, Samaria, and as far as the end of the earth" (Acts 1:8). This worldwide mission is depicted by representing the primitive glossolalia as the power to communicate with a multitude of foreign visitors in their own tongues (Acts 2:5–13). Judea and Samaria are penetrated (Acts 8), and the conversion of the Samaritans is carried through and ratified by a mission of the chief Apostles from Jerusalem (Acts 8:4–25). Saul (Paul) is called and converted to lead the Gentile mission (Acts 9:16, etc.). This mission begins formally in Antioch (Acts 13:1–3), and we know from Paul himself that the admission of Gentiles to the Church was a subject of contention between him and major leaders (Cephas/Peter, James of Jerusalem, and Barnabas are all blamed in Galatians 2:11–13). Luke rewrites the history, making Peter the pioneer of the Gentile mission (Acts 10:1–11,18), associating Barnabas closely with it (e.g. Acts 11:19–24; 13:2–3), and even making James a mediating figure (Acts 15:13–21; 21:17–25).

Luke–Acts is thus a landmark in constituting Church history, but is also a distorting glass, surer evidence of the way Luke perceives the Church than of the events he describes. To the three points outlined, other features must be added about church officers and church consultations. First, the Church is formally founded upon the Apostles, the remaining eleven duly listed in Acts 1:13–14, and the twelfth added by election (or drawing lots) in Acts 1:16–26 before the Spirit is bestowed. This process of ordaining Matthias (1:23–6) is presumably modeled on what Luke knew about appointing presbyters or bishops in his own time. Similarly the election and ordination of deacons is given apostolic origin (Acts 6:1–6), ostensibly so that the Apostles may not be diverted from "the word of God" to administering charity. Paul and Barnabas pay a return visit to churches founded on their missionary journey, to exhort them to steadfast faith under persecution, and to commit them prayerfully to God, first "having ordained for them presbyters in each church" (Acts 14:22–3), and it is such "presbyters of the church" he gathers for his farewell charge at Ephesus (Acts 20:17). The church in Jerusalem is governed by the Apostles, who remain when persecution scatters the flock (Acts 8:1), but for judicial discussions there gather "apostles and brothers" (Acts 11:1–2) or "apostles and presbyters" (Acts 15:1 and throughout the chapter), who issue their judgement as "apostles and presbyters, brothers" (15:23). Later, James of Jerusalem with "all the presbyters" confronts Paul on his last visit. James is presumably "the brother of the Lord" (Gal. 1:19), since James the brother of John was already executed (Acts 12:2): the brothers and mother of Jesus had been present in the congregation on which the Spirit fell (1:14 with 2:1–4). All of this implies a practice of government by senior males (presbyters) like that among the Jews; the "presbyters of the Jews" are often mentioned in the Gospels and Acts alongside the priests (e.g. Acts 4:23). It is easy to see how the settled congregations in a Jewish context naturally adopted the synagogue pattern, where elders, president, and assistant provide a pattern for what became universal in the Church: presbyters, bishop, and deacon.[4] Acts includes, however, a residue of a more varied pattern of authority. The leading ministers in 1 Corinthians 12:29–30 (cf. Eph. 4:11) are "first apostles, second prophets, third teachers", a trio which appears also in Didachê 11, and we find church life directed by prophets (some female) in Acts 11:27; 15:32; 21:9–10. It is a distinguished group of "prophets and teachers" who in Antioch resolve to send Barnabas and Saul (Paul) on their first missionary expedition. Significantly, they do so with a formal ordination including laying-on of hands (Acts 13:1–3). Given that the Church is seen as in various ways an ordered society, it is not surprising that formal consultation processes are present. The question of how far Paul's Gentile converts must conform to Jewish practices was the subject of spontaneous private visits of Paul to Jerusalem (Gal. 1:18–19; 2:1–2). Luke makes this into what moderns call "the council of Jerusalem," with reports, questions, set speeches, and a written conclusion circulated to the churches by appointed deputies (Acts 15:1–33). This naturally became an authoritative model for church government; but it also reflects the actual practice known to Luke late in the first century.

At the outset the Church had no special buildings, but met in the great houses of its patrons. In major cities there would be a number of these, and this is clearly true of Corinth.[5] Each congregation would naturally have the householder as its president, who might also be called a presbyter or bishop. At Rome such an arrangement prevailed until the ordination of Fabian in 236 according to Brent, when the system of one bishop with seven district churches managed by presbyters and deacons was finally consolidated. While this late dating of the rise of Roman monepiscopacy may be questioned (see below), it is likely to be true in principle. The powerful status of urban presbyters at Carthage in 250 and in Alexandria about 320 suggests that the same was true there.

We possess from the first half of the second century *The Shepherd*, an apocalyptic compilation by a Roman prophet and proprietor called Hermas.[6] The whole compilation reveals the Church as a community which is built up like a tower of various kinds of stones, in various stages of perfection. The function of the Church and the angel-spirits who supervise it is to achieve purity by cleansing, correction, or rejection of its members. The Church itself is depicted as a female figure, virginal and maternal: "She was created first of all things; . . . because of her the world was constructed" (8.1 = Vision II 4,1); she is also a tower in building. Hermas receives these prophetic visions once for all, so that the offer of repentance cannot be repeated; but the view, which has had some currency among critics, that this is intended to be only a single event before the End, is to be rejected. What is offered is a single second chance for the baptized believer who has fallen into sin, and a call to the leaders to exercise this discipline properly.[7] This large compilation was read as Scripture widely in the second century: written in Rome, it was used by Irenaeus in Lyons, by Clement of Alexandria, and by Tertullian in North Africa in about 200.[8] These instructions for the functioning of the Church were to be copied by Hermas to Clement, who is responsible for "the outside towns", and to Grapte, who "will instruct the widows and orphans": "But you will read it in this city with the elders who preside over the church" (8.3 = Vision II 4,3). This portrays an ecclesial organization in Rome which tallies with other evidence, and this must be examined next.

Late in the first century the church in Rome sent a long letter to that in Corinth, which is preserved as *The First Letter of Clement* in some ancient New Testament copies (we shall call the author "Clement").[9] Rome complains about the divisions in the Corinthian church, where jealousy has robbed it of its former tranquillity, charity, and devotion. There has been a rebellion of young against old, and presbyters of long standing have been removed from office and replaced. The whole church must turn from jealousy, which has killed martyrs and ruined nations, and restore good order by proper submission to the will of God, repenting before his impending judgement. The Church is likened to a well-organized army or a human body (using St. Paul's metaphor: 1 Cor. 12:12–30; Eph. 4:11–16). The novelty of Clement's treatment is his discovery that just as the condemnation of the rash rebels is in Scripture (1 Clement 39), so there is revealed a parallel between the biblical priestly sacrificial system and the life of the Church (40–2): God appointed through Moses distinct tasks for high priest, priest, Levite, and layman, and similarly sent his Christ, who sent his Apostles, and "they preached from district to district, and from city to city, and they appointed their first converts, testing them by the Spirit, to be bishops and deacons of the future believers" (42.4), fulfilling prophecy (Isa. 60:17 [Septuagint]). Clement has apparently discovered this meaning of the ancient priestly system, and uses it to make the point that the long-standing presbyters have God's authority, and should not be removed: Moses had miraculously demonstrated God's choice of Aaron as priest against his critics, and the Apostles had been instructed by Christ to anticipate strife, not only by appointing their first converts as bishops and deacons, but by instituting a system of continuance after their death (44–5); it is therefore a grave sin to remove them without good cause, and those who did so should step down, repent, and submit to the presbyters (46–57). The terms here need clarification. First, Clement knows the appointed ministers as "bishops and deacons," terms he found in his Greek Bible. This pairing also stands in the New Testament (Phil. 1:1; 1 Timothy 3:1–13) and in *Didachê* 15.1. Clement also refers to the bishops as "presbyters": "It will be no small sin for us, if we remove from the episcopate those who have blamelessly and religiously offered the gifts. Happy are those presbyters who made their journey before, who received their release fruitful and entire" (44.4–5). These are presumably the same presbyters to whom the founders of the schism are to submit (57.1). Presbyters are also called "bishops" elsewhere (Acts 20:17 and 28; Titus 1:5 and 7; Irenaeus about AD190 still uses "presbyters" to refer to bishops (as in Eusebius, *Hist. eccl.* 5, 24, 16). "Bishop" means "overseer" in religious or secular matters; "presbyter" means "elder," and has wide use in secular and religious contexts, including the governing bodies of Jewish synagogues. "Deacon" means "servant," and often has menial connections; but it can also refer to an official of high standing, as "minister" can in English. The church order presupposed for Rome and Corinth by Clement appears to involve government by a number of presbyter-bishops who have (though we have little detail) deacons to assist them. His argument is that this organization, including a system of succession, is divinely appointed by Christ through the Apostles, and that to depose lawful presbyters is a great sin. These presbyter-bishops are like those to whom Hermas reported his prophecies in Rome and may originally have been the leading householders, the patrons, in whose houses the first churches gathered. There are however complications.

Church organization was not uniform. We have two other early documents, the *Didachê* and the *Letters* of Ignatius, which suggest the opposite. The anonymous *Didachê* or *Teaching of the Twelve Apostles*[10] is a late first-century version of a manual for Christian living. Besides providing material for baptismal preparation, baptism, prayer, and eucharist, this gives regulations for visiting teachers, apostles, and prophets (*Didachê* 11) and for the settled prophet "worthy of his food." Settled prophets are to be given the firstfruits of every crop, "for they are your highpriests" (13). Prophets have a special role in commanding and conducting the eucharistic meal (10.7; 11.9). In what is usually held to be a later supplement, a regular eucharistic assembly on the Lord's Day is commanded (14) and consequently a regular ministry is needed like that in Clement: "Appoint therefore for yourselves bishops and deacons worthy of the Lord . . . for they also minister to you the ministry of the prophets and teachers" (15.1). *Didachê* thus represents a congregation shifting from a predominantly prophetic ministry, like that suggested in 1 Corinthians 12–14, where apostles, prophets and teachers figure large (1 Cor. 12:48), to one where the spiritual functions belong to appointed officers.

Ignatius of Antioch probably wrote seven letters during a journey towards martyrdom in Rome between AD100 and 118.[11] He is concerned for the unity of the churches he addresses in Asia Minor and Rome, and probably for that of his own in Syrian Antioch.[12] Faced with disputes over Jewish ideas at Philadelphia, and over the fleshly reality of Christ at Smyrna, he calls on each church to rally round its bishop. He says he had spoken inspired words at Philadelphia: "Give heed to the bishop, and to the presbytery and deacons" (*Philad.* 7.1); "Do nothing without the bishop . . . love unity, avoid divisions" (*Philad.* 7.2); "See that you follow the bishop, as Jesus Christ follows the Father, and the presbytery as if it were the Apostles. And reverence the deacons as commanded by God" (*Smyrnaeans* 8.1). The Church is nothing without him: "Wherever the bishop appears let the people be present, just as wherever Jesus Christ is, there is the universal Church," and the bishop is needed for valid eucharist, baptism, and love-feast (*Smyrnaeans* 8.2). Ignatius sees the one bishop as symbolizing the unity of God, and the officers as representing Christ and the Apostles: "Let all respect the deacons as Jesus Christ, even as the bishop is also a type (model) of the Father, and the presbyters as the council of God and the college of the Apostles" (*Trallians* 3.1). As against Clement, Hermas, and *Didachê* there is only one bishop, whose singularity symbolizes the unity of God; with his local congregation the bishop also symbolizes Jesus Christ and the "universal" (catholic) church. This figuration appears to be mystical rather than historical: while insisting on the bishop's role in expressing and achieving unity, Ignatius nowhere writes of the succession of bishops from apostles or other bishops in the way Clement does. His model is, however, the one which came to prevail, one in which a single bishop is supported by a council of presbyters and by one or more deacons. Those scholars (like Schoedel) are probably right who see Ignatius fighting to impose his scheme, which we call "monepiscopal," on churches which may have resisted it, including his own in Antioch. It is an interesting fact that in every letter Ignatius addresses or mentions the bishop of the church personally, except when he writes to Rome about his impending martyrdom; we may assume that this is because there is no single presiding bishop there.

Ignatius' monepiscopal model probably derives ultimately from the Jewish synagogue system, as we have described. His own city, Antioch, originally knew no single bishop, if the ordination of Paul and Barnabas is historical (Acts 13:1–3). The presiding role of James of Jerusalem and his martyrdom, before the fall of the city in AD70, may have contributed to the rise of monepiscopacy elsewhere. It is also likely that Ignatius' own martyrdom encouraged acceptance of his ideas. His letters were collected by Polycarp of Smyrna for the use of the church at Philippi, and Polycarp's own reputation as champion of orthodoxy and as martyr both became prominent, as we shall see. If we look for a reason for this development, one clue lies in the proliferation of theological thinking. A city church consisting of a number of distinct houses, with patrons, perhaps dignified as bishops or presbyters, but of varied spiritual gifts and competence, governed their churches in conjunction with charismatically-gifted travelling apostles, teachers, and prophets, and with settled prophets and teachers. The Bible consisted of what we call the Old Testament, the limits of which were not known, and the books of which not all might be available in any particular place; the New Testament was yet to be firmly identified, though some letters attributed to Paul and a number of Gospel records and Acts were in circulation; there was no fixed creed, no universal baptismal formula; many pious fictions about Jesus and the Apostles, and various visions and apocalypses were in circulation. It is not surprising that a city like Smyrna might have some groups, either households or "schools," meeting and worshipping on their own, without reference to others. Ignatius insisting, "Do nothing without the bishop," offered a clear adjudicator of what was and what was not proper. Similarly the disciplinary questions, which arise when the sins of baptized believers threaten the purity of the prayers of the community, and are dealt with at length by Hermas, benefit from the appointment of a final judge, even if he sits with assessors. This judicial function is perhaps that alluded to when the deposed presbyters at Corinth are said to have "blamelessly and religiously offered the gifts" (1 Clement 44.4), even though there is no monepiscopate yet: one of the functions of a high priest in 1 Clement is to inspect offerings for blemishes (42.2).

Earnest believers might deplore breaches of unity and discipline, but they also embellished their view of the Church as a spiritual body. Hermas saw it as the first created being, for which all else was made. An early homily, perhaps addressed to those being baptized, is preserved as *The Second Letter of Clement*.[13] It says that those who do God's will belong to "the first Church, the spiritual one, created before the sun and moon" (2 Clement 14.1). It is also Christ's body, and the spiritual Church was made manifest in his flesh (2 Clement 14.3). The believer must not abuse the flesh (by sin), or he "will not receive the Spirit, which is Christ," the marvellous gift prepared for the elect (2 Clement 14.5). Other writers develop this notion of a heavenly, pre-existent, and spiritual Church, already suggested in Hebrews 12:22–3 ("the congregation and assembly of the first-born registered in heaven"). For some of those usually classed as "Gnostics" this heavenly Church exists as one of the "aeons,"[14] the primary beings who constitute the Fulness (*Pleroma*) of spiritual reality. If correctly reported, the "true and holy Church" was for the Ophites itself the unification of the Father, the Son, and the Holy Spirit with the pre-existent Christ.[15] In *The Second Treatise of the Great Seth*[16] the Word (Christ) tells how he addressed the assembly (Church) of spiritual beings to gain their consent to his mission to rescue kindred spirits in the nether regions, as he now promotes the same mission in an assembly on earth.[17] For some the pre-existent Church meant those predestined to be restored to the Fulness when they are illuminated by Jesus Christ.[18] The malignant powers had mixed their own seed with this elect Church, but Christ came to separate the kinds, and its members attain their appropriate levels.[19] The corresponding spirituality can be strong and moving: those who repent, assent to the Church, and share her sufferings, at the hands of men and of angels, with those of the incarnate Christ.[20] Insofar as such writings are not "orthodox," it is in aspects derived from other doctrinal features. Typically, for example, many make use of the threefold distinction of body–soul–spirit, corresponding to three kinds of humanity, choic–psychic–pneumatic, which are then extended to the three elements in Jesus Christ and three constituents in the Church.[21]

Unity of doctrine is the prime concern of Irenaeus, bishop of Lyons from about 177 to about 200.[22] His chief writing, *Against the Heresies*, was provoked by a successful movement in his own vicinity led by one Markos, which Irenaeus judged in breach of true doctrine, tradition, and good order. He presents the teachings of various groups which he judges heretical, beginning with some whom he regards as Valentinians.[23] Against these and all other deviations he appeals to the one universal Church.[24] The Church, he says, is one and the same in all countries and times. It received from the Apostles some general principles, variously described as "the Tradition," "the Proclamation", or "the Rule of Truth," a concept we meet in other writers, and which is usually referred to as "The Rule of Faith." Its basic points are: one God the Creator and Father, Jesus Christ his Son who came from heaven to earth to restore all things, the Holy Spirit, and the coming Resurrection and judgement of mankind. By this he tests the doctrines and biblical interpretations of teachers and sects, and declares them wanting. Most of them posit a divinity above the Creator, and see Jesus Christ either as an inferior being, or as so spiritual as not to be concretely material, or as a combination of various persons. To support his position he insists upon the Old Testament (which various teachers had regarded as products of an inferior Creator or of angelic beings) and argues for the genuine written works of the Apostles, using various arguments for four and only four Gospels, the same which did indeed establish themselves in the New Testament canon. Some of his history is faulty: the apostolic origin of much of the New Testament is questionable, and the unanimity of the churches before his time plainly false. Some of his own ideas, like the earthly millennium of Christ's kingdom and the physical shape of God, are ones the Church has since rejected.[25] However, it is the way he based doctrine on the tradition and unanimity of the Church which makes him important.

In his third Book, Irenaeus deals with the claim of his opponents that their teaching was derived from the Apostles, given secretly to spiritually-gifted individuals. His response is to use the ideas of Clement and Ignatius, arguing that the Apostles appointed the first bishops (also called presbyters) in the churches, and would not have hidden from them any secret teaching of the kind described: "When we face them again with the tradition of the Apostles, which is guarded by the tradition of the presbyters in the Church, they oppose the tradition, saying that they are wiser not only than presbyters, but even than Apostles, and have found the pure truth, because the Apostles mixed up provisions of the [Jewish] Law with the Saviour's words."[26] Irenaeus goes on to claim that he can enumerate the episcopal succession in all the churches which the Apostles founded; but it would be tedious to enumerate them all, so he takes as his example "that tradition which it has from the apostles and faith announced to men, of the greatest, oldest, and universally known church, founded and constituted at Rome by the two Apostles, Peter and Paul, coming right down to us through the successions of bishops." This church has a preeminence such that every one agrees with it, and people from all over the world maintain its apostolic tradition. Irenaeus would probably be hard put to it to list any other such apostolic succession, but he offers one for Rome, some of which is probably a pious fiction.[27] First, The Acts of the Apostles and Paul's letter to the Romans show that Peter and Paul did not found the church in Rome, whatever they may have done to lead or organize it. Secondly, when Irenaeus reminded Bishop Victor (c.AD190) of his illustrious predecessors, the presbyters who preceded Soter, he went back only to Xystos or Sixtus, whose name means "Sixth."[28] Aware of this meaning as he is, Irenaeus needed here to fill out the list with five predecessors. Linus is the last named male in what was thought to be Paul's last letter from Rome (2 Tim. 4:21), and Irenaeus names this source. A few verses on in the New Testament, it says, "The bishop must be *anenkletos* (irreproachable)," and it is not far-fetched to suppose that Irenaeus took that as a name, *Anenkletos*, in Latin *Anacletus*, giving him as second bishop. His third is Clement, whom he knows as the writer of *1 Clement*. Such deductions came naturally to one who could argue for four and only four authentic apostolic Gospels on the basis of the four quarters of the earth, the four winds, and the four living creatures in Revelation 4:7.[29] How he arrived at Euarestus and Alexander to make up the five is not obvious. One might suppose that Sixtus actually marks the beginning of episcopal monarchy in Rome, a decade or two after the martyrdom there of Ignatius. If so, the other house-churches continued, and schools and sects flourished there, even if one house, that of the bishops Eleutherus and Victor with whom Irenaeus corresponded, was the largest. Whatever the case, Irenaeus uses the idea of succession from the Apostles to establish one point only: the authentic apostolic message was passed to their presbyteral/episcopal successors, and their testimony is unanimous. Their doctrine gives a clear answer to the speculations and errors of Valentinians, Marcionites, and "Gnostics" of various kinds. Repeatedly Irenaeus emphasizes that the Church is the seat of all truth, all grace: "Where the Church is, there is the Spirit of God; and where the Spirit of God is, there is the Church and every grace, and the Spirit is Truth."[30]

Soon afterward Clement of Alexandria was writing similar things about the originality of apostolic truth, the unanimity of the Church's teaching, and her supernatural status, preceding the creation of the world, naming those intermediaries through whom the sects falsely claim to have received secret apostolic teaching.[31] Notably, however, he does not mention the succession of presbyters. His own teaching is based on what he learned from distinguished older teachers, all so far as we know unordained.[32] The unity of teaching is sustained by the spiritual grace of the enlightened teacher, who calls his hearers to join him among the ranks of the true "knowing ones" or Gnostics, who constitute the true, eternal Church. In contrast to the shrines and idols of the pagans, the Church is the creature, pre-eminent in holiness, in which God chooses to dwell, and it consists of those who have attained knowledge, and those who are on their way to it.[33] His Alexandrian successor, Origen, shares Clement's ideal of the spiritual and intellectual Gnostic, but has more regard to the outward, institutional Church. The churches throughout the world shine like stars in the created order, their officers morally superior to their civil counterparts.[34] Together they constitute a single body, its members infused with the vivifying power of God's Logos, in a way comparable to the union of the Logos with Jesus himself.[35] Bishops and clergy have a special obligation to pursue holiness to match their teaching; Christ is the true bishop of all.[36] The power of the bishop to bind and loose like Peter depends upon his sharing the faith of Peter,[37] and the spiritual layman is superior to worldly clergy, who disgrace their profession.[38]

Questions of the sins of members after baptism, and how their sinfulness is to be reconciled with the holiness of the Church, already exercised Clement of Rome and Hermas, as we have seen. A movement began in Phrygia and the Roman province of Asia (in the west of Asia Minor) during the second half of the second century, which called itself "The New Prophecy," but was labelled "Montanism" by later heresiologists, after its ostensible founder, Montanus. This allowed prophets, female as well as male, to speak and rule on spiritual matters. On the duty of martyrdom and the reconciliation of the lapsed it was particularly severe. The movement spread from Asia to Rome and Carthage, and with it went controversy. There were large gatherings of churchmen in Asia Minor which considered and ruled upon the New Prophecy, and these probably included the councils at Iconium and Synnada which ordered the rejection of Montanist baptisms as invalid.[39] Such gatherings, whether of the leaders of congregations in one city, or of those from various places in a region, had probably been usual from an early date, as the "council of Jerusalem" (Acts 15) indicates. In the same period, though the date is uncertain, one Noetus of Smyrna was condemned for misconduct and heresy, removed from the clergy and expelled from the Church by "the blessed presbyters," presumably a council of bishops in Roman Asia.[40] The church in Lyons, which had strong connections with Asia, became involved in the dispute, and sent an account of a particularly brutal local persecution in support of a more lenient view.[41] Leading Christians and their slaves, about forty in all, were rounded up, and variously tortured to get them to confess to atrocities like cannibalism. Some yielded under pressure at the first hearing, but most of them, persuaded by the others with whom they were kept in prison, recanted their denial, and went on to become martyrs: "Through the living the dead were brought back to life; the martyrs bestowed grace on the non-martyrs; and there was great joy in the heart of the Virgin Mother [the Church], who received her stillborn children back alive".[42] There is no indication that those who had so griev-ously lapsed were put to the kind of penance or ceremonial absolution which was usual: those who had testified to their faith at the first hearing themselves performed the reconciliation, and their work was ratified by God, inasmuch as the lapsed themselves received the crown of martyrdom.

These issues would grow in importance, especially in the West. Tertullian of Carthage, the first Latin theologian, wrote on many moral and doctrinal themes. A fluent speaker and writer, he tends to be sharply argumentative, even extreme, in his views. In his later career he defended and promoted the New Prophecy and its severe disciplines. The idea that he led or belonged to a sectarian Montanist congregation is now generally rejected.[43] Tertullian uses various images from Scripture and life to depict the Church: an ark or ship for safety from the flood or storm threatening the world; a military camp prepared for war with its encamped enemies, the world and the devil; a mother whom all need and the heathen and heretics lack (a favourite figure), a virgin in purity. He presents the ideas of apostolic foundation of churches and the Rule of Faith in similar terms to Irenaeus, exaggerating the historic claim.[44] The most remarkable development, however, is perhaps the strong distinction he makes between clergy and people,[45] for whom he borrows the Roman civil terminology of *ordo* and *plebs*. The offices of bishop, presbyter, and deacon were instituted by the Apostles, and therefore of universal validity. Through them the people are trained, guided, shepherded towards holiness. It is the very high sense of the duty of the clergy which probably leads to his castigating them so severely. At the same time the Spirit of God controls the Church, and speaks of teachers (such as Tertullian himself, who was probably a layman) and, in his later writings, prophets. *On Modesty* (*De pudicitia*) sets out the issues. A senior bishop[46] has declared that he will, after due process of penance, remit the sin of adultery to a penitent. This infringes the virginal purity of the Church, says Tertullian, and encourages further sin. He concedes that the Church in principle has the power to remit even the three gravest sins, homicide, idolatry, and adultery, but it should not do so, because it will merely encourage more sin. The bishop is wrong, because he goes against the Spirit, which is the life of the Church: the Church is Spirit expressed in a spiritual man; it is not a gathering of bishops (*numerus episcoporum*).[47] In certain circumstances the Spirit might make exceptions, but this would be announced through prophets. Under the influence of the New Prophecy, Tertullian has turned against his former views. Earlier his rigorism had expressed itself in *On Penance*, where, like Hermas, he had summoned all to the "second plank of salvation," the repentance by which the Church restored penitent sinners from among its number; now Hermas' book is repudiated explicitly as "the Shepherd which loves only adulterers."[48] So strong is his moralism that even the suffering death of a martyr, which he regards as the proper conclusion of the baptized life, can only atone for the martyr's own sins, and not for any other.[49]

The career of Cyprian, bishop of Carthage from 249 till his execution in 258, is well documented from his writings and a collection of letters.[50] From the start he was faced with internal dissent in his church and with the disasters of persecution and plague. The emperor Decius tried to restore good order in a politically collapsing empire by restoring the old religion. All citizens were required to sacrifice to the gods before witnesses, under threat of confiscation, torture, imprisonment, and death. Whole churches complied, as did many lay people in churches where leaders resisted. They thereby committed idolatry, one of the gravest sins in Tertullian's list. Leading bishops, including those in Rome and Antioch, died in the persecution. Others tried to save the situation by going into hiding, and that included Cyprian and his colleague in Alexandria; flight in persecution was usually regarded as permissible (though not by the later Tertullian).[51] With the emperor distracted and finally killed on the far-off Danubian frontier, persecution faded, and many lapsed Christians assumed that they could revert to their Christianity. Some clergy in Carthage, those who resented Cyprian, were lenient. They were abetted by "confessors," that is, those who had suffered arrest and trial, perhaps torture and imprisonment, but had survived. The tradition that such confessors possessed extraordinary authority was strong: we noted it among the martyrs at Lyons. Cyprian worked very hard to establish principles on which this question could be resolved. That involved the repeated calling of councils of bishops from the area of which Carthage was the natural provincial center. Similar gatherings happened in Rome and other places. The negotiations moved at first along severe lines. Cyprian and a leading group of clergy and confessors in Rome would shut the door to those who had actually sacrificed, and even to those who had cheated by getting hold of certificates of sacrifice without doing the deed; only on the deathbed could a genuine penitent be restored to communion. Later, as renewed persecution impended, penitents were restored, on the assumption that the circumstances made clear their sincerity. But all this was complicated by the problem of Novatian.

Novatian was a leading presbyter in Rome, who became correspondent for the clergy there during the vacancy, after Bishop Fabian was killed early in 250. When in the spring of 251 the gathered synod elected Cornelius as bishop, one who was believed to favour leniency to the lapsed, three bishops were found to ordain Novatian as bishop instead. He had a following among the Roman clergy and confessors, and won some support in other places, like Syria, Gaul, and Asia Minor. His position was simple: there was no reconciliation available to those who sinned gravely, whether by lapse in persecution or otherwise; God might forgive, the Church had no such power. The arrival of Novatian's agents in North Africa complicated an already difficult situation. Faced with the attempt to take over his church and its funds, Cyprian returned to Carthage in the spring of 251 armed with two books. *On the Lapsed* described the enormity of the disaster, the gravity of post-baptismal sin, and the need for caution in restoring the lapsed. *On the Unity of the Catholic Church* argued how wicked it was to divide the church by schism, on whatever pretext, and to break away from the bishop.[52] Cyprian argues that the life of the Church depends upon the bishops: the episcopate is one, and so is the Church. A tree cannot survive if cut off from its root; a ray of sunlight disappears if cut off from the sun. To leave the episcopal church and join another body is to join an adulteress. However seemingly virtuous (he will later write, even if he gives his body to be burned as a martyr), "he is an alien, an outcast, an enemy; he can no longer have God for a Father, who has not the Church for a mother."[53] The book appears to have had two editions, one of which asserts the absolute authority of the bishop, symbolized by the uniqueness of Peter among the Apostles.[54] The other text is longer, and concentrates on the unanimity of the bishops throughout the Church.[55] This second edition was aimed at a council of bishops the next year (252), or perhaps later, as Bévenot argues. Both aspects are important to Cyprian, but whereas the shorter text was aimed at his own clergy and flock, the longer was designed to deal with the new emergency. This was caused by the setting up of a new church in Carthage which repudiated Cyprian and his supporters, and by the agitation of Novatian's agents, who plainly unsettled the African clergy. Novatian was attractive to them, because they shared Cyprian's rigorism toward the lapsed, which Novatian himself appears to have upheld against the laxity of Cornelius. Cyprian, however, was persuaded by the simple principle that there could be only one bishop in a Catholic church: Novatian was no bishop, because there was no vacancy in Rome to ordain him to. At this stage compromises were reached, in which both Roman and Carthaginian bishops, and those in various other places such as Alexandria, arrived at agreement over the reconciliation of the lapsed after due penance. For Cyprian, since the authority of the bishop, and the integrity of the episcopate throughout the world, were upheld, his ideal of a spiritual Church, bonded by the common universal episcopate, stood firm.

The situation changed with the rapid death of Cornelius and his successor Lucius in 253–4. In 254 Stephen I succeeded, and drove his church in directions offensive to Cyprian. Cyprian held that the grace of God in the Church, the presence and action of his Spirit, depended upon the holiness of its members. If a baptized person committed grave sin, he was cut off from the life of Christ. If any set up a congregation against or separate from the bishop, they did not belong to the Church at all, and outside the Church there is no salvation. If a bishop committed the grave sin of idolatry, he was no longer a bishop: none can pray to God with soiled hands. It was defaulting bishops who first attracted Stephen's support, and led to protests from Cyprian and his supporting African churches. The Gallic churches looked successfully to Cyprian for support, when a leading one of them, Marcian of Arles, adopted Novatian's policies toward the lapsed, and Cyprian rebuked Stephen for not ratifying the deposition.[56] The Spanish churches had deposed the bishops of Leon and Merida for alleged compromises with paganism; these asked and received support from Stephen for their remaining in office, and Cyprian's synod protested.[57] More serious, however, was the conflict over baptism. Stephen caused great offence to Cyprian, and to Cyprian's friends like Firmilian of Caesarea in Cappadocia, by insisting that all baptized persons from any group whatsoever were to be accepted with penance and laying-on of hands, and not baptized again.[58] Cyprian insisted that only the one true Church could baptize, and so all outsiders must be initiated and baptized on coming to the Church. Both parties to the dispute believed in one and only one baptism: the question was whether it was the one baptism of the individual, or the ceremonies of the one Church. Cyprian had past decisions in North Africa to lean upon, and there had undoubtedly been decisions in the East rejecting the Montanists' baptisms on doctrinal grounds. Firmilian and Cyprian were particularly angry that Stephen should cite the general practice of the sects, presumably in Rome, of recognizing each other's baptisms. This was perhaps a relic of the days when there were many different house-churches and schools in that city. About thirty-five years earlier, Hippolytus in Rome had castigated Bishop Calixtus I (*Kallistos*) for accepting sinners expelled from other groups into his school, and that perhaps reflects the precedent to which Stephen appealed: "Let nothing be done beyond what is traditional," he wrote.[59] A variance of traditions thus threatened the unanimity of the bishops, and exposed Cyprian's doctrine as fanciful. Stephen seems to have threatened to excommunicate the North African and other churches which did not accept his practice. He probably regarded them as treacherous, in that they appeared to side with his local and more pressing enemy, Novatian. The matter remained unresolved when Cyprian met his martyr-death in 258 under the new persecutor, Valerian. Stephen also died. So the issue was to lurk ready to explode during the next great persecution early the following century, when the competence of compromising clergy, and the validity of schismatic baptisms, formed the chief points of conflict between North African Donatists and the main body of the Church. It was Stephen's view of the permanent effects of baptism and ordination which were to prevail; but even in setting Cyprian's conclusions aside, Augustine would value his argument that the schismatic who divided the Church, whatever his grievances or virtues, was out of love, and even martyrdom profited him nothing.

By Cyprian's time, while some churches had spread to the east, especially in Persia and India, it was those within the Roman Empire which determined Christianity's future. The strong Christian communities in Syria, Egypt, Asia Minor, and Rome caused persecutors like Decius to try to reverse the trend until 311. But assimilation continued. The Church's chief officers, the bishops, tended to reflect the status of their imperial counterparts: the bishop of a great city like Rome, Antioch, or Alexandria exercised hegemony and authority over a whole province, adjudicating disputes and assembling councils of bishops (synods) for consultation or ordinations. Persecution might disrupt, but disruption increased the need for synods to meet and resolve common problems on a provincial or interprovincial basis. Such actions, together with the day-to-day administration of judgments, property, and charitable funds, meant bureaucratic record-keeping. The episcopal network came to reflect the pattern of imperial government, no doubt accelerated when men trained for public office, like Cyprian, became bishops. The Church was becoming a worldly institution, fulfilling the destiny perceived in The Acts of the Apostles. This process would further accelerate after the rise of Constantine as Emperor in 306. But what of the heavenly being, the spiritual Church, the indivisible proprietrix of truth, the eschatological people of God? Tertullian, Novatian, and Cyprian tried to sustain that holy identity of the Church by excluding sinners or by damning schismatics. Spiritualizing sects still offered a higher gnosis to the chosen few, and left the "psychic" church to its lower destiny. Perhaps, however, the pragmatism of Hermas, Cornelius, and Stephen may have grasped better what holiness means: the Church is holy by its work of sanctification, the Mother correcting her erring children, as in the Gospel pictures of the good shepherd seeking the lost sheep and the father's arms open to the returning prodigal. A comparable development affects the unity of the Church as vessel of truth. The argument of Clement of Rome about the historic origins of the presbyterate (and perhaps those of Acts), are imaginary, though grounded in the spiritual interpretation of the Old Testament. Irenaeus used the idea to claim that the apostolic truth had always been the same everywhere, a grace of truth bestowed on successive bishops, when it is plain that the first believers, and the Apostles, disagreed from time to time. His notion led to an overestimate of the infallibility of bishops in council, which would wreak havoc in the fourth century. Truth, like forgiveness of sins, needs openness and tolerance, not just the imposing of authority. Clement of Alexandria and Origen did in part perceive that. The Church, if it is to be true to its origins, must be like Jesus sitting with his rabble of sinners and objectionable religious hypocrites, eating and drinking and telling stories, very much in the world, even if essentially not of it.

Notes

1 Roloff (1990), p. 412.

2 In this article "Church" is used to refer to the one, universal Church, "church" for the local congregation or assembly, and in adjectival uses like "church officers."

3 Plümacher (1978), pp. 515–20.

4 That the Church's ministry originated so is the theme of Burtchaell (1992).

5 Kirner (2002) reports the present state of research comprehensively. Different writers apply social-historical norms in various ways.

6 *Apostolischen Väter* (1992), pp. 325–555; *Apostolic Fathers* II (1913); *New Eusebius*, pp. 50–2.

7 Following the analysis of Schneider (1999), who provides ample discussion and bibliography.

8 See Staats (1986), pp. 106ff.

9 *Apostolischen Väter*, pp. 77–151; *Apostolic Fathers* I, pp. 1–121; *Early Christian Fathers* I, pp. 33–73; *New Eusebius*, pp. 7–9.

10 *Apostolischen Väter*, pp. 1–21; *Apostolic Fathers*, I, pp. 303–33; *Early Christian Fathers*, pp. 159–79; *New Eusebius*, pp. 9–12.

11 *Apostolischen Väter*, pp. 176–241; *Apostolic Fathers*, I, pp. 165–277; *Early Christian Fathers*, pp. 74–120; *New Eusebius*, pp. 12–17. The seven letters could be a late second-century forgery, but the arguments of Hübner have not convinced most scholars (see Lindemann, 1997). If the letters are later, they still represent a significant early view of the Church.

12 Schoedel (1985), pp. 10–14.

13 *Apostolischen Väter*, pp. 152–75; *Apostolic Fathers*, pp. 123–63; *Early Christian Fathers*, pp. 181–202.

14 Naassenes in Hippolytus, *Refutatio* VI 29, 7, and often; cf. *Gnosis*, pp. 244–312.

15 Irenaeus, *Haer.* I.30.2.

16 *The Nag Hammadi Library*, pp. 329–38.

17 Nag Hammadi Tractate VII, 2 50, 1–24: *Nag Hammadi Library*, p. 330.

18 Theodotus, p. 58; *Gnosis*, pp. 150–1.

19 Nag Hammadi Tractate II, 5 124, 25–125, 14: *Nag Hammadi Library*, pp. 177–8.

20 Nag Hammadi Tractate I, 3 120–3; 124, 25–125, 11: *Nag Hammadi Library*, pp. 90–2.

21 Naassenes in Hippolytus, *Refutatio* V 6, 7.

22 Texts and French version in *Sources chrétiennes*; English extracts in *Early Christian Fathers*, pp. 341–97; *New Eusebius*, pp. 111–20.

23 Irenaeus I.1–8; *Gnosis*, pp. 123–45.

24 Irenaeus I.10; *Early Christian Fathers*, pp. 360–2.

25 Irenaeus V.6.1; 16.2; 32–6; cf. *Early Christian Fathers*, pp. 391–7.

26 Irenaeus III.2.2; *Early Christian Fathers*, p. 371.

27 Irenaeus III.3.2–3; *Early Christian Fathers*, p. 373; *New Eusebius*, pp. 114–15. On Christian teachers in Alexandria, see Neymeyr (1989), pp. 40–105.

28 Letter in Eusebius, *Hist. eccl.* V.24.14; *New Eusebius*, p. 140.

29 Irenaeus IV.11.8; *Early Christian Fathers*, p. 382; *New Eusebius*, pp. 117–18.

30 Irenaeus III.24.1.

31 Clement of Alexandria, *Paid.* VII.105–8; *Alexandrian Christianity*, pp. 161–3.

32 Clement of Alexandria, *Paid.* I.11 and Eusebius, *Hist. eccl.* V.11.3–5; *New Eusebius*, p. 180.

33 Clement of Alexandria, *Strom.* 7 5.29; *Alexandrian Christianity*, p. 110.

34 Origen, *Contra Celsum* III.30.

35 Ibid. VI.48.

36 Origen, *Comm. Mt. ser.* X.

37 Origen, *Comm. Mt. ser.* XII.14.

38 Origen, *Homin Num.* 2.1; *Comm. Mt. ser.* XII.

39 Eusebius, *Hist. eccl.* V.16.10 (*New Eusebius*, pp. 102–3) with VII.7.5.

40 Hippolytus, *Contra Noetum* 1.1–7; *New Eusebius*, pp. 145–6.

41 Eusebius, *Hist. eccl.* V.1–4; *New Eusebius*, pp. 34–44.

42 Eusebius, *Hist. eccl.* V.1.45.

43 Rankin (1995), esp. pp. 27–38.

44 Tertullian, *De praescriptione*, 20–2, 36; *New Eusebius*, pp. 164–6.

45 Rankin (1995), pp. 126–42.

46 Tertullian, *De pudicitia* 1.6–9; his target is to be identified as a bishop of Carthage, not of Rome; see Hall (1981), against *New Eusebius*, p. 176.

47 Tertullian, *De pudicitia* 21.19.

48 Tertullian, *De pudicitia* 10.12.

49 This is the studied conclusion of Bähnk (2001), and it applies to all periods of Tertullian's writings.

50 Good selection in *New Eusebius*, pp. 213–50.

51 Bähnk (2001), pp. 168–93.

52 See *Cyprian*, De lapsis *and* De Ecclesiae Catholicae Unitate.

53 *De unitate*, cf. 14, and repeatedly in the *Letters*.

54 The so-called "Primacy Text" of chapters 4–5; as Bévenot shows, it was written without any thought of the Roman primacy over other churches.

55 The "Hartel" or "Received Text." In *New Eusebius*, pp. 228–9 the first two sentences of chapter 5 are printed as though they appear in both texts, when in fact they belong only to this longer, later text. Unanimous reading begins at, "/the episcopate is one. . . ."

56 Cyprian, *Ep.* 68; *New Eusebius*, pp. 233–4.

57 Cyprian, *Ep.* 67; *New Eusebius*, pp. 235–7.

58 Cyprian, *Ep.* 74, 75; *New Eusebius*, pp. 238–43.

59 Cyprian, *Ep.* 64.1.

Bibliography

Wiebke Bähnk, *Von der Notwendigkeit des Leidens. Die Theologie des Martyriums bei Tertullian* (Göttingen, 2001) (Forschungen zur Kirchen- und Dogmengeschichte 78).

Allen Brent, *Hippolytus and the Roman Church in the Third Century. Communities in Tension before the Emergence of a Monarch-Bishop* (Leiden, 1995) (Supplements to *Vigiliae Christianae* 31).

Allen Brent, *The Imperial Cult and the Development of Church Order. Concepts and Image of Authority in Paganism and Early Christianity before the Age of Cyprian* (Leiden, 1999) (Supplements to *Vigiliae Christianae* 45).

Colin Bulley, *The Priesthood of Some Believers. Developments from the General to the Special Priesthood in the Christian Literature of the First Three Centuries* (Carlisle and Waynesboro, GA, 2000) (Paternoster Biblical and Theological Monographs).

James Tunstead Burtchaell, *From Synagogue to Church. Public Services and Offices in the Earliest Christian Communities* (Cambridge, 1992).

Hans Conzelmann, *The Theology of St. Luke* (London, 1960–); translated from *Die Mitte der Zeit. Studien zur Theologie des Lukas* (Tübingen, 2nd ed., 1957, 5th ed., 1964) (Beiträge zur historischen Theologie 17).

ἐκκλησία: *A Patristic Greek Lexicon*, ed. G. W. H. Lampe (Oxford, 1961), pp. 429–33.

Exegetical Dictionary of the New Testament, ed. Horst Balz/Gerhard Schneider, 3 vols. (Grand Rapids, MI, 1990) trans. from *Exegetisches Wörterbuch zum Neuen Testament* (Stuttgart, 1978–80).

Stuart George Hall, "Calixtus I," *Theologische Realenzyklopädie* VII (Berlin, 1981), pp. 559–63.

Stuart George Hall, "Stephen I of Rome and the Baptismal Controversy of 256," *Miscellanea historiae ecclesiasticae* VIII, (Bruxelles and Louvain, 1987), pp. 78–82 (Bibliothèque de la revue d'histoire ecclésiastique 72).

Reinhard M. Hübner, "Thesen zur Echtheit und Datierung der sieben Briefe des Ignatius von Antiochien," *Zeitschrift für Antikes Christentum* 1 (1997), pp. 44–72.

Guido O. Kirner, "Apostolat und Patronage I–II," *Zeitschrift für Antikes Christentum/Journal of Ancient Christianity* 6 (2002), pp. 1–37; 7 (2003), pp. 27–72.

Andreas Lindemann, "Antwort auf die 'Thesen zur Echtheit und Datierung der sieben Briefe des Ignatius von Antiochien,'" *Zeitschrift für Antikes Christentum* 1 (1997), pp. 185–94.

Christoph Markschies, *Zwischen den Welten wandern. Strukturen des antiken Christentums* (Frankfurt am Main, 1997) (Europäische Geschichte).

Gerhard May, "Kirche III. Alte Kirche," *Theologische Realenzyklopädie* XVIII (Berlin, 1989), pp. 218–27.

Ulrich Neymeyr, *Die christlichen Lehrer im zweiten Jahrhundert. Ihre Lehrtätigkeit, ihr Selbstverstandnis und ihre Geschichte* (Leiden, 1989) (Supplements to *Vigiliae Christianae* 4).

Eckhard Plümacher, "Apostelgeschichte," *Theologische Realenzyklopädie* III (Berlin, 1978), pp. 483–528.

Douglas Powell, "Clemens von Rom," *Theologische Realenzyklopädie* VIII (Berlin, 1981), pp. 113–20.

David Rankin, *Tertullian and the Church* (Cambridge, 1995).

Joachim Rohde, ἐπισκοπή, ἐπίσκοπος, *Exegetical Dictionary of the New Testament* (see above) II, pp. 35–6.

Jürgen Roloff, ἐκκλησία: *Exegetical Dictionary of the New Testament* (see above) I, pp. 410–15.

Athanasius Schneider, "PROPTER SANCTAM ECCLESIAM SUAM". Die Kirche als Geschöpf,

Frau und Bau im Bußunterricht des Pastor Hermae (Studia Ephemeridis Augustinianum 67) (Rome, 1999).

William R. Schoedel, *Ignatius of Antioch. A Commentary on the Letters of Ignatius of Antioch* (Philadelphia PA, 1985) (Hermeneia).

Reinhart Staats, "Hermas," *Theologische Realenzyklopädie* XVI (Berlin, 1986), pp. 100–8.

Christine Trevett, *Montanism. Gender, Authority and the New Prophecy* (Cambridge, 1996).

François Vouga, "Urchristentum," *Theologische Realenzyklopädie* XXXIV (Berlin, 2002), pp. 411–36.

The Early Church in the World

G. R. Evans

Explaining the Fall of Empire: Christian Contributions to the Providence Debate

Our period coincides with a time of dramatic decline and change in the society in which Christianity was "rising." The Roman Empire became "officially" Christian, in the sense that its rulers approved and embraced the Christian religion only in the last generations of its glory. It is important not to lose sight of this context, for it affected the story of exchange of ideas and the growing sense of a Christian "identity."

The late antique world was self-conscious about what was happening and looked about for somewhere to lay the blame. Christianity came in for criticism as a bad influence; it was seen to have the wrong priorities. In the second century, the philosopher Celsus was critical of Christians for lack of interest in the State. Marcellinus, in a letter to Augustine,[1] conveys a concern which was apparently being discussed quite widely by then, that the ethical principles to which Christians adhered brought no benefit at all to the conduct of the State. He points to its precepts: render to no one evil for evil (Romans 12:17); turn the other cheek; give your cloak to anyone who asks you (Matthew 5:39–41); go two miles with anyone who asks you to go a mile. These practices are not politically sound, say Christianity's enemies. It is a nice paradox that, conversely, in the letters of Cicero and Pliny are embedded ethical principles which Christians were far from finding to be unhelpful.

Christianity began in a world whose governing authorities, the imperial regime of ancient Rome, were finding it increasingly difficult to maintain control. In late antiquity, after the reign of the first Christian emperor, Constantine, but probably before the end of the fourth century, an unknown Latin author who saw the way the wind was blowing wrote a treatise on the arts of war and related matters. He is an ancient whistle-blower, but a polite one, well aware that he is likely to cause offense in high places. He hides behind the instructions he claims to have received from Providence. *Providentia divinitatis* has put these ideas in his head, for it is Providence's supervision which keeps the Empire prosperous.

This author is unusual in combining a pragmatic approach with his literary pretensions. He writes to the emperor of his day with a plain man's suggestions for practical improvement, particularly in the matter of the *largitates* or misplaced imperial generosities which cause offense to those who do not receive them, and waste resources (Chapter 1 is *De inhibenda largitate*). He locates the problem which is causing the decline of empire in economics, and in particular in the lavishness of emperors.[2] The main part of the treatise contains a series of equally practical suggestions for inventions which will improve the mechanics of warfare and assist the authorities in retaining control. The final chapter (XXI) suggests to the emperor a remedy of a quite different kind, by way of the removal of confusions and contradictions in the laws.[3]

Many authors were thinking and writing about this increasingly alarming political and social situation. Something had visibly been lost in these later days of the Empire, and it was not merely the secure control of an enormous area of Europe by a rich and confident government, but a style and tone in public affairs; a number of hitherto secure assumptions about standards in public life and the purposes of society could no longer be taken for granted. In the days before the decline of Rome, Cicero's *Republic* and *On Laws* are both much preoccupied with the importance of the preservation of justice. He construes it widely, so as to encompass much of what keeps government on the right course. Cicero had sketched three sound forms of government and the tendency of each to degenerate (*De republica*, I.35–71)[4] when justice disappears. "When the ruler begins to be unjust, that form of government is destroyed and the ruler is a tyrant" (*De republica*, I.xlii.65). In the first century AD, Quintilian still assumes that only a good man can be a good public servant. Nevertheless, the link between integrity and satisfactory conduct in high office was already growing more tenuous, and the slide into incompetence and corruption in public office in the State coincided with the emergence of Christianity and the development of an institutional Church.

By the fourth and fifth century it was hard for contemporaries not to be conscious that cultural standards were slipping, as well as standards in public office, and there are gloomy reflections about the general decline of culture in which are embedded further social comments. Sidonius Apollinaris writes in the 470s to compliment Johannes for keeping Latin alive in Gaul.[5] He is a second Demosthenes or Cicero (VIII.ii.1). Now the degrees of rank are swept away (*remotis gradibus dignitatum*); a knowledge of letters becomes the only mark by which, in future, nobility can be identified: *erit posthac nobilitatis indicium litteras nosse* (VIII.ii.2).

The successful invasions of the barbarians were both a symptom and a cause of the decay of the previous good sound principles of public life. There is a good deal of anxious comment on the complexities of relations with these intruders, for from quite early in the history of the Christian Church they were having to be allowed to stay within the borders of the Empire and given courtesy and recognition as "allies." Leo the Great (d. 461) comments in a sermon that it is for Christians to give thanks to God for the mercy which has led him to free Rome from the clutches of the barbarians, in imitation of the solitary grateful individual among the lepers Jesus healed (Luke 17:15); for it is God not any influence of the planets which has rescued Rome.[6] When Constantine made the Empire officially Christian in the early fourth century, he did so in the face of the barbarian emergency.

Faced with these incompatible signs of the times, Christians and pagans alike wrote a good deal about providence. The intentions of the gods, or of God, for the future of the Empire were much in their minds. For the "hermetic" thinkers of third-century Egypt the chain of necessity which binds all things together is destiny.[7]

In a sermon, *De urbis excidio*, a parallel is drawn between the decline of Rome and the destruction of Sodom and Gomorrah (Genesis 18:23–32), for it seemed fair to ask why God did not spare the city of Rome for the sake of the just who lived in it. A distinction is drawn between the destruction of the cities of the plain and the fall of Rome. Sodom was completely destroyed by fire. Rome's citizens did not all perish. Some had gone into exile; some remained in the city and escaped death; some took refuge in holy places and had sanctuary.[8] Besides, it is pointed out, there are different measures of righteousness. If one measures by the standard of perfect righteousness, there were no just men in Rome. If the standard is the ordinary human one, there were a thousand.[9]

The habit of asking what is the purpose of providence is linked quite naturally in the early Christian centuries with the debate about the imminence of the old age of the world. A considerable literature survives in which authors, pagan, Jewish, and Christian, discuss the widespread contemporary perception of the late antique centuries that the end of the world is at hand, or that the world is at least in its old age. There are several strands of opinion on this matter, for it was not a new question; though it did now seem to have a new urgency. One theory was that the state of the world went in cycles of renewal. Another was that it was in long-term decline towards a final, perhaps appointed, end.

The first idea is to be found in Plato (*Timaeus* 22Bff.). It is held that there is a cycle in the affairs of the world, with destruction (by fire or flood) followed by a period of rebirth and renewal. Macrobius explores the idea in his commentary on Cicero's *Dream of Scipio* (II.x.9 and preceding).[10] This theme is taken up by Philo in *De aeternitate mundi*,[11] where he asserts that destruction belongs to that which is created and indestructibility to the uncreated and goes on to explore the implications of the theory that the God who made the world could destroy it or allow it to be destroyed, or make another; he also examines the question in *Vita Mosis* II.x.53–xi.6.[12] This is also one of the themes of the *Hermetica*.[13]

Either line can be made compatible with a belief in divine providence, for on either view (the cycles of decay and revival or the steady decline) God (or the gods) may be working out a plan. But for Christians a theory that things were hastening to the appointed end of the world was the natural preference; it was not only the first generation which had expected the end of the world to come quickly (1 Thess. 4). Cyprian (c.AD251) says, "you must know that the world has now grown old" (*scire debes senuisse iam mundum*);[14] and there is a long passage of explanation of the implications of God's intention that the world shall age and come to an end (CCSL 3A, p. 36). Lactantius (early 4th c.), in the *Divinae institutiones*,[15] sets out an eschatological prophecy, in which he refers to Seneca's seven ages of Rome.

This acceptance that something was coming to an end could be construed in different ways as indicating the position Christians should take. The optimistic view of the period of the early Christian Empire was that the enemies of God would now receive their punishment. Constantine's biographer Eusebius in his *Life* of the emperor explains that the downfall of those who opposed Constantine was a token that in God's eyes they were attacking the Church: "The disastrous end of the life of each one indicated the manifest punishment for their hostility to God, just as the end of Constantine made plain to everybody the rewards of the love of God".[16]

Augustine was forced to find a different explanation altogether for the fact that in his lifetime it appeared that God's enemies had taken over the Empire. The task occupied him throughout the years when he was writing *The City of God*. He explains the sack of Rome as something Christians ought to accept in the spirit of Jeremiah 5:4, with a willingness to be disciplined and to learn from what has happened to them. The only tenable Christian position at the end of a Christian Empire is that there is something to be learned from times of trial, a positive *utilitas* in such episodes (PL 40.723).

The early fifth-century author Orosius was greatly influenced by Augustine in his own remarks in this area. He says at the beginning of his *History against the Pagans* that he has "obeyed Augustine's instructions" (*Praeceptis tuis parui, beatissime pater Augustine*) (Prol. 1.1).[17] "You told me to write against those whose 'vain-speaking wickedness' (*vaniloquam pravitatem*) is leading the Roman world to forget its history. They are not interested in the future; they either forget or know nothing of the past" and they misrepresent the present (Prol. 1.9).[18] So he is consciously composing a history because it is important for people to know their history (Prol. 1.16), and he is drawing conclusions about the lessons which must not be lost sight of.

The explanation that the disaster of the decline of empire is God's will and has an educational purpose for Christians is carried forward by Quodvultdeus in the same generation, also heavily under Augustine's influence. His theme is the promises of God in the Old and New Testament "up to now and at the end of the world," with a "brief period" (*brevi spatio*) in which Antichrist is let loose.[19] In Book III he considers modern times and the future, with some reference to the period of Antichrist's rule. There are so many disasters, "which we know have come upon us because our sins deserve them" (*quas meritis peccatorum nostrorum super nos venire cognoscimus*).[20]

Against this line of argument the remaining pagans were keen to tell their different "story" of what was happening and the reasons for it. A number of "histories" such as those of Eunapius, Olympiodorus, Priscus, Malchus, survive in fragments in which this is attempted.[21] For it would not be accurate to suggest that all barbarian invasion was destructive. Theodosius, emperor from 379 to 95, not only defeated but also temporarily pacified the Goths. He was able to make Arianism illegal. A century later, Theodoric the Goth was a hostage at Constantinople in his youth and he developed an alliance with the emperor Zeno, which became a battle for supremacy. Zeno despatched him in 478 to overthrow Odoacer, who had usurped the throne of Italy. Theodoric took power himself, and held it for thirty-three years. But he was a benevolent and largely non-interfering ruler, holding together as subjects Arians and Catholics. But the overall picture is of a huge pressure on the old structures at a time when they were being undermined by events.

The Church's Role in the Maintenance of Order

Decisive inroads were first made into the Empire's direct control of lands in the West by the Huns in the 370s. The invading Goths then had to be allowed to settle in Gaul as pretended "allies" (*foederati*). Alaric the Goth (c.370–410) was recognised as *magister militum* and was permitted to demand tribute from the cities of Illyricum; the failure to hold him off allowed him to lay siege to Rome in each of three years leading up to the sack of Rome in 410. The Vandals similarly had to be allowed to settle in Spain. In 406, Germanic peoples crossed the Rhine, sacked Mainz, and burnt Trier. The Huns were permitted to settle in northern Germany. The Emperor Valentinian III was assassinated in 455 and there followed a disappearance to all intents and purposes of the figure of the emperor of the West. There remained a mere "imperial puppet" of the barbarian leaders, who was not taken seriously in the Byzantine world or regarded as more than a usurper. Sidonius Apollinaris was conscious of a change of a new order of magnitude when Roman rule in Provence ended in 476.[22] The monastic leader Severinus ("Apostle of Austria") successfully held until his death in 488 the border fortifications in the area of the Danube.[23]

In the confusion of the decline of empire and the aftermath of its fall, the Church was important as the main continuing institution through which some form of order could be maintained, in the cities especially, and practical matters such as the supervision of food supplies and the restoration of supplies of drinking water could be seen to in emergencies (and even as a matter of routine).[24] In the mid-530s, the bishop of Milan was organising the distribution of grain from the Milanese grain stores.[25] Such concerns are still highly visible in the *Register* of the letters of Pope Gregory the Great (c.540–604).[26]

This was not merely a matter of keeping things going. Where the barbarians had seized power they were also inclined to seize booty. That meant that newly "appointed" governors were grabbing the local food resources to feed their soldiers and were imposing taxes as they chose. Only the senior churchmen remained of the old ruling families to defend the people against injustice and hunger.[27]

With the decline of provincial government, many civil responsibilities fell to the leaders of the Church, including military affairs (captives were sometimes ransomed with church plate).[28] Bishops are to be found acting as diplomats and negotiators with the barbarian invaders (Pope Innocent I as an emissary to Alaric the Goth in 409; Leo I to Attila the Hun in 452).[29] And the Church's role was more than one of rescue and repair; there was positive intervention too. Some bishops of the fourth century were actively aggrandizing the Church's role through the building of new and impressive basilicas such as Santa Sabina, Santa Maria Maggiore, Santa Croce, and the Baptistery of the Lateran.[30]

In the eastern half of the Empire, the emperor Theodosius II put out a code of laws in 438 which was later to be largely swallowed up in the code of Justinian compiled in the mid-sixth century, in a story told by Clarence Gallagher in the next chapter. It was badly needed, for there was no codification of laws to enable litigants or their representatives to check what the law was. It is of importance as an indicator of the ways in which the Church was influencing the administrative, legislative, and judicial needs and practices of the dying Roman world. The architect of Theodosius' code was probably Antiochus, former quaestor and praetorian prefect, and chairman of the commission which (after a false start), eventually did the work and published a code which could be declared to constitute an official reference point on all imperial legislation enacted since 312.[31]

Justinian closed the Academy and prohibited pagans from holding positions in which they could have an educational role. His Code (I.5.18.4, and see 1.5 in general, and 1.11.10) identified and banned heretics, apostates, and traitors. The driving force of Roman legislative development by now was beginning to be the hard cases which revealed anomalies or unclarified points and led to references to the emperor for clarification,[32] but the imperial will now ran with the Christians.

So, although the barbarian invasions progressively undermined the administrative structures, Christianity was, to a striking degree, keeping things going at a practical level. It was able to do this because it was developing a sophisticated institutional organization, though again this was uneven, because its force depended a good deal on whether the locale was urban or rural, in East or West.

Diocletian established a system of twelve "dioceses," extending through the whole Empire. In some of these there was a city of recognized importance. Rome remained supreme in the West, but Milan and Ravenna and Trier were important provincial capitals. In the East there was no obvious single capital until Constantine built his city at Constantinople; Thessalonica, Antioch, Nicomedia had imperial residences from which government would and did take place at different times. The Church also had its dioceses, episcopal regions in each of which a bishop and his people formed "the Church in each place." The bishop of an important city tended to become the "metropolitan" for a larger area, meeting in local councils with its bishops. The Bishop of Rome in the West could claim Petrine authority for his leadership. In the East four patriarchs emerged, of Jerusalem, Antioch, Alexandria, and Constantinople. The battle for the supremacy of Rome among the ancient patriarchates lies outside the scope and the period of this book, but the seeds were already being sown.

In this sea of troubles, Christianity, and especially the administrative system of the Church, made a significant contribution to the survival of the culture of antiquity when it could not longer be sustained by the failing Empire's own structures. Not all the "first Christian theologians" write about this; but none of them was unaffected by it.

Notes

1 Augustine, *Letter* 136.2 (CSEL 44, pp. 95–6).

2 Anon., *De rebus bellicis*, Pref., 1, ed. and trans. E. A. Thompson (Oxford, 1952), p. 91.

3 *Ut confusas legum contrariasque sententias, improbitatis reiectio litigio, iudicio augustae dignationis illumines.*

4 Cicero, *De republica*, ed. Clinton Walker Keyes (London and Cambridge, MA, 1928) (The Loeb Classical Library).

5 *Letters*, ed. W. B. Anderson (London and Cambridge, MA, 1936), 2 vols., Vol. 1.

6 Sermon 84, PL 54.433–4.

7 *Hermetica* (1924), I, p. 360.

8 PL 40.717–18.

9 PL 40.720.

10 Macrobius, *In somnium Scipionis*, ed. J. Willis (Teubner, 1970), p. 126.

11 Loeb edition, vol. IX, pp. 27–150.

12 Ibid., vol. VI, II.x.53–xi.6.

13 *Hermetica* (1924), vol. III, p. 181.
14 Cyprian, *Ad Demetrianum*, 3, CCSL 3A, p. 36.
15 Lactantius, *Divinae institutiones*, VII, 15.10, PL 7.784–90.
16 Eusebius, *Vita Constantine*, ed. F. A. Heinichen (Leipzig, 1868–70), I.10.4.
17 Orosius, *Historiarum adversum paganos*, p. 1.
18 Orosius, *Historiarum adversum paganos*, p. 3.
19 Quodvultdeus, *De tempore barbarico*, ed. G. Morin, PL, *Supplementum 3*, 1 (1963), pp. 287–98, p. 12.
20 Ibid., p. 287.
21 Blockley (1983).
22 Jill Harries, *Sidonius Apollinaris and the Fall of Rome* (Oxford, 1994), p. v.
23 Herrin (1987), p. 74.
24 Ibid., p. 73.
25 Ibid., p. 73.
26 Ed. D. Norberg, CCSL, 40 (1982), 2 vols.
27 Herrin (1987), p. 75.
28 Ibid., p. 73.
29 Ibid., p. 74.
30 Krautheimer (1980), pp. 45–53.
31 Jones (1964), vol. 1, p. 476.
32 Ibid., p. 349.

Bibliography

R. C. Blockley, *The Fragmentary Classicising Histories of the Later Roman Empire* (Liverpool, 1983).

Allen Brent, *The Imperial Cult and the Development of Church Order. Concepts and Image of Authority in Paganism and Early Christianity before the Age of Cyprian* (Leiden, 1999) (Supplements to *Vigiliae Christianae* 45).

James Tunstead Burtchaell, *From Synagogue to Church. Public Services and Offices in the Earliest Christian Communities* (Cambridge, 1992).

J. B. Bury, *History of the Late Roman Empire* (London, 1923; repr. New York, 1958).

Judith Herrin, *The Formation of Christendom* (Oxford, 1987).

H. M. Jones, *The Later Roman Empire* (Oxford, 1964), vol. 1, p. 476.

R. Krautheimer, *Rome: Profile of a City, 312–1308* (Princeton, 1980), pp. 45–53.

J. H. W. G. Liebeschuetz, *Barbarians and Bishops. Army, Church and State in the Age of Arkadios and Chrysostom* (Oxford, 1990).

J. Meyendorff, *Imperial Unity and Christian Divisions. The Church 450–680* (New York, 1989).

Daniel H. Williams, *Ambrose of Milan and the End of the Niceno-Arian Conflicts* (Oxford, 1995).

The Imperial Ecclesiastical Lawgivers

Clarence Gallagher, SJ

Introduction

Since the time of Constantine, the Roman emperor was recognised as having an important role in the life and administration of the Church. Within this one body there was a double authority: that of the ordained episcopal authority and that of the lay imperial authority. This double authority came from God and in its exercise there was a division of labor. The religious understanding of the emperor's role that had grown up in pagan imperial Rome did not disappear with the conversion of Constantine. The emperor continued to be regarded as the divinely appointed protector of the Church and the imperial power was expected to provide the Church with freedom and protection. The sacred character of the emperor was brought out in the ceremonies of the imperial court, and the old Roman vocabulary in addressing him was preserved from pre-Constantine days. All this is eloquently expressed in the oration delivered by Eusebius, bishop of Caesarea (c.260–340) in 336. The bishop sees in the emperor the divinely-appointed agent who was destined to see the triumph of Christianity: "Like the radiant sun . . . he illuminates his subjects in the remotest corners of the Empire with the piercing shafts of his brightness."[1] He is the messenger of God and God's instrument on earth. This was, of course, the language of an official court panegyric, but it expressed a portrait of the ideal emperor which would have been taken for granted in his time. It would be very influential in later patristic and Byzantine thinking and constitute a principal difference between Byzantine and Roman ideas about the nature of the Church.

The subject of this chapter is the state of ecclesiastical law between 379, when Theodosius I was declared emperor, and 565, the year in which Justinian I died. In these two centuries the foundations were laid for the development of canon law in the legislation promulgated by the councils of the Church, both ecumenical and regional. But in this same period there was issued a much more extensive body of imperial law concerning church affairs (often referred to as "ecclesiastical law," to distinguish it from the canon law promulgated by church councils). This imperial law can be found in the *Codex Theodosianus*, issued by Theodosius II in 438, in the

Codex repetitae lectionis, promulgated by Justinian in 534, and in the later *Novellae* of Justinian. Among the principal lawgivers of this period were Theodosius the Great (379–95), his grandson, Theodosius II (408–50) and especially Justinian I (527–65). My aim is to place the emperors in their historical context, then briefly describe the ecclesiastical legislation promulgated and, in conclusion, to reflect on the role the emperor was thought to have in the Church of those centuries.

The Theodosian Dynasty

Theodosius was born in Spain in 347 and died in Milan in 395.[2] His father, Flavius Theodosius, was a general under Valentinian and had played an important part in the campaigns on the Rhine. His son, Theodosius, became a skilled commander himself and, in 374, was given his own command in Moesia. After the execution of his father at Carthage in 475, he returned to his estates in Spain. He married Aelia Flaccilla who bore him a daughter, Pulcheria, and a son, Arkadios. Towards the end of 378, after the disaster of Adrianople, Theodosius received Emperor Gratian's urgent message from Sirmium, with the offer of supreme command in the East. He immediately proceeded to Sirmium where he scored a victory over the Sarmatians who were threatening the western Danube frontier opposite Pannonia. On 19 January 379, at Sirmium, Theodosius was acclaimed Augustus with direct rule over all the Eastern provinces. He now shared with Gratian the rule over the Roman Empire.

The problem facing Theodosius was the survival of the Empire. Since Adrianople, the Romans had lost the military initiative. Sections of the eastern Danube were no longer functioning frontiers. The Visigoths were on the march through the Balkans causing great destruction. Theodosius adopted a strategy of recovery that was pragmatic and cautious. His immediate need was to secure an eastern capital, so he went south-east to Salonika, the well-protected imperial capital with a great harbour on the Aegean, to which supplies could be imported from Egypt and Asia. In February 380 he fell ill and seemed to be dying; he received the sacrament of baptism. By the spring he had fully recovered, which he attributed to his Christian baptism and the prayers said on his behalf. Through arms and diplomacy he had ended the Visigothic threat by 382 and brought about the recovery of the Empire after the disaster of Adrianople and the Gothic invasions. He was an outstanding emperor and his reign marked a turning point in the history of the late Roman Empire.

Theodosius died in 395 and was succeeded by his two young sons, Arcadius in the East and his younger brother, Honorius, in the West. Arcadius was only 18 years old when he became emperor of the East and his reign was dominated by powerful personalities in his court.[3] There is relatively little ecclesiastical legislation in this period though there was a growing movement against paganism during his reign and we see more severe laws against heretics. He died in 408 when he was only 31 years old. Honorius continued as ruler in the West until 423.

Theodosius II, the grandson of Theodosius the Great, was born in Constantinople in 401 and was only 7 years old when he succeeded his father, Arcadius, as emperor in 408. Theodosius II was not a soldier; his interests were in theology and culture. As emperor he was dominated by strong-minded women such as his aunt Pulcheria and his wife Athenais-Eudokia, as well as by civil officials. His reign saw the construction of the walls of Constantinople, the founding of the University of Constantinople (425) and the promulgation of the *Codex Theodosianus* in 438. In religious matters he convoked the council of Ephesus in 431 which condemned Nestorius, whom Theodosius had appointed patriarch of Constantinople. Under pressure from Cyril of Alexandria, he agreed to accept the condemnation of Nestorianism and the imposed exile of Nestorius. He favoured Eutyches (378–454), archimandrite of a monastery in Constantinople, who, in his opposition to Nestorianism, went to the opposite extreme and maintained that there was one "nature" in Christ "after the union." He was deposed by the patriarch, Flavian, but appealed to the emperor and was given a retrial at the "Robber" council which Theodosius summoned at Ephesus in 449 and was acquitted. Theodosius upheld the decisions of this council in spite of the opposition of Pope Leo I and Valentinian III and Pulcheria. However, he died unexpectedly in a riding accident in 450, and at the council of Chalcedon, summoned by the emperor Marcian in 451, Monophysitism was condemned and Eutyches was deposed and exiled.

Codex Theodosianus[4]

What we are concerned with here is imperial legislation on matters concerning the Church. This is to be found in the *Codex Theodosianus* (CT), promulgated by Theodosius II in 438.[5] The compilation of this code was ordered by Theodosius II in 435. It was promulgated in Constantinople and Rome in 438 and came into force on January 1, 439. The commission had been instructed to collect all the general imperial laws that had been enacted by Constantine and the emperors after him right up to Theodosius II. It was also given wide powers to alter, emend, clarify, and bring up to date the imperial laws and omit those that had been abrogated. It could also divide up constitutions so as to fit into the rubrics of the code. The *Codex* contains more than 2500 laws dating from 311 to 437. It is divided into 16 books each of which is divided into titles, and within each title the laws are arranged in chronological order.

Book XVI deals with ecclesiastical legislation and what this law dealt with can be seen from its 11 titles:

1 On the Catholic faith (4 laws);
2 On bishops, churches, and clerics (47 laws);
3 On monks (2 laws);
4 On those who dispute about religion (6 laws);
5 On heretics (66 laws);
6 Holy Baptism may not be repeated (7 laws);
7 On apostates (7 laws);
8 On Jews and Samaritans (29 laws);
9 A Jew may not have a Christian slave (5 laws);
10 On pagans, sacrifices, and temples (25 laws);
11 On religion (3 laws).

Many of the laws in Book XVI deal with the rights and duties of bishops and clerics and with the protection of churches and church property. But a very large number concern heretics, apostates, Jews, and pagans. Theodosius I maintained and extended the existing legislation penalizing religious dissent. A large number of such constitutions were issued at the very start of his reign, when he proclaimed his support of what became Catholic orthodoxy.[6] He deposed the Arian patriarch of Constantinople and replaced him with St. Gregory of Nazianzus. In 380 he issued an edict declaring the true faith to be that held by Damasus of Rome and Peter of Alexandria. In the following year he summoned the first council of Constantinople at which Arianism was condemned.[7] He believed in using the law in favour of religious uniformity and proceeded to implement this council by a mass of legislation[8]: heretics were deprived of their churches;[9] they were not to be allowed to hold meetings,[10] or to consecrate bishops or ordain clergy;[11] and it was an offence to allow a meeting of a heretical sect to be held even on private property.[12] Most numerous among the heretics in the East were the Arians, and many of the laws were directed against them. All this anti-heretical legislation was continued by Arcadius and Theodosius II.

The anti-pagan legislation was similar to that against heretics. The laws at first were focused on the prohibition of blood sacrifice.[13] But in 391 Theodosius prohibited all pagan ceremonies in Rome and in 392 he outlawed every form of pagan worship, public or private, throughout the empire. The laws were particularly severe against the Manicheans. They were deprived of their right to make wills or to benefit from them. Moreover, Manicheans could be sought out by informers, brought to court, and punished, and in some cases even executed.

The legislation about Jews is more favourable; a number of laws are much more tolerant and are aimed at protecting the rights that the Jews enjoy in law.[14] These laws continue a tradition started by Constantine.[15] However, the legal position of the Jews deteriorated considerably. In 423 the Jewish patriarchate was abolished and Jews were forbidden to build new synagogues and were excluded from the imperial service.[16] In the fifth century there was much anti-Jewish legislation.[17] "Pressure on the Jews by their neighbours led by monks or bishops was now increasing. We hear of synagogues being confiscated or destroyed, even though the law continued to protect them and the remaining civic rights of the Jews".[18]

From the time of Constantine it had been accepted by the Church that it was the emperor's duty to use the secular power to enforce religious unity.[19] Theodosius acted according to the prevailing theory that the emperor enjoyed extensive authority in regulating church affairs. Anyone who did not subscribe to Catholic Christianity was seen as a threat to the dominance and the purity of the one true faith, and to the community of the faithful. It was therefore not only the right but also the duty of Catholic rulers to defend their faith by all the measures at their disposal. It is clear from a number of the laws in the *Theodosian Code* that their main purpose was the conversion of heretics and the protection of the Catholic faith by the repression of heretics if they did not convert. Penal sanctions would be avoided by repentance, whereas unrepentant sectarians would be excluded from the rest of the Catholic community.[20] All penal measures should be primarily aimed at the offender's reformation and salvation. The anti-heretical legislation aimed at eventual reconciliation and should therefore exclude the death penalty as inappropriate for crimes of heresy.[21]

The question arises, of course, about just how effective all this severe legislation was. It seems clear, in fact, that much of it was not strictly enforced. The historian, Sozomen, writing in the mid-fifth century about the anti-heretical legislation of Theodosius, says, "The penalties which he attached to his laws were no doubt severe, but he did not put them into execution; what he aimed at was not to persecute his subjects, but to frighten them, so as to bring them to be of the same mind as himself in divine matters."[22] Arians, for instance, continued to live and worship in Constantinople and to hold high positions at court.[23] As a recent historian has observed, "one might generalize that these laws represented a demonstration of religious commitment, and readiness to support bishops or officials who wanted to take action against non-Catholic religion, much more than a set of rules which the government was bound to implement throughout the empire."[24]

Justinian I (527–65)

Justinian became sole emperor in 527 and for the next 38 years provided strong and imaginative leadership. He inaugurated a new era, determined to reconstitute the Roman Empire and recover the provinces that had been overrun by the "barbarians." Within a few years he had retaken Africa from the Vandals and begun a successful campaign to regain Italy and Spain.[25] He had a great interest in theology and in 532 held theological discussions with Syrian Orthodox bishops with a view to healing the divisions within the Church.[26] With a view to reconciling the "Monophysites" of Egypt, he convoked the second council of Constantinople in 553 which condemned the famous "Three Chapters" for being tainted with Nestorianism.

The *Corpus Iuris Civilis*

From the very first years of his reign, Justinian promoted a wide-ranging legislative reform that was to have far-reaching effects on the development of both civil law and canon law. In 429 he promulgated a codex of imperial constitutions.[27] Then he commissioned a collection of excerpts from the writings of the famous classical Roman jurists. Tribonian and his collaborators produced a collection consisting of 50 books, each book divided into titles, and each title subdivided into chapters. It was completed in 533 and became known as the Digest. It was in Latin, of course, because Latin was still the official language of the law. To ensure that lawyers were trained to use the new collections, Justinian also ordered the publication of the *Institutiones*, a manual for students of law. Then he commissioned a second edition of the codex, known as the *Codex repetitae lectionis*. This is the version that has come down to us. So, by the year 534, Justinian had promulgated what became known as the *Corpus iuris civilis* which was to have a lasting influence on the development of law.[28]

In his legislation on church matters Justinian went into many more matters than his predecessors. His ecclesiastical legislation is in the *Codex repetitae lectionis*,[29] Book I, Titles 1 to 13. This constitutes a revised version of the *Codex Theodosianus*,

Book XVI, Titles 1 to 11, with a number of additional constitutions by Justinian concerning bishops, clergy, and church property. He omitted many of the earlier laws against heresy, probably because they were repetitious, but he added a number of severe laws. From the *Codex* it is clear that Justinian, right from the beginning of his reign, enacted very severe measures for the repression of heresy, Judaism, and paganism.[30] Repressive measures were taken throughout the Empire against the Monophysites. Justinian was particularly intolerant of the Manichees who became liable to the death penalty.[31]

However, by far the greater part of his ecclesiastical legislation is contained in the constitutions he issued between 534 and 565. These are called *Novellae* (new constitutions) and constitute the third volume of the *Corpus iuris canonici*. This contains a very large body of ecclesiastical law: from a total of 168 constitutions more than 30 deal with church affairs.[32] Consider, for example, the following *Novellae*: n. 3, on the clergy of Constantinople; n. 5, on monks; n. 6, on the ordination of bishops and other clerics, and on church expenses; n. 46, on the alienation of church property; n. 56, on simony; n. 57, concerning the clergy; n. 67, on oratories; n. 83, that the clergy must go before their own bishop and after that to the civil judges; n. 123, a very long *Novella* dealing with bishops, priests, and monks. *Novella* 131 is an important law concerning the clergy. Its first two laws are particularly interesting: the first confirms the canons of the ecumenical councils and puts them on a par with imperial constitutions;[33] the second assents to the primacy of the Roman see and places Constantinople second after Rome.

These laws had a particularly strong influence on the discipline of the clergy and on matrimonial law, as a few examples will show. Justinian's style in imperial legislation about the clergy can be seen in his edict of 528 – only a year after becoming sole emperor – concerning the selection of candidates for the episcopate:

> Taking every forethought for the most holy churches and for both honour and glory of the Holy Immaculate and Consubstantial Trinity, through which we have believed that both we ourselves and the common polity will be saved, and also following the holy apostles' teaching . . . by the present law we ordain that, so often as in any city whatsoever it should happen that the episcopal see is vacant, a vote by the persons inhabiting the said city should be taken concerning three persons who have borne a character for correct faith and holiness of life and the other virtues, so that from these the most suitable should be selected for the episcopate.[34]

Another clear example can be seen in the Justinian constitutions regulating the life of bishops. In the fourth and fifth centuries there were married bishops and the law did not prohibit this. Justinian's law made it obligatory for bishops to observe continence and laid down that a candidate for the episcopacy should not have children or grandchildren.[35] *Novella* 123 of AD545 is a complete treatise on the life and behaviour of the clergy. It includes such laws as: a man could not marry after priestly ordination; and married men could be ordained, though not if they had been twice married. The minimum age is established for episcopal and priestly ordination – 35 and 30 respectively.[36]

Marriage is treated extensively in Justinian's legislation.[37] Marriage between a Christian and a Jew is forbidden.[38] Holy Orders constitute a diriment impediment to marriage.[39] While it is clear that the marriage of clerics already in major orders was unlawful in the fourth and fifth centuries, it is not clear whether or not such marriages, if they took place, were considered to be null. Justinian declared all such marriages invalid.

Justinian promulgated what became the definitive law on divorce for the Eastern Empire. In 535 he issued a new code on divorce, *Novella* 22, which was a complete revision of the law. Noonan observes that the divorce legislation in *Novella* 22 seemed to "reflect a view that divorce was undesirable for its effect on the property rights of the children, not because of its severing a natural or indissoluble bond."[40] In 542, Justinian promulgated another constitution on marriage, *Novella* 117, in which he aimed to strengthen the status of marriage entered into by affection alone, without a dowry, and to protect the rights of the children of marriages which had been broken by divorce.[41] Justinian's final legislation on divorce was issued in 556 in *Novella* 134. Divorce by consent was once again forbidden, and it was reiterated that divorce was only permitted on the grounds enumerated in the law.

The emperors who introduced this legislation never made any assertions that marriage was indissoluble. Moreover, they fully intended that their legislation should be in harmony with the Church's teaching. Justinian was well read in theology and regularly sought the counsel of theologians. His Code began "in the name of our Lord Jesus Christ," and went on to set out the emperor's confession of faith.[42] All this gives the impression that there was as yet no clear and definite official church teaching on divorce and remarriage. Only very gradually did a matrimonial canon law develop. Justinian's legislation influenced greatly the whole theory and practice concerning divorce in the Church in Constantinople. There is no convincing evidence to show that the Church formally prohibited divorce and remarriage from the very beginning, and many Christians continued to regard marriage as dissoluble.[43]

These are a few examples to indicate how much imperial constitutions were taken up with what we now consider ecclesiastical matters. As one writer has observed: "The *Codex* and the *Novellae* contain a set of laws concerning the Church which cover a much wider range of ecclesiastical functions and activities than does the entire conciliar legislation before and after Justinian."[44]

Conclusion

These imperial ecclesiastical laws were to be seen as just as authoritative for the Church as the canons issued by church councils. In 545 Justinian had given the conciliar canons the force of law in the Empire.[45] All this makes an important statement concerning the place of the emperor in the Church. Justinian, like the emperors who had gone before him, considered himself responsible for religious discipline throughout the Empire. No legal text gave the emperor such power, but it came to be generally accepted that he should be a sort of supervisor of church affairs. Justinian's legislation became a constituent part of the Church's legal tradition in Constantinople.

It is important to remember that imperial laws were enacted, for the most part, on the basis of a proposal by some official: "Laws concerning heresies and other church matters read as if the emperor had thought of the idea himself, but presumably the proposals came from bishops or holy men, perhaps filtered through pious imperial ladies."[46] So the initiative for these laws would often have come from bishops and others.[47]

How Justinian considered this imperial duty of supervision in church affairs is set out in the preface to *Novella* 6, a constitution addressed in 535 to Patriarch Epiphanius, in which he lays down the regulations that should be followed concerning the ordination of bishops and other clergy. Justinian described the two great blessings they had received from God – priest and emperor – and these both came from the same divine source, the emperor to be the ultimate source of earthly law and the priest to look after spiritual matters.[48] The emperor clearly regards it as his duty to see that there are worthy bishops and clergy in the Empire and he legislates accordingly.[49]

For his legislative and administrative acts, the emperor had complete freedom. There was no organ of state that had the constitutional right to control what the emperor could or could not do. He was the supreme legislator, above the law (*solutus legibus*) as we read in the Digest.[50] The Roman emperor had a God-given task to perform within the Church. He was the anointed delegate of God – the icon of Christ – and his sphere of authority included the ecclesiastical as well as the secular order. It was the emperor who convoked ecumenical councils and saw to the promulgation of their decrees. He appointed the patriarch of Constantinople from a "terna" presented to him by the Permanent Synod.[51] Of course, he had to be a Christian and he took an oath in which he confirmed the decrees of the ecumenical councils and the privileges of the Church.

The juridical collections we have looked at briefly in this chapter – the *Codex Theodosianus* and the *Corpus iuris civilis* – had a profound influence on the later development of both civil and canon law in the East and in the West. Honoré is accurate in his comment: "Theodosius' achievement spurred Justinian to outdo his predecessor; and without Justinian Europe would neither have acquired nor transmitted to the rest of the world its unique legal-political culture."[52]

Notes

1 In *Praise of Constantine*, 2, GCS, 7, 201, quoted by J. Meyendorff in *Imperial Unity and Christian Divisions. The Church 450–680* (New York, 1989), p. 32.

2 For an account of the reigns of Theodosius I and Theodosius II, see Honoré, *Law in the Crisis of Empire*. See also Williams and Friell, *Theodosius* and Liebeschuetz, *Barbarians and Bishops*.

3 See Bury, *History of the Late Roman Empire*, vol. I, pp. 106–58.

4 No complete copy of the *Codex Theodosianus* is known to exist. The best edition we have is by Mommsen and Meyer, *Theodosiani libri XVI*. The *Constitutiones Sirmondianae* are sixteen imperial constitutions, almost all of which are concerned with church affairs. The latest is from 425. ET: Pharr, *Theodosian Code and Novels*.

5 On the formation and structure of the *Theodosian Code*, see Matthews, *Laying Down the Law*. Harries and Wood (eds), *Theodosian Code*. Tony Honoré, "The Making of the Theodosian Code," ZSS 103 (1986), pp. 133–222. Honoré, *Law in the Crisis of Empire*.

6 CT, xvi, 5.5 (379).

7 This was attended by 150 Eastern bishops. It endorsed the faith of the first council of Nicaea (325) and was accepted at the council of Chalcedon (451) as an ecumenical council. What is now known as the Niceno-Constantinopolitan Creed was attributed by Chalcedon to this council.

8 See Liebeschuetz, *Barbarians and Bishops*, pp. 146–65.

9 CT, xvi, 5.8; 5.30.

10 CT, xvi, 12 (383), 20 (391), 24 (394), 26 (395).

11 CT, xvi, 5.13 (381), 21 (392), 22 (394), 24 (394).

12 CT, xvi, 21 (392).

13 CT, xvi, 10.11 (391), 12 (392), 13 (395).

14 CT, xvi, 8.10 (396), 11, 13; CT, xvi, 8.2 (330). Also CT, xvi, 8.13.

15 CT, xvi, 8.2 (330); xvi, 8.8 (392); xvi, 8.15 (404) and 21 (420).

16 CT, xvi, 8.25, 27 (423).

17 See CT, xvi, 8.22 (415), 25, 27, 16, 28.

18 Liebeschuetz, *Barbarians and Bishops*, p. 151.

19 See Liebeschuetz, *Continuity and Change*, p. 293.

20 See CT, xvi, 5.41; xvi, 5.63; xvi, 5.64.

21 It is true that Bishop Priscillian of Avila was condemned as a Manichean and executed in 386, together with his supporters, but this was exceptional and was condemned by St. Martin of Tours, St. Ambrose, and Pope Siricius.

22 Sozomen, *Historia ecclesiastica*, VII, 12, PG, 67, 844–1630; GCS, 50.

23 See Liebeschuetz, *Barbarians and Bishops*, 152–3.

24 Ibid., p. 153.

25 For the age of Justinian, see Evans, *Age of Justinian* and Browning, *Justinian and Theodora*. See also Averil Cameron, *Procopius and the Sixth Century* (London, 1985). This is primarily a study of the writings of Procopius but Cameron sets Procopius securely in his historical context.

26 Sebastian Brock, "The conversations with the Syrian Orthodox under Justinian (532)," *Orientalia Christiana Periodica* 47 (1981), pp. 87–121.

27 Justinian's new codex made a collection of the constitutions to be found in the three previous collections: *Codex Gregorianus* (AD219), *Codex Hermogenianus* (AD295) and the *Codex Theodosianus*, as well as the new constitutions that had been promulgated up to those of Justinian. The emperor decreed that only the constitutions included in the new revised codex would have the force of law. See Justinian's decree to the senate promulgating the revised code in 534, Paul Krueger (ed.), *Corpus Iuris Civilis*, vol. II, *Codex Iustinianus* (14th edn., Dublin and Zürich, 1967), p. 4.

28 For a brief account of Justinian's legislation, see W. Kunkel, *An Introduction to Roman Legal and Constitutional History* (Oxford, 1966), pp. 152–64; also H. Jolowicz, *Historical Introduction to the Study of Roman Law* (London, 1952, 2nd edn.), pp. 488–516. For a detailed account of the methods by which Justinian's *Corpus* was produced, see Tony Honoré, *Tribonian* (London, 1978).

29 *Codex Repetitae Lectionis*: Krueger (ed.), *Corpus Iuris Civilis*. See also the *Collectio Tripartita*. This is a collection of Justinian's laws on ecclesiastical subjects. It is divided into three parts. The first section contains a Greek version of the first 13 titles in the first book of the *Codex Iustinianus*, along with four Greek constitutions. The second section contains Greek summaries of texts from the *Digest* and the *Institutes*. The third part contains the first 3 titles of a version of the *Novellae* by the late sixth-century Athanasius of Emesa. See *Collectio Tripartita. Justinian on Religious and Ecclesiastical Affairs*, edited by N. van der Wal and B. H. Stolte (Groningen, 1994). The *Collectio Tripartita* has been published in Migne, PG, vol. 138.

30 See *Codex*, I.1.5.12–22 – the laws enacted in the first years of his reign.

31 This is seen in a number of his own laws, but the *Codex*, in I.1.5, adds "ultimo supplicio tradendis" – a penalty that was not contained in the original law of 428 (CT, xvi, 5.65).

32 For an edition of the *Novellae*: Schoell and Kroll, *Corpus Iuris Civilis*. vol. III, *Novellae* (Dublin and Zürich, 1972).

33 *Novella* 131 (AD545): "Therefore we confirm that those holy ecclesiastical rules have the force of law, which were issued or confirmed by the four holy councils; that is, by the 318 fathers at Nicaea, and the 150 holy fathers at Constantinople, and in the first [synod] at Ephesus in which Nestorius was condemned, and at Chalcedon, in which Eutyches was excommunicated along with Nestorius. For we accept the dogmas of the above-mentioned four councils just like Holy Scripture and we keep their rules just like laws": Schoell and

34 *Codex Iustinianus*, I, 3, 41.

35 *Codex Iustinianus*, I, 3, 41, 2. See also *Novella* 123, ch. 1.

36 *Novella* 123, ch. 1,1; ch. 13.

37 *Novella* 22 in 535; *Novella* 111 and *Novella* 117 in 542; *Novella* 134 in 556.

38 *Codex Iustinianus*, I, 9, 6.

39 A diriment impediment in canon law indicates a condition that renders a person unqualified for certain acts.

40 John T. Noonan, Jr., "Novel 22" in W. Basset (ed.), *The Bond of Marriage* (Notre Dame, IN, 1968), p. 60. For a discussion of Justinian's legislation on marriage, see P. L. Reynolds, *Marriage in the Western Church. The Christianization of Marriage during the Patristic and Early Medieval Periods* (Leiden, 1994), pp. 28–65.

41 *Novella* 117.

42 *Codex Iustinianus*, I.1.5.

43 See Brundage, *Law, Sex and Christian Society*, pp. 96–7.

44 J. Meyendorff, *Byzantine Theology. Historical Trends and Doctrinal Themes* (New York, 1983).

45 *Novella* 131, AD545.

46 Honoré, *Law in the Crisis of Empire*, p. 133, with a reference to Sozomen, *Historia ecclesiastica*, 9.1.5–6.

The opening reference: Kroll, *Corpus Iuris Civilis*, vol. III, *Novellae*, p. 655.

47 See D. Hunt, "Christianising the Roman Empire: The Evidence of the Code", in Harries and Wood, *Theodosian Code*, pp. 143–58.

48 Professor Haldon comments on this: "As God represented the ultimate source of law, so the emperor chosen by God was the ultimate source of earthly law; a formulation which – by defining the priestly authority strictly in terms of ministering to 'matters divine' – left some considerable scope for dissension thereafter." John Haldon, *Byzantium. A History* (Gloucestershire, 2000), p. 132.

49 *Novella* 6, On the appointment of bishops and other clerics. Preface: "The greatest gifts of God to men, granted by a heavenly providence, are the priesthood and the imperial power; the former has care of sacred things, the latter presides over and takes care of things human. Each proceeds from one and the same source and sets in order human life. Therefore nothing is so greatly desired by the emperors than the dignity of the priests, and they are always making supplication to God on their behalf." Schoell and Kroll, *Corpus Iuris Civilis*, vol. III, *Novellae*, pp. 35–6.

50 See J. B. Bury, *The Constitution of the Late Roman Empire* (Cambridge, 1910), 9.

51 See E. Herman, *The Cambridge Medieval History*, vol. IV, Part II (Cambridge, 1967), ch. XXIII, "The Secular Church", pp. 105–33.

52 Honoré, *Law in the Crisis of Empire*, p. 128.

Bibliography

Robert Browning, *Justinian and Theodora* (revised edn., London, 1987).

James A. Brundage, *Law, Sex and Christian Society in Medieval Europe* (Chicago and London, 1987).

J. B. Bury, *History of the Late Roman Empire* (London, 1923; repr. New York, 1958).

J. A. S. Evans, *The Age of Justinian. The Circumstances of Imperial Power* (London and New York, 1996).

Jill Harries and Ian Wood (eds.), *The Theodosian Code. Studies in the Imperial Law of Late Antiquity* (London, 1993).

Tony Honoré, *The Law in the Crisis of Empire 379–455AD. The Theodosian Dynasty and its Quaestors* (Oxford, 1998).

J. H. W. G. Liebeschuetz, *Continuity and Change in Roman Religion* (Oxford, 1979).

—— *Barbarians and Bishops. Army, Church and State in the Age of Arkadios and Chrysostom* (Oxford, 1990).

John F. Matthews, *Laying Down the Law: A Study of the Theodosian Code* (New Haven, CT, 2000).

J. Meyendorff, *Imperial Unity and Christian Divisions. The Church 450–680* (New York, 1989).

P. L. Reynolds, *Marriage in the Western Church. The Christianization of Marriage during the Patristic and Early Medieval Periods* (Leiden, 1994).

Stephen Williams and Gerard Friell, *Theodosius. The Empire at Bay* (New Haven, CT, 1994).

Rival Traditions: Christian Theology and Judaism

Philo of Alexandria

David T. Runia

The Tretyakov Gallery in Moscow contains the most famous of all Russion icons, the Old Testament Trinity by Andrei Rublov.[1] Painted in the most ravishing hues, it depicts three angels sitting on stools around a low table. The angel in the middle at the back inclines his head to the left, as does the angel at the right. The third angel at the left inclines his head in the other direction toward the other two. The colours of their robes are surely not without significance. The central figure has a dark crimson robe, with a copious royal blue cloak cast over his left shoulder. The other two have tunics of the same colour, with other colours for their cloaks, in the one case light green, in the other a silken brown-red, turning to light blue where it catches the light. The colours of their dress thus show their diversity in unity, as befits the Trinity. In the middle of the table there is a golden chalice with some food in it; it is surely meant to suggest the Eucharist. But why is there a rather spindly tree behind the left shoulder of the central angel and why, further to the left, is there the outline of a house with an arched doorway? And what exactly is that food in the chalice? These are the details that give the scene away. The tree is the oak of Mamre and the house is the domicile of the patriarch Abraham. The food in the chalice is a calf's head. The scene thus depicts the visit of the three men to Abraham in Genesis 18, interpreted in terms of the divine Trinity. It might seem natural that the Christian Church should develop an interpretation of this kind for that rather enigmatic biblical story. In fact, however, the origins of the interpretation precede the beginnings of Christian exegesis and theology. They are to be found in the writings of a Jew, Philo of Alexandria.

Philo was an almost exact contemporary of Jesus Christ. He was born in about 15 BCE and lived all his life in Alexandria, home of the largest and most influential Jewish community in the Diaspora. He belonged to one of the leading families of the community. From a young age, it seems, he was attracted to philosophical and theological studies. From his copious writings it is plain that he had a thorough training in Greek philosophy and scientific knowledge. He was a prolific author, and many of his writings have survived, either in the original Greek or in Armenian translations. His 50 extant treatises occupy 12 volumes in the Loeb Classical Library.[2]

Later in life, he tells us, he was forced to set aside his studious pursuits and take up the political cause of his people, leading an embassy to the Emperor Gaius Caligula in 39 CE to protest against the anti-Jewish sentiment that had built up in Alexandria. It was a risky business, but he managed to return home with his life intact and probably lived for about another decade. The episode illustrates his strong loyalty to Judaism, which is combined with a deep immersion in the cultural and intellectual life of the great eastern metropolis.

Philo has been called "the first theologian."[3] The title is not inappropriate for at least two reasons: first, on account of his attachment to the Jewish religion, for his thought is more theocentric than anything we find in Greek or Roman philosophy; secondly, and for our purposes more significantly, the phrase is suitable on account of the particular orientation of Alexandrian Hellenistic Judaism and Philo's own leading place in it. Alexandrian Jews thought and spoke in Greek. Their Bible was the Septuagint, translated from the Hebrew in the third and second centuries BCE and regarded as no less authoritative than the original.[4] This Hellenized form of Judaism was more open to other cultural influences than the Judaism found in Palestine, and certainly very different from what we find in the writings of Qumran, with which it is often contrasted. Philo was clearly exceptional in his knowledge of Greek philosophy. In his writings we find a tendency to approach the contents of religious faith in a dogmatizing frame of mind. A remarkable passage is found at the end of his exposition of the creation account in Genesis, the treatise entitled *On the Creation of the Cosmos According to Moses*, where he summarizes his treatment as follows:[5]

> By means of the creation account which we have discussed Moses teaches us among many other things five lessons that are the most beautiful and excellent of all. The first of these is that the Divinity is and exists . . . The second lesson is that God is one . . . The third lesson is that the cosmos has come into existence . . . The fourth lesson is that the cosmos too is one . . . The fifth lesson is that God also takes thought for the cosmos . . . He, then, who first has learnt these things not so much with his hearing as with his understanding, and has imprinted their marvellous and priceless forms on his own soul . . . this person will lead a blessed life of well-being, marked as he is by the doctrines of piety and holiness.

The great American scholar E. R. Goodenough called this "the first creed in history," and he certainly has a point.[6] Philo speaks explicitly of doctrines (*dogmata*) and affirms that belief in them will lead to a blessed life. Often a distinction is drawn between Judaism as a religion of orthopraxy (right observance) and Christianity as a religion of orthodoxy (right belief). This distinction certainly does not work with the kind of Judaism that Philo represents; right thinking about God and his relations to the world is of the greatest importance. This attitude makes him into an important precursor of Christian dogmatic thought.

On the other hand, it should not be thought that Philo is a dogmatic theologian who writes treatises about dogmatic subjects or even produces a systematic theology such as we have become accustomed to in the Christian tradition. Matters can be quite deceptive in this regard. For example, one of his better known treatises is called *On the Immutability of God*, and it does discuss the question of whether God stays the same or is prone to changing his mind. When we look at the contents of the treatise, however, we find that it consists entirely of exegesis of Genesis 6:4–12, the passage where God determines to launch the great flood on account of human wickedness, but makes an exception for Noah, who finds favour in his sight. The question of divine immutability is raised by the text of Genesis 6:6: "And the Lord was sorry that he had made humankind on the earth." Almost all Philo's writings are fundamentally exegetical in nature, whether giving an allegorical interpretation of the first chapters of Genesis (in the so-called Allegorical Commentary, 21 treatises) or giving a detailed account of the Mosaic law (in the Exposition of the Law, 10 treatises) or giving piecemeal answers at both the literal and the allegorical level to questions raised by the biblical text (in the *Questions on Genesis and Exodus*, 8 treatises). When elaborating his exegesis Philo certainly takes theological issues into account, and it is not difficult to discern coherent theological ideas in the background. It is not possible, however, to reduce his thought to a single systematic theology. Partly this is the result of Philo's method; partly it is caused by his tendency to preserve traditional exegetical material, which often results in differing perspectives on the same questions.

The predominantly exegetical nature of Philo's thought should be continually taken into account when reading the remainder of this contribution. I shall present an outline of the more important ideas that he developed in the area of theology. It will be an account that is deliberately slanted towards the later development of theology in the Christian tradition. The reader should bear in mind, however, that the author of these ideas was a loyal Jew, whose Scripture was the Hebrew Bible in Greek translation. In fact, even that statement needs further qualification. Philo's thought is almost solely based in the first five books of that Bible, the so-called Pentateuch. He is convinced that these books were authored by the great prophet and lawgiver Moses, who was divinely inspired when writing them. They represent the summit of what human wisdom is capable of reaching. Philo regarded it as his life's work to expound that wisdom to his disciples and readers.

Theology starts and end with God. As we noted above, the existence and the uniqueness of God are the first two articles of Philo's creed. They correspond to the injunctions of the first two commandments of the Decalogue. In its history Israel had experienced the nearness of the divine presence. All of Israel's religious observance is focused on this one God. At the conclusion of his exposition of the first two commandments Philo writes:

> We the disciples and pupils of the prophet Moses shall not cease in our quest for the One-who-IS (*tou ontos*), regarding as the goal of our well-being knowledge of Him and also age-long life, in accordance with the Law which states that those who hold fast to God shall all live (cf. Deut. 4:4), laying down a necessary and philosophical doctrine. For truly the godless are dead in their souls, whereas those who have joined the ranks of the God-who-IS (*tôi onti theôi*) live a life without death.

Knowledge of God for Philo is not just recognition of his existence. It also involves trying to understand who God is and what He does. For this quest Philo makes extensive use of the conceptuality of Greek philosophy.

If we examine the text just quoted in more detail, it will be observed that it not only uses the usual Greek term for God, *ho theos*, but also speaks of God as Being (translated as "the One who IS"). In the first instance this may remind us of Plato, for in his works he often describes the transcendent world of the ideas, which he considers to be the realm of the divine, as *to on*. If we pressed Philo, however, he would certainly claim that the description of God in terms of Being is fundamentally Mosaic. In the Septuagint the self-disclosure of God at Exodus 3:14 is translated as *egô eimi ho ôn* (I am he-who-IS). The difference between the Platonic phrase and the Septuagint translation is that the one is neuter, the other masculine. The former corresponds more to the philosophical concept of God, the latter to Israel's personal experience of the divine and numinous presence. It is characteristic of Philo that he uses both interchangeably. In the text cited above the phrase is used in the genitive, so that it is impossible to determine which of the two he means. In fact, it may be surmised that he is happy to let the ambiguity stand.

Philo is convinced that God's existence should not just be accepted as a matter of faith or experiential conviction. There are rational grounds for accepting its validity. Various texts in his writings affirm the cosmological argument that God's existence and creative activity can be deduced from the ordered design and functioning of the cosmos.[7] In his allegories Philo polemicizes strongly against the Chaldeans, a group of thinkers whom he identifies with the view that the cosmos is autonomous and not dependent on God for its creation and continued existence.[8] In a famous text he goes a step further and claims that it may be possible to know God not just from his works, but also from Himself. Just as we see the sun through its own light, "so those who pursue truth envisage God through God, as light through light."[9] This has been interpreted as involving "an inner intuitive illumination, constituting a rational process of an analytical type," somewhat parallel to the famous ontological argument for God's existence.[10]

There is, however, a further step that those who are engaged in the quest to know God might wish to take, namely to know God as He really is in his essence. Philo is convinced that this is impossible for human beings. The paradigm instance is the great Moses himself who climbs the mountain in Exodus 33 and asks God to reveal himself. God replies, in Philo's words:[11] "Your zeal is praiseworthy, but the request cannot be suitably granted to any creature. I freely bestow what is appropriate for the recipient. For not everything that is easy for me to give can be received by a human being." God is thus unknowable in his essence, and this means that he is also unspeakable and unnameable. No description or name can give accurate expression to his nature.

Philo thus has both a positive and a negative theology. There can be no doubt that he is indebted to Greek philosophy for the basic approach. The arguments for God's existence and some of his characteristics are found both in the Stoa and in Platonism. The combination of positive and negative theology is strongly reminiscent of chapter 10 on theology in the *Didaskalikos* of Alcinous, a Middle Platonist handbook.[12] Some scholars have suggested that negative theology actually originates with Philo, but this cannot be proven and is not, in my view, likely. Rather we may conclude that Philo is a witness to a change in the general direction of theology during this period. The positive flavour of theology in the Hellenistic period is starting to give way to a less confident approach that is above all convinced of the utter transcendence of the supreme Being.[13]

But if God as Being is truly unnameable, what about the names that He is given in Scripture? A fascinating text that raises this question is found in the treatise *On the Change of Names* (1–33).[14] The starting point is the biblical text Genesis 17:1: "And the Lord was seen by Abraham and said to him, 'I am your God.'" This verse, says Philo, should not be taken to mean that God is seen by the eyes of the body; only the mind can do that with its spiritual light. But it should not be supposed that the Existent (*to on*) can be comprehended by a human being. As Moses discovered, by his very Nature the Existent is unknowable, and as a logical consequence no proper name can be assigned to him. When He says "I am He that IS," this is equivalent to saying, "my nature is to exist, not to be pronounced." But so that the human race would not lack a title for Him, He allows Himself to be called Lord God (*kyrios ho theos*), as in Genesis 17:1.

The most common names for the supreme being in the Septuagint are thus taken to express not his essential nature, but something about him. Philo takes these names to refer to God's Powers (*dynameis*). The name *theos*, etymologically linked to *tithêmi* (I set in place), refers to God as Creator of the universe. The name *kyrios* (Lord) refers to him as ruler and supreme authority. A little further in the same text Philo argues that the words "I am your God" are used by license of language and not exactly. The Existent considered as Existent (*to on hêi on*, the Aristotelian phrase) is absolute and fully self-sufficient; he is certainly not relative to anything such as a human being. The divine Powers can be said to be relative, for God as Creator is in a sense relative to the universe and God as Ruler is ruler of someone. Philo's distinction between God's essence and his Powers is strongly reminiscent of the famous chapter on theology in the Pseudo-Aristotelian treatise *On the Cosmos*.[15] Elsewhere we find more elaborate schemes of God's Powers, including an exegesis of the Golden Ark, which is taken to symbolize six Powers.[16] The schema of the Existent and two chief Powers is, however, the one most commonly used.

But Philo has another way of approaching the problem of God's essence and his relation to creation which has become even more famous in the history of theology. In addition to speaking of God's Powers, he also speaks of God's Logos. Philo's Logos doctrine is notoriously difficult, and certainly not always fully consistent, but in general terms we may say that the Logos represents the face of God (or of Being) as it is turned to created reality.[17] The Logos is identified with God's presence in the cosmos, pervading physical reality and maintaining its order. The Stoic background of the doctrine is obvious, but without any materialistic connotations. In a sense it comes closer to the Platonic doctrine of the World-Soul. But the Logos can also have a role that transcends the physical realm. In his exposition of the Mosaic creation account it is portrayed as God's thought as he engages in the creative work, and is identified with the realm of the ideas as blueprint for creation.[18] Here the background is resolutely Platonist, the ideas having become the objects of divine thought. The chief difficulty posed by Philo's doctrine of the Logos is the following: sometimes Philo speaks of the Logos as if it were simply an *aspect* of the divine nature, namely that aspect which is accessible to human thought precisely because it is related to that which follows it. At other times, however, the Logos is treated as a *hupostasis*, i.e. a self-subsistent theological entity that is at least to some degree independent of God himself (the issue is complicated even further when Philo talks of angels as *logoi*). In the latter case we might suspect that the doctrine of God's Oneness, as prescribed by Jewish monotheism, is endangered, but this does not seem to be a matter of concern for Philo. As we saw earlier, he strongly affirms God's unicity in his "credal" statement (which does not mention the Logos). There are some links to Philo's Logos doctrine in Greek philosophy (particularly in Plotinus). But the strongest connections are with the Christian tradition, for example in the Prologue to John's Gospel and the Christological hymn in Colossians 1:15–20.

The doctrine of the divine Spirit (*pneuma*) is not quite as prominent in Philo as the Logos doctrine, but it is certainly present. It primarily denotes the divine presence within humanity, taking as starting point the celebrated text Genesis 2:7, in which God the Creator breathes his Spirit into the face of the first human being.[19] Humankind has received the gift of the divine Spirit in its makeup, but does not always live in accordance with it. With reference to Genesis 6:3, Philo distinguishes between those people in whom the Spirit abides and those who succumb to the flesh.[20] It cannot but remind us of the Pauline distinction between the *pneumatikoi* and the *sarkikoi*. The presence of the divine Spirit is also the foundation of prophecy, as practiced by Moses and other men of God.[21]

The three components of the Christian doctrine of the Trinity, God the Father, God the Son (as Logos),[22] and God the Spirit, are thus prefigured in various ways in Philo's writings. But what about the doctrine of the Trinity itself? Here we should return to the subject of Andrei Rublev's celebrated icon. Naturally Philo knows the story of Abraham and his visitors very well, and expounds it on various occasions. In his *Life of Abraham* he gives a complex allegorical interpretation with as chief theme the doctrine of the divine Powers.[23] The central figure is the Father of the Universe whom the Scriptures call Being (*ho ón*). The other two are his two chief Powers, the one called God, the other Lord. But why, Philo asks, does the biblical text sometimes speak of three persons and at other times of just one? It is a matter, he argues, of theological perspective. To the mind that is highly purified, God appears as one, but to the mind that has yet to be introduced to the greater mysteries, the Existent cannot be apprehended on its own, but only through its actions, whether as Creator or as Ruler. This is certainly not the doctrine of the Trinity. Philo is and remains a monotheistic Jew. But it does share some interesting features in common with that doctrine.

The survival of Philo's many writings, virtually alone among all the products of Alexandrian Judaism, is quite remarkable. But we can now easily understand how it happened. The early Christians felt an affinity to Philo's writings and thought they were worth preserving.[24] They regarded them as a repository of valuable exegetical and theological ideas. A fascinating illustration of their attitude is found in a letter of the fifth-century desert monk, Isidore of Pelusium. Isidore knows full well that Philo is a Jew, but nevertheless he strongly argues that the Alexandrian recognized something of the truth of Christian orthodox religion. Some passages are worth quoting:[25]

> I admire the truth for the way in which she has induced the souls of intelligent men
> even to combat the preconceived opinion they have of their own doctrines. For the

teaching of the truth has embedded the concept of the holy Trinity so clearly and lucidly also in the Old Testament for those who wish to observe it that Philo, though a Jew and a zealous one at that, in the writings which he left behind comes into conflict with his own religion ... When he attempted to interpret the expression "God and Lord" he gained a conception of the most royal (or highest) Trinity. He that asserts that God is one does not run up against the numerical unit of the monad, but rather against the mystery of the Trinity, which is more unified than wholly discrete entities but richer than what is truly monadic. Indeed this teaching of the truth took hold of his soul with such force that he was compelled both to declare it quite explicitly and leave it behind in his writings. He declared that there were two powers of Him that IS, of which the one, he says, IS the creative and beneficent power and IS called God (*theos*), the other IS the royal and punitive power and IS called Lord (*kurios*). In so doing he moves not very far from the one who said "Christ the power of God and the wisdom of God (1 Cor. 1:24)", not a unsubstantial power but one with a separate existence, all-powerful, creator of the hypostases, of equal strength to the one whose Power he is.

It is apparent, therefore, that when we admire Rublov's icon of the Old Testament Trinity, we should also pay homage to the Jewish theologian from Alexandria, for in his writings we find the initial impetus for this doctrinal interpretation of the scene. It is a fine illustration of how the interface with Hellenistic Judaism contributed to the development of Christian theology.

Notes

1 An illustration of the icon can be easily be found on the internet, e.g. at www.marquette.edu/history/Slides/Byzantine

2 But it is not fully complete. For further details see the bibliography at the end of the chapter.

3 By W. Bousset in his well-known handbook, *Die Religion des Judentums im späthellenistischen Zeitalter* (Tübingen, 1926, 3rd edn.), p. 445.

4 Philo recounts the legend of the 70 translators in *On the Life of Moses* (LCL, VI) 2.25–42. An earlier account is found in the *Letter to Aristeas*. (References are to *Philo in Ten Volumes* [see Bibliography].)

5 *On the Creation of the Cosmos* (Loeb I), 170–2 (abbreviated).

6 E. R. Goodenough, *An Introduction to Philo Judaeus* (Oxford, 1962, 2nd edn.), p. 37.

7 Cf. *Allegories of the Laws* (LCL I), 3.97–9; *On the life of Abraham* (LCL VI), 72–80; *On the Decalogue* (LCL VII), 59–60; *On the Special Laws* (LCL VII), 1.32, 3.187–9; *On Providence* (LCL IX), 2.63.

8 Cf. *On the Migration of Abraham* (LCL IV), 178–81; *On the Life of Abraham* (LCL VI), 69.

9 *On Rewards and Punishments* (LCL VIII), 44–6. This text furnished the title of Goodenough's brilliant but flawed monograph, *By Light, Light: The Mystic Gospel of Hellenistic Judaism* (New Haven, CT, 1935).

10 D. Winston, *Contemplative Life*, p. 28.

11 *On the Special Laws* (LCL VII), 1.43.

12 See the translation and commentary by J. Dillon, *Alcinous: The Handbook of Platonism* (Oxford, 1993).

13 For Philo's theology in the context of ancient philosophy, see my article, "The Beginning of the End: Philo of Alexandria and Hellenistic Theology," in D. Frede and A. Laks (eds.), *Traditions of Theology: Studies in Hellenistic Theology, Its Background and Aftermath*, Philosophia Antiqua 89 (Leiden, 2002), pp. 281–316.

14 Only a bare summary of this rich text can be given here. Detailed analysis is found in my article, "Naming and knowing: Themes in Philonic Theology with Special Reference to the *De mutatione nominum*," which is article XI in my collection of essays, *Exegesis and Philosophy*, cited in the bibliography.

15 Especially in the comparison with the Great King of Persia, 398a10–b25. The dating of the work is controversial. Some scholars date it to the 1st century BC, i.e. close to the time of Philo; others regard it as belonging to the early Hellenistic period.

16 *Questions and answers on Exodus* (LCL XII), 2.68.

17 The formula of David Winston, *Logos and Mystical Theology*, p. 50.

18 *On the Creation of the Cosmos* (LCL I), 16–20.

19 See esp. *That the Worse Attacks the Better* (LCL II), 79–85. In Philo's doctrine of man there is a kind of rivalry between the two central texts Gen. 1:26–7 and 2:7. The "image" in the former text is linked to the divine Logos.

20 See esp. *On the Giants* (LCL II), 19–31.

21 Cf. *On the Giants* (LCL II), 60; J. R. Levison, "Inspiration and the Divine Spirit in the Writ-

ings of Philo Judaeus," *JSJ* 26 (1995), pp. 271–323.

22 In a number of texts Philo calls the Logos "son" or "first-born" or both; cf. *On agriculture* (LCL III), 51; *On the confusion of tongues* (LCL IV), 63, 146; *On dreams* (LCL V), 1.215. These texts greatly impressed early Christians.

23 *On the life of Abraham* (LCL VI), 119–32.

24 The history of Philo's reception in early Christianity is traced in my *Philo in Early Christian Literature: A Survey*, CRINT III 3 (Assen and Minneapolis, MN, 1993).

25 *Letters* 2.143. See further my article, "Philo of Alexandria in Five Letters of Isidore of Pelusium," in *Philo and the Church Fathers: A Collection of Papers*, Vigiliae Christianae, Supplements 32 (Leiden, 1995), pp. 155–81.

Bibliography

The text and translation of Philo's writings preserved in Greek, and some of the writings preserved only in Armenian, are found in *Philo in Ten Volumes (and Two Supplementary Volumes)*, with an English translation by F. H. Colson, G. H. Whitaker (and R. Marcus), (London and Cambridge, MA, 1929–62) (The Loeb Classical Library). A more complete translation is found in *The Works of Philo Complete and Unabridged*, translated by C. D. Yonge, with a foreword by David M. Scholer, (Peabody, MA, 1993), but this 1855 translation is based on a defective text. An full anthology of important Philonic texts, ordered according to topic, can be found in D. Winston, *Philo of Alexandria: The Contemplative Life, The Giants and Selections*, The Classics of Western Spirituality (New York and Toronto, 1981).
Complete annotated bibliographies of Philonic scholarship since 1937 can be found in R. Radice and D. T. Runia, *Philo of Alexandria: An Annotated Bibliography 1937–1986* (Leiden, 1992, 2nd edn.), *Philo of Alexandria: An Annotated Bibliography 1987–96* (Leiden, 2000), and in yearly updates in the journal *The Studia Philonica Annual*.

The best recent introduction to Philo's life and writings is P. Borgen, *Philo of Alexandria: An Exegete for his Time* (Leiden, 1997). Two older introductory accounts well worth reading are H. Chadwick, "Philo and the Beginnings of Christian Thought," in A. H. Armstrong (ed.), *The Cambridge History of Later Greek and Early Medieval Philosophy* (Cambridge, 1967), pp. 137–57; J. Dillon, *The Middle Platonists: 80BC to AD220* (London, 1977, 1996, 2nd edn.), pp. 139–83.
An excellent study of Philo's theological ideas is found in D. Winston, *Logos and Mystical Theology in Philo of Alexandria* (Cincinatti, 1985). See also my collection of papers, *Exegesis and Philosophy: Studies on Philo of Alexandria* (London, 1990), esp. papers XI–XIII. A comprehensive ordered list of texts on theological themes is found in the "Sachweiser" to the German translation of Philo, prepared by W. Theiler, *Philo von Alexandria, Die Werke in deutscher Übersetzung*, edited by L. Cohn *et al.*, 7 volumes (Berlin, 1964, 2nd edn.), 7.396–402. For other writings on Philo's theology see the footnotes.

Christian Theology and Judaism

Paula Fredriksen and Judith Lieu

To compare "Christian theology" and "Judaism" is difficult, because the terms do not quite correspond: "theology" is a particular type of philosophical enterprise; "Judaism" is an umbrella term for the social and religious activities of ancient Jews. Systems of thought do not influence or interact with each other: people do. To address our topic, then, we need to do both intellectual history and social history; to consider not only ancient ideas, but also ancient people, in their social contexts. The picture that emerges from our consideration will, necessarily, be complex. And that complexity attests, in turn, to the vigor, vitality, and variety of Christian/Jewish interactions in antiquity.

The Context: The City, Paideia, and Theology

In modern parlance, "theology" often functions to mean something like "religious thoughts." In antiquity, the term had greater precision. Its component words reveal its original meaning. *Theos* in Greek means "divinity" or "god"; *logos* – a term with a very broad semantic range – means "word, order, reason." "Theology," then, means something like "rational discourse on the nature and function of divinity." The point of theology was to present, in a systematic and coordinated manner, conceptualizations of the ways that divinity related to other aspects of reality: cosmos, soul, mind, body, and so on. Its dependence on rational categories and systems of thought meant that, intellectually, theology was from the beginning a species of philosophy.

Philosophy provided the tools and principles for constructing theology. But traditional narratives of profound cultural and political importance – initially, the various myths of classical antiquity – provided theology's occasion and, in a sense, its incentive. The High God of the Hellenistic curriculum was conceived as radically stable, impassive, incorporeal, eternal, free from change; these categories defined "good" in a metaphysical (not necessarily ethical) sense.[1] The more he (or "it": either pronoun could serve) became transcendent, the more the gap – metaphysical and moral

– between him and the universe became filled with various intermediaries: stars and planets; lower gods; angels; demons; the demiurge ("craftsman") or *logos* who ordered the cosmos according to divine principles. But the great ancient epics, poems, and dramas of the Greeks presented divinity as personalities: characters who appeared to have bodies; who forgot and remembered; who grew angry or calm; who plotted, raged, raped. These divine characters did not oblige the categories of philosophy.

To spin the straw of traditional religious narrative into the gold of philosophic-ally coherent and elevating theology, Hellenistic intellectuals availed themselves of *allegory*. (*Allos* in Greek means "other"; *agoreuein* means "to speak.") Allegory enabled the enlightened reader to see through the surface level of a text to its spiritual message, to understand what the text truly meant in contrast to what it merely said. Grammar, rhetoric, philological finesse: all these tools of classical paideia might be brought to bear on an ancient story to turn it into a philosophically lucid statement of timeless truth.[2] The curriculum of the urban *gymnasia* that educated young men to become leaders in their cities saturated them with all these literatures, philosophical, rhetorical, mythological. As civic leaders, they would fund, legislate, and oversee the cults connected with the traditional gods; as educated men, they might conceive such worship as expressing philosophical truths. In brief, theology in antiquity was first of all an intellectual expression of pagan culture, dependent on a post-classical pedagogy that rested socially and literarily on the ancient gods.[3]

Jews and, eventually, Christians (whether Jews or Gentiles) in their turn, produced theologies also. To do so, they depended on educations that were intrinsically, profoundly pagan. The Jewish encounter with and internalization of pagan paideia preceded by some four centuries the Christian encounter. In many ways, educated Jews rehearsed the experiences, convictions, and arguments of the later Christians.

Jewish populations of the fourth and third centuries BCE had followed Greek ones in the wake of the armies of Alexander the Great. In the new Hellenistic urban foundations diffused throughout Asia Minor, Egypt, and the Near East, immigrants as well as conquered indigenous peoples moved from their native vernaculars to Greek. Migrating Jews took their sacred writings with them. When their community shifted vernaculars, their Scriptures shifted too. By 200BCE, in Alexandria in Egypt, a huge collection of Jewish sacred writings, originally written in Hebrew or, occa-sionally, Aramaic, was becoming available in the international language. The Semitic-language "Tanakh" (Torah, the "five books of Moses"; Nevi'im, "prophets"; and Ketuvi'im, "writings") had become the Greek Septuagint (LXX).

Translation invariably affects meaning, no matter how accurate translators strive to be. The God of Israel, newly available in Greek, took on new aspects. The divine name revealed at the Burning Bush became ὁ Ὤν, "the Being" (Exod. 3:14); when this god established the heavens, he did so τῷ λογῷ, "by the Logos" or "Word" (Ps. 32 (33):6). Philosophical concepts, thus, did not need to be read into Scripture: they were already there, by virtue of the new language of the text.

The Greek text of the Bible in turn presented new interpretive opportunities for educated Hellenistic Jews. Many Jews in the Diaspora acquired their education through the *gymnasium*, nurtured, like their pagan counterparts, on grammar, rhetoric, and poems and stories about the classical gods. And again like their pagan counter-parts, Jewish intellectuals also had to struggle to make systematic sense of their own ancient religious literature. Biblical stories no less than Homeric ones depicted divinity in ways that contrasted sharply with the principles of philosophy. Thus, and again like their pagan counterparts, many Jewish intellectuals relied especially on the interpretive techniques of allegory. Allegory enabled Greek-speaking, educated Jews to retrieve philosophical meaning from the stories constituting their own religious and ethnic patrimony.

But western Jews did much more than acquire paideia, or apply it to their own traditions. They utterly appropriated paideia, and claimed it as their own. Again and again the theme emerges in Hellenistic Jewish literature: what the Greeks got right – mainly philosophy, but also mathematics, or music, or astronomy – they actually got from the Jews.[4] Plato, some Jews argued, had studied Torah and developed his doctrines in Egypt, from a (lost) Greek translation of the Bible made several centuries prior to the LXX.[5] One Jewish writer depicted Abraham as the bringer of culture to the Egyptians – another argument for superiority, in a culture where older was better.[6] Hellenistic Jews forged pagan prophecies, wherein ancient sibyls praised Jewish ethical and religious culture in proper Homeric hexameters.[7] Others presented "histories" according to which the LXX was translated at King Ptolemy's request; he had wanted this renowned book of Jewish wisdom to grace his library in Alexandria.[8] In one account, the young Moses received instruction from the wisest teachers both Egyptian and Greek, but of course outstripped them all; in another, Moses taught music to Orpheus. Jews turned out Judaizing verses while ascribing them to Aeschylus, Sophocles, Euripides, and other heroes of the classical curriculum. Centuries later these turn up, piously repeated in the writings of the church fathers.[9] In all these ways, educated Hellenistic Jews gave philosophy, and thus theology, a new "native" culture: their own.

Centuries later, by the second century CE, some Gentile Christians in their turn began to theologize. That is, they strove to make systematic, philosophical sense out of the revelation of Christ as they saw it mediated in the LXX and, eventually, also in various specifically Christian texts. To think about the Bible theologically and, thus, philosophically, they drew deeply from the springs of Hellenistic Jewish apology. Many of these Hellenistic Jewish texts (such as the entirety of Philo's exegetical opera) survive exclusively in Christian recensions.[10] Indeed, in some cases scholars remain undecided whether a particular text should be labeled "Jewish" or "Christian." And when arguing against Gentile pagan contemporaries, Gentile Christians readily availed themselves of this Hellenistic Jewish arsenal. Their utilitarian appreciation in fact accounts for the patristic preservation of these originally Jewish apologetic traditions.[11]

These Christian theologians and apologists of the second and third centuries waged a hermeneutical battle on many fronts simultaneously. They fought to define their community and to establish the superiority of their own understanding of philosophy and paideia against Gentile pagans.[12] They also strove to establish their readings of the LXX, and the practices that they saw enjoined there, against the understandings of other Christians,[13] as well as against those of the various Jews. All of these arguments affected all the others. Our concern here is to trace the particular development of the arguments *contra Iudaeos*.

Here, as we shall see, the battle was waged over the text and the interpretation of Scripture, the LXX. The Christians' faith in Jesus Christ as the fulfillment of the promises of the Bible and as the key to its meaning determined their rejection of any "Jewish reading." Allegorizing the LXX by their own lights, they condemned Jewish readings as insufficiently philosophical. Advocating "spiritual" over "carnal" interpretations of biblical texts, they renounced Jewish practice as literal-minded, thus missing the intent of the text's divine author. As they read Jewish scriptures through the lens of Christian Passion traditions, these churchmen condemned the Jews as murderers of Christ. Indeed, they urged, using the prophets as proof text, the Jewish murder of Christ confirmed his status *as* Christ.

Finally, some Gentile Christian writers turned the vicissitudes of Palestinian Jewish history in the early Roman period to their own advantage, arguing that current events sustained the Christian view. Roman armies had destroyed Jerusalem and its temple in the course of the First Revolt (66–73 CE). Later, the bar Kochkba revolt led to the erasure of Jewish Jerusalem (132–5 CE). Hadrian established a pagan city, Aelia Capitolina, on its ruins. Why else would God have permitted such disasters unless he, too, had lost patience with Jewish practice, Jewish custom, and the general Jewish refusal to acknowledge the truth of Gentile Christian claims?[14]

This antagonistic theme within Gentile Christianity has been much studied.[15] Its near-ubiquity in our surviving ancient sources, and its relationship to and resonance with the violent anti-Judaism of recent European history, enhance its visibility to the point that much of the positive social and religious interaction between Jews and Christians – as between Jews, pagans, and Christians – lies obscured or overlooked.[16] We know from many of these same sources that Christian theologians consulted with Jewish scholars on the meanings of words and phrases in their shared Scriptures, and also for the meaning of Aramaic or Hebrew words appearing in the New Testament.[17] We also know that Gentile Christians – as well as Gentile pagans – frequented Diaspora synagogues, where they would hear Scriptures, take vows, worship together, and eat with Jews. There they would seek cures, as also in pagan temples, by "incubating" overnight, that is, sleeping in or near the sanctuary in order to receive healing or celestial advice.[18]

Long after one stream of Gentile Christianity became a form of Imperial Roman culture – a process that begins and proceeds, in fits and starts, throughout the fourth century – the canons of church councils still provide oblique testimony to the free social and thus religious interactions between members of all these groups, the pronouncement of the ideologues notwithstanding.[19] Indeed, this comfortable intimacy between groups may well have spurred the increasing shrillness and invective of official – especially episcopal – theological screeds on Jewish religious and moral degeneracy: the heat of their polemic betrays their frustration in trying to effect a principled separation of communities. Patristic theology conveys a clear separation of ("true") Christianity from ("false") Christianities, from paganism, and from Judaism. Real life blurred these distinctions.

Thus throughout late antiquity, pagans, Jews, and various Christians continued to mix in synagogues; to encounter each other at civic athletic and cultural events; to meet in town council halls and at the baths. Those of the upper economic and cultural strata, further, were bound together also by the intellectual principles of philosophical and rhetorical paideia even as they were divided by the particular texts that they regarded as vessels of revelation. These elites also shared a prime social matrix of high culture: urban institutions of education. This cultural connection perdured well after the conversion of Constantine. Augustine's *Confessions* (397CE) present one glimpse of this shared universe. The son of a fervently Catholic mother and catechumen father, Augustine learned through mastering a literature peopled with such characters as Dido, Aeneas, and the old Roman gods.[20] The letters of Libanius, the great pagan rhetorician of fourth-century Antioch, provides yet another glimpse. He writes to the Jewish patriarch Gamaliel to console this *vir clarissimus* about his son's lack of academic aptitude; the boy, sent by his father from Tiberias to further his rhetorical education, had skipped out on Libanius' lectures.[21]

Theology and Identity: Defining "Being Jewish"

In what way, then, can we speak of Christianity and Judaism as "rival" traditions? To do so is to adopt a perspective from which the relationship between the two can only be seen as competitive socially and antithetical theologically. Yet to assess such a perspective we must first establish context.

The earliest "Christian" texts – a portion of which were collected and canonized as the New Testament over a period extending into the fourth century and beyond – are irreducibly "Jewish." This is so both because they are thoroughly indebted to Scriptural tradition (the LXX), and because they rely on contemporary patterns of Jewish interpretation and thought. Written in Greek, they belong to the Hellenistic Diaspora.[22] Indeed, it is partly for this reason that these writings do not belong themselves to a distinctive Christian *theology* so much as to its sources.[23]

Distinctive about these is the various ways in which they configure allegiance to Christ within an understanding of the biblical covenant with the people Israel, shaped by the promises to Abraham and by the giving of the Torah to Moses at Sinai. Paul's characterizations of Israel "according to the flesh," John the evangelist's antithesis of Jesus' community to that of "the Jews," the author of the Epistle to the Hebrews' presentation of a "new covenant" that "has made the first obsolete" (8:13): within a first-century intra-Jewish context, all these arguments would sound like claims about the right way to be Jewish. That right way would be the way urged by the Jewish writer of the text. Thus the high rhetoric of these sectarian Jewish texts – not unlike that of their near-contemporary Judean counterparts, the Dead Sea Scrolls – denies any legitimacy to a construction of "Israel" or of the "people of God" or the "children of light" at odds with the new movement's own self-understanding. "Non-Christian" understandings of Judaism seem at least disavowed, if not actually repudiated.

Read by later generations of Gentiles independent of or alienated from the traditions of the synagogue, these texts established the main themes and patterns of antithesis that so characterized subsequent Christian theology. One such antithesis emerges already in the letters of the late first–early second-century bishop, Ignatius of Antioch. It may be he who coined the term "Christianity" (*christianismos*), which he set over against "Judaism" (*ioudaismos*), a term he may have learnt from Jewish sources.[24] He imagines these positions, the Christian and the Jewish, as in opposition.

"Christianity," he urges, "did not establish its faith in Judaism, but Judaism in Christianity" (*Magnesians* 10.3). Yet Ignatius also takes for granted at least some continuity between Jewish scriptures and Christian proclamation. He urges his readers to run to Christ as to the one Temple or to the altar of God – both references to the Jerusalem sanctuary – and he assures them that "the truly divine prophets" – the ones, that is, whose stories stood in Jewish Scripture – "lived according to Jesus Christ" (*Magnesians* 7.2; 8.2).

It is difficult to determine precisely what the "Judaism" and the "Judaizing" that Ignatius excoriates actually were. His disapproving references to Gentile Christians' keeping Sabbath and circumcision suggest that he objected to particular practices.[25] Yet he may have used these terms instead simply as slogans or code for what (good) Christians "did not do." Paul, some fifty years before Ignatius, had taught that Gentiles-in-Christ were not responsible for the practices mandated by Torah: those were the exclusive responsibility and privilege of Israel (e.g. Rom. 9:4).[26] Justin Martyr, some fifty years after Ignatius, taught that not only Gentile Christians, but also Jewish Christians, were not to live "Jewishly." Indeed, even for the Jews themselves such practices drew on a faulty, indeed a fleshly, reading of Scripture which, once understood spiritually, was seen not to prescribe behavior but rather to foretell Christ and his Church. However, he has to concede that there are Law-observing Christians of Jewish (and even Gentile) descent and that they may still be saved (*Dial.* 48). Ignatius, the chronological mid-point between Paul and Justin, enunciates no clear idea justifying his position that Gentile Christians are not to do what Scripture commands. (Again, at this point in time, the only collection of texts regarded as holy and authoritative by Greek-speaking Gentile Christians was the same as that used by the Hellenistic synagogue, that is, the LXX.) Yet his encounters with those Gentiles in the churches that he visited who were, in his terms, "Judaizing," angered him greatly.

This interwoven, indeed simultaneous, pattern of theological condemnation and ecumenical behavior continued long after Ignatius' period. Both Origen in the third century and John Chrysostom in the fourth denounced those in their congregations who attended synagogue on the Sabbath and celebrated various other observances with their Jewish neighbors, while Commodian scolded Jews for allowing pagans to co-celebrate with them.[27] This easy mixing of Gentiles (whether pagan or Christian) and Jews in the cities of the Empire seems not to have been an unusual phenomenon. And while ideologically articulate churchmen and much later modern historians might identify such patterns of behavior as "Judaizing," to these ancient people, such socializing may well have been simply what it meant to live in a Mediterranean city.

"Judaizing" itself as a set of behaviors was unitary neither in practice nor, probably, in motivation. Visiting the synagogue; observing some of the practices laid down in Torah; expecting other Gentile Christians to do likewise; adopting Jewish traditions of exegesis; seeking to locate Jesus in relation to an understanding of the God of the Jewish Scriptures: all of these behaviors, individually or in combination, might be followed by persons or by groups and might be inspired by an equal variety of reasons, not all theological. Sometimes a Jewish community need not have been involved at all. A fifth-century North African Christian community against whom Augustine wrote, for example, seems to have been inspired to act "Jewishly" on the basis of its own understanding of the Bible.[28]

Where such an ethos is theologically articulated and survives in literary sources (such as in the *Pseudo-Clementine* literature), scholars sometimes speak of "Jewish Christianity." Irenaeus, Hippolytus, and later writers like Epiphanius who speak of groups such as the Ebionites or Nazoreans, consider such Christians to be heretics. Some of these communities (such as ones that Epiphanius names) might themselves have been ethnically Jewish, others not. We have no clear view of how these groups would have constructed their relationship with non-Christian Jews. Nonetheless, they clearly belong to an account of the history of Christian theology, even if they represent positions that would be marginalized, at least in the West.

Yet the label "Jewish Christianity" is itself misleading if it is taken to suggest that its implied antithesis, "Gentile Christianity," is untouched by any "Jewishness." The problem with our scholarly language is that it obscures, through an excess of clarity, the social and intellectual past it seeks to describe. *All* ancient Christian writers were enmeshed in webs of continuity and discontinuity with their scriptural heritage and its subsequent interpretation. They had to account both for continuities and for discontinuities. They had to explain how they could lay claim to Jewish scriptures while eschewing, even condemning, the Jewish practices mandated therein. They sought to position themselves vis-à-vis both those who sought much more continuity (the "Jewish–Christian" response) and much greater discontinuity (the "Marcionite" response, which will be discussed below). And at the same time, they also had to give an account of themselves to those watching outsiders like the pagan polemicist Celsus, for whom the Jewish claim to being the true heirs of Jewish scriptural traditions seemed more convincing than these competing, Gentile claims.

Rivalry and Readings of the Scriptures

This tension between continuity and discontinuity marks much of the writing of Justin Martyr (d. c.167 CE). In his *Dialogue with Trypho*, Justin explains at great length why (Gentile) Christians do not observe the Law of Moses or practice male circumcision. He also demonstrates the multiple ways in which the LXX foretells both Jesus' first and second comings, his death and resurrection, and God's rejection of the Jews in favor of the Gentiles. It is the Gentiles, argues Justin, who are the "true" Israel and, thus, the always-intended recipient of God's promises of redemption.

Throughout his *Dialogue*, Justin sharply dismisses alternative, Jewish understandings of Scripture. Yet he also seems indebted to Jewish interpretive traditions. For example, when he argues that it was not the High God, but rather Jesus as the pre-Incarnate Son, who appeared in the theophanies of Genesis 18–19 and who is to be identified as "Lord", he may be drawing on Jewish angelic exegesis (*Dialogue* 56–8).[29] Jews, too, substituted angels and other intermediaries when they read narratives about appearances of the biblical God, and Justin, too, sees Christ as (among other things) a chief angel (61). Justin further presents Trypho, rather implausibly, as persuaded by all this (63). His presentation may be motivated by his desire to refute those other Christians who, as we shall see, distinguished between the God of Israel and the Father of Jesus, and so who disputed as Christians the religious value of what other Christians would eventually call the "Old Testament."[30]

Justin goes on to argue that Psalm 45:7–13 establishes that Christ is to be worshipped and that the Gentiles are summoned to leave their ancestral way of life, which is idolatrous. When Trypho suggests, in light of this interpretation, that Jews who "already worship God as Creator" and not idols need not worship Christ, so that only Gentiles need recognize Christ as Lord, Justin reacts strenuously. Indeed, he responds, Trypho's suggestion only reinforces Justin's deepest doubts about the likelihood of salvation for "any of [their] race" (63–4). For Justin, as for most subsequent writers in his stream of Christian thought, there is no room for Jews who do not believe in Jesus, or for Jewish interpretations of the Scriptures, in the Christian understanding of God, Christ, and biblical revelation.

Justin represents a pattern followed by nearly all ancient Christian writers. He both relied on the LXX and used existing traditions of biblical "proof texts" to establish that Christ and the Church were the true subject of Jewish Scriptures. In debate, he had to acknowledge that Jews possessed the Scriptures – indeed, he may have had to consult their copies. Yet, faced not only with their alternative interpretations but even with their different, and probably more stable, versions of the Greek text, he reacted by insisting that they misunderstood their own Scriptures and indeed, to spite Christians, had probably mutilated them.[31] To establish his Christological reading of the LXX against Jewish understandings, he relentlessly applied prophetic critiques of Israel's hard-heartedness and unfaithfulness to contemporary synagogue communities, while directing exclusively to his own church the prophetic promises of eschatological redemption.[32]

Yet in his *Apology*, where he pleads his case before pagan outsiders, Justin takes a different path. There, the Jewish ownership of the Scriptures becomes an independent witness to Christian claims, legitimating the Christian appeal to antiquity and philosophical priority based on that of Moses (*Apology* 31.1–5; 59.1–60.11). A generation later, the pagan anti-Christian writer Celsus used this same argument in reverse: Christians, he claimed, were apostates from Judaism, forsaking the ancient Jewish heritage while retaining all the ancient Jewish vices.[33] In brief, for Justin as for the Christian tradition he represents and helps to establish, the presence of the Jews both challenged and legitimated Christian self-understanding, while the existence of Judaism both occasioned and focused crucial issues in Christian theology.

Both Valentinus (fl. 130) and Marcion (fl. 140), Gentile Christians in the generation before Justin, had responded to the theological challenge of Judaism in ways that differed from Justin's and that would contour his own response. All three men, well-educated in paideia, made the same assumption once they turned, as Christians, to Jewish Scriptures: the busy, active deity of the LXX could not, they knew, be the High God. However, while Justin, as we have seen, saw a unity of intent between the Maker of all things and that other God or Lord, the other two concluded that the Creator God of the LXX must, by definition, be a lower god. And unarguably, given the social location of this text in the synagogues of the Diaspora, that lower god presented in Genesis was the God of the Jews. What, then, was the relation of this lower god of the Bible to the High God, the Father of Christ their Redeemer?

What did this Jewish text have to do with Christian revelation? What, indeed, did Judaism have to do with Christianity?

For Valentinus and for Marcion, this lower god was in some sense the Father's opponent, and thus also the opponent of his Son. Reading Genesis with this conviction, and enlightened by Christian revelation, Valentinus understood that the angry, intemperate deity in the Garden, the god of the Jews, represented the forces of darkness, matter, ignorance, fear – all that from which Christ had come to save his chosen. Valentinian Christians, and others of similar mind, whom scholars designate "Gnostics" (from the Greek word *gnosis*, "knowledge"), canvassed the Jewish Scriptures and the burgeoning body of Christian writings to work out their theology based on this insight: namely, that the god of the Bible was actually the villain of the piece. Their theologians produced the first Christian commentaries on parts of the Jewish Bible, and on the Gospel of John. Just as their God and his Son had little to do with the material cosmos, and nothing to do with the Jews, so too these "knowing" Christians. They knew that their redemption was spiritual, not carnal; that their true "root" lay in the upper heavens apart from the Creator God's cosmos; that, through Christ, they had the knowledge of salvation, the revelation of the God above God. This was the message of Christian redemption encoded, even disguised, they maintained, in Jewish writings. To find it there one had to read them very carefully, very cannily, always guided by the Spirit.[34]

Marcion, too, held that the lower deity of Genesis was the god of the Jews; that the High God was the Father of Christ; and that through Christ, the Christian believer had been redeemed from sin, flesh, death. But he took his cue most specifically from the rhetoric of Paul's letters. Accordingly, to the standard contrasting pairs of light/darkness, upper world/lower world, knowledge/ignorance, spirit/flesh, Marcion added what he took to be corresponding Pauline tropes, consigning to the negative pole both Law and the Jews. For Marcion, the God of the Jews proclaimed in their Scriptures was a harsh deity: dedicated unyieldingly to justice, even vengeance, and yet often inconsistent; demanding obedience through fear; threatening punishment for sin. But Christ, the Son, revealed the face of a different ("Stranger") deity, that of his father the High God. This God, through Christ, brought a message of love, not fear; forgiveness, not punishment; forbearance, not wrath; peace, not strife.

What did such a message have to do with Judaism? What indeed, asked Marcion, did or could such a message even have to do with Jewish books? In a demonstration of supreme confidence, Marcion argued for a new textual medium of Christian revelation. If Christ, as Paul taught, had freed the Christian from the Law, then the text of the Law, the LXX, had no standing as Christian Scripture. Marcion proposed a radical alternative: a collection of new, specifically Christian writings, namely the letters of Paul and one of the Gospels.[35] Let the Jews worry endlessly over food and circumcision and holy days and carnal things; let them pore over their Law and worship their lower god and await their messiah – who indeed, as they rightly maintained, had still not come. The Christian, in Christ, was free of all that.

It was these constructions of Gentile Christianity that Justin and others like him repudiated. Instead, they discovered within Genesis the pre-incarnate Christ, the Father's Son. Consequently they wrought a division deep throughout the scriptural record: the heroes of Jewish Scripture, like Abraham, Moses, David, and the prophets, they maintained, had known and acknowledged Christ as God. On the other side was a history of disobedience and rejection: the idolatrous sinners whom Moses and the prophets opposed; Jesus' contemporaries, who murdered him; later Jews up to and including these theologians' contemporaries, who repudiated Jesus' teachings as preserved in the preaching of this Gentile church – these did not and do not acknowledge Jesus as god. Instead, they remain mired in their carnal practices, enslaved to the Law. Accordingly, these theologians urged, the Jews, in some profound sense, had lost title to what had once been their own Scriptures. They did not and could not understand them *kata pneuma*, "spiritually," that is, in this particular Gentile Christian way. Unlike Valentinian Christians, this group could see a positive message in Jewish Scripture. Unlike Marcionite Christians, they did not need to repudiate Jewish Scripture. This group kept the Scriptures; they repudiated, instead, the Jews.[36]

We have seen Justin's response to these alternative Christianities when tracing his complex relation to Jews and to Judaism. A similar complexity marks many other early Christian writers, who use "Jew" as the ultimate term of opprobrium while insisting that they, and they alone, have the true understanding of Jewish tradition. Thus, since Marcion apparently supported a non-Christological reading of Jewish Scriptures – the LXX, he had insisted, had nothing to say about Christ – Tertullian labeled him an ally of the Jews, something that was clearly not the case (*Marc.* 3.6.2). Rejecting Marcion's "solution" to the problem of the relation of Gentile Christianity to Judaism and thus to Jewish scriptures, other Christian writers, from Tertullian on, justified their retaining a text whose precepts they declined in principle to practice (Sabbath, circumcision, food laws) by increasingly lambasting the Jews. In short, they held, there was nothing wrong with Jewish Scripture; the problem was, rather, the Jews themselves.

These theologians strove to prove from Scripture itself the antiquity of the Jews' failure to understand their own text or to respond to God's call. Some writers even dated this failure not just to the advent of Jesus but to the very beginning of the nation. The *Epistle of Barnabas* argued that the Jews, because of their sin with the Golden Calf, had lost the covenant at the very moment when Moses was receiving it. The covenant did, and always had, belonged only to "us" (*Barnabas* 4.7). This mode of exegesis, prying the text loose from the synagogue while preserving its spiritual value for the Church, became enshrined not only in commentary but also in other Christian literary genres: sermons, parenesis, testimonies, martyr acts, hymns. This extreme devaluation of Jews and Judaism measured the younger community's positive valuation of Jewish scripture, and the importance of protecting a claim to the continuity of the new revelation with biblical tradition.

The "Jew" as the Christian "Other"?

The view presented thus far presupposes that Judaism presented an ideological challenge to the making of Christian theology. This challenge was inherent in the ambiguities of Gentile Christian attitudes toward the Jewish Scriptures, and was made all the more unavoidable because it was embodied in the continuing encounter with the flourishing Jewish communities of the Greco-Roman Diaspora. This reconstruction is not uncontested. Other scholars have argued that, beginning from the second century, Gentile Christians had few contacts with – and thus little chance to learn from – contemporary, "real" Jews. For these scholars the "Jews" of Christian polemic, even Justin's Trypho, are a construct, a theological abstraction, a way of dealing with the ideological problem of relation of Gentile Christianity to its Jewish past, a past frozen in the biblical text.

In support of this view, these scholars can point to the artificiality of the theological "Jew"; the thinness in descriptions of, or debate about, contemporary Jewish practices; and the overwhelmingly literary quality of Christian polemical portraiture, so dependent on images and language taken directly from Scripture.[37] Finally, two documentary voids both permit and encourage this scholarly opinion: the near-total absence of Jewish writings from the Greco-Roman Diaspora after the first or second century CE with which to compare Christian writings; and the absence of rabbinic interest in engaging in debate with Gentile Christians. These data conspire in presenting a picture of little or no real contact between these communities.

The making of Christian theology, like so much identity-construction, indeed seems to have demanded an "Other" against which to shape the self. And it was the "Jews" who repeatedly provided theologians with this "Other." In this sense – the hermeneutical or ideological or theological sense – the "Jewish Other" is indeed a construct. This image was shaped by the dilemmas of Christian self-understanding, and these dilemmas included questions about the significance and meaning of Jewish Scriptures for Christian revelation. The "Jew," in this discourse, was in many ways a theological abstraction, a construct made to served as the ultimate anti-type of the Christian. Fleshly, faithless, hard-hearted, obdurate, spiritually dull: the "Jew" of patristic polemic provided a reversed image of all that was desirable and laudable in the Christian. The hermeneutical Jew confirmed by contrast the desiderata of Christian identity.

Yet there is plentiful, even if often circumstantial, evidence that this "Other" was also constructed in the face of the fact of actual Jewish communities who were not only socially well-established but who also successfully maintained their own distinctive lives of communal and religious activity, including the creative interpretation of the Scriptures. Moreover, these Jewish communities attracted outsiders, both Christian and non-Christian. Donor inscriptions, other epigraphy, legal corpora both ecclesiastical and imperial, patristic writings such as we have already referred to – Ignatius, Origen, and John Chrysostom – all evince this contact. When these authors thunder that there *can* be no commonality between Judaism and Christianity, synagogue and church, they give us the measure of the power of an alternative social reality wherein some Christians and some Jews evidently *did* experience a great deal in common.

Yet we should not simply contrast social reality ("contact") with theology ("separation"). Nor should we see theology as being only negatively shaped by the distancing from "Judaism." Judaism also contributed positively to Christian formulations. It is self-evident that Christian theology has its roots in Jewish reflection on the Scriptures and on the nature of God as revealed there. Increasingly, scholars have recognized that even aspects of Christian thought once attributed to "Greek" or "Hellenistic" influence are not, in that measure, any less "Jewish." Hellenistic Jews, as Hellenistic pagans, thought in terms of a divine *logos*, and both pagan and Jewish concepts of divine unity, as later Christian ones, encompassed ideas of mediation and multiplicity.

Jews and Christians lived among each other in the cities of the Roman Mediterranean. Christian thought (in all its varieties) developed alongside of and in interaction with Jewish thought, this development involving both dialogue and argument. Early proto-orthodox accounts of martyrs, which did so much to shape Christian sensibility, betray this much more complicated picture. Only rarely in these stories do Jews feature as aggressors alongside hostile pagans (a role that some modern writers have also cast them in).[38] Yet, in other accounts, Jews feature as sympathetic witnesses to Christian suffering.[39] And the image of the Christian martyr – the glorious athlete winning the crown of and for Christ – appears, transposed into a Jewish key, in contemporary renderings of martyr stories in *4 Maccabees*.[40] The image of Isaac and the *akedah* ("binding," in Genesis 22) provided both rabbis and Christian theologians with a biblical trope and type of atoning sacrifice. The rabbis even spoke of Isaac toiling beneath the wood of the offering "as one who carries his own cross"; Christians, of Isaac as the prefiguration of the sacrifice of Christ.[41] Tertullian's warnings about the dangers and difficulties of living among the idols in pagan cities (*Concerning Idolatry*) is framed in terms similar to those rabbinic warnings in the Mishnah's *Avodah Zarah*.[42] Indeed, the Hebrew title of the rabbinic tractate precisely corresponds to the Latin of Tertullian's.

Conclusions: Are Siblings Always "Rivals"?

What then, finally, can we say about the relationship between Christian theology and Judaism in the first through fourth centuries? As we have seen, that relationship was complex, for many reasons. No single generalization – "hostile," "dependent," "sympathetic" – adequately encompasses the range of evidence.

We may, however, question the term "rival." Rivalry implies competition. For what, then, did Jews and Christians "compete"? Modern scholarship has responded to this question variously over the course of the past century. At the turn of the last century, Christian scholars held that Second Temple Judaism (or "late Judaism", as it was then called) had become a spiritually arid and inward-looking religion, separate and separatist, to which the Temple's destruction in 70 CE had simply delivered the *coup de grâce*.[43] The force and ubiquity of antique Christianity's *contra Iudaeos* tradition, in this view, arose from images of Jews and Judaism available in the Scriptures appropriated by the Church. In reality – so went this argument – the two religions scarcely even made contact, much less competed.

Especially in the wake of World War II, scholars challenged and revised this image. They interpreted the heat of Christian anti-Jewish polemic as an index of active and energetic competitive contact. In consequence, they reimagined Judaism, recasting it in the image of the Gentile Church. In this newer construct, Roman-era Judaism became a vigorous missionary religion, thus a genuine threat to the Church's missionary efforts. Indeed, in this later view, Christianity and Judaism *were* rivals, competing for the allegiance of Gentile converts.[44]

In the fifty-odd years since, the study of ancient Christianity and of ancient Judaism has been revolutionized by the development of the study of religion within the liberal arts or humanities. Anthropology, sociology, archaeology, theories of literary criticism, the methods and interpretative strategies from many other disciplines – all these fields and schools of thought have an impact on the study of ancient religion. The discovery of buried libraries – Qumran, Nag Hammadi – has enriched our understanding of intra-religious diversity. Progress in retrieving and amassing non-literary evidence – archeological artifacts, inscriptions – means that we now have more evidence, of different sorts, than at any point in the past. The study of ancient Mediterranean religions of all kinds is an interdisciplinary, non-denominational effort. No orthodoxy, whether ecclesiastical or academic, has been untouched by these changes.

For the issue at hand, the relationship between ancient Christians and Jews, as between ancient Christianities and Judaisms, is once again being reimagined. This chapter is a contribution to that effort. Historians of each tradition (neither of which is univocal) have had to learn to think about and with the other tradition in order to grasp the social reality of either tradition. And the specific concept of Jewish missions to Gentiles – whether in a purely pagan "market" or in a pagan/Christian one – has itself been decisively challenged.[45] Absent a competition for converts, then, in what way can ancient Jews and Christians be said to "compete"? And, absent this competitive market model, how do we usefully imagine them as representing "rival traditions"?

The external contest between traditions echoes, in a different key, the internal contest within traditions over the interpretation of the Bible. Which books were to be regarded as authoritative? In which languages? According to whose transmission? What were the criteria of authority? What were the social consequences of consensus or conflict on these issues? What were the limits of acceptable diversity, and who set them, who enforced them, who cared?

As James Parkes noted long ago, both Christianity and Judaism, as we imagine them, are fundamentally products of the fourth century.[46] It was the fourth century that saw the imperially-sponsored hegemony of one particular form of Christianity and the suppression of all others; and it was the fourth century that saw the beginnings of the rabbinic consolidation that would eventually have such a profound effect on post-Roman Jewish culture. The most intact textual records that we still have – the patristic canon; the rabbinic corpora – are the survivors of this historical moment, through which history's winners both controlled their own futures (by suppressing diversity within their own communities) and determined our view of their past (by eradicating the textual evidence that may have provided us with the fuller picture).

Orthodoxies draw sharp boundaries, make clear distinctions, and assert the timeless integrity of the community's own identity. Historical reality, unsurprisingly, is much more complex. If this chapter has undermined the seeming clarity of its own title, it will have moved the student to a more adequate appreciation of the rich diversity that characterized the very various relations between Jews and Christians – as indeed between Jews, Christians, and pagans – in the cities of Mediterranean antiquity.

Notes

1 On the High God of paideia in antiquity, see most recently the essays collected in Athanassiadi and Frede, 1999. On the ways that Hellenistic astronomy and the imagined architecture of the (geocentric) universe coordinated this theology with science, and reinforced the idea of necessary intermediation, see Dodds, 1970, ch. 1.

2 Whitman, 2000: esp. Whitman's introductory essay, pp. 3–44; also R. Lamberton, "Language, Text, and Truth in Ancient Polytheist Exegesis," pp. 73–88.

3 Jones, 1940, chs. XIV ("Education") and XV ("Religion and Games").

4 See esp. Barclay, 1996; Gruen, 1998, 2002. The following paragraph is much indebted to their discussions. See also the review of Hellenistic Jewish literature in Schürer, vol. III, pt. 1 (1986).

5 Aristobulus *apud* Eusebius, *Praeparatio evangelica* 13.12.1–2 (E. des Place et al., *Sources chrétiennes* (Paris, 1974–91), on Plato's dependence on Moses and the existence of a Greek version of the Bible predating the Persian conquest (i.e., before 525 BCE!). As Barclay notes, Aristobulus intends by this claim not only to assert the priority of Jewish tradition, but also "to praise Plato for his assiduous attention to Moses" (1996, p. 151).

6 Artapanus *apud* Eusebius, *Praeparatio evangelica* 9.23.4, 27.4, 9, 12.

7 On the Jewish sibyllines, M. Goodman's discussion in Schürer, Vol. III, pt.1, pp. 618–54. For an appreciation of such "brazen inventiveness," Gruen, 2002, pp. 213–31.

8 The *Letter of Aristeas*, discussion in Schürer, Vol. III, pt.1, pp. 685–7.

9 See Schürer, Vol. III, pt.1, pp. 667–71; Droge, 1989.

10 On Philo's contribution to biblical exegesis generally, and to later Gentile Christian biblical exegesis in particular, see the relevant essays in Armstrong, 1970; Chadwick, 1966, which discuss Justin, Clement, and Origen in this connection; also Dawson, 1976, pp. 89–107.

11 See above, nn. 4–10; cf. too Origen's refutation of the pagan Celsus' critique, which drew on arguments originally generated in Hellenistic Jewish milieux, E. T. H. Chadwick, *Contra Celsum* (Cambridge, 1953).

12 On the Greek apologists see Young, 1999, pp. 81–104.

13 Thus a key theme in Justin's *Apology* (26; 56–8) is that so-called "Christians" (in particular Marcion) who deny that God the Father is also the Creator, and that Jesus Christ his Son is the Messiah spoken of by the prophets, are inspired by demons.

14 On these arguments and texts in which they appear, see Krauss, 1995; also Lieu, 1996. A patristic *locus classicus* for many of these arguments – Jewish excisions of Christological referents in the LXX, intrinsic Jewish philosophical muddle-headedness, the theological import of the revolts in Judea – is Justin Martyr's *Dialogue with Trypho*.

15 The classic work of scholarship on this issue is Marcel Simon's great *Verus Israel* (1948).

16 Fredriksen, 2003, pp. 35–63.

17 Origen claims to have consulted with Jewish scholars, *Contra Celsum* II.31; *ep. ad Africanum* 6 for discussion with full references, de Lange, 1976. Similarly, Jerome – himself no enthusiast for Jewish practice – nonetheless was prepared to consult with and defer to Jewish scholars on textual issues; Kelly, 1975, pp. 159–60. See further Jacobs, 2003.

18 On the intimacy of Jewish–Christian social interaction, see Wilken, 1983, pp. 68–94.

19 This material is collected, annotated, analyzed, and translated in Linder, 1997.

20 *Confessions* I.xiii.20–1 refers specifically to Greek literature and to Virgil; I.xiv.23 to Homer. Much later in life, Augustine, though a Christian (that is, a Manichee), won a prestigious chair of rhetoric in Milan through the good offices of Symmachus, a Roman pagan.

21 The patriarch, as *vir clarissimus*, had highest senatorial rank. Libanius' correspondence with the patriarch regarding the Greek rhetorical education of the latter's son, *ep.* 1098, LCL.

22 Paul presumes that his Gentile audience, mid-first century, will understand the terms and arguments that he draws from Scripture: if he was right to do so, some assume that such biblically literate Gentiles would only be found in the penumbra of the Diaspora synagogue. Similarly, the Evangelists, to differing degrees, evince familiarity with the LXX (see above), a collection of texts available in the first century

primarily within a synagogue ambit. See further Fredriksen, 2000, pp. 74–154.

23 Distinguishing these Jewish texts from their later, specifically anti-Jewish traditions of interpretation, e.g., for Paul: Stendahl, 1976, Stowers, 1994; for the Gospel of John, Bieringer et al., 2001; for Hebrews, Dunn, 1991, pp. 86–91, 208–11.

24 2 Maccabees 2:21; 8:1; 14:38; 4 Maccabees 4:26. See further on the difficulties of construing this term in Cohen, 1999, pp. 105–6. The date of composition of 4 Maccabees may be well into the Christian period: thus, its use of "Judaism" may reflect the influence of the term "Christianity," Bowersock, 1995, pp. 77–81.

25 *Mag.* 9.1; *Philad* 6.1.

26 Paul's own practice and what he would have preferred Christians of Jewish background to observe are matters of dispute: 1 Cor. 9:19–21.

27 Origen, e.g., *Homilies in Leviticus* V.8; *On Exodus* 12.46, Fathers of the Church 71 (Washington, DC, 1982). Chrysostom's eight sermons against the Judaizers are analyzed and set into context by Wilken, 1983; an English translation of the sermons is available in the series Fathers of the Church, vol. 68 (Washington, DC, 1979). Commodian on the pagan *medius Iudaeus* who scurries between synagogue and traditional altar, *Instructiones* 1.24 (M. Stern, *Greek and Latin Writers on Jews and Judaism*, Jerusalem, 1974).

28 *Ep.* 196.

29 It should be noted that Justin begins his *Dialogue* by establishing, with Trypho's agreement, the definition of the High God: "That which always maintains the same nature, and in the same manner, and is the cause of all other things: that, indeed, is god" (3). From this follows his overall exegetical point that the busy deity constantly showing up in biblical narrative and encountered by human characters there cannot, then, be the High God (whom he does, however, recognize as "Maker of all things"), but must be a *heteros theos*, "another god," whom he will identify as the pre-incarnate Son (56).

30 For the ways that anti-Jewish and Gentile intra-Christian debate affected each other and subsequent Christian theology, see Fredriksen, 2002, pp. 1–30.

31 Justin, *Dial.* 68; 71.1–73.4; 83–4; 120; and Lieu, 1996, pp. 124–9.

32 The classic study of this technique of Christian biblical interpretation is Ruether, 1974, with important historical corrections in Davies, 1979.

33 See *Contra Celsum* II.1–4 for the Christians as having "left the law of their fathers," and IV.23 for Celsus' mockery of "the race of Jews and Christians" which leads into his denigration of the Jews (e.g. IV.31–5; V.41–53).

34 For an excellent introduction to this sort of biblical exegesis, see the catechetical letter of Ptolemy to Flora, excerpted by the fifth-century heresiologist Epiphanius, *Panarion* 33.3–7; English excerpt in Stevenson, 1987, pp. 85–91. On the hermeneutical processes involved, see Williams, 1996, pp. 54–79. Williams emphasizes that there was no single "gnostic exegesis."

35 Where Paul seemed to speak positively of the Law ("What is the value of circumcision? Much in every way," Rom. 3:2; "Do we overthrow the Law by this faith? On the contrary, we uphold the Law," Rom. 3:31; "Do I say this on human authority? Does not the Law say the same?" 1 Cor. 9:8, and similarly elsewhere), Marcion divined the hand of later Judaizers, and so expurgated what he held to be Judaizing interpolations. The credibility for contemporaries of Marcion's views about the transmission of Paul's letters on this issue, and of Justin's, similarly, about the transmission of the LXX, reminds us of the known instability of texts in a manuscript culture.

36 The proto-orthodox repudiated Marcion's textual novum, a new canon of specifically Christian writings consisting of a gospel and the letters of Paul. Justin referred to such writings as the apostles' "memoires" (*Dial.* 105); "Scripture" for him was the LXX, and especially Isaiah. Marcion's idea eventually took hold among his opponents, however, and a larger "new" testament – Pauline and deutero-Pauline letters, four Gospels, a book of acts, various sermons presented as (pseudepigraphic) epistles, an apocalypse – took its place conjoined with the Jewish, "old" testament.

37 Long after the destruction of the Temple in 70CE, for example, the *Letter to Diognetus* mocks Jews for offering blood sacrifices to God as if such offerings could honor him (*To Diognetus* 3.4). With the demise of the Temple, the cult in reality had long ceased.

38 The accounts of the two martyrs in Smyrna, Polycarp and, a century later, Pionius, feature

Jewish persecutors. Frend, 1965 and, more recently, Robert, 1994, take such accounts as historically descriptive; Parkes, 1934, pp. 121–50, and, more recently, Lieu, 1996, see them as narrative representations of the theological "Jew," thus rhetorical rather than historical in orientation. Against the social plausibility of Jews joining with pagans against Christians in light of the Jews' vulnerability to the same charge of "atheism" (since Jews, too, did not worship the emperor's image), see Fredriksen, 2003, pp. 56–63.

39 E.g., Eusebius, *Martyrs of Palestine* 8.1; cf. *Pionios* 13.1 (*Acts of the Christian Martyrs*, ed. H. Musurillo, Oxford, 1972), where Jews during a persecution invite Christians into their synagogues.

40 Bowersock, 1995, pp. 77–81; van Henten, 1997.

41 *Genesis Rabbah* 56.3. On the Christological and rabbinic usages of the Akedah, esp. Levenson, 1993.

42 *The Mishnah*, vol. 4, pp. 1–99, trans. P. Kehati (Jerusalem, 1987).

43 A classic account of this kind is offered by von Harnack, 1904, I, pp. 1–18, 81–3.

44 A classic statement of this position may be found in Simon, 1948. For an assessment of the motivations and implications of such views, see Taylor, 1995.

45 For example, McKnight, 1991 frames the question in the context of the first Christian generation; Goodman, 1994 prescinds from generalizing about the later rabbinic period, but challenges the idea for the first several Christian centuries; Cohen, 1999 dissolves the idea for the Hellenistic and Roman periods; Fredriksen, 2003 questions the entire formulation.

46 "[T]hough neither [Judaism nor Christianity] were born in this century, . . . both are to this day, in many ways, fourth century religions," Parkes, 1934, p. 153.

Bibliography

A. H. Armstrong, ed., *The Cambridge History of Later Greek and Early Medieval Philosophy* (Cambridge, 1970).

P. Athanassiadi and M. Frede, eds., *Pagan Monotheism* (Oxford, 1999).

J. Barclay, *Jews in the Mediterranean Diaspora* (Berkeley, CA, 1996).

R. Bieringer et al., eds., *Anti-Judaism in the Fourth Gospel* (Louisville, KY, 2001).

G. Bowersock, *Martyrdom and Rome* (Cambridge, 1995).

H. Chadwick, *Early Christian Thought and the Classical Tradition* (Oxford, 1966).

S. J. D. Cohen, *The Beginnings of Jewishness: Boundaries, Varieties, Uncertainties* (Berkeley, CA, 1999).

A. T. Davies, ed., *Antisemitism and the Foundations of Christianity* (New York, 1979).

D. Dawson, "Plato's Soul and the Body of the Text in Philo and Origen," in J. Whitman, ed., *Interpretation and Allegory* (Leiden, 2000), pp. 89–107.

N. de Lange, *Origen and the Jews* (Cambridge, 1976).

E. R. Dodds, *Pagan and Christian in an Age of Anxiety* (London, 1970).

A. Droge, *Homer or Moses? Early Christian Interpretations of the History of Culture* (Tübingen, 1989).

J. Dunn, *The Partings of the Ways between Christianity and Judaism and their Significance for the Character of Christianity* (London, 1991).

P. Fredriksen, "The Birth of Christianity and the Origins of Christian Anti-Judaism," in P. Fredriksen and A. Reinhartz (eds.), *Jesus, Judaism, and Christian Anti-Judaism* (London, 2002), pp. 1–30.

—— "What 'Parting of the Ways?' Jews, Gentiles, and the Ancient Mediterranean City," in A. H. Becker and A. Yoshiko Reed (eds.), *The Ways that Never Parted. Jews and Christians in Late Antiquity and the Early Middle Ages* (Tübingen, 2003), pp. 35–63.

—— *Jesus of Nazareth, King of the Jews* (New York, 2000).

W. H. C. Frend, *Martyrdom and Persecution in the Early Church* (Oxford, 1965).

M. Goodman, *Mission and Conversion* (Oxford, 1994).

E. Gruen, *Diaspora: Jews amidst Greeks and Romans* (Cambridge, MA, 2002).

—— *Heritage and Hellenism* (Berkeley, CA, 1998).

J. van Henten, *The Maccabean Martyrs as Saviours of the Jewish People: A Study of 2 and 4 Maccabees* (Leiden, 1997).

A. von Harnack, *The Expansion of Christianity in the First Three Centuries* (London, 1904).

J. Jacobs, *Judea Sancta: Holy Land Jews and the Making of the Christian Empire* (Stanford, CA, 2003).

A. H. M. Jones, *The Ancient City* (Oxford, 1940).

J. N. D. Kelly, *Jerome: His Life, Writings, and Controversies* (London, 1975).

S. Krauss, *The Jewish/Christian Controversy from the Earliest Times to 1789*, ed. and rev. W. Horbury, vol. 1 (Tübingen, 1995).

J. Levenson, *The Death and Resurrection of the Beloved Son* (Cambridge, MA, 1993).

J. Lieu, *Image and Reality. Jews in the World of the Christians in the Second Century* (Edinburgh, 1996).

A. Linder, *The Jews in the Legal Sources of the Early Middle Ages* (Detroit, MI, 1997).

S. McKnight, *A Light Among the Nations* (Minneapolis, MN, 1991).

J. Parkes, *The Conflict of the Church and the Synagogue* (London, 1934).

L. Robert, *Le martyre de Pionios*, ed. G. W. Bowersock and C. P. Jones (Washington, DC, 1994).

R. Ruether, *Faith and Fratricide: The Theological Roots of Anti-Semitism* (New York, 1974).

E. Schürer, *The History of the Jewish People in the Age of Jesus Christ*, ed. and rev. G. Vermes, F. Millar et al., 3 vols. (Edinburgh, 1973–87).

M. Simon, *Verus Israel. A Study of the Relations between Christians and Jews in the Roman Empire,* AD 135–425 (London, 1985; French original, 1948).

K. Stendahl, *Paul Among the Jews and Gentiles* (Philadelphia, PA, 1976).

J. Stevenson, *A New Eusebius* (Cambridge, 1987).

S. Stowers, *A Rereading of Romans: Justice, Jews and Gentiles* (New Haven, CT, 1994).

M. Taylor, *Anti-Judaism and Early Christian Identity. A Critique of the Scholarly Consensus* (Leiden, 1995).

J. Whitman, ed., *Interpretation and Allegory* (Leiden, 2000).

R. Wilken, *John Chrysostom and the Jews. Rhetoric and Reality in the late Fourth Century* (Berkeley, CA, 1983).

M. A. Williams, *Rethinking "Gnosticism": An Argument for Dismantling a Dubious Category* (Princeton, NJ, 1996).

F. Young, "Greek Apologists of the Second Century," in M. Edwards, M. Goodman, and S. Price, in association with C. Rowland (eds.), *Apologetics in the Roman Empire: Pagans, Jews, and Christians* (Oxford, 1999), pp. 81–104.

Rival Traditions: Christian Theology and Secular Philosophy

Christian Theology and Secular Philosophy

John M. Rist

In the beginning Christians did not philosophize. Neither the Old Testament prophets nor Christ himself were philosophers, nor were the Apostles and Paul, the latter of whom, though debating with Stoics and Epicureans in Athens (Acts 17:18) and willing from time to time to use philosophical-sounding language, was more inclined to inveigh against "vain philosophy" (Col. 2:8; cf. 1 Tim. 6:20).[1] What exactly he meant by that is not certain; ideas which we would call theosophical may be part of the target, but he was probably also concerned with the widespread view in antiquity that all "genuine" traditions are equally to be respected as pointers to a once-common ancient wisdom.[2]

Nor at the beginnings of Christianity is there anything like what we would latterly identify as a distinction between philosophy and theology. So when we consider such beginnings we must think of the meeting of Christian *thought* with secular (Greco-Roman) philosophy. From such a meeting something like an intelligent (if only implicit) distinction between Christian theology and Christian philosophy began to take shape, though the distinction was hardly formalized before the twelfth century.[3] As individual Christians began to think about their religion, not least in order to answer the questions of both pagans and differently-minded persons who might also call themselves Christian, they began to discuss topics later styled specifically theological or philosophical or both. But in the ancient world to be a philosopher is to live and scrutinize what one believes to be the best lifestyle; to be a theologian might mean to study what we would call metaphysics (as with Justin, the first identifiable Christian philosopher [*Dial.* 2]), or more broadly to busy oneself with what is eternal and unchanging – or at worst to be a practitioner of the magic arts.[4]

Many Christians, both in antiquity and in more modern times, have been suspicious of philosophy, not least of the Greco-Roman philosophy with which Christianity early became acquainted. Those Christians in the ancient world who wanted to take the philosophers seriously and make use of their work in their own "philosophy" or "theology" had to defend themselves for so doing. For in antiquity too there were those who, more by instinct than erudition, would have agreed with Harnack and many others in a long tradition which derives, in its modern formulations at least, from Luther, that primitive and prophetic Christianity was at risk from Hellenizing dupes and quislings. Luther himself targeted Aristotle as "That fool who misled the Church," giving a latter-day legitimacy (despite the more Platonizing tones of some of his successors) to the fears of those ancient Christians who wished to be pure of worldly philosophical taint, as even of those bolder spirits who recognized that for better or worse it is necessary to talk to philosophers, that is to those who are concerned to offer *argument* in justification of their preferred beliefs and chosen ways of life.

Revelation, tradition, and authority could supply the early Christians with important facts about the world, its beginning and its end, thus providing a basis for faith; what they could less easily provide was a basis for understanding and rational apologetics, and hence for the conversion of more than the illiterate and half-educated. And it is hard to deny that the meeting of Greek thought with Christian belief could only have become significant when Christianity had largely moved out of a Jewish and into a Gentile orbit.[5]

It seems reasonable to assume that the original Christian leaders hoped that in the few remaining years before the end of the world and the Second Coming of Christ Judaism would simply turn into Christianity. That hope soon faded; the world failed to end, and as time passed Jews in the Christian fold became a small minority in a largely Gentile Church. Had Christianity continued largely Jewish, the main concern of Christian apologetic would have remained to show that Christ had fulfilled the Old Testament prophecies: a concern still of importance but not of primary importance when the number of Jewish "converts" had all but dried up. In the mid-second century Justin is still concerned to make the case against Judaism, and particularly to present the vision of the Hebrew Prophets as metaphysical truth, but also to offer a defense of Christianity addressed not to Jews but to pagans, and to propose that defense as a Christian philosopher, that is, as a searcher who has studied in various philosophical schools and still wears the philosopher's cloak after his conversion to Christianity (*Dial.* 2).[6]

For Justin, as for his Christian successors, Christianity is the true philosophy (*1 Apol.* 3; cf. *Dial.* 8.1); but to re-assure his less confident coreligionists (and to beat the pagans at their own game) he insisted that it is also the original philosophy; in the wake of a Jewish tradition which acquired a certain currency, even among the pagans,[7] about the comparative modernity of Greek thought, he maintains that Plato, while in Egypt, learned his account of matter (and much else) from Moses (*1 Apol.* 59.1–5; cf. *1 Apol.* 10; *1 Apol.* 1.60.1).[8] And he has a further argument for Christian priority: Christ is the Logos and those who at any time live in accordance with the Logos, to whatever degree, are in effect desiderate Christians. Justin's list of such includes Heraclitus and Socrates (*1 Apol.* 46.1–3). Interestingly, Clement of Alexandria adds (or alludes to) a rather different possibility, not mentioned by Justin, to his versions of the origins of Greek philosophy: it was stolen from heaven and taught by fallen angels, though the theft itself was part of God's providential arrangements for the human race (*Strom.* 1.87.1–2).[9]

Justin's attitude towards the "Greeks" had the effect of softening up his fellow Christians: it became more acceptable to cite a pagan thinker, especially since his better insights must be Christian in origin; for while the full divine word is Christ, seeds of it have informed the limited wisdom of the pagans. In modern terminology Justin is certainly a theologian, and a theologian ready to cite pagan, especially Platonic, sources; but to cite a philosopher in support of unargued positions does not make anyone a philosopher, and if Justin is to be called a Christian philosopher, he must not merely cite Greek philosophers, but use them where necessary in developing his own arguments. Strictly philosophical activity involves the formation of logical structures, and is more readily seen in arguments *against* the positions of others than in the citing of authorities on one's own behalf. Thus we can recognize philosophical activity in Theophilus of Antioch when he claims that the Platonists are wrong to suppose that God and matter are both uncreated since, if that were the case, God would not enjoy absolute monarchy (*Ad Autol.* 2.4). In modern parlance this is an argument in the philosophy of religion: Theophilus' position (to be repeated by many others) is that the concept of a God who cannot create (rather than form) matter is incoherent.

Justin tells us that he visited various philosophical schools: Stoics, Aristotelians, Pythagoreans, Platonists. He evidently had no time for Sceptics or Epicureans, but whether, as is more likely, his search was historical, or whether merely symbolic, it brings home to us that philosophy-seeking Christians had a wide choice of possibilities to sort out; it was not as clear to them as it is to us that, with Aristotelianism in comparative eclipse, the real choices were Stoicism and some form of the ever more all-embracing Platonism, which Justin met in some of its "Middle Platonic" versions, though the fact that he and his successors were inclined to accept Middle Platonic interpretations of Plato should in no way diminish the likelihood that at least some of them, and not least Clement of Alexandria, were also concerned to check Plato's writings directly – especially the *Timaeus*, *Phaedrus*, and *Phaedo*, as well as texts like "his" influential *Second Letter* which Clement failed to recognize as spurious.[10]

In arguing with Jews, it was essential for Christians to establish not only that the coming of Christ was the fulfilment of Old Testament prophecy, but that their own religion was still a monotheism, though not a monotheism of the pagan type whereby all the subordinate gods are somehow dependent on a primary God.[11] In arguing with pagans, apart from repudiating free-floating charges of cannibalism and incest which even intellectuals were not disinclined to use if convenient, the Christians faced problems at the "metaphysical" as well as at the ethical level, and the attraction of rigorist versions of Stoicism could be tempting – especially if other ethical systems might seem tainted by any condoning of sexual (not to say homosexual) license.[12] A more fundamental strike against the dominant Platonism was the difficulty of explaining the relationship of the body to the soul; how much easier if, like Tertullian, we could agree that the soul is material, as the Stoics held! That might also help with an essential Christian thesis that not only is the soul immortal (though not by nature, as the "Greeks" might suppose[13]), but that the material body can also be transformed in resurrection. Might this not seem more intelligible if both soul and body were material? In the third century Plotinus himself was to recognize more clearly than his Platonist predecessors that the problematic relationship between an immaterial soul and a material body might prove the chink in the Platonist's armour.[14]

But Platonism has two basic principles which proved overwhelmingly attractive to early Christians and put other philosophical systems in the shade: its belief – in contrast to Stoicism – in a transcendent world peopled with immaterial beings (though in the second century, for fear of Gnosticism, Christians preferred initially not to speak of Forms); and its theory of *eros*, that power – its full capacity was debatable – by which man expresses his desire for the beauty of "divine things." And the growing success of (Middle) Platonism in assimilating much Aristotelianism, Stoicism, and even Scepticism made it possible to reposition the rigorist side of Cynic–Stoic ethics within a wider Platonizing metaphysic of morals. Admittedly "immaterialism" took a long time to penetrate to the Christian grass roots,[15] but after Tertullian no major Christian thinker was to prefer the attractions of an immanentist Stoic morality to an ethic, more or less rigorous as required, defended by a Platonizing metaphysics. And as the Christian asceticism of the ascent of the soul to God developed, especially in the third century, not least from the Platonizing Judaism of Philo, no philosophical thesis provided such a convenient psychology of desire as the Platonic theory of *eros*, though even the use of that term had to be defended against its more "carnal" associations in a long tradition beginning with Origen's prologue to his *Commentary on the Song of Songs.*

In pursuing the development of Christian indebtedness to Platonism which begins with Justin, we cannot forget that thoughtful Christians would always wish to test their Platonic borrowings – when they had become bold enough not merely to cite Platonic support for revealed truth but also to develop their "theology" through the application of Platonic theory and argumentation – by what in Irenaeus, Tertullian, and Clement of Alexandria is called the "rule of faith" (*regula fidei*) or "rule of truth."[16] As Christianity developed, Christian thinkers found themselves ever torn between the desire to exploit the riches of their pagan philosophical inheritance and a growing awareness of where the limits of assimilation must be set: Is there a difference between (Platonic) likeness to God and Christian imitation of Christ? Is Plato's immaterial world a creation of God or part of God's nature? Can Platonizing metaphysics be squared with the essential and specific historical claims of Christianity, as indeed with the particular status of Jewish history?

This is hardly the place to consider how the pagan Platonists (and others) responded to Christian claims that Platonism can be appropriated in the service of the new faith – let alone why they thought they even needed to reply. Suffice it to say that Celsus, the first known anti-Christian writer, wanted to emphasize not the similarities between Christianity and Platonism but the differences. These he identified in his *True Account* as broadly of three kinds:

1   The incarnation – and more broadly the particularism of Christianity (and Judaism) – is a frivolous intrusion of history into timeless metaphysics and a blasphemous worship of a man rather than a God (4.2). Even emperor-worship hardly claimed that the emperor is the creator of the universe, while the self-abnegating behavior of Jesus is merely pathetic – obviously inferior to that of a real divine-man (like Heracles);

2   The related doctrine of the Resurrection of the Body is an unworthy and repulsive glamorization of the transient and material part of man (5.14; 8.49);

3   In rejecting the "True Account" by which all genuine traditions partake in the "great mystery" (as Symmachus was later to put it), Christians undermine not only the authorized principles of Hellenic monotheism but the basic structures of civilized society, thus showing themselves indeed the enemies of the human race. At the political level Christianity and paganism could not coexist – which turned out to be the case when the "enemies of the good and the beautiful" prevailed with Constantine.[17]

To summarize thus far: as Christians began to develop their "theology" with the aid of the Greek philosophical tradition, we can identify the following features of the intellectual scene:

1   The dominant intellectual tradition, to which others were to a greater or less degree subsumed, was what is now called Middle Platonism;
2   The Middle Platonists assumed that their readings of Plato were a genuine representation of Plato's own views – though of course there were differences, some fairly significant, within the "school" itself, not least about how to interpret Plato's "cosmological" dialogue *Timaeus*[18] and whether to interpret the *Parmenides* as a metaphysical textbook – as the "Neopythagorean" wing of the school (Moderatus, Numenius, and others) preferred;
3   The existence in the schools of such differences invited differing Christians to take sides in the debate, thus further encouraging the use of philosophical texts as sources of argument and clarification as well as mere corroboration.

But there is a further complication: the early Christian suspicion of Greek thought did not disappear, and even among the less wary there remained a strong predilection for "our own" people. Hence a specifically Christian tradition of philosophy and theology began to develop, related in its broad outlines to the activities of the pagan Platonists who had assisted at its early stages, but gradually gaining in confidence to the point where we must recognize a Christian Platonism in *parallel* to continuing pagan development. By the middle of the third century this Christian Platonism is well established – generating problems for modern readers to which too little attention has been paid. For scholars have been tempted to argue ideologically: of each specific Christian figure some will insist that his thought is, though externally Christian, in fact heavily dependent on, or even subservient to, contemporary philosophical trends. Or, if not that, the other extreme: on the surface, we shall read, he may be Platonic but everything important in his thought is purely biblical. In this latter case we are supposed to recognize a "pure Christianity" wholly free from (corrupting) pagan influences, though such an interpretation is a distortion of the more complex situation to which we have alluded: that ancient Christians normally tested at least some of their philosophical experiments against the rule of faith.

Yet here too we must be precise; detailed examination of individual thinkers will show that they may be unevenly sensitized to those aspects of pagan thought genuinely antipathetic to the rule. Some sensitivity, however, is very early; we noticed it in the recognition that the soul is not by nature but by grace and creation immortal. And some Christians, as we should expect, were less inclined to be generous to pagan thought than others. Tertullian, let us say, is arguably less generous – rightly or wrongly – than Clement of Alexandria; while – to take a specific doctrinal instance – the Christian thesis of the equal value of all human beings as formed in the image of God retained its radical character unevenly even within the writings of individual Christian authors (liable as they were to the pressures of pagan thought and culture) let alone within the developing Christian society as a whole.[19]

As confidence grew among Christian thinkers, it was reinforced by external events: the official Christianization of the Empire in the fourth century encouraged, at least among some, an intellectual triumphalism; Athanasius could boast that the schools of philosophy were now empty and the churches full (*De incarnatione* 50, 55). And the emergence of imperially supported councils of bishops at Nicaea (325) ensured that certain platonizing possibilities available to earlier generations of Christians were now closed down.[20] No orthodox Christian after Nicaea could offer a Plotinian-style "trinity" of divine hypostases (The One, Mind and Soul) as a philosophical exposition of the Christian Trinity without fear of condemnation as a subordinationist, as not believing in the full divinity of Christ or the Holy Spirit.

Since what may be styled a Christian Platonism had been broadly established at least by the mid-third century, and since on the pagan side there were by then a number of versions of Platonism available, one could attempt to get behind "modern" interpretations by going directly to Plato himself, or follow a Middle-Platonic approach, as a number of Christians continued to do even when, among the pagans, that approach was largely superseded by the Neoplatonic developments inaugurated by Plotinus (204–70). Alternatively, one could keep up with the latest Neoplatonic trends. Among later Christians, Methodius, in his *Banquet* – where the subject-matter is not simply *eros* but *eros* as chastity (in the tradition of Origen) – offered a challenge to Plato himself, while Gregory of Nyssa, who knew Plotinus well and cited him regularly, develops his own thought more in parallel to than in servile imitation of the pagan master.[21] Both Plotinus and Gregory, for example, are concerned with divine infinity, but while this theme is comparatively marginal or at least more implicit in Plotinus, it is explicit in Gregory, and the reasons for such explicitness are less a dependence on Plotinus and a desire to "develop" his insights than a concern to work out a theory of God's infinity in the context of an intra-Christian debate about divine attributes with the "Neo-Arian" Eunomius of Cyzicus.

Yet if the example of Gregory were to induce us to believe that from then on Christians were largely blind to contemporary developments within the Platonic schools, we would again be deceived: the influential sixth-century figure known to us as Pseudo-Dionysius is soaked in the most contemporary version of Neoplatonism, that of Iamblichus, Proclus, and Damascius, as well as in that of Plotinus himself. At times he will even quote Proclus at length and more or less verbatim.[22] But neither is Dionysius uncritical; much apparently non-Christian material is pruned away, not least Proclus' proliferating jungle of hypostases, and Dionysius develops an application of Neoplatonic thinking within a wholly Christian liturgical context, with much help from that "Judeo-Christian" tradition of Platonism which we can now summarize as beginning with Philo and proceeding with additions through Justin, Clement, Origen, Methodius, Gregory of Nyssa, and Evagrius. Yet Dionysius' respectful attitude to the contemporary pagans, so different from that of Gregory (or Augustine), let alone of Athanasius, only confirms the lesson that each Christian figure must be looked at individually. From the time of Justin, Christians make deals with one or other of the broadly Platonic traditions, but the exact nature of those deals can only be attained by individual inspection.

We must, however, finally return to the beginnings, for even there the study of individual figures in sequence is not enough: Justin, Tatian, Theophilus, Irenaeus, Clement, Tertullian, and the rest. We must above all look at the types of problems they try to solve, and the all-important question of the views and concerns of their individual opponents. For Clement at least had come to recognize the force of the Aristotelian claim (*Prot.*)[23] that even to offer an argument against philosophy is to philosophize (*Strom.* 6.18.162).

An important effect of the work of Justin was simply to familiarize Christians with an appeal to Greek philosophy, but, as we have seen, to appeal to philosophers to corroborate ideas derived from revelation and Christian tradition is not yet to philosophize. It may, however, lead to philosophizing because, even if unintentionally, it will draw attention to the need for conceptual clarification, either within the pagan philosophical texts themselves or within the Christian tradition which resort to those texts may appear to elucidate. Such philosophizing will be inseparable, in patristic times, from "theology."

There has been much loose talk about whether in antiquity X is or is not a "Christian philosopher."[24] More clarity can be obtained if we recognize the types of philosophical problems with which the early Christian thinkers were presented. It would then be possible to see whether these problems are treated "philosophically," "theologically," or merely ignored. Such problems were broadly of two types. First were those already hotly debated among philosophers before Christianity appeared on the scene, but which might acquire new urgency in a Christian context. Such would include difficulties about the freedom of the "will" and our responsibility for our actions – a concern already aired in Justin (*1 Apol.* 43–4) where a famous text of the *Republic* (617E4) is brought into play to exonerate God from responsibility for human wrongdoing – and the problem of evil, which though of greater consequence in Christian than in pagan thought, had already been much debated in providentialist Platonic and Stoic circles.

A second group of problems were those which arose within the Christian (or Jewish) tradition itself – such as the sense in which Christianity is distinct from that Hellenic monotheism – as defended by Celsus – where a supreme God lords it among lesser divinities – from a need either to clarify conceptual ambiguities which merely exegetical work could not resolve since the difficulties now uncovered were no concern of their original authors, or to attend to the intelligibility of long-used utterances whose strict sense might, on reflection, be hard to determine. A good example of this latter group was provided by the word "omnipotent". Versions of the term had been in the mouths of Christians since the beginning, but it took several hundred years of reflection before the major difficulties which they introduce (such as, "Can God rewrite the moral order at will?" and "Can God do literally anything?") were even satisfactorily recognized. It is a law of the history of ideas that concepts are in use long before they are identified, or apparently identified, as concepts, and investigated as such; when they are so identified the conceptual scene changes radically.

Another specifically Christian difficulty of a related sort was the sense (against the pagans) of the notion that God has created the world "out of nothing" (rather than that he has merely organized and given form to a pre-existing substrate). By the third century Origen, realizing the importance of the problem, can assert that any account of the origin of the world which does not appeal to creation from nothing is unworthy of God's majesty.[25]

A final and quite distinct type of problem facing Christians in the second century introduces another group of opponents. Gnosticism has been described as part of the "Platonic underworld," though the Gnostics were religious speculators rather than philosophers. Yet, in rebutting them, Christians like Irenaeus and Tertullian had to deploy argument to show that their more "orthodox" theology – this is not merely the writing of history by the victors – is the more intelligible, the more capable of admitting of philosophical sense. In handling the Gnostics, Christian thinkers had to recognize the importance of logic and clear thinking in directly religious debate, in distinguishing theosophy from philosophy and religion. In that learning process, they recognized – though they often tended to minimize their debt in the interest of maintaining the originality of their own views and of emphasizing that the "heretical" underworld might in some part be a Platonic "underworld"[26] – that they needed to re-deploy the resources of a pagan intellectual tradition going back to Socrates and beyond. Perhaps in the intra-religious struggle with the Gnostics more directly than in the changing relations with pagan philosophy itself and the development of a specifically Christian Platonic tradition we can recognize the beginnings of a specifically Christian (rather than merely theistic) rational *theology*.[27]

Notes

1 Questions as to the "Pauline" authorship of these Pauline texts are not relevant to the present discussion.

2 M. Frede ("Celsus' Attack on the Christians", in J. Barnes and M. Griffin (eds.), *Philosophia Togata II* (Oxford, 1997), p. 236, rightly observes that Celsus specifically defends this position against Christian attack.

3 See especially M. D. Chenu, *La Théologie comme science au XIIIème siècle* (Paris, 1957).

4 For further comment see J. M. Dillon, "Philosophy and Theology in Proclus," in *From Augustine to Eriugena: Essays on Neoplatonism and Christianity in Honor of J. J. O'Meara*, eds. F. X. Martin and J. A. Richmond (Washington, 1991), pp. 66–76. For Varro's influential distinction between "mythical," "civic," and "physical" theology (and a Christian response)

see R. Markus, "Saint Augustine and 'Theologia Naturalis,'" *TU* 81 (1962), pp. 476–9; J. Pépin, *Mythe et allégorie* (Paris, 1985), pp. 276–392.

5 The first-century Jewish thinker Philo (later to influence Christians largely through his exegetical activity) might have disagreed with this generalization, but after the fall of Jerusalem in AD70 mainstream Judaism rejected him, taking other and non-philosophical paths.

6 For an introduction to what Justin might have learned in the schools, see K. Algra, J. Barnes, J. Mansfeld, and M. Schofield (eds.), *The Cambridge History of Hellenistic Philosophy* (Cambridge, 1999); Barnes and Griffin, *Philosophia Togata II*; H. B. Gottschalk, "Aristotelian Philosophy in the Roman World from the Time of Cicero to the End of the Second

Century AD," in W. Haase (ed.), *Aufstieg und Niedergang der römischen Welt*, II.36.2 (Berlin, 1990), pp. 1079–174; J. M. Dillon, *The Middle Platonists* (Ithaca, 1977).

7   Cf. Dillon, *The Middle Platonists*, p. 143; J. Whittaker, "Moses Atticizing," *Phoenix* 21 (1967), pp. 196–201; M. J. Edwards, "Atticizing Moses? Numenius, the Fathers and the Jews", *VC* 44 (1990), pp. 64–75.

8   Cf. Tatian, *Orat.* 31 (and 40); Theophilus, *Ad Autol.* 2.12; 3.16; Clement of Alexandria, *Strom.* 1.15.68.2; 1.17.87; 2.5.22.1; etc.; Tertullian, *Ap.* 19, etc.; cf. A. J. Droge, *Homer or Moses?* (Tübingen, 1989); D. Ridings, *The Attic Moses* (Göteborg, 1995); for further ancient evidence see H. Dörrie and M. Baltes, *Der Platonismus in der Antike* Band 2 (Stuttgart-Bad Cannstatt, 1990), pp. 190–214.

9   S. R. C. Lilla, *Clement of Alexandria: A Study in Christian Platonism and Gnosticism* (Oxford, 1971), pp. 10–11; R. Bauckham, "The Fall of the Angels as the Source of Philosophy in Hermias and Clement of Alexandria," *VC* 39 (1985), pp. 313–30; Droge, "Homer or Moses?", p. 141. The fallen-angel theory apparently goes back to the Jewish apocalypse 1 *Enoch*.

10 For a corrective to the view that Clement appealed only to Middle Platonic sources, see now D. Wyrwa, *Die Christliche Platonaneignung in den Stromateis des Clemens von Alexandrien* (Berlin and New York, 1983).

11 See J. P. Kenney, *Mystical Monotheism: A Study of Ancient Platonic Theology* (Hanover and London, 1991); P. Athanassiadi and M. Frede (eds.), *Pagan Monotheism in Late Antiquity* (Oxford, 1999). But pagan and Christian monotheism should not be too enthusiastically assimilated; "monotheism" is a slippery term. Frede grossly exaggerates in stating that various pagan thinkers were monotheists "in precisely the sense the Christians were" ("Monotheism and Pagan Philosophy in Later Antiquity," in *Pagan Monotheism*, p. 67).

12 For concern among the Platonists about homosexuality, note Plotinus' furious reaction to a proposed defense of Alcibiades' attempted seduction of Socrates, as described in Plato's *Symposium* (Porphyry, *V.P.* 15). For Plutarch's defense of heterosexual rather than homosexual *eros* see J. M. Rist, "Plutarch's *Amatorius*: A Commentary on Plato's Theories of Love?", *CQ* 51 (2001), pp. 557–75.

13 For attacks on the doctrine of "natural" immortality, which would carry the corollary that "we" are at bottom "pure" spirit, untainted by sin, see (e.g.) Justin, *Dial.* 6; Tatian, *Orat.* 1.13; cf. Tertullian, *An.* 24.

14 See recently S. R. L. Clark, "Plotinus: Body and Soul" in L. P. Gerson (ed.), *The Cambridge Companion to Plotinus* (Cambridge, 1996), pp. 275–91 and J. M. Rist, "Is Plotinus' Body Too Etherialized?", in *Prudentia* (Supplement 1993), pp. 103–17 (= *Man, Soul and Body, Essays in Ancient Thought from Plato to Dionysius* (Aldershot, 1996), essay XV).

15 See especially F. Masai, "Les Conversions de Saint Augustin et les débuts du spiritualisme en Occident," *Le Moyen Age* 67 (1961), pp. 1–40.

16 See E. Osborn, "Reason and the Rule of Faith in the Second Century AD," in R. Williams (ed.), *The Making of Orthodoxy, Festschrift for Henry Chadwick* (Cambridge, 1989), pp. 40–61; P. Grech, "The *regula Fidei* as hermeneutic principle yesterday and today," in *L'Interpretazione della Bibbia nella Chiesa* (Collezione Atti e Documenti 11) (Vatican City, 2001), pp. 208–24. The Greek term *kanon* is of philosophical (but not Platonic) origin.

17 For an introduction to the attitude of the defeated Platonists, see H. D. Saffrey, "Allusions antichrétiennes chez Proclus le diadoque platonicien," in *Revue des sciences philosophiques et théologiques* 59 (1975), pp. 553–63.

18 Cf. M. Baltes, *Die Weltentstehung des platonischen Timaeus nach den antiken Interpreten* (2 vols.) (Leiden, 1976–8).

19 For an introduction see J. M. Rist, *Human Value: A Study in Ancient Philosophical Ethics* (Leiden, 1982), pp. 153–63.

20 Cf. F. Ricken, "Nikaia als Krisis des altchristlichen Platonismus," *Theologie und Philosophie* 44 (1969), pp. 321–41.

21 See J. M. Rist, "On the Platonism of Gregory of Nyssa," *Hermathena* 169 (2000), pp. 129–51.

22 The basic work on this was done by H. Koch, "Proklus als Quelle des Pseudo-Dionysius Areopagita in der Lehre vom Bösen," *Philologus* 54 (1895), pp. 438–54 and J. Stiglmayr, "Der Neuplatoniker Proclus als Vorlage des sog. Dionysius in der Lehre vom Übel," *Historisches Jahrbuch* 16 (1895), pp. 253–73, 721–48.

23 Aristotle's Fragments, ed. Rose (51).

24 See the discussion in C. Stead, *Philosophy in Christian Antiquity* (Cambridge, 1994).

Stead, thinking only in terms of contemporary Anglo-American philosophy (and aware that to cite a philosopher is not yet to philosophize), is mistakenly inclined to award the title "philosopher" to very few Christians before the fourth century.

25 See G. May, *Schöpfung aus dem Nichts* (Berlin, 1978), English translation as *Creatio ex Nihilo* (Edinburgh, 1994); J. Fantino, "L'Origine de la doctrine de la création ex nihilo," *Revue des sciences philosophiques et théologiques* 80 (1996),

pp. 589–602; J. Torchia, *Creatio ex Nihilo and the Theology of St. Augustine: The Anti-Manichaean Polemic and Beyond* (New York, 1999), pp. 1–64.

26 We owe the happy phrase to Dillon, *The Middle Platonists*, p. 384. Recall Tertullian's *Doleo bona fide Platonem omnium hereticorum condimentarium factum* (*An.* 23).

27 My thanks must go to Eric Osborn for constructive comment on earlier drafts.

Justin Martyr

Eric Osborn

Justin Martyr and the Love of Truth

The second century is one of the turning points in the history of human thought. Christian claims were emerging in a group of writings known to us as the Christian Bible. To the Roman world they seemed as impenetrable or ambiguous as they seem to the secular modern who picks them up in a hotel room. Their message had to be explained in terms accessible to the culture of the day. Justin, like Irenaeus and Tertullian, used classical ways of thinking to explain the Christian kerygma in a way which superseded rival accounts. In doing this he began a tradition of thought which produced a civilization. The structure of this thought follows New Testament kerygma rather than fourth-century creeds.

If we think of a great bay which flows into an ocean, we can understand most simply what they were doing. The bay of the kerygma flows into the ocean of the contemporary discourse. Yet there is complexity because the bay has its tributaries and currents and all is ruled by changing tides. Concepts group and regroup with subtle changes of meaning. We may also compare the transition from Scripture and kerygma to theology with other transitions from one discourse to another, as for example from science to religion. Such transition is made through a variety of argument and masses of imagery. So Justin and his immediate successors call for conceptual stamina and display the two intellectual virtues which one of them, Clement of Alexandria, identified as audacity and wisdom.

Justin was born of Roman descent at the beginning of the second century in Flavia Neapolis (now called Nablus) in Samaria, close to the ancient town of Shechem. He travelled by way of Asia Minor to Rome where he taught and argued. He wore a philosopher's cloak and passed rapidly through Peripatetic, Pythagorean, Stoic, and Platonic schools before finding truth in Christ and the prophets. Two of his written works are known to us: one is an *Apology*, with an appendix which is commonly called a "second apology," and the other is his *Dialogue with Trypho*, a Jew who is a representative character or type rather than an historical person. Justin writes as an apologist. He looks at prevailing objections against Christianity and rebuts them one by one; yet there are connections across his work and an underlying unity in his thought. His main ideas are found again in later writers. His longer work, the *Dialogue*, is a quiet and reasoned discussion which moves from philosophy to prophecy. Justin complains that Jews curse Christians (*Dial.* 16.4; 93.4; 95.4; 96.2; 108.3) and curse Jesus (*Dial.* 95.4; 133.6). When it is possible they kill Christians (*Dial.* 95.4; 133.6) but in present circumstances they are not permitted to do this by their rulers (*Dial.* 16.4; 96.2).

Truth

Justin calls himself a "lover of truth." He aligns himself with the Apology of Socrates and takes up the position that truth, right conduct, and speech are more important than life itself. It does not matter whether Plato or Pythagoras ever supported a particular opinion; all that matters is whether it is true (*Dial.* 6.1): "Reason directs those who are truly pious and true philosophers to honour and love only what is true, to decline to follow traditional opinions, if these be worthless" (*1 Apol.* 2.1). Justin uses the term "lover of truth" rather than "philosopher" (lover of wisdom) and challenges his opponents for failing in love of truth when they do not follow the rules of argument (*Dial.* 67.4).

Justin himself had earlier rejected the common slanders against Christians, when he saw that they were "fearless in the face of death and all that men count fearful" (*2 Apol.* 12.1). He regarded martyrdom as testimony to truth. In the fourth Gospel and the Apocalypse, martyrdom is seen as witness to the truth and not as the sacrifice of the martyr. According to John, Jesus says before Pilate, "For this I was born and for this I came into the world to be a witness to the truth" (John 18:37). Justin is also strongly influenced by Plato's account of Socrates' trial and defence.

The universal Logos, who spoke through the prophets and who first made man, is the source of truth. His own words as the incarnate Christ have a special power, deflecting the wanderer from the wrong path and bringing rest to those who receive them. Justin's passion for truth is intensified because, following John and Paul, he saw the truth personified in Christ, who became the focus of his loyalty and his supreme love.

Prophecy

Justin finds truth in the words of prophets, who alone "saw the truth and spoke it to men, caring and fearing for no man, not subject to opinion, but only speaking what they heard and saw when they were filled with the Holy Spirit." They were able to see the truth because they were filled with the Holy Spirit (*Dial.* 7.1). The truth of prophecy is confirmed by its fulfilment in events. The prophets did not offer simple solutions. They spoke in types, hiding the truth so that those who sought for truth would have to work and think (*Dial.* 90.2). Typology demands the use of reason. As interpreted on consistent principles, the prophets set out God's plan and provide a basis for Christian theology, supplanting the forms of Plato. The mind, as Plato claimed, grasps transcendent objects of thought, but philosophers did not see accurately as did the prophets. Therefore their words and images supersede the schools of philosophy.

Justin's bible does not have the clear shape and full content which we find in his successors. He quotes the Old Testament freely, adapts the text to his own meaning, joins different quotations together, attributes texts to wrong authors, and quotes the same text differently in different places. He uses a Christian handbook of prophetic testimonies. Yet he also goes beyond these testimonies to the whole text of Scripture and sometimes his exegesis does not fit with the extended text which he or a later scribe quotes.

Instead of written Gospels Justin uses collections of the words of Christ, representing Christ as speaking rather than an evangelist as reporting. Yet he also refers to written Gospels as "Memoirs of the Apostles" (*1 Apol.* 66.3) in which he finds all things which concern Jesus Christ. Oral tradition and memory also play a part in his citations.

God and Logos

Justin draws on both Scripture and Plato for his account of God, who is the only unbegotten and immortal being, all other things being begotten and perishable (*Dial.* 5.4). There can only be one uncaused cause, or else we are lost in infinite regress. Polytheists who worship idols are driven to all forms of injustice and stupidity. In relation to them, Christians are rightly called atheists, but they are not atheists with respect to "the most true God, the father of righteousness, moderation and other virtues, untainted by evil" (*1 Apol.* 6.1). Strictly God is beyond human language. The titles which we give him (Father, God, Creator, Lord, and Master) are not names, but forms of address. They act as supports to our mind, says Justin, and as ways in which we can speak to him.

The Logos of God is nearest to God and the head of creation. As God's first offspring he is prior to all creatures (*Dial.* 129.4). As the first born of God, the Logos is God (*1 Apol.* 63.15). He remains God's word after God has spoken. Yet the Logos is distinct in number from the Father: "We see that fires kindled from one fire are separate fires, while the original fire is in no way diminished. Many fires can be kindled from it, but it remains the same" (*Dial.* 128.4).

In contrast to the Father, the Logos has many names. He is angel, God, lord, man (*Dial.* 59.1), king, priest, god, lord, angel, man, chief, captain, stone, and child (*Dial.* 34.2). These names, which come from Scripture, declare his universality. The universal Logos scattered seed on every human: "For the Logos both was and is he who is in every human, who foretold through the prophets the things which were to happen and taught through himself those things when he had taken our nature upon himself" (*2 Apol.* 10.8). As a result, completely uneducated men, as well as philosophers, have scorned glory, fear, and death to die for Christ. What they have known is an activity of divine power and not a mere human construct (*2 Apol.* 10.8). Those who have lived "with Logos" are Christians whether they have been Greeks like Socrates and Heraclitus or barbarians like Abraham, Ananias, Azarias, Misael or

Elijah. Those who have lived without Logos have been enemies of Christ and of all who have lived with Logos. Those who either have lived or are now living with Logos are Christians (*1 Apol.* 46.3–4).

There are degrees of participation or sharing in the Logos and there is also a difference between being the Logos and merely participating in him. Plato, the Stoics, the poets and writers of old, all had a part of the spermatic Logos, the divine seed which the Logos has scattered, but they did not have sure understanding and irrefutable knowledge. Yet, according to Justin, whatever they spoke according to the Logos "belongs to us Christians" (*2 Apol.* 13.4).

For Christians, the Logos is not merely something implanted in man: he is a living person who is known and loved. The seed which he sowed gave a dim perception of his reality, but it was never more than a "copy given in proportion to strength" (*2 Apol.* 13.6) as distinct from the reality itself, which is participated in and imitated by the seeds. Justin here joins the Stoic notion of spermatic Logos or seminal reason with the Platonic idea of participation. In this way, he gives to those who have followed Logos, both past and present, a clear status which is distinct from the direct knowledge of Christ. The direct participation of the believer is superior to the indirect participation of the unbeliever.

Christ rounds off the divine plan (*oikonomia*) in his Incarnation. He completes the dispensation, which was the will of his father (*Dial.* 67.6). The long process of preparation for Christ, both in prophets and philosophers, is needed because man must choose for himself whether to obey God or not. Justin argues against the Stoic concept of fate, because men and angels have free will. Fate would mean that all people should be either good or bad or that there is no real difference between goodness and badness (*1 Apol.* 28.1–4).

God's plan of salvation thus includes law as well as Logos. Just as the Logos came in part to men of old and then fully in Christ, says Justin, so the old law was an anticipation of the new law in Christ. The law of Moses was given, first, to encourage those who had shown the hardness of their hearts in failing to perform what is good and just (*Dial.* 45.3). Secondly, the law was concerned to set right what had gone wrong. When the Israelites had shown their foolishness in making a golden calf, God gave to his people a law, which was appropriate to their immaturity. However, the law was inadequate because it did not stop people from sinning and did not touch people other than the Jews. It fulfilled a temporary purpose and looked forward to the coming of a perfect law. It had been written that "there should be a final law and covenant supreme over all which now all men should keep if they wish to pursue the inheritance of God . . . And Christ was given to us as an eternal and final law and a faithful covenant after which there shall be no law, no precept, no commandment" (*Dial.* 11.2).

Creation and Evil

Against Marcion, an influential Christian teacher, who separated the inferior world-creator from the God of love, Justin declares that the world was made for humanity's sake. When Justin says, "we have been taught that God has made the world, not haphazardly, but for the sake of the human race" (*2 Apol.* 4.2), he is indebted both to the Bible and to the Stoics. But if God made the world and saw that it was good, why is there so much evil within this world?

Drawing on Jewish-Christian tradition and Plato's *Timaeus,* Justin tells how some angels deserted their prescribed place and disobeyed God. In falling, they lost their supremacy and were subdued by intercourse with women. From this intercourse came the demons, who have enslaved the whole human race (*2 Apol.* 5.2–4). They persecute all who proclaim the truth and they oppose the work of the Logos at every point. Their leader, Satan, has produced many blasphemies and imitations or distortions of truth.

Yet evil will not triumph. The devil will be destroyed and all his angelic followers will be condemned to endless punishment with fire (*1 Apol.* 28.1). Already, demon-possessed people in every place are exorcized by the name of Jesus Christ, crucified under Pontius Pilate. Many magicians have failed where the name of Christ has achieved victory (*2 Apol.* 6.6).

Justin speaks in detail of the future coming of Christ, the Resurrection, and coming judgement. He is the first writer to speak of a "second" coming (*Dial.* 54.1). It was prophesied that there would be two comings: one when Christ came in humility and one when he came in power. At present we live between the two (*Dial.* 51). Justin defends Resurrection as essential to Christian belief. The strangeness of this event is no argument against its truth, because the formation of the human body from human seed is equally strange. God will raise again the bodies which he first made and his people will live for a thousand years before the final judgement.

The Christian Life

Baptism is preceded by instruction, penitence, faith, a commitment to follow Christ's way and fasting. Members of the community fast and pray together with the candidate who is led to water and immersed with the formula of the threefold name. The eucharist of bread and cup is offered by Christians throughout the earth (*Dial.* 117.1). On Sunday, the day of creation and Resurrection, Christians gather for worship. The "Memoirs of the Apostles" and the writings of the prophets are read, a sermon follows, and then after prayer the bread, wine, and water are brought. He who leads in worship later distributes money from a free-will offering to those in need, such as orphans, widows, invalids, and prisoners (*1 Apol.* 67.3–6).

Justin pioneers a proud use of the name "Christian." Christians are the people of Christ, the true Israel, because they have no racial boundaries and are universal in their mission. Persecuted for their name (*2 Apol.* 2), slandered by Jews (*Dial.* 17.1) whom they regard as brothers (*Dial.* 96.2) divided by schism (*Dial.* 35), they are found among every human race as they offer "prayers and thanksgivings to the father and maker of all through the name of Jesus crucified" (*Dial.* 117).

Justin's Contribution

Justin contributed to early Christian discourse not only a concern for truth, but also a way of using reason and argument to give an account of Christian belief. In the account of his martyrdom we find that he is addressed as the man who thinks he knows the truth. He replies that after trying to learn all teachings he accepted the true teachings of the Christians, whose one God made and shaped all things seen and unseen, and whose son Jesus Christ, proclaimed by the prophets, has brought salvation and taught (*Mart.* 2).

During the prefecture of Junius Rusticus (162–8), six other Christians were martyred together with him. He says that he had taught in a house in the *Via Tiburtina*, and when further challenged, is confident that, after death, he will ascend to heaven and receive his reward. With his companions he refuses to offer sacrifice to the gods of Rome: "Do what you will, for we are Christians, and do not sacrifice to idols" (*Mart.* 4).

Bibliography

L. W. Barnard, *Justin Martyr, His Life and Thought* (Cambridge, 1967).

H. Chadwick, *Early Christian Thought and the Classical Tradition* (Oxford, 1966).

H. Chadwick, "Justin Martyr's Defence of Christianity", *Bulletin of the John Rylands Library* 47, 2, 1965.

E. R. Goodenough, *The Theology of Justin Martyr* (Jena, 1923).

C. Munier, *L'Apologie de Saint Justin philosophe et martyr* (Fribourg, 1994).

E. F. Osborn, *Justin Martyr* (Tübingen, 1973).

O. Skarsaune, *The Proof from Prophecy: A Study in Justin Martyr's Proof-Text Tradition* (Leiden, 1987).

Irenaeus of Lyons

Eric Osborn

cha
pter

10

One of the great paintings in the world is found at Rome in the Sistine Chapel where the walls and roof are covered with incidents from the Old and New Testaments. On the one side there are pictures from the life of Moses, on the other side there are incidents from the Gospels. Above, the story of creation is set out and the prophets and sibyls foretell the coming of Christ.

The front of the chapel is dominated by the figure of Christ in judgement, his raised hand revealing the wound in his side. The centrality of Christ is supported by the detail of the picture in which everything points to him. Everything that the Bible has told of God's dealing with man finds meaning in one point: the person of Jesus Christ. Splendid as is the triumph of Michelangelo, the conception is not new. From the beginning, Christians have seen their faith expressed in awareness of one God and his plan for human salvation which culminates in Jesus Christ. This is the primitive Christian kerygma.

No one has set out this account of the Christian message in written form more clearly than did Irenaeus, who was bishop in Lyons after the persecution of 177. He was a man of vision (*homme de voir*) who combined imagery with argument to transpose the message of Scripture into public discourse. Lyons was and is a great city where the Roman forum is set on a hill overlooking the confluence of two rivers, the Rhone and the Saône. Irenaeus came here from Asia Minor, where at Smyrna he had listened to the teaching of Polycarp, a bishop who, like Irenaeus' predecessor at Lyons, died a martyr. What Irenaeus had to say, his account of God, who created the world and guided its history and then came himself in Jesus Christ, has dominated the culture of the Christian West. Michelangelo's great painting is the clearest expression of this culture in visual form as Handel's *Messiah* is the clearest statement in music. They attempt to express the message of the Christian Bible which shapes the puzzling narratives and the account of God. There are four things that the Bible, Michelangelo, and Handel want to tell us and Irenaeus put them better than anyone else: the goodness of God; his saving plan; its perfection in Christ; and the offer of salvation.

Irenaeus' major work, *Against the Heresies*, survives in fragments, but a Latin translation from about 380 is complete. It is stimulated but not determined by opposition to Gnosticism, a form of theosophy which today attracts interest and sympathy. Some take the exuberance and composite nature of this work as an excuse for neglect, but its main ideas are powerfully clear. His *Demonstration of the Apostolic Preaching* is a brief work, known in a sixth-century Armenian translation since 1907. It expresses the same themes as the longer work.

With his two criteria of logical truth (Is it logically coherent?) and aesthetic fitness (Is it aesthetically harmonious?), Irenaeus develops four concepts which underpin the first comprehensive Christian theology. These concepts are the good mind of God (divine intellect), God's plan of salvation (divine economy), the summing up of all things in Christ (recapitulation), and the sharing of the believer in God's salvation (participation). The first and last point to optimism and growth, while the middle concepts show the way in which growth is achieved.

Divine Intellect

For Irenaeus, God is universal intellect, holding all things in knowledge and vision, indivisible and simultaneous, entire and identical, the source of all good things: "His greatness lacks nothing, but contains all things, comes close to us and is with us" (*Haer.* 4.19.3). Instead of rejecting the philosopher's concept of God as ultimate being, Irenaeus joins philosophy with the biblical witness to develop his account of the divine intellect. We learn from Scripture that God is one and three: one Father, one Son and Holy Spirit (*Haer.* 1.10.1; 5.20.1).

Against those Gnostics who had divided the divine fullness into a multitude of eons, Irenaeus draws on the pre-Socratic philosopher Xenophanes, who supplanted the many gods of Greece with a universal mind who "sees all, thinks all and hears all".[1] Anthropomorphic subdivision of the divine mind is foolish and presumptuous. God simply is, while man "becomes". God makes, while man is made. God is always the same, while man grows from a beginning, through a middle, to an end. God's goodness is poured out on man who grows from creation to final glory.

Irenaeus identifies the concept of divine intellect with active goodness to make a theocentric optimism. God's goodness precedes his action (*Haer.* 4.39.2). Optimism springs from confidence in the goodness of Creator and creation. Irenaeus describes Gnostics as restless and dissatisfied; they are always seeking but never finding (*Haer.* 5.20.2). In contrast, Irenaeus puts forward a love of what exists. The divine perfection needs a contingent creature to receive the goodness which it gives. The diversity of the world is ordered to become a splendid harmony from the composer of a wonderful universe (*Haer.* 2.26.3; 2.25.2; 4.4.2).

Irenaeus develops the common human awareness of a divine being into the forceful claim: God is a universal, intelligent being, who sees all, who knows in advance every creature's need, and who displays his love and glory everywhere, but especially through his prophets and supremely in his Son.

Salvation History/Economy

The divine economy or plan of salvation begins with creation. To explain creation, Irenaeus use two biblical analogies: God as Wise Architect and God as Sovereign King (*Haer.* 2.11.1). The Wise Architect produces order from disordered matter; the Sovereign King produces by word, will, and power. God, not an inferior demiurge, produces the varied beauty of the world (*Haer.* 2.2.1–3). While the Architect needs material in order to create, the King does not. By joining the two images together Irenaeus formulates a concept of creation from nothing.

The divine economy is the way in which the Wise Architect, God, proceeds and "draws up the plans for the edifice of salvation" (*Haer.* 4.14.2). It is packed with artistic detail and gives order to the story of God's dealing with mankind, without losing continuity in time or comprehensiveness in space. The functions of the economy – accustoming of God to man and man to God, progressive revelation and human development – are never abstract. They all have a human orientation.

The idea of "accustoming" meets an obvious challenge to Christian belief: why had God left it so late to send his Son to save the world? Irenaeus ingeniously replies that man had to be accustomed to God and God had to be accustomed to man. Abraham, Isaac, and Jacob prefigured what was to come as God accustomed his people to live as strangers in the world and to follow his word (*Haer.* 4.21.3). The Incarnation is the climax because in Christ man is able to see God, to contain God and to participate in God; at the same time God is accustomed to live in man (*Haer.* 3.20.2).

The economy thus describes the ascent of man. Irenaeus' human optimism has long excited enthusiasm. At the Renaissance he inspired Erasmus. In the twentieth century he enthused those who, like Teilhard de Chardin, were driven by science to see human evolution to Christ as the omega point.

Irenaeus' account of the ascent of man to Christ has been contrasted with the fall of man as it is later described in Augustine. This contrast is oversimplified, for Irenaeus also speaks of the fall of man in Adam, and does not diminish the catastrophe. Yet Adam was an infant and God was able to take him and bring him, even in his fallen state, to perfection in Christ. Man, a mixture of soul and flesh, is created by God through his hands, the Son and the Spirit (*Haer.* 4.20.1). Adam has never left the hands of God, who made him and finally perfected him in Christ (*Haer.* 5.1.3). Irenaeus' many-sided development of the Adam–Christ typology takes the restoration of divine sonship and immortality in new directions. He develops the Pauline defence of the flesh and of human status as creature, against the spiritualizing tendencies of Gnostics.

The economy of salvation presents a progressive revelation of God. Revelation begins with creation and continues through the law and the prophets to end in the Incarnation of the Son. Here all creation sees its King, and in the splendid flesh of the Lord, man finds and receives the light of the Father (*Haer.* 4.20.2). The plan of salvation is defined by its climax in recapitulation.

Summing up/Recapitulation

Salvation history leads to the summing up or recapitulation of all things in Christ. In this event, end is joined to beginning, omega to alpha, and death is changed to life.

The first meaning which Irenaeus links with the concept of recapitulation is that of correcting what has gone wrong with human history. With this concept of correction are linked the ideas of the liberation of captive sinners, the justification of the ungodly, repetition, restoration, and reconciliation.

God is in Christ reconciling the world to himself. The world (sinful humanity) is summed up, united, and included in Christ just as it had been included in Adam. The action is repetitive in that it returns to the point of error and replaces the wrong deed with the right deed, thereby rectifying the ancient fault.

The mass of detail which Irenaeus uses to describe recapitulation reflects his desire to include everything. Christ is not merely Head, Chief, or Summit, but the one who unites a vast plurality. To Romans 5:12–21 (Christ as second Adam) and 1 Corinthians 15:25–8 (subjection of all things to Christ), must be added Ephesians 1:10 (summing up of all things) for an appreciation of Irenaeus' cosmic view.

Secondly, recapitulation means perfection. The whole history of salvation is resumed by the Gospel, so that beginning, middle, and end are brought together (*Haer.* 3.24.1). The supremacy of Christ over all things is established; just as he reigns over the unseen world, so he is Lord of the visible world, which he supports by the axis of his cross. All things are restored, renewed, and set free. Creation achieves its purpose; it is not merely repaired but brought to perfection.

Thirdly, recapitulation means the inauguration of a new humanity: "The glory of God is a living man and the life of man is the vision of God" (*Haer.* 4.20.7). Irenaeus has his own account of man as the image and likeness of God. Because the incarnate Son is the archetypal image, every human possesses shape and flesh similar to him. At baptism every believer receives the power of assimilation (likeness) from the Holy Spirit as a dynamic which gradually transforms the image until it is finally perfected by Resurrection.

Adam was weak, incomplete, an infant, possessing by the Spirit a likeness to God which he lost through disobedience. God led Adam to penitence (*Haer.* 3.23.5), life (*Haer.* 3.23.7), immortality (*Haer.* 3.20.2; *Dem.* 15) and communion with himself (*Haer.* 5.27.2). Lost possibilities were restored by Christ whose fullness now excels what was given during his earthly life. The new life is marked by immortality, for the Father will receive the righteous into incorruption and everlasting refreshment (*Haer.* 4.6.5), as his order of salvation moves forward to liberate his servant, adopt him as son, bestow on him an incorruptible inheritance, and so perfect humanity (*Haer.* 4.11.1).

Finally, recapitulation points to resurrection. The resurrection of Christ concerns the substance of his flesh. Our resurrection, like his, must be a resurrection of the flesh, for he will raise us by the same power, which he used in his own resurrection. The reality of his flesh was proved when he showed the marks of the nails and the wound in his side. Our mortal bodies will be raised as he was raised. This is the work of the Spirit, whose power we already know in his pledge which prepares us for future incorruption. Those who possess this pledge of the Spirit are subject to the Spirit and serve the Spirit rather than the flesh.

Irenaeus' millenarian eschatology is the necessary act of a God who renews creation. The return of Christ in glory will display and prove his saving work (*Haer.* 3.16.6). The restoration of human lives, which is the present concern of the Church, will be complete in a restored universe. The inauguration of a new humanity is fed by the hope of final glory. Recapitulation and final consummation are thus tied together, and the whole of recapitulation is oriented to the end when creation and redemption fulfill their purpose.

A good image for Irenaeus' exuberant thought is that of an hourglass lying on its side so that it presents a movement from left to right. God begins with creation and ends with the consummation of all things. The first half of the hourglass bears on its sides the message of the prophets. Their visions represent the mind of God, and for Irenaeus take the place of the world of Platonic forms. The narrow neck of the hourglass is the recapitulation of all things in Christ, and the second half of the hourglass bears on its side the message of the prophets and the words of Christ and the Apostles.

Participation

Participation, the fourth of Irenaeus' key concepts, takes many forms. His first three concepts, we have seen, are unitive and point to one God, one saving economy or plan of salvation, one summing up. Participation is distributive, for God shares his life, truth, beauty, and goodness with humans in many ways. Humanity cannot live without life, which comes from participation in God. True knowledge works through divine/human exchange (*Haer.* 5.1.1), God becoming what we are so that we might become what he is. Irenaeus claims that this exchange, in a single stroke, destroys the dualism of the heretics (*Haer.* 5.1.1). Moreover, God finds joy in the work of salvation. He is the good shepherd, who "regaining his own, hoists the lost sheep on his shoulders to carry it back with joy to the fold of life" (*Haer.* 5.15.2).

Humans participate in God's truth through faith and reason. A canon or rule of truth was central to Hellenistic philosophy, but Irenaeus was the first Christian theologian to speak of the rule of truth or rule of faith, which is the original true and firm knowledge of God which the Church preserves. This has been handed down in succession from the Apostles (*Haer.* 3.3.2–3). Irenaeus sets out the succession for the church of Rome as an example. Other churches have a similar succession and will agree with Rome because they too hold apostolic doctrine. Irenaeus belonged to a church which had accepted a canon of four Gospels and he was the first writer to have a complete Christian Bible before him. He sought out what was clear and unambiguous in Scripture by applying the classical criteria of logic (what is true) and aesthetics (what is fitting).

Humans find beauty in the light of God's glory and participate in God's life through the breath of his Spirit. Finally, they participate in God's goodness by loving those who wrong them. God's glory shines not in supernal heights but in a living human being. From the vision of God who is light comes life. The glory of

God is thus revealed in the flesh which he first made (*Haer.* 5.3.2–3) and which bears the imprint of his fingers (*Haer.* 4.39.2).

We began our account of Irenaeus with a reference to Michelangelo's great painting. This is appropriate, for Irenaeus has been called an *homme de voir*, and visual metaphors abound. We turn to a detail of that painting to explain where Irenaeus found the centre in his ocean of imagery. The uplifted arm of Christ in judgement reveals the wound in his side. For Irenaeus the cross is central. Paul had found the summing up of the law in the command to love. Irenaeus has two extended passages of argument where he moves first from the summing up in Christ to the love command and then from the love command to the recapitulation of all things (*Haer.* 3.18–20; 4.13–16, 20). The end of each complex argument is to identify the apex of Christ's summing up with his utterance on the cross: "Father forgive them, they know not what they do." This is an unforgettable claim of Irenaeus. While few writers call for conceptual stamina as often as he does, few reward it so richly.

Note

1   G. S. Kirk, J. E. Raven, M. Schofield, *The Presocratic Philosophers* (Cambridge, 1983), p. 170.

Bibliography

John Behr, *Asceticism and Anthropology in Irenaeus and Clement of Alexandria* (Oxford, 2000).

Jacques Fantino, *La théologie d'Irénée* (Paris, 1994).

R. P. Fernandois, *El concepto de profecía en la teología de San Ireneo* (Madrid, 1999).

R. M. Grant, *Irenaeus of Lyons* (London and New York, 1997).

F. R. M. Hitchcock, *Irenaeus of Lugdunum. A Study of his Teaching* (Cambridge, 1914).

E. P. Meijering, *God, Being, History: Studies in Patristic Philosophy* (Amsterdam and Oxford, 1975).

Denis Minns, *Irenaeus* (London, 1994).

A. Orbe, *Antropología de San Ireneo* (Madrid, 1969).

Eric Osborn, "Love of Enemies and Recapitulation", *Vigiliae Christianae* 54, 1(2000), pp. 12–31.

—— *Irenaeus of Lyons* (Cambridge, 2001).

B. Sesboüé, *Tout récapituler dans le Christ, christologie et sotériologie d'Irénée de Lyons* (Paris, 2000).

G. Wingren, *Man and Incarnation. A Study in the Biblical Theology of Irenaeus* (Edinburgh, 1959).

Clement of Alexandria

Eric Osborn

Clement (probably born in Athens) came to Alexandria between 175 and 180 and left during the persecution of 202. This was a period of comparative peace for the Church. When the emperor Marcus Aurelius died in 180, his son and successor, Commodus, exercised tolerance towards Christians, despite sporadic persecutions. Septimius Severus, the next emperor, was at first tolerant towards Christians, but in 202 he issued an edict against them. Clement then left Alexandria to spend the remaining ten years of his life in Palestine.

During the second century Asia Minor had been the most creative centre of Christian thought. Rome was important for its sense of order and government, but not for ideas. Alexandria, the intellectual center of the world, constituted the third major center of Christian life and thought, and here Christians developed the rigorous study of the Bible, theology, and philosophy.

Clement came to Alexandria after travelling widely in southern Italy and Palestine, where he had learnt from different teachers (*Str.* 1.1.11.2). In Alexandria, he found his greatest teacher in Pantaenus; here he remained to study and then to teach in what has been known as a catechetical school. His three main writings, he explains (*Paed.* 1.1.1–3), follow a progressive structure of exhortation, instruction, and advanced teaching. In the well-written and powerful first work, *Exhortation to the Greeks* (*Prot.*), he exhorts pagans to turn to Christian faith. He shows an extensive knowledge of Greek literature, religion, and philosophy and calls on Greeks to come to the Logos who will give them life and a place within the structure of the divine reality.

Clement's second work, the *Instructor* (*Paed.*), is different in tone and matter. He instructs Christians in the way they should live and the virtues they should try to acquire. Morality includes all the detail of daily life. Philosophers provide assistance. Clement was not speaking to poor people but to those whose wealth brought the temptations of luxury, gluttony, and intemperance. The effects of overindulgence in food and drink are vividly portrayed. The kiss of peace was a perilous part of worship. Liturgical kissing can be noisy, insincere, and morally poisonous. Bathing must be done with propriety and not too frequently. General principles hold together the remarkable detail of moral teaching while the account of God, Father and Son, shapes the whole.

The third main work, *Miscellanies* (*Str.*), is more difficult to read and there is no agreement concerning its purpose. Clement had announced that he would produce a final, crowning work, the *Teacher* (*Didaskalos*), where he would lead his readers on to highest knowledge. Many people believe that the disordered structure of the *Stromateis* excludes the possibility that this work could be the promised *Didaskalos*. Certainly, the *Stromateis* do not resemble the handbook of Alcinous, which is his *Didaskalikos*. Yet philosophy does not fit well with handbooks. There is strong ground for finding in this work, for all its disorder, the best of all that Clement had gathered concerning philosophical and theological questions.

Clement's other works include the discourse "Who is the rich man, who is saved?," a well-constructed account of Christian use of material wealth and a good introduction to his ideas. Of special value is his *Excerpta ex Theodoto* where, in response to a Gnostic work, he sets out some striking ideas. There are fragments of lost works, such as the *Hypotyposeis*, notes which Clement wrote on the exegesis of Scripture. A copy of this work was seen two hundred years ago in Egypt at the Monastery of St. Macarius, according to the comte d'Antraigues, but it has not been seen since.

Clement, like Justin, describes the universal activity of the divine Logos and the value of Scripture as the source of prophetic signs which point to divine truth. He does not name Justin or Irenaeus as a source. In relation to Irenaeus he makes the important innovation of naming Greek philosophy as a preparation for the coming of the Gospel. Just as the law was given to the Jews, so philosophy was given to the Greeks to prepare them for the final truth in Christ. Salvation must be universal: "How could he be saviour and lord, if he be not saviour and lord of all?" says Clement (*Str.* 7.2.7.6). The divine saving power is like a magnet which draws all men; some through their own choice reach the highest point, others come lower down, while some simply fall away and do not receive salvation.

Divine Reciprocity

Behind the disorder of the *Stromateis*, Clement has a clear structure of thought. Everything that exists depends on an ultimate reciprocity of the Word, who was with God and was God. Clement learned of this reciprocity from chapter 17 and the Prologue of the Fourth Gospel. In reciprocity the Father glorified the Son that the Son might glorify the Father; the witnesses to the authority of Jesus were not one but two, for the Father confirmed the witness of the Son. Clement found a reciprocity like this in Plato, where the form of the good and the world of forms were related in similar dependence. Plato's form of the good was inaccessible apart from the world of forms, which it united and held together. Clement's saviour unites the world of saving powers. Contemporary Platonism recognised a distinction, expounded by Plato in his *Parmenides*. Unity could be simple and unique (like a pinpoint) or complex (like a spider's web). Those of Pythagorean tendency placed the different kinds of unity in a hierarchy. In Clement, however, as in Plato, there was a relation of reciprocity rather than a hierarchy. There could be no simple unity, a one-one, without a complex or universal unity, a one-all.

Clement's adoption of this pattern of thought was supported both from his understanding of Plato and from the Platonic tradition of his time, which is known as Middle Platonism. However, despite the numerous parallels between his language and that of people like Alcinous, his position was his own.

Philosophy and Faith

Clement's account of his use of philosophy is similar to that of Justin. Whatever has been "well said" is the property of Christians and the eclectic whole of these ideas is what Clement calls "philosophy." The inevitable question is: "what do Clement and Justin mean by 'well said'?" The answer would be: "whatever elucidates an obscurity or amplifies an element of Christian thought." Philosophy could help Christians to make certain distinctions. When Justin and Clement wanted to distinguish between the truth which was found in pagan authors and the truth which was to be found in Christ, they used the notion of participation or sharing; this Platonic concept allowed for different levels of participation in a universal idea. Such terms helped Christians to elucidate problems which were parallel to earlier philosophical problems. Clement owed a special debt to Philo, the Jewish Platonist of Alexandria, who lived early in the first century. Philo pioneered the way to join the Bible and Greek philosophy. Clement frequently borrowed from Philo; he either adopted a useful phrase or modified a whole passage to carry a Christian meaning. For example, when Clement took over Philo's allegorical interpretation of the vestments of the high priest, he explicitly related the allegory to the universal sovereignty of Christ.

Clement defended Christian faith against the objections of philosophers who claimed that "only believe!" was the irrational demand of Christians. Clement argued that in all philosophy there was an important place for faith, that philosophers had spoken of faith in different ways: as necessary perception, decision, anticipation, criterion, or a point of ultimate dependence. These philosophical claims, Clement argued, were taken from what Scripture said about faith. They showed that there could be no knowledge without faith and that the Greeks had seen this as clearly as the Christians. Faith was the beginning of knowledge and must advance, both logically and spiritually, by argument, by meditation, and by prayer, to become knowledge which ended in love: "Unless you believe," the prophet Isaiah (LXX 7:9) had said, "you will not understand." Faith was the beginning, knowledge the way and love the end. Faith was never superseded: no matter how great knowledge grew, it still depended on faith. Indeed there was a reciprocity between faith and knowledge, similar to that between the Father and the Son. Clement insisted: "neither is faith without knowledge nor father without son" (*Str.* 5.1.1.3).

Ethics and Knowledge

The same pattern of simple unity and complex unity, noted earlier, was to be found in Clement's account of the good life. God was the transcendent Good, and virtue was the manifold participation of humans who followed God. Clement was able to use the Platonic theme of assimilation to God (*Theaetetus* 176ab) to explain the dependence of human virtue on a unique, transcendent Good. It was easy for him to do this, because he wrongly believed, as did many others, that the Greeks had found all their ideas in the Hebrew Scriptures and stolen them for their own use.

As with faith and knowledge, so the life of virtue was marked by movement upwards towards a higher virtue, towards the final goodness of God. Here was the vision "face to face," of which Paul had spoken. Virtue and reason joined in Clement's account of Christian perfection. He spoke of the sage or true Gnostic, the man of knowledge, in contrast to the false Gnostic whose lack of vision and lack of reason disqualified him from opportunity for Christian growth. There were no ordinary Christians, for all must be pressing on to greater virtue and greater knowledge. The mediocrity which Tertullian acknowledged (*mediocritas nostra*) was always a threat to Christianity. It was this weakness which the Gnostic heresy had singled out.

Clement's use of logic is directed to the interpretation of scripture. Scripture, he said, is complex, not bald in its simplicity, and those who would understand it must divide and join its imagery and propositions so that they ascend the true dialectic of the true philosophy and finally gaze on God himself (*Str.* 1.28.177–9). Logical skill is needed to distinguish between particular and universal claims of Scripture. The failure to make this distinction is, says Clement, the source of most error. He adds to the *Stromateis* a handbook of logic, which indicates the importance which he gave to this discipline.

Just as Plato joined logic and vision in his philosophy, so Clement spoke of the vision, by which the Christian lived and grew. Christ had turned sunset into sunrise. The light of Christ cast no shadow but illumined all who received its presence. Whatever the Christian was doing, whether he was ploughing a field or sailing the sea, his prayer to God never ceased, as he silently gave thanks and drew near to God every minute of his day.

As Paul claimed in his Corinthian letters, on which Clement often draws, it is Christ himself who is true knowledge and wisdom. Clement found in these letters an antidote against heterodox perfectionism. Corinthian enthusiasts was just as keen to leave simple faith behind as were Clement's contemporaries. At no point did Clement's Christian move beyond the vision of Christ, and at no point did this vision come to an end.

In general, Clement found, in Paul and John, problems like the relations between faith and knowledge, between human virtue and divine grace, between free will and freedom, between the Word who is with God and who is God; these problems needed elucidation. His own environment demanded answers to ethical questions related to sex and marriage, right use of wealth and many details of Christian living. To all these questions Clement brought an active mind which was stored with the heritage of Greek philosophy and literature. No Christian writer of his time did more to bring Athens and Jerusalem together.

Bibliography

C. Bigg, *The Christian Platonists of Alexandria* (Oxford, 1913).

H. Chadwick, in A. H. Armstrong, *The Cambridge History of Later Greek and Early Mediaeval Philosophy* (Cambridge, 1967), pp. 137–92.

A. van den Hoek, *Clement of Alexandria and his Use of Philo in the Stromateis* (Leiden, 1988).

J. L. Kovaks, "Divine Pedagogy and the Gnostic Teacher according to Clement of Alexandria," JECS 9 (2001), pp. 3 25.

A. Le Boulluec, "Pour qui, pourquoi, comment? Les 'Stromates' de Clément d'Alexandrie," in *Patrimoines, religions du livre*, pp. 23–36.

S. R. C. Lilla, *Clement of Alexandria: A Study in Christian Platonism and Gnosticism* (Oxford, 1971).

C. Mondésert, *Clément d'Alexandrie. Introduction à l'étude de sa pensée religieuse à partir de l'Ecriture* (Paris, 1944).

E. Osborn, *The Philosophy of Clement of Alexandria* (Cambridge, 1957).

—— *The Beginning of Christian Philosophy* (Cambridge, 1981).

—— "Clement of Alexandria's Hypotyposeis: A French Eighteenth Century Sighting." *Journal of Theological Studies*, 36 (1985) (with Colin Duckworth).

—— "Clement of Alexandria, A Review of Research, 1958–1982," *The Second Century*, 3, 4, pp. 219–44.

—— "Arguments for Faith in Clement of Alexandria," *Vigiliae Christianae* 48, 1(1994), 1–24.

D. T. Runia, *Philo in Early Christian Literature: A Survey* (Leiden, 1993).

—— *Philo and the Church Fathers* (Leiden, 1995).

D. Wyrwa, *Die christliche Platonaneignung in den Stromateis des Clemens von Alexandrien* (Berlin, 1983).

Origen

Rowan Williams

Probably no single figure in the Greek-speaking Christian world had an influence comparable to that of Origen. For the three centuries after his death, it was his system that set the agenda for the most significant theological debates in the eastern Mediterranean churches, even if their conclusions were often deliberately framed to avoid his ideas. The sheer volume of his work, especially in biblical commentary, gave him a unique authority; and his skilful deployment of some of the canonical themes of late classical philosophy left a lasting mark especially upon the language of contemplative and ascetical literature. Controversy followed him in life and death, but – despite the condemnation of certain views ascribed to him in the sixth century – it proved hard simply to dismiss him overall as a heretic. Intensely revered in his lifetime by his disciples, he never became the object of an official cultus. Just as Augustine of Hippo could be called "the father of both reformations" (Catholic and Protestant), Origen could rightly be seen as the father of both sides of the great theological controversies of the fourth century, a hero equally to writers who repudiated each other's ideas with unqualified vigor.

And therein lies one of the difficulties in gaining a fair picture of Origen. Later ages read him through spectacles ground in the controversies of a later age. In reading him now, we have to keep firmly in mind the fact that he lived in an age before "general" councils had evolved to give the Church a means of settling disputes, and that his method of biblical interpretation inevitably involved speculative and idiosyncratic readings. He is himself quite clear both that speculation is legitimate (indeed, that it is an obligatory part of the intellectual maturation of Christians) and that it can only be exercised in those areas where the Church in general has not yet declared a common mind. In his nearest approach to a full statement of his system, the treatise *On First Principles*, he distinguishes carefully between those matters that are part of the *ecclesiastica praedicatio*, the official proclamation of the Church, and those that are deliberately left uncertain, so that keener minds among believers may have the chance to display their love of wisdom by exploring the deeper meaning of Scripture (*Princ.* I, praef. 3ff). It is also important to remember that he is committed to expounding his ideas primarily, if not indeed exclusively, as a reading of the Bible.

In an age when philosophy was commonly done as commentary on ancient and authoritative texts, Origen does his Christian philosophy by doing exegesis; the fact that it is a style of exegesis profoundly strange to most post-enlightenment readers should not blind us to the fact that his interpretation of the Bible establishes him in his context both as a faithful orthodox Christian and as a recognizable intellectual of the period.

The former clearly mattered to him in his maturity, though his earlier years may have been a little less "safe." Most of what we know of his life derives from the lengthy memoir written by the church historian Eusebius of Caesarea some fifty years after Origen's death, to be found in Book VI (1–39) of Eusebius's *Historia ecclesiastica*. Eusebius was a largely uncritical admirer of Origen, and is evidently concerned at several points to make it plain that his hero was at no point infected with heresy; but the text hints at quite close contacts with circles that would later be regarded as suspect. The truth is that Origen grew up in an environment where groups later identified as orthodox existed alongside others almost as substantial which taught rather different doctrines. That was the atmosphere of Alexandria in the late second century. Eusebius tells us that Origen's father was executed in 202, when the emperor Septimius Severus attempted a purge against Roman citizens prominent in public life who had converted to Christianity or were involved in instructing converts; Origen was 17 when this occurred (which establishes his year of birth as 185/6), the eldest of seven children. Since his father's estate was forfeit, he had to support the family, initially by work as a *grammatikos*, a routine instructor in language and literature. It is during these years that, Eusebius admits (*Hist. eccl.* VI, 2, 14), Origen is involved with unorthodox Christians; Eusebius insists that he never shared their views, but, given the rather chaotic state of the Alexandrian church in these years, when the bishop had fled the city, it may well be that things were less clear-cut. However, the next few years saw Origen gradually gaining stature as a specifically Christian teacher. He had a reputation for holiness and extreme simplicity of life (the legend that he castrated himself out of ascetical enthusiasm relates to this period; its historicity is highly suspect), and Eusebius reports that he was in regular danger of arrest, and spent some time being passed from one Christian "safe house" to another. Many of his pupils died as martyrs. By the time persecution was over (c.210), he was the most revered spiritual guide in the city; which did not make his relations with the now returned bishop, Demetrius, any easier.

The chronology of his life in the decades following is far from clear, and still the subject of much scholarly debate. He visited Rome at some point, and also spent time in Caesarea, where he made some important friendships, but he is likely to have been back in Alexandria by 219. The 220s were a productive decade, in which he began work on his monumental commentary on the fourth Gospel, pursued textual researches on the Bible (he learned at least some Hebrew and prepared the first really critical text of the Old Testament, the *Hexapla*), and (probably) wrote the summary of his teaching and method already mentioned, the *First Principles* (adopting a title familiar to contemporary students of philosophy from similar essays by non-Christian teachers). However, the early thirties saw the most significant upheaval of his career. He was ordained priest in Palestine by a friendly bishop of Caesarea, and this gave Demetrius an excuse for acting against him. He sent out a condemnatory circular letter and made it plain that Origen would not be welcome to continue his work in Alexandria. Origen settled in Caesarea, where he spent the rest of his life, apart from a number of journeys. He continued work on his commentaries, preached regularly (leaving an enormous corpus of sermons on most of the books of the Bible), and, between 245 and 250, completed a major work of apologetics, *Against Celsus*, replying to one of the most important critics of Christianity in the preceding century. From this period we have a full and enthusiastic account of his teaching methods by a former pupil, later to become a bishop in Asia Minor, and a brief but intriguing report of a meeting with Porphyry, the disciple of Plotinus and one of the most significant figures in the development of Neoplatonist philosophy. Porphyry was clearly baffled by the combination of intellectual sophistication and Christian piety, and lamented the waste of a good mind. In 250, the emperor Decius renewed the state persecution of Christians. Origen was imprisoned at some point and tortured; although dates and details were obviously unclear, Eusebius suggests that he was released but died shortly afterwards, in 253 or 254. He was buried in Tyre, where his grave was still being shown in the Middle Ages.

Whatever the truth about Origen's relations in his youth with heterodox groups, his mature work reflects an intellectual programme specifically designed to combat the most popular and coherent alternatives to what was to become ecclesiastical orthodoxy. The teachings of Marcion and Valentinus attracted substantial followings; and both, though in very different ways, presupposed a major schism within the whole universe, a radical alienation between the supreme God and the world. Marcion denied that the supreme God was at work in the history of the Old Testament; Valentinus held that the creation of the material world was the result of the tragic "fall" of the heavenly power Sophia, Wisdom, which overreached itself in eagerness to fathom the unfathomable mysteries of the ultimate deity. Origen's theology can be seen as a consistent and passionate attempt to defend the coherence of the universe in the providence and love of God. *First Principles* begins with a firm declaration that God is one, the same God at work in the prophets and in Jesus: "This just and good God, the Father of our Lord Jesus Christ, himself gave the law and the prophets and the gospels; he is both the God of the apostles and of the Old as well as the New Covenant" (*Princ.* I, praef. 4). Hebrew Scripture reveals the same God as Christian Scripture. But also, every aspect of Scripture reveals the same coherent universe. The need to comment upon every book of the Bible rests on the importance of showing that intellectual consistency underlies even the most diverse texts. At the beginning of the sixth book of his commentary on John, Origen explains the importance of completing the work of interpretation: it is the building of a house in which Christians can live and think in peace. It is positively dangerous not to finish off such work: people fall off the roof of a house without a properly built parapet. And this is given more acute urgency by the fact that other interpreters are at work who will be propagating different beliefs. Origen's commentary on John was stimulated by the existence of a commentary written from a Valentinian perspective by Heracleon, so that he has to counter rival readings at many points (there is a significant example at *ComJn* II.8, where he sets out to refute Heracleon's idea that, when John says that all things were made through the Word, he must mean only the inferior parts of the universe).

These considerations make sense of two of the dominant themes in practically all Origen's writing: the place of the Word, the Logos, in the universe, and the correlation between the way we read the Bible and the way we are actually constituted as human beings. It is impossible to pull these apart: to understand Origen's exegesis you also need to understand what he thought about the universe itself and the nature of humanity in particular. Certainly, the fact that the Bible was regarded by contemporary pagans as a set of texts far inferior in both style and morality to the literature of the classical world added urgency to the need for a sophisticated reading of Scripture (see, for example, *Cels.* IV); and Origen was able to appeal to the existing use of allegory in the Greek world as a way of making sense of ancient and ambiguous texts. If we assume that God is communicating with us through the text in a consistent way, and if we have good reason to think of God as both rational and loving, we cannot rest content with the surface meaning of biblical passages. But what is distinctive in Origen's thinking is the way in which the appeal to allegory is correlated with a theory of human nature itself. Biblical texts have three levels of meaning (confirmed for Origen by the Septuagint's translation of Proverbs 22:20: "Write these things down for yourself in a threefold manner"); human nature has three levels of reality. St. Paul's reference in 1 Thessalonians 5:23 to "spirit, soul and body" is picked up by Origen in the second and third chapters of book IV of *First Principles* as a summary of what should be believed about our constitution as human beings. Thus all biblical texts possess three levels of meaning corresponding to the three levels of human existence.

There is a "bodily" sense: texts deal with matters in the external world, present reality or past history. They give us an impression of situations in this world, and they may, by God's grace, give us simple good examples and instructions as to how God's providence works in the visible world – though they may also create problems and present apparent contradictions that can only be resolved by appeal to the deeper senses. There is a sense corresponding to the soul, the *psyche*, whereby we learn how to discipline our unreasoning instincts. And there is the spiritual sense, the level of *pneuma*, where the character of God's own life and its relation to the deepest structures of the universe are set out. The literal, bodily sense is accessible to all; but not everyone immediately progresses to the deeper senses. This schema evidently owes something to the distinction in Valentinian Gnosticism between the three grades of human beings, material, "psychic" (stuck at the level of routine morality) and spiritual (capable of contemplating ultimate mysteries); but Origen of course refuses any suggestion that there are fixed frontiers between these types and finds all levels in each human self. We are all summoned to develop our capacity for deeper understanding. But even if some refuse, the mercy of God allows the literal sense to give some benefit to the reader.

This theory is elaborated most fully in the fourth book of *First Principles*, though there are anticipations of it in the earlier sections; in practice, Origen's commentaries were meant to explore the spiritual sense of the texts, while his homilies, aimed at a wider audience, dealt with the "psychic," the level of the animating soul that by its habits and choices gave shape to a bodily life. Very loosely, you could say that the homilies are about moral and ascetical matters, the commentaries about the deep structures of the Christian universe. The literal sense tends to be regarded by Origen most frequently as a source of problems; he is fond of taking some unlikely text from Leviticus or some disedifying story from the historical books and challenging the Christian reader to defend a purely surface interpretation; these are God's deliberate mistakes, designed to alert us to the need to look deeper. For the modern reader, one of the paradoxes of Origen is that he both holds to a robust doctrine of biblical inspiration and completely refuses to understand this as guaranteeing the historical accuracy of the text: there may be literal errors, non-historical details or incidents, placed by God to help us recognize his call to understand more fully. This was one area in which his work attracted unfavorable comment in his own lifetime, and it remained a controversial issue, especially in regard to his dismissal of a literal historical ground for the narratives of creation and fall in Genesis.

Indeed, it is his version of creation that grounds the theory of human nature and the corresponding method of exegesis; and this was in some ways the most contentious of all his beliefs for centuries. God is himself wholly unlike any kind of bodily substance; thus it is rational that his first creation is incorporeal, a world of reasoning spirits. But reason entails freedom; and, for anything less than God, freedom entails a choice between the possibilities of good and evil (*Princ.* I.7.5 and elsewhere). There is no element in us that prompts or compels us to evil (a point clearly made in *Princ.* IV.3), only the presence of free will in our spirits. The fall is when these created free spirits become weary of contemplating their origin in the Father's perfection; in turning away from God, they condemn themselves to frustration and irrationality (*Princ.* II.8 ii, the Greek text), so God steps in to limit the damage. He clothes the fallen spirits with bodies, so that they may develop their spiritual capacities once more through the challenge of overcoming bodily instinct: the world of human bodies is a kind of gymnasium for spirits that have become lazy (*Princ.* I, 4 and 5; and the whole of III on free will). And once again, we can see how Origen contests the worldview of his Gnostic adversaries: the material world is not the result of either a rebellion or a mistake; it is the providential gift of a good and just God, who does not want to see his beloved creation ruined. At every stage, the governing principle of a *coherent* universe is being defended. The same impulse is no doubt behind Origen's suggestion that different kinds of material life correspond to different levels of spiritual maturity or integration; heavenly bodies (the stars) represent a higher spiritual purity than terrestrial ones. And this is connected with the idea, touched on here and there by Origen, but never systematically expounded, that our spiritual attainment in this life determines the next stage of our journey to God in a different kind of body. This is not "reincarnation" in any easily recognizable sense, since the spirit is certainly not recycled within the material order with which our senses are familiar; nor does it reappear in another human body. The point seems to be that each new level of spiritual mastery over the body is accompanied by a new material environment for it to work in and grow through (*Princ.* II.11.6, *HomNum* 27).

What worried Origen's critics in his lifetime and later was the implied separation between the spirit, the "essential" in the human constitution, and the particular body actually functioning on earth. Although Origen is clear about the goodness of the material order as made by God, he tends to regard any specific aspect of the material world as simply instrumental to spiritual growth and thus dispensable. What then happens to the biblical doctrine of the Resurrection of the Body? Origen is aware of the complexities and seems a little unsure of how to reconcile this quite satisfactorily with his scheme (e.g. *Cels.* VII.32); but he does seem to be clear that, as there is no absolutely incorporeal reality but God (*Princ.* II.2.2), all spirits must have *some* kind of embodiment in their future life. His problem – from the point of view of majority orthodoxy – lay in the implication that the present body might be discarded completely in favour of a more ethereal vehicle, more transparent to the spiritual glory within. But for Origen the true identity of each subject is its spiritual core; and while it may always need a body in order to be distinguishable from other spirits, it cannot be assumed that it always needs the same body.

It is by no means a fully consistent picture, but it shows Origen's concern both to hold on to the central elements in biblical thought as received by the orthodoxy of his day and also to work out a metaphysically serious framework for such belief. It is the one area of his thinking where signs of embarrassment appear: in the verbatim transcript of a discussion with a synod of Arabian bishops, the *Dialogue with Heraclides* (unknown to scholars until its discovery in 1941 in Egypt), Origen, addressing a not wholly sympathetic audience, is careful to distinguish his position from a straight-forward assertion of the immortality of the soul. But it is no simple matter, for him or his modern readers, to establish this with clarity.

One significant aspect of his treatment of this topic is the admission that there is no real diversity without some sort of materiality (*Princ.* II.1.4). Since God alone is completely beyond multiplicity, the implication would seem to be that even the pre-existent spirits created by God prior to the material world as we know it were endowed with some kind of "bodies"; but it is difficult to find this plainly stated. It corresponds to the belief of Plotinus that there is an element of passivity even in the intellectual world: the intelligible forms of things are eternally active in some sense, and so must have something to act on. There must be an eternal "matter," though it is quite unlike what we mean by matter in the world of the senses. If Origen is difficult here, he shares the problem with the foremost mind of his age.

But it is a reinforcement of the insistence that even the pre-existent spirits are contingent. They do not, Origen believes, have a beginning in time: since God is always creator, there must be an eternal creation (*Princ.* I.4.3). Origen's critics argued that this was to place alongside God a second "first principle" or first cause. But he himself is clear enough about the difference between the eternal exercise of God's power to create what is other than God or less than God and – on the one hand – the shaping of the world as we know it (*Princ.* I.4.5, *ComJn* XIX.22), and – on the other – the natural "outflowing" of the eternal Word from God. But here is another area in which Origen's teaching provoked confusion and hostility in later periods. The Word, the Logos, which is God's everlasting expression of his rationality, is never separable from God the Father; but its status as expression or emanation means that it is somehow less than the Father, who alone is *autotheos*, "God as such", or *ho theos*, "the one who is God" (*ComJn* II.2) – distinctions which owe something to the work of the Alexandrian Jewish philosopher of the first century CE, Philo, who clearly influenced Origen in many ways. From the perspective of the fourth century, this looked very suspicious. But it makes excellent sense in the context of Origen's carefully graded universe. As the very full discussion in the first two books of the

Commentary on John explain, the Logos is the ground and beginning of the world of plurality, containing within itself all the diverse possibilities creation might realize. All the created spirits, *noes*, are activated by the Logos and participate in the Logos's activity of contemplating the Father. The Logos is on the very boundary between divine simplicity and created plurality, capable of being described under a number of diverse conceptual and metaphorical terms (*epinoiai*), but holding all the potential diversity of creation together by directing it to the unity of the Father in praise and contemplation.

In virtue of that ceaseless and undistracted contemplation, the Logos can be said to share in the nature of God the Father as no other being can (*ComJn* I.27, 34, II.2, *Princ.* II.2.2). The Logos can be called a "second God", just as in Philo and some Hellenistic philosophers (*ComJn* VI.39, *Cels.* V.39). But it is misleading, in Origen's eyes, to say that the Logos derives from the *ousia*, the substance, of the Father, as that might imply that the divine life of the Father was capable of being divided or diminished: the Logos must have an *ousia* of its own (e.g. *ComJn* XX.18, 20, 24), must be a *hupostasis* in its own right (*Cels.* VIII.12). The point Origen is making is clear enough: the Logos is neither an impersonal aspect of the divine life (it is an active agent, loving and gazing at the Father), nor a split-off portion of divinity. However, the language of *ousia* and *hupostasis* is still conceptually untidy in many respects, and does not receive decisive clarification until the debates of the following century; Origen's vocabulary seemed highly problematic to fourth-century readers, and reinforced suspicions against his orthodoxy. He certainly seems to deny that *homoousios*, "of the same substance," is an appropriate word to use for the relation between the Father and anything else (*ComJn* XIII.25). Yet a fragment from his lost commentary on Hebrews suggests that the Logos may be called *homoousios* in the sense that light from a flame or steam from water might be thought of as sharing the "substance" of the originating reality.

Whatever the exact nuance of his terminology, what is clear is that the Logos is eternally a partner with God the Father (God is always what he is, so if he is essentially Father, he must have an eternal Son: *Princ.* I.1.9, 2.3, 4.4), and enjoys a relation with the Father quite unlike that of any other being. The Logos is unlike the Father in the sense that it or he is "originated" (*genetos*), a reality brought into being by the initiative of another. As we have noted, there cannot be two "first principles" in the universe. From one point of view, the gap between Logos and Father is greater than that between Logos and creation (*ComJn* XIII.25). From another point of view, however, we could say the exact opposite (*ComMt* XV.10, *Cels.* V.11) – and this latter perspective seems to be what Origen prefers to stress in his later works. Likewise, for certain purposes you can call the Logos a "created being" (*Princ.* IV.4.1, though this is a textually difficult passage; cf. *Cels.* V.37) in the sense that it is produced by God's act; but it would be wrong to conclude that Origen saw the Logos as in any way simply a member of the class of created beings, since it is only through the Logos that anything else exists and relates to the Father.

This theology of the Logos combines with Origen's general view of creation and the soul to produce a highly distinctive and innovative doctrine of the incarnation, elaborated most fully in *First Principles* II.6. The pre-existent spirits first made by God are, as we have seen, liable to change and decline according to their own free will; but one of these spirits never falls away from union with the contemplative activity of the Logos. It is one with the Logos as iron is one with the fire in which it is heated; it is "one spirit" with the Logos (cf. 1 Cor. 6:17). Thus it is possible for this spirit and this spirit alone to descend into the material world not because of its decline from primitive purity but because of its identification with the rational and loving purpose of God. When God seeks to restore fallen humanity, he does so by allowing this spirit which is perfectly united with the Logos to take on flesh. Because of its unique relation to the flesh, it is not subject to the earthbound and self-centred desires and habits that imprison our spirits and which require lifelong ascetic monitoring. It demonstrates for us that by God's gift we can be made capable of overcoming fleshly instinct; it reveals to us our true nature as spirit and rekindles the spirit's urge for reason and contemplation. Although Origen occasionally uses the language of sacrifice for the effects of Christ's death, he generally means no more than that Christ's life and death are a perfect self-gift to the Father rather than a literal propitiation for sin (this is dealt with in the *Commentary on Romans* III).[1]

Sacramental life in the Church is seen by Origen mostly in terms of inner maturation symbolized by the outward activities of the sacraments, rather than some sort of objective efficacy in the acts themselves. More significant is the life of personal prayer, to which Origen devoted an important treatise, *On Prayer*, in which he combines practical advice (pray three times daily, turn eastwards, retire to a quiet place) with theological analysis: he discourages prayer directly to the Logos or to Christ, since the logic of prayer is that we stand *with* the Logos addressing the Father. Once again, this was misunderstood in later ages as an attempt to play down the full divinity of Christ. Interestingly, this treatise is one of the few places in Origen's vast output where he finds a clearly intelligible role for the Holy Spirit. Always formally Trinitarian, his interest is really in the pattern of mediation by the Logos between God and universe, and the Spirit's place in such a scheme is hard to clarify; but when he turns to discuss prayer, it is evident. The Spirit is the gift by which we recognize Jesus' lordship and are enabled to call God "Father." Origen's account of spiritual maturation also provides another variation on the threefold structure of human existence: in the introduction to his *Commentary on the Song of Songs*, he distinguishes between moral development, rational perception of divine wisdom through the rational order of the universe, and direct contact with the mystery of God. To these correspond the three books under Solomon's name in the Bible – Proverbs (for morality), Ecclesiastes (for rational wisdom) and the Song of Songs (for ecstatic, loving contemplation). Origen's views in this area had immense influence in all later accounts of mystical contemplation, and he is the first serious "mystical" commentator on the Song.

It should be clear from this rapid overview that Origen's theology, despite its ambitions of providing a comprehensive and coherent reading of the Bible, fit to stand with a conviction about the rational unity or harmony of the universe, fell short in some areas of consistency or systematic thoroughness. Its loose ends inevitably created problems in a more doctrinally exact and anxious age. Origen's speculations about the possible salvation of all reasoning beings, including Satan, caused difficulties during his life; and within fifty years of his death there was sharp controversy over many of his other teachings. The formidable theologian Methodius of Olympus (from Asia

Minor) attacked several features of Origen's thought in the early years of the fourth century, criticizing aspects of his allegorical exegesis, his unclarities (as Methodius saw it) over free will and his doctrine of an eternal creation. Various elements in his theology of the Logos and the Incarnation, as well as allegory and doubtful eschatology, were challenged by bishops and teachers from Syria and Asia Minor during the years of the persecution of Diocletian, when Christians from diverse churches were thrown together in imprisonment; and this prompted the composition by Eusebius of Caesarea, Origen's biographer, in collaboration with his own teacher, Pamphilus, of a *Defence of Origen* (*Apologia pro Origene*). This survives only in part, and in a Latin translation which regularly misunderstands the concerns of the original compilers but remains a useful source. Lists of charges against Origen were to reappear regularly in the fourth century, and the end of that century saw a bitter and violent controversy breaking out between supporters and critics of his teaching in the monastic communities of Egypt. Theologians and hierarchs from elsewhere were drawn in, and the controversy poisoned relations between whole provinces for decades. The debate over Pelagius' teaching in the Latin-speaking world early in the fifth century was in part shaped by anxieties connected with "Origenism." The sixth century saw formal condemnations of views ascribed to Origen, under the direction of the emperor Justinian and his ecclesiastical allies. Relatively few were able to appreciate Origen's tentativeness in putting forward speculations in areas as yet undefined or underdefined, or to appreciate how he is willing to shift emphasis and even conceptual structure according to the context of his arguments: Athanasius of Alexandria calls Origen *philoponos*, "painstaking" or "devoted to work," suggesting some recognition of this flexibility and of the need to read him with careful attention. Not many others shared this sensitivity.

Yet, as we have already observed, the language of Greek Christian spirituality was heavily marked by his influence. The threefold analysis of the human constitution and the corresponding threefold pattern of spiritual maturation are assumed by many leading spiritual writers of the centuries that followed. They were given a new precision at the end of the fourth century by Origen's greatest disciple, Evagrius of Pontus; and he was building upon the use of Origen's ideas in some of the work of the Cappadocian Fathers (Basil of Caesarea and Gregory of Nazianzus had collaborated in producing an anthology of Origen's teaching on the spiritual life under the title of *Philokalia*, "The love of the good [or beautiful]"). Despite condemnations of "Origenism," which meant that many of Evagrius' works survived only under the names of other authors or in translations into languages other than Greek, a good deal of the general structure of his account of the nature and destiny of the created spirit survived in the eastern Christian world. Even where it was not uncritically accepted, it provided the framework for discussion. And the continuing importance of the allegorical method in both eastern and western Christendom can hardly be overestimated.

Origen is a writer very much of his time in his attitude to texts, to the nature of the divine and to the relation of the world of sense to the world of understanding. We know from the account of his teaching by his pupil Gregory how Origen led his pupils through the study of the natural world and the exploration of the nature of good actions towards *theologia*, the study of the nature of God as the philosophers and poets had described it; he encouraged them to roam around in the literature of several contemporary philosophical schools (avoiding only the "atheistic" Epicureans), and we can gather from Porphyry's account of Origen that he was familiar with the main Platonic writers of the second century, including Numenius and Longinus, as well as some Stoics. Certainly, Platonism and Stoicism are the main intellectual influences visible in Origen's work. The characteristic problems of the period – how to understand the relation between "passion" (non-rational impulse or force) and virtue, how to explain the transition from divine unity to the multiplicity of things in the material world – are clearly high on Origen's agenda. He is concerned to define a distinctively Christian response to the questions exercising the educated public of his day.

Yet reading Origen leaves you with surprisingly little sense of someone collating the opinions of others. When all is said and done, he seems strikingly independent of "influences," for all that he is undoubtedly participating in a real contemporary intellectual conversation. You can understand something of Porphyry's puzzlement. Even earlier Christian writers do not figure conspicuously in the background: Clement of Alexandria, the most important local teacher of the generation immediately senior to Origen, is never mentioned and probably never even alluded to. There are obviously points of contact, notably in a common debt to Philo and to Stoic ethics, but nothing in Clement really compares with the complex interweaving in Origen's work of cosmology and anthropology.

And the explanation is in large part given by what Gregory says about the final stages of Origen's pedagogy. When all the general work on physics and ethics had been done, and when current concepts of God had been explored, Origen introduced his students to the spiritual reading of the Bible, the deciphering of which revealed a system of signs which laid out for the believer the consistency of God's character and action. It sounds rather eccentric to call Origen a "narrative theologian," but that is in an important sense what he was. His concern is to trace as fully as possible the *process* of the universe's history as Scripture puts it before us (Scripture read, of course, with his allegorical perspective, not simply as the record of earthly events), and to locate the human vocation and potential within that process. Thus there is no real gap between theology, ethics, spirituality, and exegesis; there is simply one seamless activity of reflection on who and what we are in a universe existing because of the loving act of a God who first invites the eternal Logos to share his life in contemplation, then extends that invitation to all the rational spirits whose existence the Logos makes possible, then provides, in the creation of a material world, for corrupted spirits to make their way back to their true calling, and reveals in the material world how that world may be subjected to the energy of undistracted spirit, through the Incarnation of the one faithful spirit that is eternally united with the Logos. And within all this, Origen can speak of our hoped-for union with the Logos not only in "intellectualist" terms, but with a personal fervour which makes it clear that he saw intellect itself as the supreme form of love set free from "passion." We may raise an eyebrow at his description of the joys of heaven in terms of an eternal *schola*, a lecture-room; but this is a lecture-room in which the students are oblivious to themselves in the exhilaration of a discovery of unfailing generosity, patience, and beauty.

Note

1   Ed. C. P. Hammond Bammel (Freiburg in Breisgau, 1990–8), 3 vols.

Bibliography

Henri Crouzel, *Origen* (Edinburgh and San Francisco, 1989); probably the best general introduction.

Jean Daniélou, *Origen* (London and New York, 1955); valuable on the wider intellectual background.

R. P. C. Hanson, *Allegory and Event* (London, 1959); a comprehensive but unsympathetic study of Origen's exegesis.

Nicholas de Lange, *Origen and the Jews* (Cambridge, 1976).

J. W. Trigg, *Origen: The Bible and Philosophy in the Third-Century Church* (London and Atlanta, 1983); a helpful guide to Origen's practice as an exegete, but somewhat uncritical in its adoption of Pierre Nautin's radical proposals about the chronology of Origen's life and other matters.

Karen J. Torjesen, *Hermeneutical Procedure and Theological Method in Origen's Exegesis* (Berlin, 1986).

B. F. Westcott, "Origenes," in the *Dictionary of Christian Biography* (London, 1887), vol. 4, pp. 96–142; still one of the finest surveys of all aspects of Origen's life and work, though overtaken by modern discoveries in some areas.

There is a larger selective bibliography of books and articles at the end of R. Williams, "Origenes/Origenismus," in the *Theologische Realenzyklopadie*, vol. 25 (1995), pp. 397–420.

Tertullian

Eric Osborn

To move from Clement to Tertullian is to move from east to west, from Greece to Rome, from Greek to Latin. Tertullian lived (160–225) in Carthage, the foremost city of Roman Africa, where Hadrian (117–38) had built a great aqueduct and Antoninus Pius (138–61) had rebuilt the forum. We know almost nothing of his life (claims that he was a lawyer and son of a centurion have been disproved); but 31 works, written in his own lively Latin, have survived. Earlier ideas of Irenaeus and Clement are evident: the universal good God and his saving plan, the perfection of all things in Christ, and the call for all to share in salvation. When Christ follows the way of human life to the end on the cross, all is summed up, for the end has been joined to the beginning and he can say, "It is finished." For Tertullian, "Just as Alpha rolls on to Omega and then Omega rolls back to Alpha, so he might show in himself the way from the beginning to the end, and the way from the end to the beginning" (*Mon.* 5.2).

Tertullian is a lively and verbal Christian, skilled in rhetoric, who believed that the mind could only function in a warm climate and that it grew torpid in the frozen North. He enjoyed invective. Marcion of Pontus, who came to Rome about 140 and died in 154, had claimed that Christ could not have had a human body. Tertullian responded that it was possible to imagine a man without heart or brain, like Marcion, but that it was impossible to think of a man who had no body. For many the rigor of his argument and the sharpness of his wit are too violent and conceal his creativity, a creativity which anticipated later formulations concerning the person of Christ and the Trinity.

Tertullian needs to be read several times to appreciate a series of aspects of his writing. A first reading is impressive for the vigor of his language and imagery. He regrets that he is "always sick with the fevers of impatience" (*Pat.* 1). Yet there is subtlety everywhere, and overstatement is rare. After expounding, with sympathy, the barbarous biblical theology of the Deuteronomist (God always rewards good and punishes evil) (*Marc.* 2.14.1) he tells how God took on himself the suffering due for human salvation: "God himself died" (*Marc.* 2.16.3). After recounting the disadvantages of matrimony, he tells his wife that no second marriage could regain the happiness they had known, for the angels in heaven alone can tell of the blessedness of husband and wife who share in prayer and service to God (*Ux.* 2.8.6–9). When arguing for the resurrection of the body, he insists that humanity does not have to fit into the end of things, but the end of things has to fit around humanity (*Res.* 59). His images hold his thought together: God sits as judge over earthly judges; the Christian fights for Christus Victor; the heavenly city looms over earth. We could call him the "laughing Stoic" were it not that he rejected philosophical labels for any form of Christian faith.

Reason and Paradox

Like all who bridge diverse cultures and invent new vocabularies, Tertullian is best understood by those who follow his arguments. Failure to do this has produced two common misconceptions: first that he rejected Greek culture and philosophy; and, secondly, that he was an irrational fideist.

Some Christians rejected philosophy, in obedience to Paul (Col. 2:8). They saw philosophy as the source of heresy. Tertullian prefers to follow the claim of the kerygma that all is fulfilled and perfected in Christ. What indeed, he asks, has Athens to do with Jerusalem? What concord is there between the Academy and the Church? What common ground between heretics and Christians? "Let them beware who put forward a Stoic, Platonic, dialectical form of Christianity. For us there is no need of curiosity after Christ, no need of inquiry after the gospel. When we have believed we have no desire to add to our faith. For this is our primary faith that there is nothing further which we ought to believe" (*Praescr.* 7.11–13). Tertullian claims that there is no place for curiosity *after* Christ or for inquiry *after* the gospel, because the perfection of Christ cannot be surpassed. Like Justin, who saw seeds of Logos in others, Tertullian believed that the whole Logos had come in Christ. He encouraged philosophers to move on to the "better philosophy" in Christ. To suggest that anything should be added to Christ was to deny the finality of the gospel. To improve on the gospel was to deny it, for the rule of faith (*Praescr.* 13) declared that all is perfected in Christ. Earlier ideas may be used to explain but never to modify the gospel.

A second misconception concerning Tertullian arises from his claim that the incarnation is "credible because inept (inappropriate, unfitting)" (*Carn.* 5). Here he is arguing against a Marcionite claim that Christ, as God, could not have had a real human body. Tertullian explains that, because God is wholly other, differing from man and all else, then, if he is joined to man in a way which is not shameful, inappropriate, and impossible, it would follow that either God is no longer God or man is no longer man. When God is joined to man in a way which is shameful, inappropriate, and impossible, then God is credibly God and man is credibly man. The inept is theologically the most apt. This is a paradox because, in other cases, what is inappropriate is false. This treatment of the paradoxes and opposites of faith is typical of Tertullian's use of reason in argument, which needs to be carefully followed and rehearsed.

A favourite word for Tertullian was *ratio* or reason. He uses reason to defend the rule of faith against those who would oppose it. There is nothing mechanical about his thinking. He treats different opponents with different methods. Hermogenes, a thoughtful dualist, is met with careful exposition and argument; Valentinians, who deal in stories and visions, are ridiculed. The difference is of great importance. Hermogenes presented argument; Valentinians offered myth. Tertullian responds to this difference, with argument for one and satire for the other. His final work on the philosopher's *pallium* shows a respect for philosophy: "Lower your eyes and revere the philosopher's gown which attests that its wearer has renounced error" (*Pall.* 4). The detachment of the philosopher points to the rational responsibility of each person who enters and leaves the world alone (*Pall.* 4). Neglected in the Middle Ages, Tertullian returned to great favour among Renaissance humanists, only to lose favour in the nineteenth and twentieth centuries.

Goodness and Justice

Tertullian's largest work, *Against Marcion*, was directed against Marcion's argument that there were two Gods, one the Just Creator and the other the Good Redeemer. God, said Tertullian, is the supreme Greatness, supreme in form, reason, strength, and power, who made one world, with man at its centre: "God is not, if he be not one" (*Marc.* 1.3.1). Where Marcion saw God the Creator as a limited being and ridiculed the insects he had made, Tertullian observed that Marcion himself could not imitate the skills of bee, ant, spider, silkworm or any other of God's tiny creatures. All things come from God, who produces opposites. He makes things corporeal and incorporeal, animate and inanimate, vocal and silent, mobile and static, productive and sterile, dry and wet, hot and cold (*Marc.* 1.16). Tertullian enjoyed the beauty and harmony of creation.

In order to save mankind, God endured human limits and the humiliation of the cross: "In fact the whole of what you find disgraceful in my God is the sacrament of man's salvation." While Marcion demands goodness from God, he despises these ultimate acts of divine kindness (*Marc.* 2.27.7ff.). Tertullian shows that all the contradictions or antitheses that Marcion cannot accept are capable of rational solution and can be united in one God: "the two attributes of goodness and justice together make up the proper fullness of the divine omnipotent being" (*Marc.* 2.29.1).

Trinity and Incarnation

Where Marcion divided God into two, Praxeas denied any distinction between Father and Son and merged God into one identity. Tertullian responded with an account of Trinity, which eventually won total Christian acceptance: "God so willed . . . to be believed as one in a new way, through the son and spirit" (*Prax.* 31). The three are one in quality, substance, and power, but distinct in sequence, aspect, and manifestation (*Prax.* 2.4).

Tertullian's chief argument, which reappears later in Augustine, uses the Stoic genre of "relative disposition" which arises out of the distinction between "sweet and bitter" on the one hand and "father and son" on the other. "Sweet and bitter" point to intrinsic qualities which are also related in a certain disposition to one another. "Father and son" do not point to intrinsic qualities but only to a disposition. When a son dies, the father may cease, *without any internal change*, to be a father. Tertullian thus argues that father and son have their existence in their disposition alone; therefore, when that disposition is denied, they cease to be. Father and son are no more identical than day and night. Neither can be both. A father makes a son and a son makes a father. Since Praxeas makes father identical with son, and son identical with father, both father and son no longer exist (*Prax.* 10). God is three persons and one substance. The tension between the three and the one points to relative disposition or substantial relation. God is one God; but father and son are mutually necessary to each other, and never identical. Identity would destroy them; their difference is the ground of their unity.

Equally important for Tertullian was the distinction between spirit and flesh, between God and man in Christ. Stoics distinguished three different types of mixture: in the first, things were simply placed beside one another; in the second, they both disappeared into a third substance; in the third there was a total blending, "when certain substances and their qualities are mutually coextended through and through, with the original substances and their qualities being preserved in such a mixture."[1] The persistence of the blended constituents was proved from the fact that they could be separated artificially: an oiled sponge, when placed in a blend of water and wine, would absorb water and leave the wine.[2] Tertullian insisted that in Jesus, spirit remains spirit and flesh remains flesh. God remains God and man remains man: "We see a twofold state, not confused but joined in one person, God and man, Jesus" (*Prax.* 27). There are two substances, twofold quality, two natures, which interpenetrate in "total blending."

Cohesion of Opposites

Tertullian finds a different duplicity in mankind when he develops a doctrine of original sin. Mankind's likeness to God was lost by Adam's sin and restored by grace (*Bapt.* 5.7). Human effort is inadequate, for all mankind, sprung from the seed of Adam, is infected by his sin (*Test.* 3.2). Adam knew what he was doing and chose freely; since his fall, sin has acquired natural status and compulsive force (*An.* 16.1). Corruption is passed on from every parent to every child. Tertullian's views of human history, therefore, like those of Irenaeus, are catastrophic as well as evolutionary and dialectic.

In his ethics, Tertullian joins final apocalypse to natural law with characteristic cohesion of opposites. The beginning in creation is joined to the end in the paraclete, who brings no strange novelties but testifies to Christ "with the whole order of God the creator" (*Mon.* 2.4). As *restitutor* rather than *institutor*, the paraclete restores mankind to its ancient beginning (*Mon.* 4.2). Moreover, Christ, who is both Alpha and Omega, brings humankind back to paradise (*Mon.* 5.3).

His general defence of Christianity follows another dialectic. In his *Apologeticum* (*Ap.* 48) he explains that the world is governed by the strife of opposites – of light with darkness, of good with evil. Within this conflict, justice or reason must balance all things, suppress evil, and encourage good. Tertullian's first claim is that the persecution of Christians destroys this harmony and undermines the moral structure of the world. Governors execute Christians to gain popularity with the mob; yet the Christians thrive: "we spring up in greater numbers the more we are mown down by you; the blood of Christians is seed" (*Ap.* 50.13). God's plan of salvation or economy runs unbroken from creation to the man Jesus, the seed of the martyrs, and the final judgement. The cross persists in those who are tortured and afflicted. Out of their suffering, salvation is proclaimed and out of their seed the Gospel grows.

Naturally Christian

Tertullian's second main claim in the *Apologeticum* is that Christian faith is a recognition of the God who is universally known. God may be proved from his works, by which we are preserved, and from the testimony of the soul which is naturally Christian (*Ap.* 17.4ff.). The invisible God may be seen, the incomprehensible may be known by grace. He may be found by all except those who "refuse to *recognize* him, of whom they cannot be ignorant" (*Ap.* 17.3). The soul names God: "Good God! Great God! . . . O testimony of the soul which is naturally Christian!" (*Ap.* 17.6). Faith is not merely the substance of things hoped for but the recollection of things past: "What is our sin, I ask you, if we believe the future also, as we have already learned through two stages to believe it (*Ap.* 20.5)?" Natural order and prophecy have already provided a past and present knowledge of God. Faith is the recognition of this knowledge and welcomes God as one already known. The soul is naturally Christian (*Ap.* 17.6), yet Christians are made rather than born (*Ap.* 18.4). In another work, he claims that prayer is natural. Birds spread their wings in the form of the cross and make a prayerful noise. When cattle rise from rest they lift their heads to heaven and bellow (*Orat.* 29). ("Hush, hush, whisper who dares? Ferdinand the Bull is saying his prayers!")

Church and Prophecy

His sense of order in the natural world was matched by a recognition of church order. Yet, although he enunciated a doctrine of threefold ministry and apostolic succession, Tertullian was highly critical of bishops and the "sordid church." He was deeply influenced by the "new prophecy" which began in Phrygia with Montanus. Jerome and others named him as a Montanist but he knew nothing of the extravagances of the movement. Austerity marks all his writings: "We would have arisen as prophets to ourselves" (*Iei.* 12). Of his 31 writings which survive, 8, written after 213, display the stringency of the "new prophecy." He was not disowned by the Church which he criticized from within. Cyprian, the pillar of church order and right belief, claimed him as "master" and read him daily. Yet there is a marked severity in some of his later writings where he sets himself against the practice of other Christians who are "animal" rather than "spiritual." In *Scorpiace* 10–11 and *On Flight* 5, he declares that it is wrong to avoid martyrdom: the Bible offers no compromise with idolatry and total love of God requires a readiness to die for him. Flight in persecution was a temporary expedient and against the general principle. In *Monogamy* 9, second marriages are seen as adultery. Celibacy, as Paul said, is preferable to marriage. In *Fasting* Tertullian defends the stricter practices of Montanists against the moderation of others. God does not welcome fat Christians but the lions and the bears will (*Iei.* 17.9). In his later work *On Modesty* Tertullian is more opposed to the remission of sins than in his earlier work, *On Penitence*. Sins against man may be remitted but not sins against God. Those guilty of sexual sins have defiled the body, which is the temple of God, and cannot be absolved. Nor can confessors grant letters of indulgence, for martyrs expiate their own sins and only God can expiate the sins of others. Apostates who have failed under persecution have a much stronger claim to absolution than fornicators.

Resurrection

Tertullian's final set of opposites is the end which is a new beginning. Jean Daniélou claimed that Tertullian's treatise on the resurrection of the flesh (natural physical body) was his masterpiece and strikingly relevant for today. God who made the body will find it easier to remake it (*Res.* 11.10). The cycle of the world includes making and remaking, day and night, light and darkness, life and death which again revolves to life (*Res.* 12.2). Creation by God proves the goodness of the flesh, which is the "hinge" on which salvation turns (*caro salutis est cardo*) (*Res.* 8.2). The same flesh in which we have sinned and in which we struggle, that same flesh will behold God's salvation or damnation (*Res.* 59.3). Do we doubt God's power to renew? We have seen ships, whose structure had been battered by storms, later remade so that they could venture out as before (*Res.* 60f.). Our renewal and perfection depend on the uniting of flesh to spirit, which union the two natures of Christ already declare (*Res.* 63.1ff.).

> In a flash, at a trumpet crash,
> I am all at once what Christ is, since he is what I am, and
> This Jack, joke, poor potsherd, patch, matchwood, immortal diamond,
> Is immortal diamond.[3]

General Conclusion

The four main Christian writers of the second century offer a richness and vitality which invite exploration. What are their strengths and weaknesses? Justin's strength is his intellectual passion, his love of truth, while his weakness is the lack of precision in his ideas. The strength of Irenaeus is the majestic clarity of his four main concepts (divine intellect, divine economy, recapitulation, participation); his limitations are the disorder of his multiple sources and the exuberance of his argument. Clement's strength is his variability and his philosophical awareness of problems; his weakness is the disorder of the *Stromateis* which makes heavy demands on his readers. Finally,

Tertullian has the virtue of dividing his opponents and demolishing them in turn; his weakness is a lack of moderation. If, as Clement claims, audacity and wisdom are the intellectual virtues, Tertullian has plenty of both but not enough patience.

Notes

1 Alexander of Aphrodisias, *On mixture* 216, 14–218, 6 (H. von Arnim, *Stoicorum veterum fragmenta* (Leipzig, 1903), 2.473; Long and Sedley, 48C).

2 Stobaeus, *Eclogues*, 1.155,5–11 (von Arnim, 2.471; Long and Sedley, 48D).

3 "That Nature is a Heraclitean Fire and of the Comfort of the Resurrection" in Gerard Manley Hopkins, *A Selection*, ed. W. H. Gardner (London, 1953), p. 66.

Bibliography

J. Daniélou, *The Origins of Latin Christianity* (London, 1977).

J. C. Fredouille, *Tertullien et la conversion de la culture antique* (Paris, 1972).

A. A. Long and D. N. Sedley, *The Hellenistic Philosophers*, 1 (Cambridge, 1987).

C. Munier, *L'apologie de Saint Justin philosophe et martyr* (Fribourg, 1994).

—— *Petite vie de Tertullien* (Paris, 1996).

Eric Osborn, *Tertullian, First Theologian of the West* (Cambridge, 1997).

G. Prestige, *God in Patristic Thought* (London, 1936).

David Rankin, *Tertullian and the Church* (Cambridge, 1995).

M. Spanneut, *Tertullien et les premiers moralistes africains* (Gembloux, 1969).

A. Viciano, *Cristo salvador y liberador del hombre* (Pamplona, 1986).

The Hermetica

G. R. Evans

It is not easy to reconstruct the process of the Christianizing of Egypt. There is almost no evidence dating from before the end of the second century when there was already an active Church and a catechetical school in Alexandria.[1] Even that seems to have been precarious. Dionysius of Alexandria describes a grim scene of diminishing population and local warfare in the Alexandria of the 260s AD.[2]

Within this uncertain and patchily "Christian" environment there came to birth around the third century AD, a cult or sect known as "hermetic," after the Greek name (Hermes) for the Egyptian god Thoth.[3] "Hermetic" writings survive in the form of short reports or teachings, on topics which were of peculiar interest to adherents.[4] These *Hermetica* manifestly have strong Egyptian associations; among the "Egyptians" named in the various reports of dialogues and conversations on this distinctive concatenation of teachings are Tat and Ammon. Clement of Alexandria, writing of course in Egypt, refers to 42 books of Hermes.[5] There are references to the existence of a considerable corpus, reaching far beyond this figure, which is striking enough in itself. Iamblichus attributes to "Hermes" the collecting together of 20,000 books.[6] Others credited him with amassing 36,555 books. Even if these improbable figures were once correct, relatively few items now survive. Among them are 87 orphic hymns,[7] and a number of writings we shall touch on in more detail in a moment. The modern editor of the medieval *Book of the Twenty-Four Philosophers* regards this latter-day "hermetic" work as a rendering of a Hellenistic Greek original.[8] The astrological *De triginta sex decanis* also seems to be a medieval Latin survival of a much earlier hermetic text,[9] as may be the Arabo-Latin texts of astrology and divination also recently edited.[10]

It is not a straightforward matter to say how Christian beliefs and hermetic teachings were understood at the time to be related to one another. We find ourselves deep in a process of what modern missionary theology would call "inculturation," in which the trick for the would-be Christian faithful was to avoid syncretism. Didymus the Blind (c.313–98), head of the catechetical school in Alexandria in the late fourth century, attempted to treat the *Hermetica*, with its frequent references to the Logos, as prophecy of Christian revelation.[11] Augustine too notes that the Sibyl, Orpheus,

Hermes, and various "seers, sages and pagan philosophers are said to have foretold the truth about the Son of God or God the Father".[12]

A deliberate cultivation of the mystery, a *disciplina arcani*, in the texts known as the *Hermetica*, adds to the modern scholar's difficulty in penetrating into hermetic beliefs. The adherents of the sect seek to remain "exclusive," maintaining that that which deals with the highest themes and evinces the most profound reverence must not be profaned by a throng of curious listeners and hangers-on.[13] There is a paradoxical echo here of Jesus' words about throwing the children's bread to the dogs (Mark 7:27–8), testing the woman who came to him for help because her daughter was possessed by an evil spirit.

Some Principal Teachings

Poimandres

The *Poimandres* of "Hermes Trismegistus' begins with a vision, in which there are clear affinities with some elements of Christian teaching. The author says he was visited by a Being of infinite size who showed him an immense expanse of light. From the Light came forth a holy Word (Logos). The Being, who called himself Poimandres, explained that the Light is Himself, Mind, the First God and the Logos is His Son. He described the way the sensible world came into being, from the will of God, which created a likeness of the beautiful world of his own ordered intellectual Being. The watery substance of the sensible world received the Word and was brought into order; elements were created and from them came forth living creatures.[14] There follows a description of the way creation was designed to be administered and how God, in due course, loosed the bonds binding things together so that the hitherto bisexual creatures became separate males and females. Then they increased and multiplied by giving birth to offspring. This prompts the distinctively "hermetic" reflection that he who knows himself has entered into the Good which is above all being, for he understands that he is made of Life and Light; but he who has been led by fleshly desire to love the body wanders in the darkness of the world of sense and is mortal.[15]

In his *Confessions* IV.xiii.20, Augustine describes how, during his decade as a teacher of rhetoric in North Africa he was "in love with beauty of a lower level and it was dragging [him] down." As the "hermetic" tradition understands it, human beings have the potential to become more godlike by being virtuous, just as they can become more "beastly" by behaving like animals and giving way to the vices. In the *Hermetica*, there are awful warnings to human beings who fail to strive to become more godlike, more spiritual (by *deificatio*), that they will find themselves as a consequence becoming more like beasts.

Book II of the *Poimandres* takes the form of a "conversation" between Hermes and Asclepius on cosmology, taking as its starting point the notion that everything that moves is moved "in" and "by" something.[16] The third Libellus concentrates on the notion that God is the First and the Source and that both the universe and nature are themselves divine.[17] Libellus VI identifies God with the Good; it also emphasizes the Platonic notions that the highest Being is without passion and incapable of alteration or disturbance.[18] The same idea is the focus of Libellus X, going on to explore the changes the soul undergoes as it passes to a happier or a more wretched state by adhering itself to the Good or remaining enthralled in its bodily condition. A soul's vice is to lack knowledge, to be blind to the Light, and when it is in that state it cannot be, as it should, "contrary" to the body.[19] Strands of Gnosticism appear, for example in Libellus XVI, where a chorus of demons is described as subject to the Sun.[20] In the same passage are astrological borrowings, for these demons act under orders from the planets.[21]

The Asclepius

One of the most important of the hermetic works from the point of view of its relationship to Christianity, is the *Asclepius*. The *Asclepius* purports to be a "holy book" of Hermes Trismegistus addressed to Asclepius. Augustine certainly knew the Latin version of the *Asclepius* and he connected it with Egypt (*haec vana deceptoria, perniciosa sacrilega Hermes Aegyptius*),[22] but he did not attribute it to Apuleius. In any case, Apuleius cannot be the author because his lifetime (c.125–80) places him too early.

The Greek originals preserved or gave rise to three distinguishable texts (*Asclepius* I, II, III) which were brought together in Latin translation sometime between AD280 and 426.[23] *Asclepius* I (not before the second century AD) appears to be free of Christian influence.

Asclepius I discusses souls and their relation to the corporeal world (*mundus*).[24] It emphasizes the extreme difficulty of understanding the divine. To some men, though few, falls the high good fortune of having pure minds, so that they may raise their eyes to heaven (*Aliqui ergo, ipsique paucissimi, pura mente praediti, sortiti sunt caeli suspiciendi venerabilem curam*). But for most their mixed being, body and soul, means that they are weighed down by the burden of their bodies and look to lowlier things.[25]

Asclepius II (150–270) is concerned with the problem of evil, again from the essentially dualist viewpoint which identifies matter with the tendency to evil and sees it as in eternal conflict with spirit. The author seeks to answer the question why God did not ensure that there was no such thing as evil. He says God did not have the power. Evil is in the world as an inseparable part of it (*ita enim in mundo est, ut quasi membrum ipsius videatur*). All that God could do he did, that is, to endow men's minds with intellective powers (*sensu, disciplina, intelligentia*).[26]

Only with *Asclepius* III, written in about AD270, is there an unambiguous indication of the encounter with Christianity and then Christianity is presented as the enemy threatening to dominate the religious world and bring about the end of paganism.[27] *Asclepius* III 24–5 contains a telling denunciation of Christianity and the danger it poses to the continuance of pagan beliefs. There is a "prophecy" that cruel, unbelieving foreigners will invade Egypt and kill many of the local population. Then the Egyptians will become cruel and faithless themselves and the religion they have held in the past will die away. This makes plain the real fear of at least these "hermetic" pagans that their way of life and belief was under threat.

For the author(s) of the *Asclepius*, Egypt is an image of heaven (*imago sit caeli*); it is, to be more exact (*quod est verius*), a place to which the business of ruling the universe has been transferred from heaven itself (*translatio aut descensio omnium quae gubernantur atque exercentur in caelo*). Egypt is, in other words, the temple (*templum*) of the whole universe.[28] Men make their gods in their own image. They make statues, but animated statues (*statuas animatas, sensu et spiritu plenas*), which know the future and can predict it, which can inspire prophecy and cause dreams and make people ill and heal them (the verbs are active).[29] But the time is coming when the gods will go back to heaven and Egypt will be conquered. The Nile will run with blood. In that time the very Egyptians will lose their faith and religion will vanish from the earth. The sense of wonder which prompts worship will be gone when men contemplate the universe. Ultimately God will restore religion.[30]

Conclusion

The *Hermetica* thus illustrate several aspects of the problematic character of Christianity's relationship with contemporary thought and belief with which the last few chapters have been concerned: the mutual fear and suspicion, coupled with a powerful mutual attraction; the territoriality, both geographical and conceptual, which led to defensiveness and exclusivity in the case of sects; the overlap and interpenetration of ideas; the multilayered character of the thought, ranging from debased and popular ideas to the most intellectually refined.

Notes

1 *Hermetica*, ed. and trans. Scott, I, p. 64.
2 Ibid.
3 *Corpus hermeticum*, vol. 1, p. I. *Hermetica*, trans. Copenhaver.
4 *Hermetica*, ed. and trans. Scott, I, p. 2.
5 *Hermetica*, trans. Copenhaver, p. xxxiii.
6 Iamblichus, *On the Mysteries of Egypt*, ed. E. de Places (Paris, 1966), 8.1.260–1.
7 *Hermetica*, trans. Copenhaver, pp. xxvii–xxviii.
8 *Liber XXIV philosophorum*, p. IXff.
9 Hermes Trismegistus, *De triginta sex decanis*.
10 Hermes Trismegistus, *Astrologica et divinatoria*.
11 See *De Trinitate* II.3.26–8, ed. I. Seiler (Meisenheim am Glan, 1975); and see Fowden, *The Egyptian Hermes*, p. 179.
12 *De Civitate Dei*, CCSL 47 (1955), XVIII.xxiii; *Contra Faustum* 13.1, 1, 15, 17.
13 *Hermetica*, ed. and trans. Scott, I, pp. 286–8.
14 Ibid., I, pp. 66–7.
15 Ibid., I, p. 124.
16 Ibid., I, p. 134.
17 Ibid., I, p. 144.
18 Ibid., I, pp. 164–6.
19 Ibid., I, pp. 186–92.
20 Ibid., I, p. 268.
21 Ibid., I, pp. 268–70.
22 *De Civitate Dei*, VIII.xxiii, CCSL, pp. 241–73.
23 *Hermetica*, ed. and trans. Scott, I, pp. 51–81.
24 Ibid., I, pp. 288–90.
25 Ibid., I, p. 302.
26 Ibid., I, p. 314.
27 Ibid., I, pp. 55ff.
28 Ibid., I, p. 340.
29 Ibid., I, pp. 338–40.
30 Ibid., I, pp. 342–8.

Bibliography

Hermetica, ed. and trans. Walter Scott (Oxford, 1924).

Corpus hermeticum, ed. A. D. Nock and A.-J. Festugière (Paris, 1945), 4 vols.

Liber XXIV philosophorum, ed. F. Hudry, CCCM, 143A (Turnhout, 1997).

Hermes Trismegistus, *De triginta sex decanis*, ed. S. Feraboli, CCCM, 144 (Turnhout, 1994).

—— *Astrologica et divinatoria*, ed. G. Bos, C. Burnett, T. Charmasson, P. Kunitzsch, F. Lelli, and P. Lucentinit, CCCM, 144C (Turnhout, 2001).

Garth Fowden, *The Egyptian Hermes* (Cambridge, 1986).

Hermetica, trans. Brian P. Copenhaver (Cambridge, 1991).

The Maturing of Early Christian Theology in East and West

Athanasius and the Arian Crisis

Rowan Williams

For the churches of the eastern Mediterranean, the greatest theological problem in the latter part of the third century was the legacy of Paul of Samosata, the controversial bishop of Antioch, condemned by episcopal synods in 264 and 268. What we can reconstruct of Paul's teaching suggests that he regarded Jesus as being, not the incarnation of a pre-existent being, but a person in whom the divine reason or wisdom was present to a unique degree. Whether he thought that the Logos of God was a substantive independent reality, a *hupostasis*, is not clear; but he certainly drew a sharp distinction between the Logos, which remains in heaven, and the earthly Jesus, who is anointed by grace. There are traces here of an exegetical debate over scriptural texts that mention the "anointing" of the saviour (the problem is discussed by Origen); Paul seems to have been concerned to avoid any language implying that the heavenly Word could be the subject of an act of divine grace (symbolized by the vocabulary of "anointing"). It is likely that he reinforced this by insisting that the Logos belonged to the very substance of God, since his critics repudiated the use of the word *homoousios*, "of the same substance", for the Logos.

Several concerns are in evidence here, all of them significant for the great doctrinal crisis of the fourth century. Paul's view was clearly seen as jeopardizing the distinctness of the Logos as in some sense a heavenly subject or subsistent – a conclusion hard to reconcile, for early Christians, with both scriptural and liturgical language. It was also interpreted as driving a wedge between the heavenly Word and the earthly redeemer, coming dangerously close to those earlier heresies that had presented the relation between Logos and Jesus as contingent (the Word abandoning the dying Jesus on the cross in one such doctrine), or to certain Jewish-Christian notions that played down the concept of direct incarnation. Some saw Paul's scheme as suggesting that Jesus "earned" his quasi-divine status by fidelity to God – which made salvation dependent on human achievement, not God's gift. Paul's teaching, in short, provided people with a sort of checklist of unacceptable doctrines; if someone could be convicted of teaching what he had taught, they were self-evidently outside the orthodox pale. For example, because Origen's teaching on the Incarnation avoided saying that the Logos as such became incarnate (as opposed to the pre-existent righteous spirit united with the Logos), some appear to have associated him with Paul, and to have looked for evidence of other parallels. The charges to which Eusebius and Pamphilus were responding when they drew up their *Defence of Origen* in the first decade of the fourth century were probably originally of this kind, though the extant Latin translation obscures this.

Securing a proper distinction between God and the Logos was a priority for theology, both because of exegetical concerns and because of a worry that without such a distinction the very concept of God was made incoherent. A God who, as it were, cut off a portion of himself to produce a separate being could not be (as God must be) immaterial. A God who had eternally alongside him a second divine subject could not be the sole source of all. Very generally speaking, up to the beginning of the fourth century, such philosophical sources as had been used by theologians had belonged within the intellectual world of "Middle Platonism," modified by certain Stoic themes; and Middle Platonism had been content to think of divine life or power as possessed wholly by God, and mediated to lower levels of reality through a secondary "divinity" who was, so to speak, the divine mind in action. This fitted quite well with third-century theology; but philosophy was changing, and the new readings of Plato (and Aristotle) that shaped the system of Plotinus and the world of neoplatonism made life more complicated for theologians. They stressed the absolute mysteriousness and transcendence of the first cause much more strongly, and so made it harder to go on using the language of a sort of "trickling downwards" of divine life. In other words, the desire to clarify the difference between God and the Logos because of exegetical and polemical concerns could have found an unexpected ally in some of the new trends in philosophy. And while it is unlikely that many theologians were particularly well-informed on these trends, we know that there was some coming and going between theology and the philosophical schools, and that a few Christian teachers picked up at least some of the slogans and vocabulary of current philosophy.

One further matter is worth mentioning. Part of the exegetical commitment to an independent heavenly Logos was connected with the language of Jewish speculation about angels and the worship of the heavenly sanctuary. Already in the New Testament, we can see the figure of Jesus being interpreted through the lens of this mythology; and many early texts draw extensively upon it, depicting Jesus and the Spirit as the two angels flanking the throne of God (like the cherubim on either side of the Ark of the Covenant, or the seraphim of Isaiah 6). There is some evidence that this imagery was used in the Church's worship: Christ and the Spirit are the leaders and enablers of our worship, taking us into the heavenly sanctuary to stand with them before the Father. Here is another motif in the widespread concern that the distinction between Father and Son should not be eroded: that difference is precisely what secures *our* place in heaven, sharing the Son's adoration of the Father.

Few if any intellectual crises are precipitated by purely intellectual factors. What brought all this into practical focus was the situation of the church in Alexandria in the first two decades of the fourth century. The persecution of Diocletian had affected the Egyptian church as severely as the Palestinian and Syrian churches, with the usual result of a weakening of hierarchical authority in the community. Bishop Peter of Alexandria eventually met his death by martyrdom in 311, but he had been absent from the city for long periods in hiding. Just as with Bishop Demetrius a century earlier, his authority suffered: a major schism broke out when another bishop began ordaining clergy for Alexandria on his own initiative. It is also clear that in Alexandria the presbyters of the city churches enjoyed considerable independence in any case: there are hints that several of them saw themselves as "schools" gathered around charismatic teachers, not as subgroups in a single, episcopally-dominated fellowship.

At some point in the second decade of the fourth century, Bishop Alexander (d. 327) attempted to standardize exegetical and doctrinal teaching in the city, and met sharp resistance from some of the presbyters. His leading critic was Arius (d. 336), pastor of the Boukolia or Baukalis church (the mausoleum of St. Mark and of the bishops of Alexandria according to some sources), a popular preacher and spiritual director, and a man with some technical training in philosophy. The course of events is obscure; but it is clear that when Arius was challenged by the bishop, he replied with a critique of the bishop's own theology as expressed in his public teaching. The two disagreed over the interpretation of Proverbs 8:22 ("The Lord created me at the beginning of his ways"), since this provided a clear exegetical crux in respect of the difference between God and the Logos. If the Logos is created by God, he cannot be eternal alongside God; he must exist because God wills him to exist. Thus he is not in any way part of God's intrinsic nature, and "there was when he did not exist" is the most notorious of Arius' slogans.

We have a credal statement drawn up by Arius and his supporters and submitted to the bishop around 320 or 321, in which these points are made with great clarity. "We acknowledge," they write, "one God, the only unbegotten, the only eternal, the only one without cause or beginning, the only true, the only one possessed of immortality, the only wise, the only good . . . the begetter of his only Son before endless ages . . . giving him subsistence by his own will . . . the perfect creation of God, but not like one among other creatures." The text goes on to distinguish this teaching from various heresies and errors which make God out to be a material and divisible being by suggesting that the Logos is a *homoousios* portion of divinity, or which reduce the Logos to an impersonal function of God or to one among other aspects of God. It is obvious that Arius' main concern is to secure the uniqueness of the Father and the dependence of the Logos on the Father's decision; and in the last section of this manifesto, he addresses an issue that had evidently been raised in Alexandria over several generations. Origen, it will be remembered, had taught that, although the Logos depended on the Father, there was no interval "prior" to the generation of the Logos, as God's self-expressive action must be eternal. This was taken up by later Alexandrian writers (including Bishop Dionysius in the 260s), and seems to have been pressed by Alexander (who summed it up epigrammatically as "always God, always the Son"). Arius carefully repudiates this argument from logical correlation as coming unacceptably close to the "two first principles" error he is keen to rule out (you will find a similar anxiety in the work of Methodius of Olympus in the first decade of the fourth century): the Son is not born "in" time, admittedly; but his generation is the beginning of time, and the Father is "before" the Son in the sense that the Father is strictly timeless. Arius' language is under strain here, and it is not surprising that this led to misunderstanding.

A further set of concerns appears not in Arius' own work but in the lengthy attack on his views set out by Alexander in a circular letter to other bishops written around 321, when Arius had left Alexandria and was soliciting support in the churches of Palestine, Syria, and Asia Minor. This document is a rather laboured, even confused response, but it picks up Origen's insight that there is a distinction between eternal existence and independently necessary existence: an eternal Son, sharing in all the Father's qualities without reserve except for the single fact that the Father has no origin, is quite reconcilable with belief that the Father alone is the source of all. But what is here said about the Son entails that the Son does not exist because of God's choice: he is the natural expression of God's nature, the eternal image and radiance of what the Father is. Themes from Origen are deployed to defend the conviction that there is no "gap" between Father and Son, and the scriptural language of the Son as perfect image is central to this argument. However, it is worth noting that in a later letter (drafted by his assistant and eventual successor, Athanasius), Alexander also claims that Arius is teaching a novel doctrine about Christ. If only the Father is incapable of change, the Logos must be changeable; so if the Logos is capable of change, his eternal virtue must be the result of his free choice. *In principle*, he could choose evil. As with Paul of Samosata's theology, this raises the spectre that salvation depends on something other than God's grace. Alexander is thus able to associate Arius with just the theology to which Arius is most passionately opppposed. Whether Arius did explicitly teach this, or whether Alexander is simply pushing the implications of his teaching, is not clear; the bishop claims that some of Arius' party had admitted that this was implied, but nothing directly from Arius bears it out. It is a common technique of theological debate in this period that an opponent can be held responsible for possible implications of his teaching, even if he does not say it in his own right, so we should not rest too much on this in interpreting Arius' actual doctrine.

But it relates to another set of issues, again to do with exegesis, which are raised in both the letters under Alexander's name. Jesus in the gospels is represented as suffering, being uncertain, being subject to the contingencies of this world. God cannot be vulnerable in this way; but the heavenly Logos, who is not by nature invulnerable and immutable, is capable of this. So Arius' scheme avoids the embarrassment of ascribing vulnerability to God by involving God directly in the Incarnation, and allows us to read the Gospels with full realism. Origen, like Clement before him, had found the ascription of real mental suffering or doubt to Jesus profoundly difficult: in this, as in other respects, Arius cuts the Gordian knot. Alexander's letter makes it plain that part of the attraction of Arius' system was that it provided a way of dealing with such passages, and this reminds us once more of the central importance of questions about how to read the Bible in the development of this controversy.

Arius gained some support from influential church leaders in Palestine and Asia, including Eusebius of Caesarea – who initially saw him as the natural heir of Origen, in doctrine and in relations with the hierarchy in Alexandria – and Eusebius of Nicomedia, a consummate politician and organizer with links to the imperial household. The bishop of Nicomedia was also a former pupil of Lucian of Antioch, martyred a few years earlier, and one of the most learned and significant exegetes of the age; his disciples included several senior figures in the churches of the eastern Mediterranean, and Eusebius was able to draw on their skills and support (Arius implies that he too studied with Lucian, but, as we shall see, he can hardly be reckoned a disciple). Something of a pamphlet war followed in 322–3, interrupted by a brief but fierce outbreak of persecution. This was ended when, in 324, Constantine gained power over the entire Roman Empire; already sympathetic to the Church, he wanted to use it to cement loyalty and unity within the State, and thus had a great interest in resolving what was by now a violently disruptive quarrel in the churches. His response to intensive lobbying from all sides was to call a council of as many bishops as possible; it met at Nicaea in the early summer of 325.

By this time, Arius had published a statement of his views in verse, a work dubbed the *Thalia* ("Dinner Party Songs") by his opponents. This survives only in part, but is the most important source for grasping what mattered to Arius; and it draws together all the significant issues already mentioned – God as the only transcendent being, the Logos as the greatest and most graciously endowed of all other beings, consumed in the contemplation and praise of God, although he never fathoms the divine mystery, the impossibility of treating the Logos as a portion or aspect of God (the word *homoousios* is again rejected). Some elements of this text must have alarmed his supporters; Lucian and others had tended to stress the perfect likeness of Son to Father and not at all to emphasize the unspeakable mystery of the divine being (indeed they were wary of the possible Gnostic implications of that sort of language). When the Council opened, Arius had few unequivocal supporters; those who backed him were probably more concerned to rule out what they saw as the erroneous doctrines of Alexander's party. But, largely through the influence of the emperor's main religious adviser, Bishop Hosius of Cordova, the Council was persuaded to adopt a formula tightly crafted to exclude any hint of Arius' views and containing the fateful word *homoousios*. And it condemned explicitly all who taught that the Logos was created or that there was a time when he did not exist.

Although this was received by an overwhelming majority (Eusebius of Nicomedia and a handful of others voted against or abstained, and were duly deposed and exiled), it did not represent a workable consensus. Eusebius of Caesarea, who had initially supported Arius, voted for the definition, but was not happy about it, and wrote a none-too-convincing justification of his stance for his home church; in his later biography of Constantine, he mentions neither Arius nor the creed of Nicaea. He had realized, it seems, how different Arius was from Origen, but continued to believe that the great danger for theology was anything that obscured the distinctness of Father and Son. The record of the years that followed Nicaea is one of monumentally complicated maneuvers to find another unifying formula. Most eastern bishops thought that the use of *homoousios* could imply that the all-important point of the Logos' difference from the Father had been sacrificed for a Sabellian doctrine of the successive "modes" of divine being. Matters were not helped by the fact that some supporters of Nicaea – notably Marcellus of Ancyra, vigorously attacked by Eusebius of Caesarea – really did teach something not too far removed from this. However, this should not be seen as support for "Arianism"; there was really no such thing as Arianism in the fourth-century Church, as the distinctive doctrines of Arius were definitely not held or defended by any outside Arius' immediate circle. Even some of the strongest critics of Nicaea make a point of distancing themselves from him; and a group of bishops meeting at Antioch in 341, five years after Arius' death, insist that they are not "followers of Arius." The general consensus was to see the Logos as the perfect and eternal image of God, existing independently but in such a way as to reveal God definitively, even fully (the Son is the image of "the substance and will and power and glory" of the supreme God). Arius' stress on the "infinite qualitative difference" between God and the Logos was not welcome. By the 350s, there was a substantial group who supported the term *homoiousios*, "of similar substance," as a designation of the Son's relation to the Father; but these were outflanked by sharper logical minds who could see that *homoios kat'ousian*, "similar in substance," was not at all clearly distinguishable from the doctrine that Father and Son were two equal members of a class of divine beings – which revived fears of a "two first principles" model. This new group, hostile to Nicaea but also to the middle ground represented by the *homoiousios*, were often called "Anomoians," because of their belief that Father and Son were *anomoios*, "dissimilar," in substance. Since the Father was *agennetos*, "unbegotten", and since that was a fundamental property of divinity, the Son, who was begotten, could have nothing in common according to his substantial definition with the Father. This view, propagated with great energy and skill by the idiosyncratic Aetius and his pupil Eunomius (later bishop of Cyzicus), echoed Arius' concern to emphasize the absolute uniqueness of the Father as sole God, but took a quite opposite line to his in respect of whether the nature of God could be known; Aetius and Eunomius popularized the belief that *agennetos* was a comprehensive definition of the divine substance, so that, if you knew that definition, you knew the essence of God.

This doctrine, combined with the aggressive tactics of Aetius and Eunomius and their supporters, was deeply offensive to those who held the sort of consensus represented by the synod of 341 and subsequent meetings like that at Seleucia in September 351. But the Anomoian group gained powerful political support, and, by the end of the 350s, had succeeded in securing the deposition of many leading Homoiousians. We shall return to the factors that produced a revolutionary change after 360; but it should be noted that the involvement of secular political power had become more and more intrusive since the 320s. Constantine had forced the vote at Nicaea by his personal endorsement of the *homoousios* solution, but had later given support to some of its critics, and had been impatient with those who insisted on the letter of Nicaea. His son Constantius had been a fairly consistent supporter of Nicaea's enemies; initially unsympathetic to Anomoians, he had increasingly backed them in the late fifties against the Homoiousians. Throughout the period, bishops had had to devote a not very edifying amount of energy to gaining and keeping the favour of the emperor and his advisers; few were willing to resist openly.

Theologically speaking, we can see how the agenda shifted during these years. Arius is concerned to secure the grounds for believing in a separately subsisting Logos, in order to preserve both the utter supremacy of God the Father and the personal Incarnation of a heavenly being as the hinge of our salvation, revealing to us all we can know of God and leading us to share his own adoration of the divine mystery. But as the controversies developed, the emphasis fell more on the need for perfect revelation, less on the gulf between God and the revealer. Anomoianism boldly combined the most outspoken formulation yet about the distance between God and Logos with the most sweeping statement yet about the fulness of revelation. But the profound unease with which it was met in most of the eastern Church shows that the theme of underlining the substantial distinction of Father from Son had lost what popular enthusiasm it might once have had. The threat of Paul of Samosata had become remote for most Christians, and there were new fears that the whole notion of revelation was being jeopardized, either by reckless assertions about divine unknowability or by what seemed absurd and trivializing claims that revelation was (as for Eunomius) essentially a matter of clarifying concepts. By 360, there was an urgent need for some sort of new consensus.

The fact that this consensus finally consolidated around the creed of Nicaea is actually quite surprising, given the history of the preceding decades; and it is attributable to two major factors. First, and very practically, the political climate changed abruptly in 361, with the accession of a passionately anti-Christian emperor, Julian "the Apostate." Julian was even-handedly hostile to Nicenes, Homoiousians, Anomoians and everyone else in the Christian world; he allowed most exiled bishops to return to their sees, so that factions could fight their battles directly, without state intervention (his hope naturally being that they would effectually destroy each other). This suddenly removed the power base of the Anomoians, and led many to look for new alliances in this new and precarious situation. Secondly, Nicene theology began to look attractive in such a context, largely because it had been defended with single-minded consistency for decades by one of the most able and prolific Christian writers of the age, Athanasius (c.295–373), successor to Bishop Alexander at Alexandria, a man who had never allowed political advantage to determine his convictions. He had emerged as a significant figure when he was a young deacon in Alexander's entourage in the early 320s, and (as noted above) had drafted for him an important synodical letter circulated on the eve of Nicaea, in which he crisply summarized Arius' theology and marshalled an assortment of biblical texts against it. However, his main contributions to the debate were made in the decades that followed, during which he was repeatedly dethroned and exiled by political and theological opponents. His three treatises, *Against the Arians*, composed probably in the early 340s during one of his exiles from Alexandria, tackle systematically the main exegetical problems that might give some credibility to Arius' scheme – notably those which ascribe weakness or changeability to the incarnate Christ – as well as clarifying what it might mean to see God as eternally and necessarily "productive," generating the Son timelessly because that is his very nature. In II.2 and III.62 especially, he spells out some implications of this: God's will is not arbitrary, but a consequence of God's nature. So if God wills to create, this must be because there is something about his very essence that makes this possible; once we accept that he is eternally engaged in generating the Son, we see that he is always producing what is other – first by nature, then by free action relating to what is outside his own life. Creation would make no sense without eternal begetting; they are two radically different categories, yet there is an analogy such that one is impossible and unintelligible without the other. This in turn dismisses the "Arian" point that God must beget the Son either by free will (as Arius held) or by necessity (which would be inappropriate to the unconditioned being of God). For Athanasius, the opposition is not between will and necessity but between free self-determination and the preceding character of the self that is determining its acts. To deny that this prior reality is as it is because of an act of will is not to say that it is as it is because of an imposed necessity, an external constraint, simply that it is naturally what it is.

But the most important elements in Athanasius' arguments here have to do with two basic insights about the character of salvation. In the first place: in Arius' system, the Logos receives a grace which he passes on to us; but if there is a fundamental problem about how God communicates with creation, if there is an immeasurable ontological gulf, how can even the most exalted creature help in the process? If the incarnate Son makes us sons and daughters of the eternal Father, what does it mean to say that the Son too has to be *made* a son? Does he also need a mediator, since God is so profoundly alien to all created nature? What the Son gives he must first have; if what he has he has by grace not by nature, there must be a process by which he acquires these gifts; so the risk yet again appears of making salvation dependent on actions other than God's. In short, for the Son to give God's gifts, the Son must act with God's action, and not be passive to the act of grace (see especially I.38, II.19ff., III.25 of *Against the Arians*).

What is emerging here is an argument for continuity of substance between Father and Son on the basis of continuity or identity or "indiscernibility" of *action* (cf. I.35–6, II.67ff., III.4–5, 41). In creation and redemption, God does one thing, but does it in a pattern of interwoven self-relation, does it *through* the active inter-dependence of the giving and receiving of love within the one divine life (which for Athanasius is clearly distinguishable from the giving and receiving of the kind of specific grace appropriate to God's dealings with what is not God). The Son and the Father share *ousia* because they perfectly share action (I.15ff., 58); we can even say that the Son is "proper to the Father's substance" (II.82), a phrase which could well have given trouble to a critic of Nicaea worried about Sabellianism, the reduction of the Son to an impersonal property of the Father. While *Against the Arians* does not explicitly defend Nicaea or the *homoousios*, the convergence of what Athanasius says with Nicaea's vocabulary is unequivocally clear.

And there is a second theme, less consistently marked, but still plainly discernible. Arius had appealed, it seems, to the archaic language of liturgy to support the idea that the Logos (with the Spirit) led the heavenly host in praising the Father. Athanasius challenges the implied doctrine that, when we address prayer or praise to the Son, we are actually adoring what is less than God; we are forbidden in Scripture to worship creatures, and, if the Son is not divine by nature, it is nonsense to worship him (II.23–4). What is more, the threefold baptismal formula cannot make sense of Arius' presuppositions: either the naming of the Son and the Spirit adds nothing (so why confuse matters?), or there is something the Father cannot do without the Son and the Spirit (which, if they are not God, means that God depends on creation for what he can do). For Athanasius, naming the Father immediately and automatically "names" the Son as well (II.40–1).

Arius had almost certainly appealed to liturgical practise; Athanasius appears to be saying, "To the liturgy you shall go," insisting that baptismal usage controls whatever else may be said or implied in the language of worship. Similar points recur later in the century in other writers defending Nicaea. Athanasius' polemic represents two rather novel sorts of argument, one appealing to what might be called the logic of redemption, insisting on maximal generosity in interpreting what is given in Christ (the divine freedom, a share in the Son's eternal relation to the Father), the other appealing to the logic of Christian practise. In one sense, Athanasius is, no less than Arius, deploying what theologians of the day called – usually disparagingly – "dialectic"; but it is a dialectic shaped not just by conceptual analysis but by the spiritual expectations and spiritual practise of believers. You might signal the shift between the beginning of the century and Athanasius' theology by saying that in the earlier period theologians were anxious to secure the belief that the Logos was a divine *agent* (so that there was a real Incarnation of a heavenly being in Jesus), while Athanasius sought to secure the belief that the Logos was a *divine* agent (so that what was bestowed through the Incarnation was genuinely the gift of divine and immortal liberty, love, and rationality). Writing outside the directly controversial context, in his apologetic works *Against the Pagans* and *On the Incarnation*, Athanasius sets out this point with great clarity: it is in *On the Incarnation* 54 that he uses the celebrated phrase of the Logos: "He became human so that we might become divine." But this would be empty if the Logos were not clearly "different from every kind of existence that owes its being to something else, from every created thing" (*Against the Pagans* 41). And in his letters to the Egyptian bishop Serapion later in his career (c.360?), we find Athanasius applying exactly the same sort of logic to establish that the Holy Spirit is fully divine (see, e.g. *Letter* 1.24): the Spirit is venerated and invoked as God in worship, and rightly so, because the Spirit gives us a share in what he possesses, the divine life.

This, then, was the theology advanced against Arius' views by his most sophisticated opponent. But for several decades, Athanasius was almost the sole articulate opponent of the consensus around non-Nicene or anti-Nicene formulae. His genius as a controversialist emerges most clearly, though, in the 350s, when he issued a series of substantial works both defending Nicaea and attacking other conciliar formulations. His purpose was to demonstrate quite simply that anything short of the Nicene definition effectively committed you to views indistinguishable from those of Arius or of the contemporary Anomoians. In other words, he was deliberately wooing the broad constituency that might have described themselves as Homoiousian, and was refining the sense of the Nicene *homoousios* to bring it as close as possible to *homoiousios*, giving great weight to the importance of distinguishing the substantive "hypostases" of Father and Son. This work was taken up and completed with much skill by the Cappadocian Fathers in the 360s and afterwards. But none of their thinking could have been possible without the extraordinary innovative thinking of Athanasius; indeed, some of his key ideas, especially the locating of divine unity in a singleness of divine action (not just a parallel exercise of divine action), sometimes go even further than most of Cappadocian theology.

So the sharp change of direction that took place around 360 was due not only to the effects of Julian's hostility, but to the fact that Athanasius had been preparing the way for a realignment of allegiances by his consistent exposure of what he saw as the flaws of Arius' teaching, and his consistent argument that only Nicaea could successfully avoid these errors. He knew when to offer compromise formulae; in 362 he presided at a synod in Alexandria designed to consolidate the new consensus, and so laid the foundations for what would be recognized as orthodoxy from then on, so that all future authoritative confessions of faith took the vocabulary of Nicaea for granted.

However, the shift was not only in terms of intellectual debate. Arius had in many respects distanced himself from the legacy of Origen, but in one important sense had shown himself Origen's heir, as Eusebius of Caesarea had initially seen him (before he realised how much separated the two teachers). Arius claimed in his *Thalia* to be a teacher "instructed by God"; he made liberal use of the idea that the charismatically-inspired teacher was more authoritative in the Church than the hierarchical leader. Athanasius was a man who wielded hierarchical authority (sometimes with ferocity, if there is even a small amount of truth in the accusations of his enemies); yet he was able in a very remarkable way to unite this juridical and institutional authority to something like the charismatic authority of earlier teachers by developing and exploiting his links with the nascent monastic movement. The life of St. Antony the Great, the major figure in the first generation of monasticism, made it plain that Antony had no time for Arius or any other critics of episcopal orthodoxy; and Athanasius' regular and extensive correspondence with monastic communities (some of which sheltered him when he was, as not infrequently happened, on the run from imperial authority) cemented the loyalty of these groups. Athanasius was largely responsible for shaping the characteristic ethos of the next generation of great bishops in the eastern Mediterranean (the foremost examples being the Cappadocian Fathers), rulers of the Church whose personal lives of asceticism gave them the sort of authority that an Origen might once have possessed.

One final point about the intellectual developments of this period should be noted, as it makes some sense of the next stage of theological controversy in the Church. Part of the concern around in the early days of the Arian crisis, as we have seen, was the exegetical difficulty raised by biblical passages ascribing weakness or suffering to the incarnate Logos. Arius had an elegant solution to the difficulty, which unfortunately wrecked much of the structure of Christian piety. Others attempted similarly elegant solutions, with equally problematic results. Apollinaris of Laodicea (c.315–92) denied that there was in the incarnate Christ any created spiritual principle; thus the Logos stood in the place of a human soul, and directed the life of Jesus with total freedom from passion or weakness. The scriptural texts were to be interpreted so as to restrict suffering to what was created and mortal in Jesus. Although this was an extreme statement, Athanasius (and other Nicene supporters) came quite close to suggesting similarly that all the suffering of Christ should be ascribed to the "lower", "fleshly" part of his humanity, while he remained spiritually free.

But by defining the Logos as in every way possessed of a fully divine nature, Nicaea had actually ruled out by implication any such compromise solution. If the Logos was fully God, then there was no way in which the Logos could, as it were, form part of a hybrid of incomplete humanity with gaps supplied from the divinity. Divine nature could not enter into a collaborative enterprise in which it performed certain functions in a composite reality, since divinity exists on a different metaphysical level. Thus nothing diminishes the full humanity of Christ; and the way is open for the further elaboration of the soteriological importance of that full humanity. For Christ to restore all of human nature, he must contain or exemplify all of human nature: Apollinaris' solution takes away the hope of a total transformation of humanity by grace (a point made forcefully by Gregory Nazianzen and others in the later fourth century). There was thus no need to be embarrassed by the Gospel records of Christ's weakness or suffering: these were a matter of his solidarity with us in his complete human nature, but they did not in any way compromise the divine.

It was out of this background that the Christological controversy grew. Some – the theologians most directly influenced by the Arian crisis in northern Syria and its dependencies – sharpened the distinction between God the Logos and the human Jesus to the point at which there could appear to be two *agents* working side by side in Jesus, united only in external form. Others, above all Cyril of Alexandria, followed Athanasius' suggestion that the human suffering was in some way so controlled by the Logos that it should not be seen as simple vulnerability in the inner life of the Lord; Cyril's provocatively paradoxical formula was to say that Christ "suffered without being passive" (*apathos epathen*). Both sides were working out the implications of rejecting Arius' created Logos as a solution to the difficulties of a suffering savior; both schemes generated their own problems. But it is impossible to see what was going on in this later quarrel without understanding that its roots are in the Arian crisis. Just as Nicaea swept away an "intermediate" level between the divine and the created, so in Christology it swept away, at least by implication, any notion of the incarnate Christ as a being intermediate in nature between divinity and humanity. The road to the settlement of the council of Chalcedon is already opened at Nicaea.

Bibliography

Khaled Anatolios, *Athanasius* (London, 1998).

T. D. Barnes, *Constantine and Eusebius* (Cambridge, MA, 1981).

—— *Athanasius and Constantius. Theology and Politics in the Constantinian Empire* (Cambridge, MA, 1993); these two studies are the best historical guides to the period.

David Brakke, *Athanasius and the Politics of Asceticism* (Oxford, 1995); excellent on the changed models of church and authority in the period.

R. P. C. Hanson, *The Search for the Christian Doctrine of God* (Edinburgh, 1988); a magisterial overview of fourth-century theology.

Alvyn Pettersen, *Athanasius* (London, 1995); a good and clear introduction.

Peter Widdicombe, *The Fatherhood of God from Origen to Athanasius* (Oxford, 1994).

Frances Young, *From Nicaea to Chalcedon* (London, 1983).

The Cappadocians

Morwenna Ludlow

Introduction

The fourth-century theologians usually known as the Cappadocians are Basil the Great, Bishop of Caesarea; his close friend Gregory of Nazianzus; and Basil's younger brother, Gregory of Nyssa. They are remembered primarily for their writings on the doctrine of the Trinity, which helped to achieve the consensus that the one God should be considered as three persons – Father, Son, and Holy Spirit – equal in honor and power, unified in will, and sharing the single divine essence. However, their theological achievements stretch beyond this and they should also be credited with some very profound reflections on the form and purpose of the Christian life, whether in the context of the church, the monastery or the home.

Context

Cappadocia was a province of the eastern Roman Empire, lying to the south-east of Constantinople in almost the exact centre of what is modern-day Turkey. Its most important town was Caesarea (modern Kayseri); Nazianzus, Nyssa, and Sasima were small, unimportant towns in the west of the province. To the north-west of Cappadocia lay the province of Galatia (chief town Ancyra, modern Ankara); to the north was Helenopontus where Annesi was situated on the river Iris; to the north and east lay the province of Armenia (chief town Sebaste, modern Sivas). Neocaesarea was found in the province of Pontus Polemoniacus, which lay between Armenia and the Black Sea. These imperial provinces all lay within the diocese of Pontus. The diocese of Asia, containing the very important bishopric of Constantinople, lay directly to the west.

Cappadocia had been a Roman dependency since 191 BC and part of the Empire since AD17. The region was not as Hellenized as some Roman provinces: although the Cappadocians' education was typical of that of many wealthy men in the Empire, it was not typical in Cappadocia. From Acts 2:9–11 it seems that there were Jews in Cappadocia at the time of Christ. 1 Peter (written between AD70 and 100) is addressed to Gentile converts in Pontus, Galatia, Cappadocia, Asia, and Bithynia; however, very little is known about early mission to the area. The first prominent Christian was Gregory Thaumaturgus – "the Wonderworker" (c.210–15 – c.270–5). He was born in Cappadocia, educated in Greek and Latin, and then traveled to Palestine. Although planning a career in the law, he spent five years in Origen's circle in Palestinian Caesarea (c.233–8). He was bishop of Neocaesarea throughout the Decian persecutions and the Goths' invasion of 257, and converted many in the area to Christianity. Basil and Gregory of Nyssa were particularly devoted to their local saint, because he had converted their grandmother, Macrina the Elder, who was very influential in their religious formation. Although they may have respected the fact that the Wonderworker had been a pupil of Origen, they were probably more influenced by his character than by his theology, which was doctrinally very basic.

In 325, in response to an ongoing debate about the nature of Christ, the council of Nicaea declared that the Son was "of the same essence (*homoousios*)" as the Father. This was intended to rule out speculations from the followers of Arius, an Egyptian priest (d. 336), that the Son was inferior to the Father, both in nature and in power and honour. Nevertheless, this declaration did not stop the debate. Particularly in the eastern Greek-speaking churches, there was anxiety that "of the same essence" might lend support to "modalists" like Marcellus of Ancyra (d c.374) who backed Nicaea but argued that Father, Son, and Spirit were merely successive appearances or modes of the Godhead, not eternal distinctions. Whilst most people were not prepared in their opposition to modalism to go as far as those Arians who declared that the Son was "unlike" the Father, many settled for the views that the Son was "like (*homoios*)" the Father or "of like essence (*homoiousios*)" to the Father. The latter view, sometimes known as "homoiousianism" (= "homoeousianism") or "Semi-Arianism", appeared for a long time in the East to be the moderate compromise position and was championed by two emperors. However, by the mid- to late fourth century a group of moderate "new Nicenes" were gaining confidence in defending the Nicene formula in such a way that it not only guaranteed the full divinity of the Son, but also was not susceptible of modalist interpretations as some "old Nicene" or "ultra-Nicene" views had been. It was at this point in the debates that Basil and the two Gregorys came to theological maturity and supported the new Nicenes' cause. (Although it was once thought that Basil was originally attracted to the "homoiousian" perspective, this is now generally doubted.) In the debates much depended on the persuasiveness of key bishops and theologians around whom groupings gathered; however, these were never organized parties in the modern sense – despite the political motives of at least some of the participants.

Cappadocian Lives

Our primary biographical sources for the Cappadocians are letters, commemorative speeches, Gregory of Nazianzus' autobiographical poem *On his own Life* and Gregory of Nyssa's *On the Life of Saint Macrina*. None of these, however, is concerned with providing a scientific history and, although scholars have been able to piece together a remarkable amount, there are still periods in the Cappadocians' lives about which little is known, and dates over which there is much dispute. The following account will rely on those areas of greatest consensus.

Gregory of Nazianzus was born at Arianzus in Cappadocia between 325 and 330. Basil was probably born in 329 or 330 in Caesarea; his sister Macrina (the eldest child) was born a couple of years earlier and their brother Naucratius a year or two later. Gregory of Nyssa was at least five years younger than Basil, being born between 335 and 340. There were four other daughters and two more brothers. The two families were similarly wealthy, land-owning, and well-established in the Hellenized élite of Cappadocia; both had been Christian for one or two generations: the Christian influence was particularly strong among the women of both families, who seem to have been largely responsible for the children's religious education. We know little of their childhoods. When Macrina was 12, the man to whom she was betrothed died; she reacted by dedicating herself to a life of celibacy and asceticism as if she had been widowed. Like many female Christian ascetics in this period, she followed this vocation at home. When her father, Basil the Elder, died a few years later, Macrina is said to have taken particular responsibility for her youngest brother, Peter, who was born after his father's death. At some point after this, Macrina, her mother Emmelia, and Peter, together with other members of their household, moved from Neocaesarea (where Basil the Elder had practised as a teacher of rhetoric) to the family's large country estate at Annesi.

Whereas Gregory of Nyssa was taught entirely in Cappadocia, Basil and Gregory of Nazianzus travelled more widely. They were educated at Caesarea in their late teens, then Basil spent some time in Constantinople before travelling to study in Athens in about 350. Gregory of Nazianzus stayed in Palestine and Alexandria before also arriving in Athens. There they met, formed a close friendship, and pursued together an education in rhetoric – the skill of public speaking. This was an extremely important intellectual and practical training in the ancient world. Originally designed to train the student for a life in law or politics, it increasingly came to be a preparation for any form of public life. Consequently, there was a demand for teachers: Basil, the two Gregorys and Basil's brother Naucratius were all teachers of rhetoric for part of their careers. Basil left Athens after five years and spent a year or so in Caesarea teaching his brother Gregory, amongst others; Gregory of Nazianzus did not return to Cappadocia until about 358. He taught briefly in Nazianzus where his father was bishop.

While Basil was still in Athens, his brother Naucratius retired from teaching rhetoric to an ascetic life at Annesi, living apart from Emmelia and Macrina's household, but probably accompanied by a few other like-minded male companions. His decision was probably influenced in some way by Eustathius of Sebaste (c.300 – after 377), an Armenian who had not only founded several monastic communities but who taught extensively about the nature and form of Christian asceticism. Basil himself was already attracted by Eustathius' ideas whilst in Athens and on his return to Cappadocia he spent only a short time teaching before embarking on a tour of monasteries in Syria, Mesopotamia, Palestine, and Egypt to find out more about the life Eustathius advocated. Whether or not Basil met him on this trip, Eustathius certainly later became a friend of the family.

On his return in 357–8, Basil was baptized in Caesarea by its bishop, Dianius and then retired to Annesi to undertake his own monastic life. There he was joined by Gregory of Nazianzus for the first of a series of visits. During one of these, Basil and Gregory are traditionally thought to have put together the *Philokalia*, a collection of excerpts from Origen's theology.

It is possible that Basil and Gregory joined Naucratius' group of monks, either before or after Naucratius' death in a hunting accident in about 358. In any case, Basil is credited with transforming the men's community into a more formal organization with an early type of monastic rule. Around this time, Emmelia joined her daughter in the ascetic life: this seems to be the point at which the family home at Annesi became fully transformed into a women's monastic community. The household slaves and their former mistresses were treated on equal terms, and the family was joined by other women who had dedicated themselves to a life of virginity. By 360, there were two communities at Annesi – or, perhaps, one community consisting of men and women who lived apart but worshipped together, a prototype of the later type of "double monastery." The form of this life had been influenced in different ways by Macrina, Naucratius, and Basil, but there is good reason to suppose that it was Macrina who was the head of the whole community, certainly by the time of her death and possibly from the time of Emmelia's commitment and the transformation of the family home.

Basil's first visit to Annesi ended in 359 or 360 when he attended the synod of Constantinople where he debated against Arian delegates. He was ordained reader by Dianius, but he fell out first with Dianius and then with Dianius' successor Eusebius (who had probably ordained Basil priest). On both occasions he retreated to Annesi, where he wrote his celebrated defense of the Trinity, *Against Eunomius*, before returning to Caesarea and the pull of ecclesiastical office. On one of these retreats he was joined by his friend Gregory who had recently been ordained priest by his father. Gregory had strong misgivings about his vocation, being unable to decide between an "active" life in the ordained ministry and the more contemplative existence of monasticism. Claiming that his father had forced him into the priesthood, Gregory abruptly fled to Annesi "like a cow stung by a gadfly" (*On his own Life* l. 350).[1] Nevertheless, he dutifully returned to work with his father within a year.

The years 361–3 saw the rule of the pagan emperor Julian ("the Apostate"). In 362 he passed legislation forbidding Christians to teach the Greek classics (a vital part of rhetorical training), but it was repealed in 364 by the new emperor, Jovian: around this time Gregory of Nyssa began to teach rhetoric. He also married, thus signaling a double difference from Basil and Gregory of Nazianzus, who had not only given up rhetoric professionally, but had also embraced certain ascetic habits, such as celibacy, even if they were unable to pursue a totally monastic lifestyle. (It was not unusual at the time for priests and bishops to be married.)

A double blow fell in the late 360s. A severe famine affected the area – charitable communities like Annesi helped the locals and took in orphan children. Secondly, Jovian's very short reign was followed by that of Valens, who opposed the Nicenes: "It was a time of exile, confiscation, banishment, threats of fines, danger of life, arrests, imprisonment, scourging" (Gregory of Nyssa, *Against Eunomius I*, p. 47).

Nevertheless, Basil, who had been elected bishop of Caesarea upon Eusebius's death in 370, managed to hold on to his bishopric. At the beginning of the 370s he met with Valens and defended his position (an event which was later much praised by both Gregorys); it is highly doubtful whether he affected Valens' doctrinal views, but the emperor recognized Basil's political talent and used him to strengthen the Empire's presence in Armenia through the Church.

Around the same time, Valens divided the province of Cappadocia in two: this resulted in Caesarea being the main town of Cappadocia Prima only, with a bishop unsympathetic to the Nicenes established in Cappadocia Secunda. With his influence thus restricted, Basil acted swiftly to create at least two new sees in Cappadocia Secunda. In 371 or 372 he made his brother bishop of Nyssa and his friend bishop of Sasima. We do not know Gregory of Nyssa's reaction to this appointment – although we do know that Basil disapproved of some of the moves he made while in this post. Gregory of Nazianzus' resentment, on the other hand, is famous: he took his appointment to the uncivilized staging point, as a snub deliberately planned to block his intended return to monasticism as soon as his father died (*On his own Life* l. 415–50). Once more he fled, this time to a retreat in the mountains, and he never formally took up the seat.

The next few years were testing times for all three Cappadocian fathers. Gregory of Nazianzus was forced by duty to return from the mountains to help his ailing father, who then died in 373, shortly followed by his mother. He was pressed by the congregation to take up his father's duties, but although he seems to have stayed for a short time, perhaps in an organizational capacity, he claims never to have administered any sacraments. Soon after, he fled yet again, this time to the convent of St. Thecla in Seleucia, where he stayed for about four years. Meanwhile, Gregory of Nyssa suffered under Valens' persecution of the Nicenes: he was accused of financial maladministration, but he appears to have eluded his opponents by fleeing from Nyssa. In 376 a synod convened in his absence formally deposed him from his seat and appointed an Arian successor. Even Basil encountered opposition, albeit from an unexpected quarter: Eustathius, his old inspiration in the monastic life, turned against him, joining the Pneumatomachians who denied the full divinity of the Holy Spirit and thus opposed Basil's whole Trinitarian doctrine. Basil fought back, amongst other things by writing his famous work *On the Holy Spirit*, but it is clear that the loss of Eustathius' friendship was a grave disappointment.

Nevertheless, the tide did turn in the late 370s. Basil's view of the Spirit began to gain ground, being ratified, for example, at a council in 376. The Nicenes' cause was further strengthened by the abrogation of Valens' decree, which allowed the return of exiles like Gregory of Nyssa in 378. Gregory of Nazianzus also returned to public life, having been invited by the small but strong congregation of pro-Nicenes at Constantinople to be their leader. It was during this period that his rhetorical talents reached perhaps their finest expression in his *Five Theological Orations*, defending what we now know as the "Cappadocian" doctrine of the Trinity.

Unfortunately, though, Basil did not live long enough to see a more decisive victory. He died in 379, apparently worn out by illness, with his brother Gregory at his side. Shortly after, Gregory also attended the death-bed of his sister Macrina. His account depicts Macrina as a much-loved and influential woman, esteemed not only by her own community, but also by the local people and the bishop and clergy of the neighbouring town (*The Life of Macrina* 33–4).

In 378 Theodosius had succeeded Valens; but his pro-Nicene sympathies only began to have effect in 380 with his edict making the doctrine of Nicaea the official teaching of the Empire and with his arrival in Constantinople a few months later. He asked the Arian bishop, Demophilus, to choose between the Nicene faith and exile, and, when Demophilus chose the latter, appointed Gregory of Nazianzus in his place. This ended Gregory's honeymoon period in Constantinople, for he immediately became embroiled in ecclesiastical and political in-fighting. This peaked at the council of Constantinople in 381: after the death of the president of the council, Meletius of Antioch, Gregory of Nazianzus was elected his successor; but delegations hostile to Gregory objected not only to his presidency but to his being bishop of Constantinople – on the grounds that he already held the bishopric of Sasima (and, arguably, that of Nazianzus too) and that transferal was forbidden. Gregory, tired, ill, and very frustrated, and possibly with the aim of gaining the moral high ground, offered to resign. His resignation was accepted and he returned to Nazianzus. Reluctantly persuaded to continue as bishop there, he eventually retired owing to ill-health and further complaints from his enemies about the legality of his position. He returned to his birthplace, Arianzus, and died several years later between 389 and 91.

Gregory of Nazianzus' experience of the council of Constantinople was obviously jaundiced: he was convinced that many delegates' quest for power had barred proper doctrinal debate. Nevertheless, the council is now remembered for its authoritative and influential ratification of the Nicene formula – this was probably the moment at which the balance was tipped decisively in favour of the "Cappadocian" doctrine of the Trinity. At a more personal level, the council also had positive results for Gregory of Nyssa, who until this point had remained in the shadows of Basil and Gregory of Nazianzus. Since his return from exile he had been engaged in defending his position in Nyssa against local Arians and in traveling to settle disputes between rival parties in other areas. Although he had been writing theology since about the early 370s, Basil's death seemed to act as a stimulus to his work: picking up the theological baton from his brother, he composed his own work *Against Eunomius*, and completed (indeed, went beyond) Basil's homilies on the six days of creation, the *Hexameron* (*On the Six Days of Creation*), with his own *Hexameron* and the very confident *On the Making of Man*. At the council of Constantinople Gregory of Nyssa was asked to give the funeral oration for Meletius, and, a few years later, those for two members of the imperial family. Soon after the council he was named in an imperial edict as one of three orthodox bishops with whom all in the diocese of Pontus must be in communion. Although this may not have given him any specific duties, he does seem to have continued to play the role of conciliator, travelling on one occasion to Arabia and then to the Holy Land (a journey which seems to have held few fond memories, for he used it as an example of why Christians should not go on pilgrimages).

Nevertheless, by the mid 380s Gregory's ecclesiastical influence began to wane, partly because some of his theological views were under attack and partly perhaps because his writing was turning away from the defense of specific doctrinal positions towards reflections on the nature of the Christian life. Writings like *The Life of Moses* and the *Commentary on the Song of Songs* are sometimes called ascetic works, but that does not mean they were programs for monasticism: although Gregory deeply respected the monastic life and although he occasionally appears to regret that it was not an option for him, in fact he seems never to have contemplated it seriously. (Being married was not necessarily an obstacle, because married couples sometimes entered a community, albeit living in separate quarters.) Rather, Gregory's very measured and moderate conception of asceticism was to see it as the ordering of the emotions and of physical needs so as to make room for and even perhaps to stimulate the search for and contemplation of God. As such, it was open to all Christians, whatever their vocation. Beyond the fact that some of his most important works were written in this period, we know almost nothing about the last years of Gregory's life. His wife probably died around 387 and Gregory himself died about ten years later.

Literary Achievements

Between them, the Cappadocians left a vast body of writings. Their inheritance from their rhetorical education was a deep conviction of the power of both the spoken and the written word to persuade, to prove, to inspire, to console, to ridicule, and to praise. A focus on their doctrinal or spiritual works alone, however, deflects attention away from the variety of subjects and genres found in their works. It also masks the extent to which Basil and the two Gregorys were men of their age and particular culture, as is clear from their letters, for example. Of the three, Gregory of Nyssa produced the most varied output, covering the whole range of genres listed below. Gregory of Nazianzus' surviving works comprise orations (including sermons or homilies), letters, and large quantities of poetry; Basil's comprise letters, homilies, dogmatic works, works about monasticism, and an essay on the benefits of a classical education. Here their writings are briefly analyzed according to subject matter (exegesis, doctrine, and ascetic and moral questions) and form (speeches, treatises, letters, poetry, biography).

Subject Matter

Naturally, much theological writing involved **exegesis**, but the two most important formal genres for the interpretation of Scripture were homilies (originally preached as sermons, often forming a series) and commentaries (usually more detailed). Particularly notable are Basil's *Hexameron* and his homilies on the Psalms.[2] Gregory of Nyssa wrote homilies on large portions of books, such as Ecclesiastes and the Song of Songs, and on short excerpts such as series on the Beatitudes and on the Lord's Prayer. He also wrote a piece of full-scale allegorical interpretation: the *Life of Moses*, which is in effect a commentary on the edited highlights of the last four books of the Pentateuch, comparing the soul's search for God to Moses' progress through the wilderness. Some theological treatises or essays were based on the detailed exegesis of a line of Scripture – see especially Gregory of Nyssa's *On 1 Corinthians 15:28*.

With regard to **doctrine**, ancient theologians did not write systematic theology in the modern sense. Even Origen's *On First Principles* is less systematic than it first appears and none of the Cappadocians seems to have tried to emulate it (although the *Philokalia* quoted excerpts from it). Gregory of Nyssa's *Catechetical Oration* was probably neither an oration nor, as once thought, intended for the catechesis of candidates for baptism: it was perhaps intended for an educated pagan audience, answering objections to Christianity. It is certainly not an attempt to set out the whole Christian faith and does not cover the theological range evident from Gregory's other writings. The Cappadocians' other dogmatic writings tend to be of two types: either defenses of a position (usually with a specific opponent in mind) or positive elucidations of a particular belief. Such doctrinal works usually take the form of sermons or treatises. Gregory of Nazianzus' *Theological Orations*, a series of five sermons preached in Constantinople in defense of the Nicene doctrine of the Trinity, became the epitome of the early doctrinal sermon. Basil too wrote sermons on the subject. Basil's and Gregory of Nyssa's works against Eunomius are clear examples of defensive treatises, as are Basil's *On the Holy Spirit* and some of Gregory's shorter dogmatic works (e.g. *To Ablabius, that there are not three Gods*; *To Eustathius, on the Holy Trinity*; and *To Theophilus, against the Apollinarians*). Their content clearly relates to the wider Trinitarian and Christological controversies of their day. By contrast, many of the works positively setting out a belief appear to be attempts to solve an addressee's specific query (e.g. Gregory of Nyssa's *On Infants' Early Deaths*); others spring from the author's own theological preoccupations: Gregory of Nyssa's *On the Soul and the Resurrection* probably emerges both from his interest in eschatology and from reflection on the deaths of Basil and Macrina. The latter is one of the most sophisticated of Cappadocian writings: a dialogue inspired by Plato's *Phaedo* boldly sets Macrina in the role of the dying philosopher (Socrates) encouraging her grieving disciple not to fear death. Whilst being philosophical in form, it deliberately challenges the orthodoxies of ancient philosophy: the beliefs that rationality is superior to faith, male to female, and soul to body. It is a demonstration (perhaps deliberately provocative) of the possibilities of the integration of Christianity with classical culture.

The final common theme is **ascetic and moral questions**. Each of the Cappadocians was very concerned with the practical demands of living a Christian life, especially with regard to the idea of living a life of ascetic simplicity, whether inside or outside a monastery. Basil in particular is remembered for formulating "rules' for monastic life, but even these are not rules in the formal sense, being a series of questions and answers on spiritual and organizational matters. Other of his ascetical writings are addressed to a wider audience and are intended to promote the same standard of moral life to all Christians – the love of God and of neighbour within a communal life – and in particular to stamp out ascetic extremism. Gregory of Nyssa addressed ascetical themes in some treatises (*On Virginity*, *On being a Christian*;[3] *On perfection*); Gregory of Nazianzus in some of his poems (I.2.1 on virginity, and I.2.10 on virtue[4]). Homilies too were used for reflection on moral questions, sometimes on vices or virtues (Basil, *Homily* 10 on anger; 11 on envy; 14 on drunkenness; 4 on the giving of thanks; 20 on humility[5]), sometimes on social issues such as the treatment of the poor (Gregory of Nyssa, *On Generosity* [*or On Loving the Poor*][6]) or the 368 famine (Basil, *Homily* 8).

Form

As rhetoricians, public speaking was second nature to the Cappadocians. Their speeches usually took the form of **sermons** (sometimes called homilies), often used for exegesis, and for doctrinal and moral questions, as we have already seen. In addition, there were several types of celebratory sermon: marking feast days (Nazianzen's *Oration* 38 on Christmas; 39 on Epiphany; 41 on Pentecost; Nyssen's *Easter Sermons*; *On the Nativity*; *On the Ascension*); honouring a sacrament, especially baptism (Basil's *Homily* 13; Nazianzen's *Oration* 40; Nyssen's *On the Baptism of Christ*); or commemorating martyrs and saints (Basil's *Homilies* 5, 18,19; Nazianzen's *Orations* 15, 21, 24, 44; Nyssen's *On Stephen*; *On Theodore*; *On the Forty Martyrs*; *On Gregory Thaumaturgus*). We have already noted that Gregory of Nyssa was called to give several funeral sermons; we also have examples from Gregory of Nazianzus (*Orations* 7, 8, 18). Both Gregorys wrote sermons commemorating Basil (Nyssen *On Basil*; Nazianzen *Oration* 43).

Treatises were usually doctrinal, although their essay-like form was sometimes used to treat more general issues, for example Basil's *How Young Men can Derive Profit from Pagan Literature* and Gregory of Nyssa's *On Fate*.

Letters were important to the Cappadocians not only for private communication, but also for the public dissemination of their ideas (letters originally addressed to one person were often passed on). Basil left over three hundred letters from which we can learn much about his personal and private relationships, about his plans for the organization of the Church and monastic life, and his views on doctrine, society, and pastoral issues. (The identification of some letters' authorship is problematic: Basil's letter 38 on the Trinity is now generally thought to be Gregory of Nyssa's, and several others are by Gregory of Nazianzus. The collection also contains some letters from Basil's correspondents.) By contrast, Gregory of Nazianzus' preoccupation seems often to be the perfection of the letter as a literary form (he was the first Christian writer to make a collection of his own correspondence). This means that it is sometimes difficult to excavate personal or historical information from beneath their polished form – his poetry is more revealing of his personality. The few surviving letters from Gregory of Nyssa cover personal, pastoral, doctrinal, and ecclesiastical themes. Some are addressed to pagan friends. Gregory too was a skilled exponent of the conventions of ancient literary letter-writing and his letters are full of references to classical literature; however, they also provide an insight into his sensitive character which is often hidden in the rest of his writing.

Gregory of Nazianzus wrote some 17,000 lines of **poetry**. Whilst this choice of form makes him unusual among Christian writers, he generally adapted conventional classical forms and themes without much originality of style, but with frequently striking expression. The poems are variously didactic (dogmatic, moral), consolatory, and reflective. However, one poem – *On his own Life* – stands out for its innovation and captivating narrative, and adds something new to ancient autobiography.

Gregory of Nyssa's *The Life of Saint Macrina* produced an original sort of prose **biography**, fusing elements from biography, autobiography (his own reactions to Macrina's death), hagiography, funeral orations, and treatises on asceticism.

Theological Achievements

The Doctrine of the Trinity

The Cappadocians are often credited with the decisive development of the Christian doctrine of the Trinity: the Nicene formula was defended and given a more nuanced interpretation by the Cappadocians so that, after a period of semi-Arian dominance, the council of Constantinople finally reiterated this particular reading of Nicaea. The "Cappadocian settlement" of the doctrine of the Trinity is often summarized by the phrase, "one *ousia*, three *hupostases*" – one essence, three persons. However, it has recently been argued that this formula is convenient modern academic shorthand, rather than a phrase used frequently by the Cappadocians themselves, and even that the word *homoousios* features surprisingly rarely in their writings.[7] Furthermore, it is difficult to assess precisely what influence the Cappadocians had at Constantinople: Basil was dead, Gregory of Nazianzus was embroiled in the dispute surrounding his election as bishop of Constantinople, and we have no record of the role played by Gregory of Nyssa beyond his giving of Meletius' funeral oration.

Clearly, however, the Cappadocians' Trinitarian writings were influential. Why was this, and what were their actual achievements? First, the highly-educated Cappadocians were well-placed to combat the intellectual precision, sophisticated argumentation, and rhetorical ploys of Eunomius, who, like them, was rhetorically trained. Equally importantly, they understood the qualms of those who feared that Nicaea might be taken to condone a form of modalism. Consequently, they stress that although the Son shares the Father's essence or nature they are eternally distinct. Finally, Basil (and, to a lesser extent, the two Gregorys) had the personality and the ecclesiastical influence to convince other churchmen that it was this interpretation of the doctrine of the Trinity, and not that of the semi-Arian homoiousians, which was the moderate and truthful way forward.

Although they advocated essentially the same doctrine, the three can be argued to have made distinct but cumulative contributions.[8] It is with Basil that we first find the emphasis that *ousia* denotes what is common and *hupostasis* what is particular – perhaps a grammatical more than a philosophical distinction. Basil then argued not only that all three persons are equal, because the same essence is common to them, but that the essence is common to them because it is communicated from the Father to the Son and to the Spirit. Thus he asserted that the Father is cause of, but in no sense superior to, the other two persons (a theory sometimes confusingly referred to as the Father's "monarchy", from the Greek *monarchia*, meaning "being sole cause of"). Gregory of Nazianzus was the first to analyze the differences between the persons in terms of their relations (and not other qualities, such as goodness or power, which must be identical in each person; or faculties, such as will or power, which all three must share if they are not three gods). Gregory of Nyssa carried on these lines of reasoning, by reemphasizing that each person is involved in *every* divine action (they are not distinguished by doing different things): the Father initiates, the Son is the means, and the Spirit completes. He seems to think that these causal relations between the three persons in the economy in some way parallel their relations in their shared essence: the Father is the cause, the Son is begotten, and the Spirit is breathed. He also attempted to explain further the application of the analogy of three people to the Trinity, which had drawn accusations of tritheism.

The Cappadocians also differed in their approach to the Holy Spirit. Whilst it is very clear that Basil regarded the Spirit as sharing equally in the divine essence with the Father and the Son (*On the Holy Spirit* 13–16) and was particularly insistent that the Spirit should not be called a creature, he hesitated to call the Spirit "God" and to say explicitly that the Spirit is *homoousios* with the Father and Son. The two Gregorys were much happier to say that the Spirit was God, but they added little to Basil's views and to their doctrine of the Trinity which had in fact always entailed the Spirit's divinity, even if much of the debate focused on the Son.

The Cappadocians' use of imagery and vocabulary for the Trinity was highly influential. In their arguments against Eunomius they steered a line between his pseudo-scientific verbal precision and an empty agnosticism: God's essence cannot be defined, they argued, but we can learn about the three persons from Scripture and from God's action in the world. Consequently, they did make some theological language more precise – in particular, distinguishing *ousia* and *hupostasis*, which had earlier often been used interchangeably. Although many of their analogies, such as sunlight, the scent of perfume, a river, were not original to them (many deriving ultimately from Scripture), they developed them in new and memorable ways – whilst at the same time warning that no analogies (especially no physical analogies) could be adequate to explain God.[9]

The Cappadocians claimed not to be innovators compared to Eunomius, whom they insisted was imposing new restrictive definitions on God (e.g. Basil, *On the Holy Spirit* VI:13). Nevertheless, in their distinction of *ousia* and *hupostasis*, in their examination of how the being and the persons of God are related, and how the persons are related one to another in being and action, in their use of traditional biblical vocabulary and images in new ways, they can justly be credited with very significant developments in the Christian doctrine of the Trinity.

Christology

Apollinarius of Laodicea (c.310–c.390) was a strong supporter of Nicaea, a friend of Athanasius and correspondent of Basil (Basil, *Letters* 361–4). However, by around 375 his views on the person of Christ were becoming suspect and they were condemned at the council of Constantinople in 381.

A strong defense of the divinity of the Son naturally leads to the question of how to explain the Incarnation: either the humanity of Jesus Christ is an illusion, or there is the problem of how to explain the full union of the human and the divine. The former view – docetism – had been held by some Gnostics and was vigorously denied by many Christian writers. Apollinarius explained the union of divine and human analogously with the union of soul and body in humankind.[10] This had the advantage of explaining why Christ was sinless: he lacked a fallible human soul.

Basil died before the controversy became very heated, but did affirm that Christ had a human soul – partly because this had to be what experienced human suffering, or Christ's divinity would not be perfect. The two Gregorys played a more important role and both were clearly influenced by Origen's emphasis on Christ's human soul (the "Logos-Anthropos" (Word-Human) model). Gregory of Nazianzus summed up the theological problem inherent in Apollinarius' solution with his famous – and typically pithy – "what has not been assumed cannot be healed".[11] He recognized that it was precisely sinful human nature in both aspects, body and soul, that needed redeeming, and that a savior who had assumed a human body alone could not redeem the fallible soul. This viewpoint rests on a theory of redemption which stresses the Incarnation much more than the cross; it sees salvation in terms of healing[12] and of divinization – the divinization of the man Jesus Christ by the indwelling of the divine Word being the epitome of the divinization of each believer.[13]

Gregory of Nyssa's writings against Apollinarius (*Against the Apollinarians*; *Reply to Apollinarius*; *Catechetical Oration* 9, 10, 27; *Against Eunomius* III.3) attempted to clarify some of the issues left unresolved by explanations such as Nazianzen's – in particular the question of how Jesus Christ can be said to be one person, if he is both fully human and fully divine. This led to a more complex and subtle argument, but one lacking Gregory of Nazianzus' clarity. It is particularly confusing if judged by the standards of later Christological debates: Gregory sometimes seems to assert that Christ had two natures, sometimes that he had one. The best explanation of his view is that Christ's human and divine natures become gradually less and less distinct until humanity is overwhelmed by divinity.[14] Gregory suggested that ultimately Christ's human nature was renewed by being mixed with the "overwhelming" divine nature, just as mixing a drop of vinegar into the sea makes it appear to be seawater, because all its natural *qualities* (e.g. acidity) disappear "in the infinity of that which overwhelms it," although its constituent *parts* never cease to exist.[15] Gregory of Nyssa's Christology thus reflected his wider conception of redemption: while he emphasized the goodness and importance of the material body, he suggested that eschatologically, through participation in God, individuals would be taken up into a higher spiritual realm which would transform the qualities, but not destroy the matter of the physical body.[16]

Salvation History

The connection between both Gregorys' Christology and their concept of redemption reminds us that the Cappadocians' reflections on the Trinity and on Christ are set in a wider theological framework. Their view that we cannot define God's essence is not purely negative: it reflects a profound belief that God's actions reflect his true essence, albeit in a refracted and indirect manner. Hence their thought is set within their conception of the divine *oikonomia*, or economy (a Greek word literally meaning "management of the household" which Christians used for God's dealings with the world). They believed that because God created and sustains the world, it has a fundamental order – despite all appearances to the contrary – which will be perfected at the end of time. Thus Basil's and Gregory of Nyssa's works on creation stressed its proper order and explained why different stages of creation and different creatures have forms and characters appropriate to their functions (Basil, *Hexameron*; Gregory, *Hexameron*[17] and *On the Making of Man*). They used contemporary science to show that Christianity was not superstition, but a rational faith reflecting the rational order of the universe. (They also sought to distinguish the Christian doctrine of creation *ex nihilo* both from pagan ideas of emanation and from the Father's begetting of the Son.)

The *Philokalia* contains a large section of extracts from Origen on human free will: they show it is part of the divine economy of salvation and that God's apparently cruel acts in the Old Testament merely punish people in order to reform them. Gregory of Nyssa's eschatology is focused on the same conception of purificatory divine punishment: like Origen he claims that since God is good and cannot fail in his purpose, all people will eventually be punished, purified, and thus saved (e.g. *On the Soul and the Resurrection* NPNF V, p. 451). Gregory of Nazianzus appears to have shared this universalistic view (*Oration* 30:6), but placed very little emphasis on it; Basil believed in an eternal hell.

The Christian Life

Whereas eschatology infuses nearly all of Gregory of Nyssa's thought, it did not play such an important part in the writings of the others. Nevertheless all three emphasized the continuing transformation of the individual through divine grace in this life. For precisely this reason, moral questions for the Cappadocians were not side issues: virtue is the human free response to and participation in the divine economy. They did not mean that humans could earn salvation though good deeds; rather, they thought that the potential for divinization lay in God's gracious creation of humanity in his own image. Gregory of Nyssa developed the notion of *sunergeia* ("working with God") in the Christian life.[18] It is found in the ideas of the imitation of Christ (e.g. *Homilies on the Beatitudes* I:2) and of pilgrimage (the progress through the desert: *The Life of Moses*; climbing "the mountain of the Lord" or Jacob's ladder: *Homilies on the Beatitudes*). This dynamic notion of discipleship as movement forward and upward takes its most original form in Gregory's famous notion of *epektasis* – "stretching out toward" – a perpetual progress toward and participation in God in love and knowledge: *perpetual* because humanity is finite and God infinite, but always a *progress* because God graciously allows us to move toward him in such a way that we are paradoxically always satisfied, yet always left seeking more.[19] Although this notion was original to Gregory, the idea of participation in God was common to all three Cappadocians and explains a tension in their writing. On the one hand they emphasize that the Gospel's call to discipleship is addressed to all, whatever their walk of life. On the other hand, all three men hankered for the time and space for the contemplation of God in prayer (usually within monasticism), because they thought it was the purest precursor of participation in God in the life to come. Thus they were attracted to this life of devotion, whilst seeing it as a luxury, recognizing that it pulled them away from their practical ecclesiastical concerns and fully acknowledging that it was not to be advocated for all people.

Connected with this is their moderate approach to asceticism: although they acknowledge the benefits of ascetical discipline, they always urged against excess and sometimes remarked that the point is not so much physical denial, but spiritual devotion (Basil, *Homily* 1 on fasting; Gregory of Nyssa, *On Virginity*). They thus left a way open for a dedicated Christian life outside monasticism, whilst warning of the distractions of a non-monastic life.

"Philosophia" and the Worldly Life

This sort of debate about what sort of life constitutes the best Christian path was memorably captured by Gregory Nazianzus in his autobiographical poem which contrasted the contemplative life which benefits its practitioner, with the practical life which is more widely beneficial (ll. 302–12). This echoed the traditional Greek distinction between a life of contemplation – *philosophia* – and a life of action. For the ancients, *philosophia* denoted not just the intellectual discipline of philosophy, but a way of life usually involving some degree of ascetic discipline and isolation. This idea was transferred over to Christian monasticism: the word Gregory of Nyssa uses for Macrina's chosen way of life is *philosophia*.

But although the Cappadocians used the contemplation–action distinction themselves, it is easy to misunderstand it, since it is used in several different ways. First, in the extract above, Gregory of Nazianzus makes the distinction in terms of *usefulness*: the difference between a life of public service and solitude. The sort of monasticism he envisages seems to be a hermit's life, the most extreme sort of solitude, unsuitable even for the study of the Scriptures (ll. 296–8). But the communal monastic life of places like Annesi involved much work for the local poor and Macrina self-consciously adopted tasks like breadmaking usually done by the household slaves. So when her brother Gregory praises *philosophia*, he sees it being opposed not to usefulness, nor to action, but to a secular life, with all the distractions imposed by a job and family. This second contrast, like the first, is between two different ways of living a Christian life, but the form of monasticism it advocates is more moderate because it is, in fact, more practical. (In such a way, the Cappadocians in fact dissented from Eustathius' more extreme form of asceticism.)

Yet, while some of the distractions of everyday life are tiresome, others are more pernicious temptations. Consequently, the contrast sometimes takes a third form: the distinction between a life of virtue (*philosophia*) and a life of the world. Since this contrast is between a Christian life (whether monastic or not) and a life which is not Christian, the Cappadocians were able to enjoin this sort of *philosophia* on all Christians, regardless of their vocation.

Finally, in late antiquity the action–contemplation contrast alluded to in Gregory of Nazianzus' poem was frequently compared with the contrast between rhetoric and philosophy: rhetoric training for the worldly life of the courts and politics; philosophy training of the soul. Rhetoric was thus attacked by philosophers for being a utilitarian tool not aimed at the truth; rhetoricians thought philosophers abdicated from the responsibilities of public duty. Some of this contrast is also found in the Cappadocians – most obviously in their attacks on Eunomius, whom they criticize for manipulating technical jargon, instead of aiming at the simple truth. But of course this attack was being made by trained rhetoricians who were every bit as capable of matching Eunomius' verbal firepower and who believed in the necessity of devoting human words to the service of the divine Word.

The Use of Philosophy

The Cappadocians' use of contemporary Hellenistic philosophy is an extremely complex issue and is best studied in relation to specific issues (such as the doctrine of the Trinity; Platonic and Aristotelian ideas; Christology and the moral life; Stoicism; the soul's participation in God; Neoplatonism).[20] Here it will be more constructive to raise some general issues. First, while the Cappadocians clearly use philosophical vocabulary, this does not always mean that they used it in the same way as philosophers did: it was quite common for some words to have both technical and non-technical meanings and for Christians either to vacillate between the two or to alter the meaning again to suit their own purposes. Thus although it is often helpful to know the previous philosophical uses of a word like *hypostasis*, the most important question must be: what did the *Cappadocians* mean by the word?

Secondly, it is difficult to know what philosophy the Cappadocians had actually read. Philosophy formed part of their senior education (even as rhetors) but the use of textbooks of excerpts was common and they may not have read many full works. A further puzzle is that Gregory of Nyssa – who claimed to have been taught by Basil – had a better comprehension of contemporary philosophy than Basil and was probably better read. He must have read some works, such as Plato's *Phaedo*, in their entirety. Scholars have managed to draw further conclusions about what the Cappadocians read, by tracing close verbal similarities between their writings and philosophical texts.

The most important general point to make is that, despite occasionally sniping at "pagan learning," all three Cappadocians were deeply infused by it. The balance between philosophy and theology varies from man to man and topic to topic, but the former never overwhelmed the latter. Nevertheless, getting rid of all trace of their classical education would have been as difficult for the Cappadocians as ceasing to write and speak in Greek.

Interpretation of Scripture

The Cappadocians' hermeneutics are largely inspired by Origen. They follow his view – as expressed in the excerpts in the *Philokalia* – that since all of Scripture is inspired by God, it must all be useful: any part which appears immoral or facile has a spiritual meaning hidden beneath the surface. This is uncovered by a variety of exegetical techniques, such as allegory or typology (seeing characters and events in the Old Testament as types or forerunners of those in the New Testament). Nevertheless, the literal meaning of the text does remain important: Gregory of Nyssa's *Life of Moses* would not make sense if Moses were not a historical figure as well as a metaphor. Although Origen's approach meant that certain texts would be difficult for the average congregation to understand, and although he recommended that some be kept for Christians of some maturity, this did not necessarily lead to elitism. First, it put the onus on the preacher to expound Scripture (hence the large number of Cappadocian exegetical homilies) and secondly, the Cappadocians' progressive concept of Christian life suggested that all Christians could at some stage reach the same point of understanding.

A few differences from Origen are apparent in the Cappadocians' exegesis. They were more interested in the text's structure (a result perhaps of their rhetorical training): in Basil's and Gregory's *Hexamerons* the sequence of the text of Genesis is central; and Gregory of Nyssa's larger exegetical works have an eschatological structure in which the beginnings and the ends of the texts are vital for the interpretation of the whole (e.g. *On the Beatitudes*; *On the Inscriptions of the Psalms*; *On the Song of Songs*). In addition, much Cappadocian exegesis was influenced by their debates with opponents. For example, in *On the Holy Spirit* Basil criticized an overly literal approach to Scripture, protesting that arguments cannot be constructed out of mere prepositions, because Scripture itself is flexible and varied in how it uses them (chapters IV and V). Gregory of Nazianzus met the Eunomians' stock of proof-texts with an overwhelming compilation of his own (e.g. *Orations* 29 and 30): not sinking to their level, but effectively showing that by concentrating on a selection of proof texts, the Eunomians did not do justice to the meaning of Scripture as a whole. Gregory also emphasized the unknowability of God's true essence, despite the revelation of Scripture (*Oration* 28); this line of thought was extended by Gregory of Nyssa into a sophisticated theory of language. In response to Eunomius he argued that although God gave humans the ability to speak, all words are human constructs and fallible tools. Even language about everyday things struggles to hit its mark; no wonder then that it is impossible for human words to talk directly of God, far less to define him. Even the words of Scripture, although divinely inspired, are human words; thus although they are the best descriptions of God we have, they are nevertheless only approximations which are heading in the right direction.

Postscript

Basil and Gregory of Nazianzus became great Fathers of the Eastern church, along with Athanasius and Chrysostom, and they are generally celebrated more prominently than Gregory of Nyssa. This was partly as a result of their ecclesiastical roles: Basil was an important and influential bishop and his monastic rules had lasting significance. Gregory of Nazianzus came to be seen as having played a key role at a key time when he preached his theological orations at Constantinople. For his clear and compelling style of address, which became a standard for later Byzantine homiletics, and for his defense of orthodoxy, he was given the title "Gregory the Theologian." Despite his affirmation as a touchstone of orthodoxy by Theodosius, Gregory of Nyssa never had the same sort of impact. His writing, although more profound, was also more complex and more capable of misinterpretation by his enemies. He later became suspect when an Origenistic form of the doctrine of universal salvation was condemned by the fifth ecumenical council in 553. Although Gregory did not teach the form of the doctrine condemned by the council, he clearly did believe that all people would be saved and this probably tainted his reputation, despite his staunch defense of Trinitarian orthodoxy. Oddly enough, however, it is his theology which is now most commented on and used as a resource by modern theologians. Although all three Cappadocians are regularly cited for their works on the Trinity and the Holy Spirit (where there has been a decided preference for Gregory of Nazianzus' writings among Protestant systematicians) and although the writings of Basil and Gregory of Nazianzus are still of great value, the sheer scope and depth of Gregory of Nyssa's work has meant that when it comes to wider theological questions, particularly those on the spiritual life, it is he whose legacy has recently provoked the widest – and most diverse – comment.

Notes

1   *Gregory of Nazianzus. Autobiographical Poems*, trans. C. White, Cambridge Medieval Classics 6 (Cambridge, 1996).
2   *Saint Basil, Exegetic Homilies*, trans. Sister Agnes Clare Way, CDP, Fathers of the Church 46 (Washington, DC, 1963).
3   *Saint Gregory of Nyssa: Ascetical Works* (including: *On Virginity, The Life of Macrina*), trans. V. Woods Callahan, Fathers of the Church 58 (Washington, DC, 1967).
4   PG 37, cols. 521–78; 680–752.
5   PG 31, no. 10, cols. 353–72; no. 11, cols. 372–85; no. 14, cols. 444–64; no. 4, cols. 217–37; no. 8, cols. 304–28.
6   In *Gregorii Nysseni Opera*, vol. IX, ed. A. van Heck (Leiden, 1967), pp. 93–108.
7   Lienhard, 1999, p. 99; Barnes, 1998, pp. 59–61.
8   E.g. Meredith, 1995, pp. 104–11.
9   Hanson, 1982, esp. pp. 104–9.
10 Grillmeier's so-called "Logos–Sarx" (Word–Flesh) Christology: Grillmeier, 1965, pp. 220ff.
11 Gregory of Nazianzus, *Letter* 101.
12 Meredith, 1995, p. 112.
13 Grillmeier, 1965, p. 280.
14 Meredith, 1995, p. 113; Meredith, 1999, p. 48; Gregory of Nyssa, *Against Eunomius*, III.3, NPNF, p. 180.
15 Gregory of Nyssa, *Against Eunomius*, III.3, NPNF, p. 181.
16 Ludlow, 2000, p. 71.
17 Gregory of Nyssa, *Apologia in Hexaëmeron*, PG 44, cols. 61–124.
18 Ludlow, 2000, pp. 105–6.
19 Ibid., pp. 62–4.
20 For a good introduction to the specifics, see Meredith, 1995, pp. 118–24.

Bibliography

(The introductions to the texts in the List of Sources are also very valuable.)

Michel René Barnes, "The Fourth Century as Trinitarian Canon" in Lewis Ayres and Gareth Jones (eds.), *Christian Origins: Theology, Rhetoric, Community* (London, 1998).

Susanna Elm, *"Virgins of God" The Making of Asceticism in Late Antiquity* (Oxford, 1994).

P. J. Fedwick (ed.), *Basil of Caesarea: Christian, Humanist, Ascetic: A Sixteen-Hundredth Anniversary Symposium*, Parts One and Two (Toronto, 1981).

A. Grillmeier, *Christ in Christian Tradition* (London), 1965, pp. 220–33, 278–91.

R. P. C. Hanson, "The transformation of Images in the Trinitarian Theology of the Fourth

Century", in *Studia Patristica* XVII:1 (Oxford and New York, 1982).

—— *The Search for the Christian Doctrine of God* (Edinburgh, 1988), ch. 21.

Joseph T. Lienhard, "Ousia and Hypostasis: The Cappadocian Settlement and the Theology of 'One Hypostasis'" in Stephen Davis, Daniel Kendall, and Gerard O' Collins (eds.), *The Trinity: An Interdisciplinary Symposium* (Oxford, 1999).

Morwenna Ludlow, *Universal Salvation: Eschatology in the Thought of Gregory of Nyssa and Karl Rahner* (Oxford, 2000).

Anthony S. J. Meredith, *The Cappadocians* (New York, 1995).

—— *Gregory of Nyssa* (London, 1999).

J. Pelikan, *Christianity and Classical Culture* (New Haven, CT, 1993).

P. Rousseau, *Basil of Caesarea* (Berkeley, CA and Oxford, 1994).

R. R. Ruether, *Gregory of Nazianzus, Rhetor and Philosopher* (Oxford, 1969).

M. Slussler, *St. Gregory Thaumaturgus: Life and Works*, Fathers of the Church. (Washington DC, 1998.)

Pseudo-Dionysius and Maximus the Confessor

Janet P. Williams

Dionysius the Areopagite

The Dionysian Corpus

According to the Acts of the Apostles, around thirty years after the death of Christ the Apostle Paul travelled to Athens to preach the Gospel: a mission not merely to a Gentile city, but to the symbolic custodians of the intellectual culture of the time.[1] The sermon recorded in chapter 17 of Acts stands, therefore, as a demonstration of the Gospel's philosophical credentials, its ability to meet Greek philosophy on the latter's own ground, and its superiority in answering the great questions. Scripture records the names of two early converts, the woman Damaris and the man Dionysius, a member of the great council of the Areopagus, the ancient law-court of Athens.

Nearly five centuries later, a group of texts ascribed to "Dionysius the Areopagite" came to attention when in 532CE certain Monophysite theologians, in debate over the nature of Christ, appealed to quotations from them to support their position. The party subsequently judged "orthodox" retorted that they did not accept the validity of the quoted texts, accounting them spurious on the grounds that earlier Fathers of the Church had neither quoted them nor apparently known them. Within two further centuries, however, such doubts had largely been glossed over, thanks to the work of two undeniably orthodox commentators, John of Scythopolis and Maximus the Confessor. More importantly, Maximus in particular reacted as many other readers of these texts have reacted since, finding contained in them a spirituality so provocative and nutritious that his own vision and expression of the Christian life was profoundly affected by them.

The theology presented in the texts ascribed to Dionysius the Areopagite, though it contains much that is original, belongs within the great Eastern tradition stretching from Clement of Alexandria and Origen, through the Cappadocian Fathers, particularly Gregory of Nyssa, on to Maximus and beyond. Partly because of the depth of that tradition, Dionysius' particular work, though important, has not had outstanding significance for the Eastern Churches; in the West, however, since other representatives of this tradition were less well known, the work of Dionysius has had more substantial impact. Froehlich commented that "Except for the Bible and perhaps the works of Boethius, no writing of the early Christian era received similar attention [in the West] in terms of translations, excerpts, commentaries, and even cumulative corpora that combined these elements into veritable encyclopaedias of Dionysian scholarship" (Luibheid, 1987, p. 33). It was believed that Dionysius the Areopagite had subsequently become the bishop of Paris, Saint-Denis, the martyr commemorated at Montmartre: the writings of such a prestigious apostle and martyr were naturally of enormous significance. The schoolmen of the early Middle Ages appealed to him as an authority not only on mysticism but also on issues of church governance; some of the mystics of the period had drunk deep of his ideas, particularly the unknown fourteenth-century English author of *The Cloud of Unknowing*, fifteenth-century Nicholas of Cusa, and the sixteenth-century Spaniard, John of the Cross. His texts were an inspiration to the humanist thinkers of the Reformation, affecting even the young Luther.

But growing interest among humanists and Protestant scholars in textual studies raised again the issue of the authenticity of the corpus. Luther came to agree with Erasmus in dismissing the work of "Dionysius-whoever-he-was," finding altogether more Greek philosophy than theology in it. At the close of the nineteenth century Koch and Stiglmayr proved that the author had depended substantially on the work of Proclus, a fifth-century Neoplatonist philosopher who was not merely pagan but explicitly anti-Christian. It now seems that these texts must have been written at some time between the maturity of Proclus (412–85CE) and their first quotation in 532, probably nearer the end of that period than the beginning. They seem to betray a knowledge of Syrian liturgy, and the earliest interest in them is also Syrian, so we may surmise that they have a Syrian origin. As to who wrote them, many fascinating hypotheses have been put forward, but the fact remains that we do not know.

Though the corpus may be promulgated under a pseudonym, it would be an overreaction to dismiss it as fraudulent and therefore worthless. It emanates from a culture in which pseudonymity was used for many more reasons than fraud, including modest homage and a perfectly respectable intellectual anonymity; and its quite considerable historical significance aside, as generations of readers have found, its contents amply justify theological interest. The corpus as we have it includes four treatises, *The Ecclesiastical Hierarchy*, *The Celestial Hierarchy*, *The Divine Names*, and *The Mystical Theology*, and in addition ten *Letters*. They include references to further texts (*The Theological Representations*; *The Symbolic Theology*) for whose existence we have no evidence: it may be that they are lost, or more likely that they too are fictions.

Major Themes

Dionysius sometimes talks as if there were two quite distinct ways of doing theology within his work: he offers in *The Mystical Theology* a distinction between cataphatic theology (making affirmations about the created order and God as Creator) and apophatic theology (denying that these statements can tell us about the transcendent

Divinity, who must be sought beyond all that derives from him); and in the ninth letter, a different division between theology which "resorts to symbolism and involves initiation" and that which "is philosophic and involves the method of demonstration" (1105D); other distinctions might center on the division between theologies employing "like" and "unlike" likenesses to God, or within the corpus itself between hierarchical/cosmological works and interior/mystical works. However, these (never entirely compatible) divisions express, rather than breach, the unity at the heart of his work: they do no more than reflect the two sides of the life of the cosmos and the human individual, in the characteristic Neoplatonist motif of procession from God's creative activity, and return to God in contemplation. These are two sides of one life process: not stages in which one succeeds the other, but complementary moments like inhalation and exhalation. Within this unified life, Dionysius' major themes include the beyondness of God, anagogy, hierarchy, divinization, apophasis, and unknowing. Moreover, these themes, embedded within descriptions of the divine, the life of the Church and the individual's manner of relation to God, are never simply analysis or description, but prepare for, and participate in, the creature's response of praise and worship to the heart-breaking beauty and generosity of its Maker.

Dionysius' God is, in a sense, utterly transcendent, and Dionysius expresses this with the Neoplatonic philosophers' trick of prefixing words with "hyper" – he thus modifies a huge number of terms to express the excessive divinity, its sheer bursting of the boundaries of all that we can think. It surpasses all being (*MT* 1000B), since all being is caused by God. It is therefore above all knowledge: all the things which we are able to think and say of God need ultimately to be unthought and unsaid. There is no name by which we can know him: "nothing that is or is known can proclaim that hiddenness beyond every mind and reason of the transcendent Godhead which transcends every being. There is no name for it nor expression. We cannot follow it into its inaccessible dwelling place so far above us and we cannot even call it by the name of goodness." (*DN* 981A) Yet Dionysius' language is of the "beyondness" of God, not of transcendence as opposed to immanence; and therefore, in a typical paradox, the divine which is beyond all duality transcends even the duality of transcendence and immanence, is known in all created works, and called by every name.[2] This is not a distant causality, but an immediate presence: "the very cause of the universe . . . is, as it were, beguiled by goodness, by love, and by yearning and is enticed away from his transcendent dwelling place and comes to abide within all things, and he does so by virtue of his supernatural and ecstatic capacity to remain, nevertheless, within himself." (*DN* 712A-B)

Dionysius' favourite term for the spiritual life is "anagogy", literally "being led upward." For him, therefore, Christian discipleship is not a simple matter of a once-for-all commitment to Gospel truth, or a "conversion" experienced whole and complete. Implicitly recalling Gregory of Nyssa's notion of *epectasis*, the never-ending penetration into God, Dionysius envisages a continual process of discovery in which God leads the soul into ever-deeper relation with himself.[3] This process occurs through all the providential aspects of Christian life. In engagement with Scripture, the disciple may begin with a quite simple understanding of God, but the very strangeness of many scriptural images will lead him or her first to question their purport, and gradually to understand that all divine images, visual or conceptual, are inadequate and need to be used for growth and then laid aside as we journey away from image and toward reality.[4] In ecclesial life, the disciple will be nourished by the sacraments – first of baptism, subsequently by the eucharist and others – and gradually drawn deeper through them into the life of the Spirit; and also by the liturgy, which Dionysius expounds in *The Ecclesiastical Hierarchy* as giving symbolic expression to the activity of God in the world. Further, Dionysius assumes, although he spends little time developing it, that discipleship also involves a progress in the moral life, a growth particularly toward becoming the self-giving love which is the very creative nature of the Godhead (*DN* 977B-C). Although he sometimes uses the term "ascent," Dionysius prefers the term "anagogy" for its clearer expression of the passivity of this progress, whereby the soul is lifted up by God, both directly and through the medium of the hierarchies he has ordained. At each stage as it is lifted up, the soul sloughs off all the limited knowledge of God acquired in prior stages – knowledge derived from sensory experience of creation, from rational reflection on experience, biblical revelation and church teaching and activity, and from its own spiritual experiences to date. Spiritual growth, therefore, is not simply a matter of progress in acquisition of knowledge or virtue or – least of all – ecclesiastical rank, but rather a progressive realization of that dying to self which Christ demanded of his disciples (Mark 8:34–5). Thus at the beginning of *The Mystical Theology* Dionysius makes it clear that the final goal of union with God is only attainable by "an undivided and absolute abandonment of yourself and everything" (1000A).

Despite his interest in what we might see as an "interior" life, Dionysius' vision is cosmic in scope, and his vision of the cosmos is thoroughgoingly hierarchical. This does not mean, however, quite what we might assume. Although a ranked and ordered universe is characteristic of the Neoplatonic framework of thought within which he is working, the term "hierarchy" is actually Dionysius' own coinage, derived from the word "hierarch," meaning a pagan high priest (which Dionysius uses to refer to the Christian bishop). In chapter 3 of *The Celestial Hierarchy* Dionysius defines his new word: "a hierarchy is a sacred order, a state of understanding and an activity approximating as closely as possible to the divine" (164D). This definition is significant for two reasons. First, whereas the philosophical motif of the "great chain of being" has existence flowing from the divine source through successive ranks of creatures, the Christian hierarchy mediates knowledge alone: in accordance with the doctrine of creation *ex nihilo*, Dionysius' God grants being directly to each creature. Secondly, although there was an element of dynamism in the philosophers' view of being, expressed in the theme of procession and return, such a stately order is radically qualified by Dionysius' insistence on the ecstasy of God, whereby the divine abandons its place of dignity at the head of the hierarchy because of its yearning love of humanity, taking on human flesh and suffering human death, and being immediately present to individual souls at the height of the spiritual ascent. Jean-Luc Marion has identified a further significance to the Dionysian understanding of hierarchy, namely that whereas the established hierarchies of Western culture stifle individuality and freedom by conferring not just being but power on the successive ranks, Dionysius' hierarchy is founded not on being and power but on the self-giving of what is beyond being. We might add too that, whereas Proclus' work was characterized by a profusion of triadic ranks descending from the transcendent One (and Dionysius echoes the triadic ranks particularly in the two works on the hierarchies, each of which is divided into three ranks of three), Dionysius' Trinitarian vision of God requires that the transcendent God is not One but One-in-Three, maintaining the dynamism of the communal life of three persons, rather than the isolation of a single self-sufficient entity, as somehow involved at the highest level at which we can conceive the divine. Dionysius' hierarchy therefore is mobile, self-giving, concerned not to maintain power or divide "lower" creatures from its peak, but to raise up all creatures by imitating and revealing God, and always open to the immediate presence of the divine lover to any and all of its members.

It is easy to read Dionysius, whose text itself is difficult and intellectually demanding, as requiring only an intellectual engagement with God: the mind travels toward God through contemplation, affirmation and negation of the divine names and the likenesses provided by Scripture. Such readings are not lacking: Turner, for example, talks of the "resolute 'intellectualism'" of Dionysian mysticism, insisting that it is the ascent of the mind, the dialectics of "knowing and unknowing" which govern his vision (1995, p. 47). While it is incontestable that Dionysius' construal of Christian discipleship is grounded in the turning-over within the mind of concepts and images provided by the Bible and the liturgy, and this to a much greater extent than many Christian writers, we must take very seriously Dionysius' insistence that what is at stake is the transformation of the whole person, intellectual and moral. Like any Platonist, Dionysius believes that truly to know something involves being like it: thus we cannot separate intellectual knowledge of God from the activities in which one emulates him, activities of love and compassion. Both Rorem and Louth have done much to demonstrate that Dionysius sees the Christian's ascent towards God in the context of a full engagement, physical, ritual, and ethical as well as intellectual, with the resources revealed to the Church. The end of his vision is not knowing or unknowing, but union with God, in which the believer by grace is deified.

The most perplexing and fascinating work in the Dionysian corpus is undoubtedly the brief *Mystical Theology*, which sets out in five lapidary chapters the way of unknowing which leads beyond all created reality to this union with the divine itself, expressed by Dionysius in the famous paradox of "brilliant darkness" (997B). He envisages two linguistic movements connecting God and humanity, another version of procession and return: the descent through assertions beginning from God and gradually following the path of creation into ever-greater multiplicity, a continuous unfolding of the riches of divine life; and the ascent by negations, beginning from the most diverse forms of life, denying that they are adequate images of the divine, gradually moving up the chain of being into higher and less diverse forms of life, toward the one source. This ascent by negations is enacted in the final chapters of the treatise: starting with the concepts "inexistent, lifeless, speechless, mindless" (technically known as "privations"), he denies that these are true of God. Then he deals with concepts derived from sensory knowledge, such as weight, shape, location in space, capacity for change, and denies that these are true of God. In the last chapter, the great affirmations of Christian faith are dealt with – God is Life, Light, Love, Goodness, Wisdom, Power, and so on – and these too are all denied: they are not true. This rejection of all the precious truths of Scripture is a breathtaking demonstration of the stripping-off of all comforts to the self. It is met at the very last by the terse statement that God, the "supreme Cause", is "free of every limitation, beyond every limitation; it is also beyond every denial." Here we have simply, as Dionysius says, run out of words: the soul has nothing left, nothing to hold on to, as it "plunges into the truly mysterious darkness of unknowing" (1001A).

The crux of Dionysius' interest, then, is in a spirituality of "going beyond": God is beyond all that we can know, and we must strive for our fulfilment in him, doing so by going through and beyond all that he has made, taking from it all that will nourish us, and then moving on by denying it. Dionysius further coined the theological language of "unknowing" (*agnosia*), distinguishing it from ignorance as the blank lack of knowledge, indicating instead a "quite positively complete unknowing" (Letter 1, 1065A) occurring when the mind is so full of God, who transcends being and knowledge, that there is no room either for any of the images which usually mark his place when he is absent, or for the sort of self-awareness which is a necessary part of discursive knowledge. In unknowing, however, Dionysius is not suggesting a spirituality of love or of activity in which the life of the mind has no place: the mind is richly fed by God through the hierarchies, and it is the mind which, coming to know God as Good, Love, Life, Light, and Beauty (and all the other names discussed in *The Divine Names*), is carried beyond itself in yearning.

Dionysian Theology

The Dionysian corpus has been subjected to a variety of theological criticisms, ranging from heretical doctrine to subtler but no less damaging types of theological inadequacy. Many have noticed the quasi-Donatist nature of Dionysius' views on priesthood and the sacraments: in Letter 8, Dionysius argues that impious priests cannot "bestow illumination" on the people. This is in sharp contrast to the Augustinian argument, accepted as orthodox, that the personal holiness of the minister was irrelevant to the efficacy of the sacraments he administered. For Dionysius, as members of the hierarchy the priests' function is also to bestow knowledge, and they cannot know God objectively without knowing him subjectively, namely in and through their own being, their own penetration into the activity of divinity. Dionysius has also been accused of inadequacy with regard both to Trinitarian and Incarnational theology; but it is less the case that he lapsed from orthodoxy on these counts, than that they appear to be marginal where they should be central. There is little to be said to defend Dionysius here, except to point to the nature – such as we surmise it to be – of his work, which is not presented as a systematic dogmatics, but as a presentation of a Christian cosmology and spirituality in terms which make clear its ability to take up the best of Neoplatonist philosophy and reshape it in Gospel terms. One might also remember that if *The Theological Representations* and *The Symbolic Theology* are indeed fictional works, we are presented with a corpus which is deliberately incomplete. Incidentally, Dionysius himself tells us that Trinity and Christology are both dealt with in the former (*MT* 1033A).

Regarding the heavier charge of heresy, the original quotation of Dionysius' work was by a group of supporters of Severus, Monophysite bishop of Antioch: arguing for the position that Christ had only one nature after the union, they cited a phrase from the fourth Letter referring to "a new activity of the God-man" (*kainen tina ten theandriken energeian*) or, in a variant reading, "a single activity of the God-man" (*mian theandriken energeian*). This is undoubtedly the sort of language more favoured by the Monophysite opponents of the Chalcedonian settlement, and their later Monenergist cousins, than by the proponents of Chalcedon, who insisted on two natures in the Incarnate Lord, both before and after their union in the birth of Jesus.[5] Equally, there is evidence for the popularity and influence of the Dionysian corpus among Monophysite circles. Nevertheless, this is a slim basis on which to construct a Monophysite identity, and as John and Maximus demonstrate, is no obstruction to a truly determined pro-Chalcedonian reading of the corpus as a whole. Whether the author was Monophysite or orthodox is a question which may have been deliberately avoided by the choice of the first-century pseudonym, not to pass off "heretical" work as orthodox, but because the whole tenor of the corpus is at odds with the waging of controversy by Christological or theological definition: if every theological word is inadequate and to be negated, and by the same token to be affirmed prior to its negation, then the Areopagite's position is an irenic refusal to take sides. This is, indeed, much the argument of *Letter 7*, in which he states: 'good men are satisfied to know and to proclaim as well as they can the truth itself as it really is . . . It is therefore superfluous for someone expounding the truth to enter into dispute with this one or that one . . . therefore I have never wished to embark on controversies' (1077B-1080A).

Possibly more significant for contemporary reactions to Dionysius than all of these is the charge that this work is at heart barely Christian, rather a cloaking of an explicitly pagan philosophy in Christian robes. Protestant theologians in particular have inclined to see the Neoplatonist flavour of Dionysian spirituality as ultimately incompatible with the truths of the Gospel. But Dionysius may be defended here too: although pagan terminology is brought in – for example, the naming of the bishop "hierarch" and the reference to Scripture as "Christian oracles" – and pagan philosophy clearly leaves its mark upon some of the discussions – the triadic ranks of the hierarchies, the overarching motif of procession and return, the selection and treatment of "Divine Names" – these nevertheless involve no real modification of Christian teaching, whereas the modifications of Neoplatonist thought are striking and radical. We have touched on some already: the insistence on the immanence of the divine, and upon the yearning love for creatures which drives it to undergo ecstasy in passion and embodiment; the deeper identity of the One with the Three-in-One; and the greater sense of dynamic movement arising from all these. Here we have the heart of this author's assumed identity: the pagan philosophy of Iamblichus, Proclus, and possibly also Damascius is neither abandoned nor promoted, but con-verted and baptized into Christianity, in order to articulate an extraordinary spiritu-ality of "living without a why." Dionysius envisages a life without certainty or permanence: nothing is to be held on to, no ideas clung to, no practices treated as completely known. One is to die daily, for a God who is never known, and only obliquely present. Dionysius' achievement is to present such a life as unimaginably precious, consoled by the diffused light of the Creator present in the communal life of an ecclesial cosmos; relentlessly driven by a yearning thirst for God, driving us beyond all that we have known ourselves to be; and finally crowned in captivity to the love God has for us, when one is lost in the life of the divine.

Maximus the Confessor

The Man and his Work

Born in CE580 into an aristocratic family, Maximus abandoned an early career in the imperial civil service to seek out a life of monastic tranquillity. He practiced in a variety of monasteries from Constantinople west to North Africa, gaining repute as a spiritual adviser to old friends and to monastic colleagues, but by the mid-640s being drawn into the controversies over Monenergism and Monothelitism. Standing firm with Pope Martin I against the imperial adoption of Monothelite Christology, he was arrested in 653, banished for treason, but recalled for further trial eight years later, when, in addition to exile, he was condemned to mutilation by the removal of the hand and tongue with which he had continued to resist the emperor. He died shortly afterwards, in 662, of the wounds which earned him the title of "Confessor." The details of Maximus' later life are sufficiently embedded in the controversies of the age as to be well-documented. For his early years, we have incompatible sources: one, a Greek biography compiled in the tenth century, is rather hagiographical and based on little evidence; the other, a Syriac version, is contemporary with Maximus' life but hostile to him and impugns his birth, education, and orthodoxy. The few details given above are supported by internal evidence in Maximus' works.

Maximus' output consists largely of occasional works: responses to questions from fellow monks, letters, explorations of problems encountered in the texts commonly studied among the monks, polemical works on the issues he was drawn into, two sets of brief explanations of theological and ascetical wisdom in the form of "centuries" for monastic practitioners, a few commentaries, and scholia on the Dionysian corpus. His thought is never entirely drawn together into a systematic whole, but in spite of this a remarkably coherent and comprehensive account of theology and practice emerges from his works – what Pelikan has called "an ample, vigorous, and profound synthesis, without doubt one of the richest in the entire history of Christian thought."[6]

Major Themes

One overarching theme conditions and unites all Maximus' varied work on doctrinal, ascetic, and spiritual matters: the Incarnation of the Logos, second Person of the Holy Trinity, in human flesh as Jesus the Christ. The entire drama of the cosmos itself, and the intimate personal history of each human individual are recognised as fragments, echoes, enactments of this pivotal act of God. Christ's work renews humanity; and we appropriate that renewal insofar as we follow Christ's model of life. But Maximus does not divide the two natures, divine and human, in Christ so that the human nature is the part which is operated upon and the divine nature is the part which operates. In that case, our participation in Christ would be in only one part of his nature. Rather, Maximus envisions a participation in the whole person of Christ: like him, we must become both human and divine. Some commentators have seen deification as the main theme of Maximus' work, but this neglects the double aspect of the Incarnation: it would be better to say that humanization and deification together are the main theme in and through which Maximus worships and safeguards the Chalcedonian understanding of the person of the Incarnate Lord. Because Christ was human, we too can become fully and properly human: one way in which Maximus says this is that in addition to the image of God, which we have always retained, we can regain the likeness which was lost at the Fall. Maximus, who spent a great deal of time in North Africa, is intimately faithful to the traditional Alexandrian insight that that which was not assumed by Christ was not healed by Christ, and to the Chalcedonian Definition that Christ was perfectly and fully man, "like us in all things apart from sin." Therefore all aspects of our nature are taken up and healed in Christ. Maximus allies to this the ancient understanding that love is the force which brings diverse realities together into one, whether at the interpersonal or the astronomical level: since God is Creator, and God is Love, then it is the mark of the divine love to integrate fractured and broken reality, healing division and bringing all things together. The Incarnation crystallizes this integrative work; Maximus famously understands the human as a microcosm – a "world in miniature" – so in the reintegration of every aspect of human being, the fractures of the cosmos itself are healed. This is why, even at such tremendous cost, it mattered so greatly to Maximus to oppose the Monenergists and Monothelites who argued that in Christ there was only one activity or only one will. With bitter irony, it might well have seemed that it was Maximus who in this controversy was preventing loving reintegration: these Christologies were formulated as compromise views under which both proponents and opponents of Chalcedonian theology could reunite, allowing political stability to be built upon ecclesial unity within the Empire. The odd accusation in Maximus' first trial: "You alone betrayed Egypt and Alexandria and Pentapolis and Tripoli and Africa to the Saracens," makes a sort of sense in this context. However, Maximus saw clearly that to admit any exception to the fulness of Christ's human nature would imperil not only our salvation (we would not be entirely saved – and of all aspects to abandon, how central to our identity is the will!) but also the establishment of God's will as "all in all" to the created universe.

On the other hand, because Christ was God we too can become divine. The full realization of this deification belongs to the heights of the spiritual life, where the soul is taken up by God "becomingly and fittingly as only he can; penetrating it completely without passion and deifying all of it and transforming it unchangeably to himself" (*Mystagogia* 23, Berthold p. 206). This is the mystical union familiar from Dionysius, which Maximus also describes as adoption to divine sonship, and, in the language traditionally taken from the Song of Songs, a marital embrace between the soul and the divine. Maximus does more than Dionysius, however, to make explicit the Trinitarian nature of the divine thus encountered, identifying mystical theology, the summit of the spiritual journey, with experiential knowledge of the Holy Trinity. Maximus also construes deification as the healing of the last and deepest division of the Cosmos – that between creature and creator. Because divine love heals all without loss, the difference between divine and human natures remains, but there is a complete integration of activity, with the soul "becoming completely whatever God is" (*Difficulty* 41, Louth p. 158). Primarily, of course, this means that the soul becomes perfectly filled with love: "For nothing is more truly Godlike than divine love, nothing more mysterious, nothing more apt to raise up human beings to deification" (*Letter* 2, Louth p. 85). But Maximus also honours the more intellectual strand of the tradition, stemming from the Platonic insight that "like is known by like," that we become more God-like by contemplating God; and the insight of the Cappadocians and the Dionysian corpus, that knowledge of God does not come by some tranquil and static meditation on revealed facts, but by painful practice of continually leaving behind all that we can know and all that we are; and that such knowledge when it comes is not merely an addition to the facts at our fingertips, but a transformation. Thus spiritual contemplation is a major element of the Christian life, equally valued by Maximus with practical or ascetic activity: he does not just discuss such contemplations, but frequently enacts them within his texts – for example in *Difficulty* 10. Maximus characteristically brings this insight back to his Christocentric focus, by identifying deification with the "eighth day," the day of Resurrection from the tomb. Thus he reminds us that the Incarnate One died, and that we too must be crucified if we wish to live the life of God. In the practice of love and of crucifying and burying the self, therefore, Maximus offers a process of deification that the believer can embark upon from the earliest stages of the spiritual life. The Cross and the tomb, he says, are to be applied to all aspects of the journey to God, at ever-deeper levels – and the Resurrection too will continually bring us rebirth into deeper realization of divine life.

The two natures of Christ thus provide the pattern for the Christian life, and it is instructive that of all the visual depictions of Christ, Maximus finds enormous theological nourishment in the Transfiguration, where both the humanity and the radiant divinity are clearly shown to the disciples in a way that one might characterize in Chalcedonian terms as "without confusion, without change, without division and without separation." In *Difficulty* 10 Maximus loads contemplation and interpretation of the Transfiguration upon each another as if he is unable to exhaust the richness of this theme, and elsewhere he writes about the deification of the individual believer in terms which suggest that the believer will then appear as the transfigured Christ did: "In this state only God shines forth through body and soul when their natural features are transcended in overwhelming glory" (*Chapters on Knowledge*, II. 88, Berthold p. 167). The other aspect of Chalcedon which the Transfiguration also demonstrates (much more clearly than, say, the image of the baptized Christ with the dove descending from heaven) is that human and divine are encountered in Christ as "one person." Thunberg has carried out detailed analyses of Maximus' theological anthropology, linking the Confessor's concern to safeguard the human mind of Christ with his concern to unravel the structures and workings of the human mind in general, knitting together the interest of the ascetic traditions of the desert in putting psychological knowledge to the service of prayer and the battles with demonic temptation, and the Christological issue of what exactly it means to be a "person." Where early disputes over the nature of Christ had sometimes been tempted to see the unity as almost a mask or character assumed in a sort of drama, Maximus develops (in perhaps his most original contribution to the tradition) a deeper and fuller understanding of personhood both in Christ and in created beings, borrowing from the Cappadocians the phrase "mode of existence" (*tropos tes hyparxeos*) in order to express the way in which a person develops over time a perfectly individual expression of the fixed nature (*logos tes physeos*) which is given to them.

A major concern expressed in such works as Maximus' earlier collection of *Difficulties* and the *Two Centuries on Knowledge* was to correct the Origenist spirituality developed in the Evagrian tradition among the monastic communities – to correct it so that it might continue to be used, and not be discarded whole. One aspect of this tradition was an understanding of salvation history as the restoration of an original harmony: the created state of souls was one of static contemplation of the divine, a contemplation disrupted by disobedience and the Fall into materiality. Maximus addresses this in many places, insisting that the idea of "rest" applies to the end of the spiritual life, not the beginning. But in Maximus' own terms, one might say that part of the problem was that the Origenists allowed no space for the person to develop in distinction to the created nature, left no gap between creation and salvation where the individual might learn from material existence how to become the adopted son of God, a fully differentiated adult participant in the community of divine love. Garrigues' analysis of Maximus' soteriology has led him to suggest that the Confessor himself grew into this appreciation as a result not only of intellectual maturation, but of his encounter with obstructive reality. Garrigues traces Maximus' development from a youthful sense of ease and serenity in the ascent to the divine, then driven into exile by the Persian encroachments in the East, to a gradual realization of the sense in which life is a constant struggle to build in the wisdom derived from experience upon the gift of being. There is a growing appreciation of the eschatological nature of this personal salvation: that the Incarnation of Christ enacts a radical innovation upon creation. Maximus' practise of homelessness (*xeniteia*) is no longer merely the intellectual and moral casting-off of achievement that we find in Dionysius and perhaps also Gregory of Nyssa, but a practical initiation into the defeats of self, certainty, and familiarity inflicted by life in the world. In a final stage, once the prospect of martyrdom for his opposition to imperial policy becomes apparent, Maximus comes to appreciate fully the character of the Trinity as kenotic love, a love which opens for individual beings not merely the way of crucifixion but also Resurrection to a sharing in the personal life of Christ. Throughout this learning-in-practice and reflection upon the Christian life as a training in personal existence, Maximus corrects Evagrian or Origenist intellectualism with his characteristic insistence on the importance of the human will, and its accession to self-emptying, and with an emphasis redolent of Macarius on the experience of grace in the life of the baptized, and on prayerful response.[7]

Two natures, therefore, in one person: this is the foundation of Maximus' spirituality, and within the person the two natures are related to one another not statically, by an external or artificial connection, but organically by a mutual adhesion of the natures. Maximus develops from a hint in Gregory of Nazianzen what becomes for him a central concept, that of *perichoresis*, or mutual interpenetration. This is simultaneously a development and a correction of the traditional understanding of the *communicatio idiomatum*, the ability of each nature to share in the properties of the other. In the tradition, this is a Christological notion, and can focus almost superficially on the propriety of a grammatical attribution of divine properties to the human nature and more controversially of human properties to the divine nature. Maximus' expansion and innovation is, first, to focus upon the underlying activity, the kenosis of each nature in loving abandonment to the other, and in this respect he does fuller justice than his predecessors to the mutuality of this process – not just divine condescension to human nature, but the true penetration of human into the divine. Secondly, Maximian *perichoresis* applies not simply to Christology but to the deification of all believers: the mutual interpenetration of human and divine is the model in which all will participate. Or even further: perichoresis comes to flavour the whole cosmic drama, so that Maximus is capable of applying it to such non-personal relations as those between the sensible and the intelligible stages of the spiritual ascent (*Mystagogia* 2), between the practical and contemplative lives (*Questions to Thalassius* 58) and between the apophatic and cataphatic theologies (*Difficulty* 10). Through this notion of mutual penetration, thus, Maximus works through the implications of his Chalcedonian commitment so as to express not simply the identity of Christ, but the entirety of the relation between divinity and created being, initiated by the Incarnation, expressed in the pouring of divine and creation into each another with loving self-abandonment, and completed in the eschaton.

The relationship between divine Incarnation and human deification is therefore not simply that of initiative and response or cause and effect: for Maximus, the mutual interpenetration of human and divine achieved in the personal life of Christ is more intimate than that. Rather, in the practise of the Christian life human persons actualize the Incarnation: Maximus regards the Incarnation as an event not limited by the historical career of Jesus the Christ, but enacted also in creation (the "natural law") and in Scripture (the "written law" – *Difficulty* 10, Louth p. 109). Once again, the human person as microcosm has a particularly pivotal role in this: as created beings and bearers of the scriptural tradition, we realize the Incarnation of Christ not merely by making Christ human, but also by divinizing him. Maximus explains: "In the active person the Word grows fat by the practice of the virtues and becomes flesh. In the contemplative it grows lean by spiritual understandings and becomes as it was in the beginning, God the Word" (*Chapters on Knowledge* II. 37, Berthold p. 156). This "Fat Jesus, Thin Jesus Lesson" continues in what follows immediately on: the enfleshment of Christ is not only by virtuous activity, but also "moral teaching" and "speak[ing] of God in positive affirmations"; the enspiriting of Christ is not only by spiritual contemplation but also by exposition of mystical theology and "speak[ing] of God negatively through negations." So the apophatic and cataphatic theologies are themselves not merely ways of approaching God, but ways of being Christ. Maximus even modified the mystical tradition he inherited in order to posit not one supreme state of union with God in "pure prayer" but two, supervening upon the enfleshment of the divine and the enspiriting of the human

(*The Four Hundred Chapters on Love* II. 6, Berthold p. 47), where the first resembles the Evagrian ideal of the rational soul's encounter with God in detachment from all sensible and intelligible elements, the second the Dionysian rapture to an ecstatic union beyond knowing.

Maximus sees the activity of theology, therefore, as a tremendously high calling – for which a theologian will be prepared to suffer. He places "theology" (or "mystical theology") at the highest stage of the spiritual ascent, identifying it with the highest stage of prayer, with union and deification itself. But we should take care not to conflate Maximus' understanding with our own. "Theology" is "God-talk," but it is not truly talk about God – perhaps that only by a sort of analogy – but rather a talking with God. In that sense there is no difference between theology and prayer. And the summit of "pure prayer" will be a conversation so intimate that no words or thoughts are formed – no wonder Maximus uses the analogy of a marital embrace! So when we do talk as theologians about God, we only repeat what God has already declared about himself in Scripture and creation and the person Christ; thus there is another perichoresis, between our speech and that of God. Maximus himself instances this mutual interpenetration, most obviously in his frequent use of citations and allusions to Scripture and the patristic tradition, but further in the playfulness of his language, his fondness for wordgames which recall the games of the Word himself (the lovely *Difficulty* 71 expounds Gregory Nazianzen's poetic reference to the Play of the Word, recalling also Paul on the "foolishness" of God – see Louth pp. 163–8). When Maximus writes of God, therefore, he prefers the vocative case to the accusative, and never forgets that invocation of the unknowable God is accomplished as much by gestures (ascetic, liturgical, or ethical) as by words. Finally, despite his understanding of the theologian's Incarnation of Christ in word and act, Maximus' "theology" is not limited to participation in the Logos alone: he connects mystical theology with prayer most especially to the Trinity (just as Dionysius began his treatise on *The Mystical Theology* with a prayer to the Holy Trinity – see Maximus' comments on the beginning of the Lord's Prayer – Berthold p. 106). Perhaps it might not be going too far to think in terms of Maximus' theology as a participation, through prayer, in the rich conversations of the Trinity.

Maximus' Theology

Little in Maximus' thought is entirely original – nor would he have aspired to originality, preferring faithfulness to tradition. His claim to our attention is based largely upon other attributes – the clarity of his insight into just what is essential to Christological commitment, the wisdom and breadth of the synthesis that he constructs out of the diverse strands of prior theological development, and the sheer attractiveness of his voice, the humour, the friendship, the practicality, the Christocentrism, the joyfulness, the cosmic vision, the acquaintance with estrangement and pain, the quiet rest in God.

In constructing his vision of the Christian life at the pivot of all creation, Maximus has practiced his own theory of the reintegration of all things, with nothing lost.

From Dionysius he has taken his understanding of the Christian life as a systematic ascent through partial revelations of the divine to the unknowable source, and the cosmic sweep of vision. From the Cappadocians he has taken his love of theology itself, and the understanding of the practical life of asceticism and virtue as a participation in the very activity of God. From Evagrius he takes his understanding of the interior life of the ascetic, while correcting Evagrius' Origenist tendencies (particularly the failure to integrate the passions into the life of the redeemed, and the overintellectualism). From the Macarian tradition he took his appreciation of the wisdom which comes through the spiritual experience of members of the community of the baptized. And all this is woven into the fabric of a consciousness molded by constant reflection upon Scripture and what it reveals of the pattern of life given us by God himself.

Nearly twenty years after his death as a witness to orthodox Christology, Maximus was vindicated by the sixth ecumenical council (680/1), which endorsed the dyothelite ("two wills") position to whose statement at the 649 Lateran council he had contributed. Since that time he has been highly venerated among the Fathers of the Church, and particularly as the last representative of the ecumenical Christian tradition before the split between Latin Catholicism and Eastern Orthodoxy. There was, nevertheless, a lack of good editions, translations, and studies of his works particularly in the West, until this began to be remedied in the middle decades of the twentieth century through the works of scholars such as Dalmais, von Balthasar, Sherwood, and Thunberg, resulting in the upsurge of interest evidenced in Nichols's summary of more recent scholarship.

Contemporary Interest

Theologians continue to take the works of Dionysius and Maximus as a rich seam of resources for Christian reflection, but in relation to Dionysius in particular there is a fascinating overflow beyond the boundaries of traditional patristic scholarship, or dogmatic theology. There is a nexus of interest (Marion, Milbank, J. P. Kenny, Kolakowski, and others) in a return to Neoplatonism: a movement from considering particular beings to a holistic view encompassing Being itself, and asking the old questions about the relation between being and goodness, aseity and being in dependence on others, and whether we can posit anything "beyond being." And a related nexus of interest among post-modern thinkers (especially Derrida) particularly concerning the relationship between language and being, and whether positing God "beyond being" might not free us to see divinity as dynamic activity, ethical or loving activity. This might free theology – and ourselves – from bondage to modernity, to philosophy, enabling retrieval not only of otherness but of our ethical debt to the other. What Dionysius and Maximus offer is an articulated spiritual theology which is freed from bondage to particular metaphysics. Ironically, what the Neoplatonist metaphysics does is to make Christianity, as A. H. Armstrong noted, "compatible with limitless criticism" – not simply with endless intellectual questioning, but with a lifetime's worth of experience and change.

Janet P. Williams

Notes

1 Acts 17:18 makes the point that Paul was not addressing only "Jews and devout persons," as in other cities, but also philosophers.
2 *DN* 593D–596A. The numbered divisions of the text derive from the critical edition by Migne, and are reproduced in the translation by Luibheid, from which all translations used here are taken.
3 This is explained in Chapter One of *The Divine Names*.
4 This is explained in Chapter Two of *The Celestial Hierarchy*.
5 It is possible that there is also a Monophysite reading of the consecration of oil in *EH* 473A–485B – a suggestion first made by Werner Strothman.
6 Introduction, p. 11, to Berthold's translation.
7 J. M. Garrigues, *Maxime le Confesseur: La Charité, avenir divin de l'homme* (Paris, 1976). Nichols offers a useful summary of Garrigues' argument in *Byzantine Gospel*.

Bibliography

G. Berthold, *Maximus Confessor: Selected Writings* (New York, 1985).
A. Louth, *Maximus the Confessor* (London, 1996).
C. Luibheid (trans.), *Pseudo-Dionysius: The Complete Works*, London (1987).

The Syriac Tradition

David G. K. Taylor

Introduction

Christianity very early established footholds in the major cities of the eastern Mediterranean provinces of the Roman Empire (modern Israel, Lebanon, Jordan, Syria, Turkey) and in the western provinces of the Parthian Empire (modern Iraq and western Iran). From these urban bases missionaries rapidly spread out and began to establish churches in the smaller towns and villages, those from centers such as Antioch (modern Antakya) – where it is reported that the followers of Jesus first received the name "Christians" (Acts 11:26) – using Greek, and those from Edessa and Nisibis (modern Urfa and Nusaybin, south-eastern Turkey) using the local Aramaic dialect, Syriac. Despite some advances in our knowledge,[1] this earliest period is still shrouded in much obscurity, but it would appear, for example, that by AD235 the church in the Sasanian Empire (which succeeded the Parthian in AD226) had approximately eighteen dioceses and twenty bishops.

By the late fourth century, when our historical sources become more reliable, it is clear that not only was Christianity flourishing throughout these regions, but local missionaries had also helped to establish thriving Christian communities in Armenia, Georgia, Central Asia, South India, Arabia, and Ethiopia. In AD535 the voyager Cosmas Indicopleustes reports having encountered Christian coreligionists 20 years earlier in ports along the South China coast and in southern India, Sri Lanka, Bangladesh, and Thailand. To the north the Christians of Persia had expanded right along the central Asian trade routes, converting Turk and Hun tribes on their way, and in 638 they consecrated their first monastery in the imperial capital of China.

This missionary expansion by the Syrian and Mesopotamian churches is of course very impressive by any standards, but it should also prompt us to reconsider our attitudes to their native region. It is only too easy to understand why, from a European perspective, Syriac Christianity has often been regarded as an anomalous offshoot which developed at the furthest eastern edge of Christendom, squeezed up against the desert frontier of the Roman Empire, whose eccentric beliefs and practices can be attributed to its peripheral and remote origins. Like some provincial cousin whose curious dress, habits, and manner of speech partly amuse and partly scandalize her fashionable urban relations, Syriac theology has often been ignored or exhibited as a peculiar relic. Viewed from a different perspective, however, the territories and sees of the Syriac churches were neither remote nor isolated, for they straddled the frontier zone that provided the meeting point for the two greatest empires of the western late antique world, a crossroads for merchants, missionaries, diplomats, and, when the latter failed, invading armies. This was no quiet backwater, but an area of constant tidal movement, sometimes shifting individuals to and fro, sometimes whole urban populations – in AD256 and 260, for example, Shah Shapur I transported large numbers of captured Roman citizens from Antioch to Persia, including numerous Christian laypeople and clergy, amongst whom was the city's bishop, Demetrius[2] – but always mingling and mixing different peoples, languages, and ideas. And like the tide it did not pay great heed to the commands of distant emperors, shahs, and patriarchs. Thus although Syria and Mesopotamia in late antiquity contained political, linguistic, ethnic, and environmental frontiers, all of these were porous, and as a consequence these provinces provided an extraordinarily fertile environment for the development and diversification of Christianity during this period. It is, therefore, impossible to isolate one Syriac theological tradition, whether in theological methodology or in theological doctrine, but in what follows an attempt will be made to sketch some of the most characteristic features and developments of Syriac theology.

Earliest Syriac Christianity

Most accounts of early Syriac Christian origins have been dominated by discussion of a Syriac text known as *The Teaching of Addai*,[3] according to which Christianity gained a firm foothold in the Syriac-speaking centre of Edessa as a consequence of the conversion of the royal family and aristocracy soon after Christ's death. (The contemporary king of Edessa, Abgar the Black, is said to have been told of Christ's teachings and sufferings in Jerusalem and to have written and offered him sanctuary in Edessa. In reply Christ is reported to have declined the offer, being bound by his duty to fulfil his Father's will, but as a reward for the king's generosity he promised to send him an apostle, Addai, to preach the Gospel after his death, a promise that he kept.) This vision of a single defining moment in which a pure apostolic Christian faith was accepted by the rulers of Edessa and passed on to the lower social orders, following an ideal pattern typified in the West by the conversion of the Emperor Constantine and in the East by the conversion of the Armenian king Trdat, yet avowedly earlier than either, is in fact a product of the early decades of the fifth century (although the correspondence with Jesus was already cited in the fourth century by Eusebius,[4] and so may have circulated independently before the composition of the final work). Thus the tradition of Addai is not referred to by any of the earliest Syriac writers, not even by the fourth-century writer Ephrem, some of whose voluminous works were written in Edessa in the last decade of his life. Such early texts as do survive[5] instead suggest that Christianity grew slowly in Edessa, drawing converts from across the social classes, including the most humble, rather than exclusively from the ruling classes.

The traditional view of the origins of Christianity in Edessa and the surrounding regions was further challenged by Walter Bauer,[6] who argued that orthodox Christianity in Edessa arose as just one of a multitude of competing sects and religions in the city. He drew particular attention to the Marcionites who appear to have been very well established in Edessa,[7] and who may even have appropriated the name "Christian" for themselves,[8] perhaps, as Bauer suggests[9] because they were the first to bring a form of Christianity to Edessa. In the second half of the fourth century they were still perceived to be numerous and threatening, as is clear both from the ferocity of the attacks upon them found in an extensive pseudo-Ephremic text[10] and in many genuine writings of Ephrem[11], who complains bitterly that in his day in Edessa the orthodox Christians of his church were a minority group unjustly referred to as "Palutians" by rival sects (after an early bishop, Palut).

Ephrem was also fierce in his condemnation of the teachings of the Bardaisanites, the followers of an Edessan philosopher named Bardaisan (AD154–222),[12] a cosmopolitan courtier of King Abgar the Great who appears to have developed a highly syncretistic form of Christianity and thus fell foul of orthodox Christians. (His system was notable for its speculative cosmology, according to which primeval darkness became mingled with the four elements to produce the created world. This world is ruled by a benevolent High God – through the agency of the seven planets – whose Logos found lodging in Jesus of Nazareth, taught a new law that enabled souls once more to return to their source after death, and would bring about a new creation purged of darkness after 6,000 years).[13] Ephrem also attacks the Manichees, followers of Mani, a prophet from these very frontier lands who grew up in a community of the Elkasite sect, who wrote in an Aramaic dialect closely related to Syriac, and whose teachings spread across the known world from the 270s on. To these disparate groups should also be added more conventional Gnostic factions such as the Valentinians, as well as lesser known groups such as the Quqites and Sabbatians.

It needs to be emphasized that the early orthodox Syriac Christians did not develop from any of these groups (although in later centuries the remnants of these sects were often forcibly converted to the Nicene faith), and neither, contrary to occasional academic claims, do they appear to have appropriated any of their theological or anthropological beliefs. (The Syrian Christians did, however, make great use, until the fifth century, of the Syriac Gospel harmony, or Diatessaron, of Tatian (fl. 172), who was alleged to hold various extreme ascetic, or encratite, beliefs, and indeed it was upon this text that Ephrem based his Gospel commentary.)[14] The religious context of the Syrian Christians, however, inevitably exercised an important influence upon their theological outlook, and to it might be attributed some of their traditional hostility to the use of pre-Christian Hellenistic philosophy to establish Christian doctrine, an emphasis on biblical revelation, in the Old Testament as well as the New, with the Paradise accounts of Genesis in particular playing a central part in their accounts of salvation and the divine economy, combined with an essential belief in divine revelation through the created natural world. Theological innovation was treated with suspicion, and links with the Great Church were maintained and fostered both politically and through the rapid translation into Syriac of the writings of key figures such as the Cappadocians, Cyril of Alexandria, Theodore of Mopsuestia, and many others.

But from what religious groups were the early converts drawn, and what was their influence on Syriac theology? The main possibilities are of course the ancient pre-Christian religions of the region. In Syria the ancient Hellenistic cults survived for many centuries after the advent of Christianity. Thus despite the account of pagan priests overturning their altars in *The Teaching of Addai*, sacrifices were still made in Edessa at the temple of Zeus as late as the end of the sixth century,[15] and many other local cults also continued to flourish for centuries.[16] Syriac Christian reaction to this Hellenistic inheritance is very mixed. It is clear from mosaics, inscriptions, and texts that Hellenistic culture had profoundly influenced cities such as Edessa and Nisibis, and that there were numerous bilingual Greek-Syriac speakers through-out the region.[17] Once texts such as Basil of Caesarea's *Ad adolescentes*, with its defense of Christian use of classical Greek literature, was translated into Syriac (perhaps as early as the late fourth century), the study of philosophical and even Homeric texts seems to have become more widespread (indeed Aristotle soon became a mainstay of formal Syriac theological education, and many Greek philosophical, scientific, and medical texts were translated into Syriac, and then Arabic, and so were preserved and restored to Western European culture at a later date).[18] It is notable that the divine triads found in certain Syrian cities have a happy coincidence with the Christian Trinity, especially in the early Syriac form (prior to the fifth century) in which the Spirit is considered to be feminine and in certain contexts can even be addressed as "mother,"[19] but this may simply have provided an opportunity for missionaries, like the sacred tree of Wotan in Germany, rather than having influenced Christian conceptions. On the other hand, it is certainly possible that the ascetic practices of certain Syrian Hellenistic religions, such as the pre-Christian stylites mentioned by Lucian of Samosata in his *De dea Syria*,[20] encouraged the remarkable early growth of asceticism in the Syrian churches.[21] Despite such points of cultural contact, many Syrian theologians were profoundly suspicious of the theological value of Hellenistic philosophy, not only on account of its ideological content and cultural assumptions, but as a methodology for gaining knowledge of God and of his divine purpose. The appeal made to Hellenistic philosophy by rival religions and sects in Syria in general, and in such Syriac-speaking centres as Edessa in particular, cannot have helped the supporters of philosophy.

In Persian territory in particular, the Syriac-speaking Christians were surrounded by Zoroastrians and members of other ancient Iranian religions, significant numbers of whom converted to Christianity over the centuries. Iranian religious influence on Syriac Christianity seems limited, but has been detected in particular in imagery relating to the judgement of the individual soul after death and of all the living in the last days.[22]

Between Syria and Persia the Syriac Christians were also heirs to the culture of Mesopotamia, and this is evident both in popular religious belief and practice – as for example in the survival of the old gods and goddesses as demonic spirits,[23] and in the preservation of the Aramaic tale and (polytheistic) proverbs of Ahiqar until the present day[24] – as well as in the official faith and practice of the Church, where one encounters occasional terms, such as "medicine of life" used of Christ, which have impeccable Mesopotamian origins,[25] not to mention the highly influential literary genre known as the dialogue or dispute poem.[26] Of Sumerian origin, these poems in which speakers argue against each other verse by verse, were quickly adopted by Christian writers who saw their potential in exploring key theological and exegetical themes in an accessible manner. Speakers such as Satan and Death, the Angel and Mary, John the Baptist and Christ, the good thief and the cherub guarding Paradise, are paired together and explore key issues. These poems were often performed in a liturgical session at key seasons of the year, as some still are.[27]

The other significant local religion was Judaism, which had numerous sizable communities spread throughout Syria and Mesopotamia, and academies mentioned by the Talmud in Nisibis and Arbela.[28] In Edessa itself there is a small group of early third-century Jewish tombs, amongst many pagan tombs, with Hebrew and Greek inscriptions, and the royal family of the neighbouring kingdom of Adiabene is known to have converted to Judaism[29] during the reign of Claudius (41–54 CE). The Syriac Old Testament, the Peshitta, which is now used by all of the Syrian churches, was translated directly from Hebrew by a number of different translators (thus excluding the possibility of a forgotten Syriac Jerome) during a period that probably stretches from the mid-second to the third century, and preserves occasional traces of Jewish exegetical traditions. If it is of Jewish origin, how did the text so quickly come into the possession of Christians? If of Christian origin, were the translators converts from Judaism, and if so, how representative were they of the larger community for which they were translating?[30] It should also be noted that an extraordinary quantity of further Jewish exegetical traditions are also preserved in subsequent Syriac Christian texts,[31] both in early witnesses such as Ephrem Syrus,[32] and in later compilations such as the sixth-century *Cave of Treasures*[33] and the thirteenth-century *Book of the Bee*.[34]

Some of these exegetical traditions have provided the starting point for major mytho-poetic accounts of Christian salvation. For example, there is an important Syriac tradition that Adam and Eve were not naked in Paradise but were clothed with robes of glory, symbolic of their immortality and their relationship with God. As a consequence of their Fall these robes were stripped off, leaving them truly naked. In his Incarnation Christ brought back these robes of glory and placed them in the waters of the Jordan, the universal waters of baptism, whence they are taken up again spiritually by every Christian on the occasion of their baptism as a pledge of the actual robes that will be restored to them in the next world. This whole scheme of salvation, which is highly influential, depends upon a reading of Genesis 3:21, in which the Lord God is understood to have made for Adam and Eve not garments of skin, but garments of light (in Hebrew 'or rather than 'or), a reading also attested in some Jewish sources. Related to this scheme is the widespread Syriac tradition of using the metaphor "putting on the body" of the Incarnation. It is found in the very earliest Syriac writings and authors (including the Syriac Peshitta text of Hebrews 10:5), was used in an early Syriac translation of the Nicene Creed, and survives in some medieval liturgical and theological texts.[35]

Despite the importance of these Jewish exegetical traditions, there is no evidence that Syriac Christians as a group maintained any traditional Jewish practices (for example circumcision, kashrut, or sabbath observance as in Ethiopia), nor that their Christological or Trinitarian formulations preserved any features that might be expected of Judeo-Christian groups. The claims, therefore, of certain scholars that Syriac Christianity is essentially the product of the conversion of a Jewish community (whether rabbinic or non-rabbinic), or that it is a descendant of early Judeo-Christianity, or is an authentic representative of Semitic Christianity (usually implying that Syriac Christianity in some sense represents an irrational, primitive, apostolic form of Christianity), should be treated with some caution. Such polarized opinions fail to take into account the multicultural, multilingual, and multireligious environment in which Syriac Christianity first developed.

Thus, far from being deprived of the theological tools that were used by their coreligionists in the Greek-speaking cities of the West, Syrian theologians had access not only to the Greek philosophical tradition, but also to the biblical, parabiblical, and exegetical resources of Jewish scholarship, and to the poetic and ascetic inheritance of Syro-Mesopotamia. The challenge facing them was to identify the most appropriate tools for engaging in theology, and for channeling the results of that theological endeavor to the Christian faithful. Needless to say, different personalities were drawn to different theological methodologies, and different methodologies were sometimes deemed to be more suitable to address particular needs, but although from the fifth century on many Syriac writers employed the analytical philosophical methodology of Western allies and opponents in the great Christological controversies of that era, in the early centuries the major Syriac theologians mostly chose to work through poetry, or through asceticism/mysticism,[36] and it is in these areas that Syriac theologians made perhaps their greatest contributions to world Christianity.

Poetry and Analogical Theology

Throughout the history of Western Christianity almost all the major theological writers have sought to articulate their arguments and beliefs through the medium of prose. For many early Syrian theologians, however, as most clearly articulated by Ephrem, a prose-based, philosophical approach to theology, which sought to pin down religious truth, by nature dynamic and multilayered, and to circumscribe divinity by the philosophical formulae and definitions so beloved of the Greek-speaking theologians, not only represented arrogance beyond belief but was ultimately futile. In part this reflects the common Hellenistic philosophical precept that a mind cannot comprehend that which is greater than it,[37] and so God infinitely surpasses human comprehension, and in part the fierce contemporary sectarianism and schismatic rivalries which seemed to observers to be the result of human arrogance and a refusal to acknowledge the limitations of humanity's intellectual capabilities. According to Ephrem, humans cannot, despite the claims of philosophers, fully understand themselves and the world around them, let alone God, without divine assistance, and even then there are limits to what can be known. God cannot be dissected by any conceivable analytical tools, he cannot be neatly categorized and labeled. Knowledge of God is entirely dependent upon his willingness to make himself known to humanity, and even then this knowledge must be communicated in ways and in forms that are acceptable and intelligible to human minds. For Ephrem, as will be discussed below, this divine self-revelation takes the form of the symbols and types that are omnipresent in Scripture and in the natural world, and the most fruitful medium for engaging in this analogical theology is poetry, because only poetry, with its multivalent images and its ability to communicate differently to each reader on each reading, was capable of hinting at the divine realities without imposing the rigidity and contrived artificiality of so much philosophical theology. (Poetry, particularly in the form of hymns, had the very practical advantage that it could be sung in the liturgy, and was highly memorable – a feature that had already been exploited by the opponents of the orthodox, such as Bardaisan and, later, Arius.) Not surprisingly then, for some six centuries many of the greatest Syrian theologians chose to write theology by means of poetry.

Odes of Solomon

With the possible exception of the Peshitta translation of the biblical Psalms, the 42 *Odes of Solomon*[38] are the oldest collection of Syriac poems yet identified, although there is little scholarly consensus about their date, original language, or place of composition. They survive in two Syriac manuscripts of the tenth and fifteenth centuries, but they must predate the mid- to late third century, when they were circulating in various languages in North Africa.[39] Their imagery, theology, and implicit dependence upon the New Testament text (all of which, it must be noted, are of very uncertain diagnostic value) seem to suggest a mid-second-century origin in bilingual Syrian Christian circles. Attempts have been made to date them much earlier[40] and significantly later,[41] but these are far from convincing, as are attempts, now almost entirely abandoned, to associate them with Gnostic groups.[42] They are an extraordinarily powerful and haunting set of poems, and few who have read them will readily forget their imagery and strangely elusive language. One of the most striking features of the *Odes* is their intense sense of prophetic inspiration, of a link between the Odist and God that is so intimate that prophet and Christ become one and their thoughts and words are barely distinguishable. This awareness of inspiration is frequently to be found at the beginning of the *Odes*, many of which are addressed to an audience by the Odist speaking in the first person, for example:

> As the wind moves through a harp,
> And the strings speak,
> So the Spirit of the Lord speaks through my members,
> And I speak through his love. (*OS* 6.1–2)

Or again:

> As the wings of doves over their chicks,
> And the mouths of their chicks are towards their mouths,
> So also are the wings of the Spirit over my heart. (*OS* 28.1)

The Odist sees himself as an instrument upon which the Spirit plays, not the source of theological wisdom, but simply the transmitter of that which is placed in his mouth by the nurturing Spirit. In this the Odist is not possessed, the passive play-thing of an irrefutable deity, but both Lover and Beloved (cf. *OS* 3), only capable of discerning love because he was first loved, only receiving wisdom and knowledge because in his turn he responded with love. Although the love of God/Christ can be described, as in the Gospels, as that of a bridegroom for a bride (cf. *OS* 42.8), it is more often portrayed as that of a gardener carefully tending the shoots he has planted (*OS* 38.17–22), or, and far more radically to our ears, as the love of a mother breast-feeding infants, e.g. God speaks:

> I formed their members,
> and my breasts I prepared for them,
> that they might drink my holy milk, and through it live. (*OS* 8.14)

and again the Odist speaks:

> And I was carried like a child by its mother,
> And he gave me milk, the Lord's dew. (*OS* 35.5)

Awareness of this divine love calls forth a similar response from the Odist:

> As honey drips from the honeycomb of bees,
> And milk flows from the woman who loves her children,
> So also is my hope in you, my God. (*OS* 40.1)

In *Ode* 19, God's overflowing maternal love for creation is described not only as a present reality and source of blessing for the Odist, but as the motivation for the Incarnation itself:

> A cup of milk was offered to me,
> and I drank it in the sweetness of the kindness of the Lord.
> The Son is the cup,
> and he who was milked is the Father,
> and she who milked him is the Holy Spirit.
> Because his breasts were full, and it was undesirable that
> his milk should be spilt to no purpose,
> the Holy Spirit opened her womb,
> and mingled the milk of the two breasts of the Father . . .
> The belly of the Virgin took it,
> and she received conception and gave birth.

In this Ode, as elsewhere, the Odist turns preconceived notions of divinity upside down: the Father produces milk like a mother about to give birth, the Son is portrayed as a receptacle, the vessel for God's outpourings, and the Spirit, which in Syriac writings is, until the fifth century, always regarded as feminine,[43] is the active agent in the process. This process continues a few verses later on (*OS* 19.10) where it is said of the Virgin that "like a man she begat by will . . . and she created with great power." The Odist is clearly picking up on various hints and allusions in the Old and New Testament, but his sense of inspiration allows him a remarkable theological confidence. By contrast, without such a relationship of love, trust, and dependence on God, theological speculation is doomed to error (e.g. *OS* 24.10–11: "And the Lord destroyed the conceits of all those who possessed not the truth, for those who were exalting themselves in their heart lacked wisdom" [cf. *OS* 26.8–10, 33.8]).

In the *Odes*, as in later Syriac theological poetry, there is no attempt to present systematically the theology of the community and church to which the Odist (and his colleagues, cf. *OS* 26) belonged, and so statements taken in isolation can be highly misleading. This is evident from much scholarship on the *Odes* which has often sought to find parallels to particular verses in the sort of apocryphal writings that were often favoured by dissident groups in the early centuries of Christianity, rather than in biblical texts or in the later writings of Syriac theologians, for example:

> And I was covered with the covering of your Spirit,
> and I lifted off my garments of skin,
> because your right hand lifted me up,
> and caused sickness to pass from me. (*OS* 25.8–9)

This has been taken by some scholars to be a Gnostic statement denigrating human flesh, and parallels are discovered in such texts as the Gospel of Thomas (20:30–4). Rather, it is clearly a reference to Christ reversing the effects of the Fall, removing the leather garments made for Adam and Eve by God (Gen. 3:21, see above), removing their susceptibility to illness and pain, and restoring their original robes of divine glory. As such it is of a piece both with other passages in the *Odes* (e.g., *OS* 7.3–6, 21.3, 33.12) and with later orthodox Syriac theology. Sometimes the Christological passages can seem a little imprecise, or even dangerously loose, by later standards, and yet the eternal pre-existence of the Son, his true humanity and true divinity, are all expressed in the following lines:

> And his Word is with us in all our way,
> the Saviour who gives life and does not despise us.
> The man who humbled himself,
> and through his righteousness was raised up.
> The Son of the Most High appeared
> in the perfection of his Father,
> and light dawned from that Word
> who was in Him at the first.
> The Messiah in truth is one. (*OS* 41.11–15)

To understand rightly such poetic formulations of theology, it is clear that Western theologians must learn to read holistically, to judge from the whole, and not to be too quick to identify flaws as though engaging with a text of linear argument.

Ephrem

Ephrem (c.306–73) is not only one of the greatest of the early Syriac theologians, known to his fellow Syrians as the "Harp of the Spirit," but he has also had a profound impact upon theologians in other traditions. Amongst the Greek Byzantine orthodox he had a major influence upon Romanos the Melodist,[44] and a large corpus of pseudonymous Syrian ascetical writings also circulated in Greek under his name.[45] He was declared a Doctor of the Church in 1920 by Pope Benedict XV, and according to John Wesley he was "the most awakening writer among all the ancients."[46]

Despite the existence of several hagiographical accounts of his life, some dating from the fifth century, only a few details are certain. He was born in Nisibis, on the Roman side of the frontier with Persia, and appears to have lived there until it was ceded to the Sasanians in 363 when he moved back across the new border to Edessa, where he died in 373. He was a deacon in the orthodox church, and a member of a proto-monastic group known as the "Children of the Covenant" (the *bnay qyama*).

Ephrem was responsible for a number of prose works: for example, commentaries on the Diatessaron text of the Gospels, the Pauline epistles, and Genesis and Exodus, as well as refutations of major local heresies,[47] but it is for his poetic works that he is best remembered. Although it is clear that many have been lost over the centuries, more than four hundred survive, the majority of which are stanzaic "teaching songs,"[48] known in Syriac as *madrashe*. These were composed in more than 45 different syllabic meters, and were intended to be sung as part of the liturgy, as some still are. Remarkably for his day, Ephrem created and trained choirs of women to sing these songs, thus not only giving women an active role in a church liturgy which was otherwise the preserve of men, but also providing them, and so their families, with some orthodox theological education in memorable form,[49] which was essential in an age when the Church was under threat not only from old rivals but also from the Arians and, briefly, the pagans who were resurgent under the emperor Julian.

Ephrem's preference for using poetry as his main theological tool was not driven primarily by propagandistic pragmatism. It was also the perfect vehicle for his developed form of symbolic or sacramental theology.[50] For Ephrem it is self-evident that a vast ontological chasm lies between Creator and creation, which no human theological investigation can bridge. God's original initiative to overcome this divide by offering immortality and perfect knowledge to humanity in Paradise failed because of Adam and Eve's freely chosen rejection of the offer, a decision which might have led to their eternal alienation from him. God's love for humanity did not diminish, so he sought again to draw them back to himself by reaching out his hand to them and inviting them to take hold. This he did by crossing the chasm and revealing himself to those with the eyes and will to see.

This divine self-revelation took several forms, the first of which is God's creation of the worlds, since through his handiwork essential aspects of God's being and his love and will for creation could be glimpsed, not in the rationalistic or forensic manner of scholars in more recent centuries who seek proofs of divine purpose and activity in the organization and running of the visible universe, but rather in the manner of one who gazes in wonder and intellectual and emotional engagement with a masterpiece painted on canvas. The tiniest of details can provide insight into the mightiest of truths, and not by chance or the independent workings of the viewer's mind, but as a direct consequence both of the divine purpose which created the detail and of divine interaction with the viewer's mind. All of creation can be viewed sacramentally, every minor detail partakes in divine reality, as long as it is approached with humility, not arrogance, and an openness to God's love:

> Whenever I have meditated upon You
> I have acquired a veritable treasure from You;
> Whatever aspect of You I have contemplated
> a stream has flowed from You.
> There is no way I can contain it.

> Your fountain, Lord, is hidden
> from the person who does not thirst for you;
> Your treasury seems empty
> to the person who rejects You.
> Love is the treasurer
> of your heavenly treasure store. [*Hymns on Faith* 32.2–3][51]

This visual divine self-revelation is accompanied by an aural self-revelation, for God was prepared in his love for creation to humiliate his divinity and to allow himself to become incarnate in human speech, both generally in human attribution to him of names, titles, and parts,[52] but more specifically in Scripture, which was inspired through his Holy Spirit, and should be read on both historical and spiritual levels (without concentrating on one to the detriment of the other, which can have dangerous results). The consequence of biblical inspiration is that even the most unlikely of passages are full of divine self-revelation to those who are prepared to listen – they contain both types (*tupse*) and symbols/sacraments (*raze*) which not only point to, but actually participate in, divine reality (*shrara*), and they are inexhaustible:

> Who is capable of comprehending the extent of what is to be discovered in a single utterance of Yours? . . . Anyone who encounters Scripture should not suppose that the single one of its riches that he has found is the only one to exist; rather, he should realize that he himself is only capable of discovering that one out of the many riches which exist in it . . . A thirsty person rejoices because he has drunk: he is not grieved because he proved incapable of drinking the fountain dry! [*C. Diat.* I.18–19][53]

If different people (or the same person at different moments) approach these symbols in faith with purity of heart or view them, in Ephrem's own words, with "a luminous eye," they will find in them an almost limitless variety of meanings, but even so only part of the infinitely complex divine reality will be revealed.

The ultimate form of divine self-revelation, however, took place in the Incarnation of the Son, and so for Ephrem it is Christ who provides the key to all the other symbols and types; he is "the Lord of symbols." All the symbols in Scripture from creation on point forward to him, just as the New Testament and the proclamation of the Church point back to his past Incarnation and forward to his Kingdom, and from a vertical perspective (in which the incarnate Word can be seen as occupying an intermediate position between Creator and creation) both the natural symbols and the revelation of God all point to him.[54] Through Christ the chasm is overcome, for he is "the hidden bridge which carries one over from death to life."

These Christocentric ideas find expression in Ephrem's poetry in various ways. Ever avoiding the dangers of speculation into the hiddenness of God and arrogant attempts to study and limit him with definitions – "the bitter poison of the wisdom of the Greeks" (*Hymns on Faith* 2.24) – Ephrem instead concentrates on the aspects of his divinity that God has chosen to reveal to humanity. For example, he makes much use of the paradoxes in revelation: the Great One who became small; the Creator who became an infant; the Lord who became a servant; the Word who fell silent in the womb; the Provisioner of all who experienced hunger and thirst. Such paradoxes do not provide a definition of Christ's being, but they lead to a true understanding of it. He also explores the parallels between the original Fall of humanity away from God and the restoration of humanity through Christ. For example, the lance that pierces Christ's side (John 19:34) removes the Cherub's sword that prevented humanity from returning to Paradise (Gen. 3:24); from the wound in his side Christ's bride, the Church, is born in the blood and water that flowed from him, just as Adam's wife, Eve, was born of the rib from his side (Gen. 2:22). Thus through the wound in Christ's side humanity reenters Paradise. Another technique is to concentrate on a particular natural symbol, for example a pearl, or oil, or fire, and turn it over and over, exploring ways in which it leads us to an understanding of God and his purpose. Ephrem is quite explicit, however, that none of these analogies should be studied in isolation, or pushed too far, for that also would lead to error. Their value lies in their ability to cast light on different aspects of the divine, but these aspects should not be regarded as constituting the whole. For Ephrem it is precisely this lack of perspective and balance which characterizes the theology of the heretics.

Councils, Creeds, and Analytical Theology

The analogical, symbolic theology in poetic form of writers such as Ephrem continued for many centuries to be the preferred method of writing theology for internal use within the Syrian churches, and it found great practitioners in East and West in writers such as Jacob of Serugh (d. 521), Narsai (c.399–c.502), and the various authors gathered under the name of Isaac of Antioch (c.5–c.6). However, in the fifth to seventh centuries, an age of international theological controversy which focused especially on the teachings of the churches in relation to the person of Christ, it became necessary for the Syriac-speaking Christians to choose sides, and to articulate their Christological teachings in a form that would enable comparison with the teachings of their neighbors, and, perhaps inevitably, this meant according to the analytical theological method of the Greeks. By the end of the seventh century the consequences of this period of controversy was that Syriac Christianity was sundered into three parts, and these divisions have remained until the present:

1   The Syriac-speaking Malkites, or "Royalists," who adhered to the Chalcedonian dyophysite ("two natures") Christological position of the council of Chalcedon

(AD451), promulgated by the Byzantine emperors, that in the Incarnate Christ there are two natures and one hypostasis. This group continued to use Syriac[55] as a major theological and liturgical language for many centuries, but it was steadily replaced by Greek and Arabic as the community was absorbed into the general Byzantine Orthodox population of the Middle East – thus the great eighth/ninth-century Chalcedonian orthodox theologian, Theodore Abu Qurrah, who was born in Edessa, wrote some texts in Syriac but composed the majority in Greek and Arabic.[56] (In the twelfth century the Lebanese branch of the Syrian churches, the Maronites, accepted the primacy of Rome and so also joined the Chalcedonian grouping. From the sixteenth century on, Catholic missionary activity amongst the Syrian churches in the Middle East and in India gave rise to a number of important Eastern Rite Catholic Churches).[57]

2   The Syrian Orthodox Church,[58] one of the Oriental Orthodox group of churches (the others being the Armenian, Coptic, and Ethiopian Orthodox Churches) which rejected the definition of Chalcedon and sought to uphold the miaphysite ("one nature") Christological formulation of Cyril of Alexandria, proclaiming that in Christ there is one nature and one hypostasis. The Syrian Orthodox have continued to use Syriac as their major theological and liturgical language up to the present, although in the modern diaspora increasing use is being made of regional languages.

3   The Church of the East,[59] the church which flourished in the Sasanian Empire and beyond, whose Antiochene dyophysite Christology is based upon the theology of Theodore of Mopsuestia (d. 428, condemned at the council of Constantinople in 553, whose exegesis and teachings became the mainstay of the great theological school of Edessa), and which from the seventh century on proclaimed that in Christ there are two natures and two *qnome* (a term which will be explained below). Like the Syrian Orthodox, the Church of the East continues to use Syriac in its liturgy and theology.

Despite the ill-informed comments found in many theological handbooks, all three of these Christological traditions agree that there is only one subject (*prosopon*) in the incarnate Christ, and all three seek to affirm that he was perfect God and perfect human. There are, however, not only differences of formulation, but also differences of emphasis, and the historical origins of this need to be examined further.

The Christology of the Church of the East

Centred outside the Roman Empire, or *oikumene*, the Syriac Church in Persia played no role at all in any of the great ecumenical councils of the Western empire – although as a consequence of the councils and the perceived growing closeness of the Roman enemy and the Western Church they suffered fierce persecution during the fourth and fifth centuries at the hands of the Sasanian authorities. Thus the canons and credal profession of Nicaea (AD325) were recognized by the Church of the East only in 410, at the synod of Seleucia-Ctesiphon (through the initiative of the Western bishop and diplomat Marutha of Martyropolis). It is noteworthy that this occurred during a period of official religious toleration, and that the synod was actually summoned by the Shah.

During the fourth century the concerns of theologians in Persia seem to have been rather different from those of their co-religionists in the West, at least in so far as this can be judged from such texts as the 23 theological treatises (or "demonstrations") that were composed in rhythmic prose by Aphrahat the Persian Sage,[60] an earlier contemporary of Ephrem,[61] in 337 and 345. Aphrahat was a leading figure in his church, and one of the major early Syriac writers, but there is no trace of any awareness of the disputes raging across the border. For Aphrahat, alongside practical issues of bolstering faith in a time of persecution, a key concern still seems to be to persuade Jews that Jesus was the true Messiah and the Son of God. In the seventeenth demonstration, which is dedicated to this theme, the emphasis throughout is on Christ's humanity and his continuity with the patriarchs and prophets of Israel, and it is argued that "Son of God" does not contravene the uniqueness of God since Moses was also called God (Exod. 6:1), and Israel was named the "firstborn" of God (Exod. 4:22). This however must be held in tension with statements, as in the sixth demonstration,[62] that the Word came down from on high, became a body, and dwelt amongst us, and on his return to Him who sent him he took back that which he had not brought with him, raising us up to sit with him in heaven. Salvation is also often described in terms of the conquering of Satan, Sheol, and Death by Christ, and a restoration and perfection of the original creation. So, as in other early Syriac theologians, Aphrahat's Christology is Orthodox, despite a marked lack of technical Christological terminology, and a willingness in his apologetic writing to base himself firmly in his opponent's territory, but it is also interesting to see how important Christ's humanity is to his theological scheme.[63]

As has already been noted, however, the frontier was not impermeable to theological ideas and influences, and this is particularly notable from the late fourth century on. The great theological school across the border in Edessa became known as "the Persian school" because of the numbers of students from the Persian Empire who studied there,[64] and it was renowned as a centre of Neo-Nicene theology, both in its Cappadocian and in its Antiochene forms.[65] Its continued espousal of Antiochene theology in the hostile climate that followed the councils of Ephesus in 431 and Chalcedon in 451, in particular that of Theodore of Mopsuestia (d. 428) who was considered the biblical "interpreter" *par excellence* by the Syrians,[66] led to its closure in 489 on the orders of the emperor Zeno. Thereupon many of its teachers and students moved across the border and founded a new school in Nisibis, where they were free of imperial interference. Theodore's emphasis on the importance of the full humanity of Christ for salvation, and his fierce rejection of Christologies such as Apollinarianism which compromised this humanity, as well as his genius for biblical exegesis, fitted well with the theological norms of the Persian Church, as found in Aphrahat. Despite this great reverence for Theodore, however, it is clear that the Syriac translators of his writings were still quite prepared, on occasion, to remove some of his more extreme dyophysite terminology when it was deemed appropriate.[67]

By contrast, Nestorius himself, the patriarch of Constantinople who was condemned at the council of Ephesus in 431, exercised only minimal influence on the developing theology of the Church in Persia. From sources such as Narsai,[68] it is clear that whilst he was indeed held in honour there, as he still is by the Church of the East, because, as another student of Theodore, he was perceived to be a martyr for the Antiochene cause, yet little, if anything, was known of his actual theology and writings. Further, we are fortunate enough to possess a text known as the Synodicon Orientale[69] which preserves the texts of the synods of the Church of the East from the fifth century on, and from this it is clear that the earliest credal statements contain nothing that is distinctively "Nestorian," and in no synod is reference ever made to the Nestorian formula of "two prosopa" – indeed Nestorius is not referred to in any synod of the fifth or sixth centuries, and he is never cited as a Christological authority. Even when Nestorius' "Book of Herakleides" was brought to Persia from the West and translated into Syriac[70] (in 539/40) none of his distinctive terminology entered the creeds. In fact, during the sixth century the creeds even started to become less Theodoran and far more Chalcedonian in language – "Christ who is in the flesh, who is known and confessed in two natures, God and Man, a single Son"[71] – although the Church of the East ultimately rejected the terminology of Chalcedon also.[72]

However, a significant change did take place in the early seventh century when the Persian Shah Khosroes II ordered a theological disputation to take place between the Syrian Orthodox, who were growing increasingly influential in Persia, and the Church of the East, headed by Babai the Great (d. 628).[73] This confrontation took place in 612, and for the first time in the official teaching of the Church[74] reference is made to "the two natures and two *qnome*" in Christ. This terminology has been a bone of theological controversy ever since. Here, as so often, much of the problem lies in the way that key terms in Greek and Syriac were understood by the various parties (and subsequent scholars).[75] In particular, problems arose because the Greek term *hupostasis* (approximately "person") was regularly translated by the Syriac term *qnoma* (plural *qnome*; approximately "particular property", "characteristic"), even though the connotations of the two terms are quite different. For the Syriac theologians of Persia *hupostasis/qnoma* is the necessary individual manifestation of nature (*physis/kyana*), which is itself considered to be generic (e.g. humanity, divinity – closely associated in this Christology with Greek *ousia*, "essence"[76]). As a consequence the Chalcedonian position that Christ had two natures but one *hupostasis/qnoma* appeared quite illogical to the Church of the East, whereas the "one nature" of the Miaphysites implied confusion and mixture of the natures. Instead Babai, and his succesors in the Church of the East, proclaimed that the *qnoma* of divinity (God the Word, perfect God) and the *qnoma* of humanity (Jesus, perfect man) are united in a single *prosopon* of sonship in an inseparable union from the very beginning of its fashioning.[77] The essential Christological orthodoxy of this profession was recognized by the Roman Catholic Church in 1994 when a common declaration of faith was issued by Pope John Paul II and Catholicos Mar Dinkha IV.[78]

As a codicil to this discussion of the theology of the Church of the East in the seventh century, it is instructive to note that the same church consecrated its first monastery in the imperial capital of China in 638, and over the following centuries its missionaries translated its key texts not only linguistically but ideologically into Chinese forms. Thus the famous Chinese Christian stele of Xian, erected in 781 by clergy whose names are engraved in Syriac, incorporates numerous Buddhist and Daoist concepts and metaphors into its summation of the faith of the "Illustrious

Religion."[79] It begins its account of creation by stating that God "appointed the cross to determine the four quarters. He stirred up the primordial wind and brought to life the two forces of nature [Yin and Yang]," thus blending ideas found in St. Basil with those from Chinese philosophy. Again, in its account of Christ's economy of salvation, Syriac and Chinese ideas are found side by side:

> He fulfilled the Old Law of the Twenty-Four Sages' discourses,[80]
> governing tribes and nation according to great principles.
> He established the New Religion of the Triune Holy Spirit's silence,
> refashioning good works according to right faith.
> He determined the salvation of the Eight Stages,[81]
> refining the earthly and perfecting the heavenly.
> He revealed the gate of the Three Constants,[82]
> unfolding life and destroying death.
> He hung a brilliant sun which scattered the regions of darkness.
> The Devil's guile he has utterly cut off.
> He rowed Mercy's Barge[83] which took him up to the courts of light.
> The souls of men he has already saved.
> His mighty task once done, at noonday he ascended into Heaven.

Such accomplished inculturation is often considered to be the hallmark of the most modern and enlightened missionary practise, and so it should perhaps give scholars some pause for thought before, as so often, they judge the theology of the Syriac Church of the East to be the product of unsophisticated, provincial conservatives.

The Christology of the Syrian Orthodox

Unlike the Syriac-speaking Christians in the Sasanian Empire, those in the eastern Roman provinces were fully involved in the great ecumenical councils, and in the theological disputes and ecclesiastical rivalries that raged from the fourth century on. In particular they had had to battle to survive the confrontation with Arianism, with its denial of the full eternal divinity of the second person of the Trinity, and they had rallied around the theological opponents of Arianism, the Cappadocians in Asia Minor,[84] Ephrem in Edessa, and in particular the great Egyptian theologians, first Athanasius and later Cyril of Alexandria, whose formula "one nature (*mia physis*), and that incarnate, of God the Word" became their battle cry. In this context Syrian theologians increasingly emphasized the importance of Christ's perfect divinity for human salvation, with the divine Word becoming fully human, assuming humanity in everything except sin. In this model of salvation the unity of Christ, his absolute oneness, was essential.

Links between these Syrians and Egypt were strong. In times of persecution Syrian church leaders had always found refuge in Egypt, and from the late fourth century on, when Egyptian monasticism became increasingly prestigious in Syrian eyes and started to replace the native forms of asceticism, would-be Syrian monks traveled to Egypt to train, and returned educated in both coenobitic monasticism and Alexandrian theology. It is evident that these alliances were reinforced at a formal theological level, for Cyril himself noted that he had sent copies of his writings – for example his *De recte fide* – to Edessa for translation into Syriac and local distribution.

Not surprisingly, such committed proponents of Alexandrian Christology found the Antiochene dyophysite approach of Diodore and Theodore abhorrent, and yet in Syriac-speaking centres such as Edessa, the Antiochene Christology still had powerful supporters, and the ensuing conflict inevitably radicalized opinions. The Chalcedonian definition of 451, therefore, with its reference to Christ being "made known in two natures . . . [both] concurring into one Person and one hypostasis," seemed to such theologians to be another articulation of Nestorianism. For Syriac writers in the West as in the East, *hupostasis/qnoma* is the individual manifestation of nature, and so for them two natures after the Incarnation necessarily implied two *hupostases* in Christ, despite the apparently illogical assertion of the Chalcedonian definition that there was only one, and this implied two Sons, and thus rendered salvation ineffective. They considered their theology of salvation to be equally imperiled by genuine Monophysites such as Eutyches whose Christological model was understood to imply that Christ's humanity was overwhelmed, even absorbed, by his divinity, and so Eutychians too were declared anathema by the Miaphysites.[85]

The Syrian Miaphysites found their great champion in the Greek writer Severus of Antioch (d. c.542), most of whose surviving writings are now preserved in Syriac.[86] In treatise after treatise, and letter after letter, he insists on the necessity of a hypostatic, or natural, union in Christ, and on the inadequacy of a prosopic union – sometimes referred to as "partnership", or "conjunction." He also carefully distinguished between "difference" and "division":

> Where, then, we confess the one out of two, Lord and Son and Christ, and one incarnate nature of the Word himself, we understand the *difference* as it were in the natural characteristics of the natures from which Christ is. But if we speak of the two natures after the union, which necessarily exist in singleness and separately, as if divided into a duality, but united by a conjunction of brotherhood . . . the notion of *difference* reaches to the extent of *division*, and does not stop at natural characteristics.[87]

This distinction allowed him to maintain the reality of Christ's perfect humanity and perfect divinity, both with respect to his hypostasis and to his activity, recognizing difference but avoiding separation or division, and to counter the charges both of confusion of natures in Christ, and of theopaschism (i.e. that divinity itself suffered pain and death on the Cross) with which the Miaphysites were frequently confronted. It also suggests that Severus' Christology and that of the Chalcedonians were, in truth, not far removed from one another.

Whilst Severus' Greek analytical theology was warmly embraced in its Syriac form by the Syrian Miaphysites since it provided them with a means of defending themselves against their opponents[88] and pressing their own claims, this theological approach did not entirely replace the old analogical methodology, particularly in texts that were produced for circulation within their own community. An interesting figure in this respect is the highly influential Syrian bishop, Philoxenus of Mabbug (d. 523), who wrote entirely in Syriac.[89] He was a close ally of Severus, sharing a very similar Christological outlook,[90] and as an educated theologian he attempted to reform many traditional articulations of Syriac theology, such as the Christological use of clothing imagery which he considered inadequate and theologically dangerous.[91] Despite this, he was unwilling to abandon other potentially misleading theological terminology that he had inherited from Syriac tradition, such as the language of "mixture." For Philoxenus this was a key concept that played an important role not only in his explanation of the union of the Christian and the Holy Spirit, or of the union of body and soul, but also of the union of humanity and divinity in Christ. He absolutely denies that this mixture involved any loss of the characteristics of humanity or divinity, or any confusion of the two, and significantly he defends his use of this language by citing the authority of Ephrem.[92] To a Syriac audience this terminology was familiar, trusted, and effective, and could not simply be put aside because of the ill-informed qualms of the Greeks. In other sixth-century Syriac Miaphysite writers, such as Daniel of Salah (fl. 542), the theological use of clothing metaphors was not only continued, despite the strictures of Philoxenus, but it was reworked and developed in order to handle new Christological challenges, such as those posed by the "phantasiasts."[93] Yet other writers, most notably Jacob of Serugh (d. 521), who may have been a student alongside Philoxenus in Edessa, chose to continue the tradition of writing analogical theology almost entirely through the medium of poetry, offering no concession to the Greek mode of theology, and barely a nod towards the Christological controversies of his day.[94]

The Syriac tradition of theology, both in the lands of the Roman Empire and those of the Sasanian Empire and beyond, is not a peculiar fossil of primitive Christian belief, but was, and is, a living organism that developed in a particularly fertile and competitive religious environment, and subsequently showed great powers of adaptation when presented with new challenges or new opportunities. It retained many of its original theological emphases and insights, often highly challenging to other expressions of Christian theology, whilst simultaneously producing numerous subvarieties that could flourish in new conditions.

Notes

1 E.g. for the spread of Christianity through the villages of northern Syria, cf. F. R. Trombley, *Hellenic Religion and Christianisation, c.370–529*, 2 vols. (Leiden, 1994).

2 Until 410 it appears that the indigenous Christian population and the Christian descendants of these Roman citizens preserved separate ecclesiastical hierarchies in Iranian cities. Cf. S. P. Brock, "The Church of the East in the Sasanian Empire up to the Sixth Century and its Absence from the Councils in the Roman Empire," in A. Stirnemann and G. Wilflinger, eds., *Syriac Dialogue* I (Vienna, 1994), pp. 69–86, p. 74.

3 G. Howard, *The Teaching of Addai* (Chico, 1981).

4 *Hist. eccl.* I, 13.

5 E.g. martyrdoms of Shmona, Gurya, and Habbib; cf. F. C. Burkitt, *Euphemia and the Goth* (London, 1913).

6 *Rechtgläubigkeit und Ketzerei im ältesten Christentum* (Tübingen, 1934), ch. 1 (*Beiträge zur historischen Theologie* 10). Bauer's work only came to exercise any significant influence with its second German printing in 1964, and with the later English translation, *Orthodoxy and Heresy in Earliest Christianity* (London, 1972).

7   Cf. D. Bundy, "Marcion and the Marcionites in early Syriac apologetics," LM 101 (1988), pp. 21–32.

8   A late sixth-century life of Mar Aba (ed. P. Bedjan, *Histoire de Mar-Jabalaha, de trois autres patriarches, d'un prêtre et de deux laïques, Nestoriens* (Paris, 1895), p. 213; German translation in O. Braun, *Ausgewählte Akten persischer Märtyrer* (Munich, 1915), p. 190, states that in an area to the east of Edessa, near the river Tigris, "krestyana," the Syriac transliteration of the Greek term "Christian," was normally used of the Marcionites, whereas the Syriac term "mshihaya" ("messianist", "follower of the Messiah") was used of the orthodox Christians.

9   Bauer, *Orthodoxy and Heresy*, p. 22.

10 D. Bundy, "The Anti-Marcionite Commentary on the Lucan Parables (Pseudo Ephrem A). Images in tension," LM 103 (1990), pp. 111–23.

11 For Ephrem's prose homilies cf. C. W. Mitchell, *S. Ephraim's Prose Refutations of Mani, Marcion, and Bardaisan*, 2 vols. (London, 1912, 1921); E. G. Mathews & J. P. Amar, *St. Ephrem the Syrian: Selected Prose Works* (Washington, 1994).

12 Cf. H. J. W. Drijvers, *Bardaisan of Edessa* (Assen, 1965); J. Teixidor, *Bardesane d'Édesse. La première philosophie syriaque* (Paris, 1992).

13 These ideas were preserved by a pupil in a Syriac text (quoted in Greek translation in the Clementine Recognitions, IX.19, and in Eusebius, *Praeparatio Evangelica* 6.10.1) that takes the form of a Platonic dialogue on fate, and refers to many early Christian communities in Europe and Asia. Cf. H. J. W. Drijvers, *The Book of the Laws of the Countries. Dialogue on Fate of Bardaisan of Edessa* (Assen, 1965).

14 Cf. W. L. Petersen, *Tatian's Diatessaron* (Leiden, 1994), and especially pp. 78–83, where the weakness of the textual evidence of Tatian's alleged encratism is set out.

15 John of Ephesus, *Hist. eccl.* 3.3.28 (CSCO 106, p. 155 [Syr]).

16 Cf. H. J. W. Drijvers, *Cults and Beliefs at Edessa* (Leiden, 1980); H. J. W. Drijvers, "The Persistence of Pagan Cults and Practices in Christian Syria", in N. Garsoïan et al., eds., *East of Byzantium: Syria and Armenia in the Formative Period* (Dumbarton Oaks, 1982), pp. 35–43; G. W. Bowersock, "The Syrian Tradition," in *Hellenism in Late Antiquity* (Cambridge, 1990), pp. 29–40; and Abbé Martin, "Discours de Jacques de Saroug sur la chute des idoles," ZDMG 29 (1875), pp. 107–47, who refers to the survival of many pagan cults throughout Syria in the early sixth century, including that of Nabu and Bel in Edessa (pp. 110–12).

17 Cf. Steven K. Ross, *Roman Edessa. Politics and Culture on the Eastern Fringes of the Roman Empire, 114–242* CE (London and New York, 2001), and D. G. K. Taylor, "Bilingualism and Diglossia in Late Antique Syria and Mesopotamia," in *Bilingualism in Ancient Society: Language Contact and the Written Word*, ed. J. N. Adams, M. Janse, and S. Swain (Oxford, 2002), pp. 298–331.

18 Cf. S. P. Brock, "From Antagonism to Assimilation: Syriac Attitudes to Greek Learning," in N. Garsoïan, et al. (eds.), *East of Byzantium*, pp. 17–32; H. Daiber, "Semitische Sprachen als Kulturvermittler zwischen Antike und Mittelalter. Stand und Aufgaben der Forschung," ZDMG 136 (1986), pp. 292–313; and for a general overview, E.-I. Yousif, *Les philosophes et traducteurs syriaques: D'Athènes à Bagdad* (Paris, 1997).

19 Cf. S. P. Brock, "The Holy Spirit as Feminine in early Syriac literature," in J. Martin Soskice (ed.), *After Eve. Women, Theology and the Christian Tradition* (London, 1990), pp. 73–88, and S. P. Brock, "'Come, compassionate Mother . . . come, Holy Spirit': A Forgotten Aspect of Early Eastern Christian imagery," *Aram* 3 1991 [1993], pp. 249–57.

20 Cf. Harold W. Attridge and Robert A. Oden, *The Syrian Goddess (De dea Syria)*, Society of Biblical Literature Texts and Translations, no. 9 (Missoula, MT, 1976), 4.28–9; J. L. Lightfoot, *Lucian: On the Syrian Goddess* (Oxford, 2003); and D. Frankfurter, "Stylites and *Phallobates*: Pillar Religions in Late Antique Syria," *Vigiliae Christianae* 44 (1990), pp. 168–98.

21 The standard, if controversial, reference work to this key feature of early Syriac Christianity is A. Vööbus, *History of Asceticism in the Syrian Orient*, 3 vols. (Leuven, 1958, 1960, 1988). These volumes need to be read critically with the aid of S. P. Brock, "Early Syrian Asceticism," *Numen* 20 (1973), pp. 1–19; R. Murray, "The Features of the Earliest Christian Asceticism," in P. Brooks, ed., *Christian Spirituality: Essays in honour of E. G. Rupp* (London, 1975), pp. 65–77; and S. H.

Griffith, "Asceticism in the Church of Syria. The Hermeneutics of Early Syrian Monasticism," in V. L. Wimbush and R. Valantasis (eds.), *Asceticism* (New York, 1995), pp. 220–48.

22 Cf. the "Hymn of the Pearl," of uncertain religious origin but now found in its earliest (Syriac) form embedded in the Acts of Thomas, which includes numerous Iranian elements; texts and detailed commentary in P. H. Poirier, *L'Hymne de la perle des Actes de Thomas* (Louvain-la-Neuve, 1981), ET by H. J. W. Drijvers, "The Acts of Thomas," in W. Schneemelcher, ed., *New Testament Apocrypha*, vol. 2 (Westminster, 1992), pp. 322–411, pp. 380–5. As an example of later religious influence, mention might be made of the belief that the righteous and unrighteous alike will have to pass through a sea of fire at the last judgement, as found in Christian form in Jacob of Serug and Daniel of Salah in the sixth century and in Zoroastrian apocalyptic texts; cf. M. D. Guinan, "Where are the dead? Purgatory and immediate retribution in James of Sarug," *Symposium Syriacum 1972* (OCA 197; Rome 1974), pp. 541–9; P. G. Kreyenbroek, "Millennialism and Eschatology in the Zoroastrian Tradition," in A. Amanat & M. Bernhardsson, *Imagining the End: Visions of the Apocalypse from the Ancient Middle East to Modern America* (New York, 2002).

23 For the apotropaic, anti-demonic incantations found on magic bowls from a variety of Aramaic religious communities of the region, including Jews, Christians, and Mandaeans, cf. J. Naveh and S. Shaked, *Amulets and Magic Bowls* (Jerusalem and Leiden, 1985), and *Magic Spells and Formulae* (Jerusalem, 1993).

24 Cf. J. M. Lindenberger, "Ahiqar," in J. H. Charlesworth, ed., *The Old Testament Pseudepigrapha*, vol. 2 (London, 1985), pp. 479–507.

25 Cf. G. Widengren, *Mesopotamian Elements in Manichaeism* (Uppsala and Leipzig, 1946), pp. 129–38, and S. P. Brock, *The Luminous Eye: The Spiritual World Vision of St. Ephrem* (Kalamazoo, 1992), ch. 6.

26 Cf. S. P. Brock, "Syriac Dispute Poems; The Various Types", in G. J. Reinink and H. L. G. Vanstiphout, *Dispute Poems and Dialogues in the Ancient and Mediaeval Near East* (OLA 42; Leuven, 1991), pp. 109–19, and R. Murray, "Aramaic and Syriac Dispute Poems

and their Connections", in M. J. Geller et al. (eds.), *Studia aramaica* (Oxford, 1995).

27 The dialogue poem genre was later taken up by Arabic and Persian writers in the Middle East, and spread west from Greek into Latin and then into modern Western languages, such as the English of the Metaphysical poets.

28 J. B. Segal, "The Jews of North Mesopotamia before the Rise of Islam," in J. M. Grintz and J. Liver, *Studies in the Bible presented to Professor M. H. Segal* (Jerusalem, 1964), pp. 32*–63*.

29 Cf. Josephus, *Ant. Jud.* xx, 17–48.

30 Cf. M. P. Weitzman, *The Syriac Version of the Old Testament: An Introduction* (Cambridge, 1999), who argues persuasively that this translation was produced by and for a group of non-rabbinic Jews, although much of the evidence cited would also be compatible with origins in an early Christian group.

31 S. P. Brock, "Jewish Traditions in Syriac Sources," JJS 30 (1979), pp. 212–32.

32 Cf. R. Murray, *Symbols of Church and Kingdom: A Study in Early Syriac Tradition* (Cambridge, 1975) and T. Kronholm, *Motifs From Genesis 1–11 in the Genuine Hymns of Ephrem the Syrian. With Particular Reference to the Influence of Jewish Exegetical Tradition* (Lund, 1978) (Coniectanea Biblica – Old Testament Series 1).

33 Ed., Fr. trans., and commentary by Su-Min Ri, *La caverne de trésors* (CSCO 486, 487; Leuven, 1987) and *Commentaire de la caverne des trésors* (CSCO 581; Leuven, 2000). Older ET by E. A. W. Budge, *The Book of the Cave of Treasures* (London, 1927).

34 E. A. W. Budge, *The Book of the Bee* (Oxford, 1886).

35 For a full account, cf. S. P. Brock, "Clothing Metaphors as a Means of Theological Expression in Syriac Tradition," in *Typus, Symbol, Allegorie bei den östlichen Vätern und ihren Parallelen im Mittelalter*, ed. M. Schmidt (Regensburg, 1982), pp. 11–38 (Eichstätter Beiträge IV), reprinted in S. P. Brock, *Studies in Syriac Christianity: History, Literature and Theology* (Hampshire, 1992, XI). Cf. R. Murray, *Symbols of Church and Kingdom: A Study in Early Syriac Tradition* (Cambridge, 1975), pp. 69–76, 310–12. It might be noted that similar clothing imagery is also to be found in early Greek and Latin texts, most notably in Tertullian who regularly employs *induere carnem* for the Incarnation.

36 Space does not allow for an examination of the Syrian spiritual literature, but its impact on early Christianity was profound, whether originally written in Greek – as in the case of Pseudo-Macarius and Pseudo-Dionysius – or in Syriac, as for example John of Apamea, Philoxenus of Mabbug, Sahdona/Martyrius, and Isaac the Syrian. Their method of doing theology has much in common with the poetic analogic methodology, and also draws upon an awareness of intimate contact with the divine. Despite belonging to the non-Chalcedonian Christological tradition the texts of Isaac in particular (but also some pieces of Philoxenus) were rapidly translated into Greek and the other languages of the Byzantine tradition where they became standard reading for monks. For an overview, cf. S. P. Brock, "Syriac spirituality," in C. Jones et al. (eds.), *The Study of Spirituality* (London, 1986), pp. 199–215; S. P. Brock, *Spirituality in the Syriac Tradition* (Kottayam, 1989); S. Beggiani, *Introduction to Eastern Christian Spirituality: The Syriac Tradition* (London and Toronto, 1991); and on Isaac, cf. H. Alfeyev, *The Spiritual World of Isaac the Syrian* (Kalamazoo, 2000).

37 It may be noted again that Ephrem was not uninfluenced by, or ignorant of, Greek philosophy, but he simply made a conscious decision not to adopt its methodology. Cf. U. Possekel, *Evidence of Greek Philosophical Concepts in the Writings of Ephrem the Syrian* (CSCO 580; Leuven, 1999).

38 The second Ode has been lost. For a convenient edition and translation, cf. J. H. Charlesworth, *The Odes of Solomon* (Chico, 1977), and, for a more detailed commentary, M. Lattke, *Oden Salomos: Text, Übersetzung, Kommentar*, 2 vols. to date (Friburg and Göttingen, 1999, 2001).

39 A Latin citation of Ode 19 appears c.AD300 in the *Divine Institutes* (4.12.13) of the North African apologist Lactantius; several odes were extensively cited in the *Pistis Sophia*, a Coptic Gnostic text, of c.280; and the Greek text of Ode 11 is preserved in Bodmer Papyrus XI of the third century, which has some marginalia indicative of a Coptic scribe.

40 E.g. J. H. Charlesworth, *Critical Reflections on the Odes of Solomon* (Sheffield, 1998), who seeks to link them to Judeo-Christian circles with connections to both the Essenes, responsible for the Dead Sea Scrolls, and to the author(s) of the Johannine literature in the New Testament.

41 E.g. H. J. W. Drijvers, "Die Oden Salomos und die Polemik mit den Markioniten," in *Symposium Syriacum 1976* (OCA 205; Rome, 1978), pp. 39–55; "The 19th Ode of Solomon," JTS 31 (1980), pp. 337–55; "The Odes of Solomon and Psalms of Mani," in R. van den Broek and M. J. Vermaseren, *Studies in Gnosticism and Hellenistic Religions presented to Gilles Quispel* (Leiden, 1981), pp. 117–30; these articles were all reprinted in his *East of Antioch* (London, 1984).

42 Cf. H. Chadwick, "Some Reflections on the Character and Theology of the Odes of Solomon" in *Kyriakon: Festschrift für J. Quasten*, ed. P. Granfield and J. A. Jungmann (1970), pp. 266–70, and J. H. Charlesworth, "The Odes of Solomon not gnostic," CBQ 31 (1969), pp. 357–69 (reprinted in his *Critical Reflections*, cf. n. 40 above).

43 Cf. n. 19 above.

44 W. L. Petersen, *The Diatessaron and Ephrem Syrus as Sources of Romanos the Melodist* (CSCO 475; Louvain, 1985).

45 Cf. D. Hemmerdinger-Iliadou, "Éphrem (Les Versions): I. Éphrem grec, II. Éphrem latin," *Dictionnaire de spiritualité* 4 (1960), pp. 800–19; D. G. K. Taylor, "St. Ephraim's Influence on the Greeks," *Hugoye: Journal of Syriac Studies* 1.2 (1998) (http://syrcom.cua.edu/Hugoye/Vol1No2/index.html).

46 Cf. G. Wakefield, "John Wesley and Ephraem Syrus," *Hugoye: Journal of Syriac Studies* 1.2 (1998) (http://syrcom.cua.edu/Hugoye/Vol1No2/index.html).

47 For these prose refutations see n. 11 above. For a comprehensive bibliography of other key texts and studies, cf. K. den Biesen, *Bibliography of Ephrem the Syrian* (Giove, 2002).

48 A translation suggested by Andrew Palmer.

49 This positive attitude towards women is also to be found in the passages of his commentaries dealing with female biblical figures, cf. A. G. Salvesen, "Themes in Ephrem's Exodus Commentary," *The Harp* 4 (1991), pp. 21–34.

50 Still by far the most accessible introduction to the theology of Ephrem is S. P. Brock, *The Luminous Eye: The Spiritual World Vision of St. Ephrem* (Kalamazoo, 1992), but also extremely useful are T. Bou Mansour, *La Pensée symbolique de Saint Éphrem le Syrien* (Kaslik, 1988), R. Murray, *Symbols of Church and*

Kingdom: A Study in Early Syriac Tradition (Cambridge, 1975), and "The Theory of Symbolism in St. Ephrem's theology," *Parole de l'Orient* 6 (1975), pp. 1–20.

51 Translation from Brock, *Luminous Eye*, p. 44.

52 Ephrem subdivides this "putting on of human names" into "perfect names," those which are eternally applicable such as Creator, Father, Son, King, and "transient names," metaphors such as rock, shield, Ancient of Days, which reveal some aspect of the divine, or his purpose, but which are not reflections of his true being and are not essential for faith. It is a permanent source of wonder to Ephrem that God allows himself to be described, so inadequately, by human speech, and he reserves his strongest anger for those, in particular the Arians, who, due to their lack of wonder and faith, abuse these metaphors to attack the eternally divine nature of God the Word.

53 Translation from Brock, *Luminous Eye*, p. 50.

54 Cf. R. Murray "The Theory of Symbolism in St. Ephrem's theology," *Parole de l'Orient* 6 (1975), pp. 1–20.

55 And, further to the south, Christian Palestinian Aramaic.

56 An English translation of his key writings, by J. Lamoreaux, is to be published in 2003 by BYU Press, in the Library of the Christian East.

57 From the Church of the East tradition came the Middle-Eastern Chaldean Church, and the Indian Syro-Malabar Church. From the Syrian Orthodox tradition came the Middle-Eastern Syrian Catholic Church, and the Indian Syro-Malankara Church (plus, under English Protestant influence in India, the reform tradition Mar Thoma Church).

58 Often referred to in older scholarly texts (and in popular works) by the old pejorative titles given to it by its rivals, such as the "Syrian Monophysites," or "Syrian Jacobites." Such terms are neither accurate nor appropriate.

59 Again, often referred to by the old pejorative title "Nestorian Church." This terminology is also misleading and is no longer acceptable.

60 There is an excellent French translation, with a very useful introduction, by M.-J. Pierre, *Aphraate le Sage Persan; les exposés*, 2 vols. (Paris, Sources chretiennes 349 (1988), 359 (1989)).

61 Ephrem appears to have known Aphrahat's work, cf. P. Botha, "A Comparison between Ephrem and Aphrahat on the Subject of Pass-over," *Acta patristica et Byzantina* 3 (1992), pp. 46–62, and S. P. Brock, "*Notulae syriacae*: Some Miscellaneous Identifications," LM 108 (1995), pp. 69–78, p. 77.

62 *Demonstration* 6.10.

63 Cf. P. Bruns, *Das Christusbild Aphrahats des persischen Weisen* (Bonn, 1990).

64 Many had fled across the border to avoid persecution.

65 Many of the writings of the Cappadocian fathers were translated into Syriac within decades of being written, as, slightly later, were the works of Theodore.

66 Theodore's exegesis influenced not only all subsequent generations of exegetes in the Church of the East, but also those Syrian Orthodox scholars, such as Jacob of Serugh, who were educated in the school of Edessa. (Outside the Syrian churches Theodore's exegetical influence is also to be seen in Latin, Irish, and Coptic commentaries, amongst others.)

67 Cf. L. Abramowski, "Über die Fragmente des Theodor von Mopsuestia in Brit. Libr. add. 12.156 und das doppelt überlieferte christologische Fragment," *Oriens Christianus* 79 (1995), pp. 1–8.

68 Most clearly in his "Homily on the Three Doctors" (Diodore, Theodore, and Nestorius); ed. and Fr. trans. by F. Martin, "Homélie de Narsès sur les trois docteurs nestoriens," *Journal asiatique* IX. 14 (1899), pp. 446–92, 15 (1900), pp. 469–525; cf. L. Abramowski, "Das Konzil von Chalkedon in der Homilie des Narsai über die drei nestorianischen Lehrer," *Zeitschrift für Kirchengeschichte* 66 (1954/5), pp. 140–3.

69 Ed. and Fr. trans. by J. B. Chabot, *Synodicon Orientale* (Paris, 1902); for a study of the Christological passages, see S. P. Brock, "The Christology of the Church of the East in the Synods of the Fifth to Early Seventh Centuries: Preliminary Considerations and Materials," in G. Dragas, ed., *Aksum-Thyateira: A Festschrift for Archbishop Methodius* (London, 1985), pp. 125–42 (repr. in his *Studies in Syriac Christianity* (London, 1992) ch. XII.)

70 G. R. Driver and L. Hodgson, *Nestorius: The Bazaar of Heracleides* (Oxford, 1925). It should be noted that the translation of key Christological terminology in this volume – and especially *qnoma* – can be highly misleading.

71 Cf. the English translations of the key texts in Brock, "Christology of the Church of the East."

72 Cf. the comments of Catholicos Isho'yahb II – whose own confession of faith was accepted by the emperor Heraklios and his Greek theological advisers at Aleppo in 630 – reported in L. R. M. Sako, *Lettre christologique du patriarche syro-oriental Išo'yahb II de Gdala (628–646)* (Rome, 1983), pp. 146–7. Cf. C. Mango, "Deux etudes sur Byzance et la perse sassanide," *Travaux et Memoires* 9 (1985), pp. 91–118.

73 Babai's major Christological treatise is his "Book of Union," ed. and Latin trans. by A. Vaschalde, *Babai Magni liber de unione* (CSCO 79, 80; Louvain, 1915). Cf. G. Chediath, *The Christology of Mar Babai the Great* (Kottayam, 1982) and L. Abramowski, "Die Christologie Babais des Grossen," *Symposium Syriacum 1972* (OCA 197; Rome, 1974), pp. 219–45, and "Babai der Grosse: Christologische Probleme und ihre Lösungen," OCP 41 (1975), pp. 290–343.

74 Reference to two *qnome* is first recorded in a report from c.562 concerning theological discussions arranged by Justinian with representatives of the Church of the East. Cf. A. Guillaumont, "Justinien et l'église de Perse," *Dumbarton Oaks Papers* 23/4 (1969/70), pp. 39–66.

75 Useful discussions of this terminological confusion and of the key terms involved can be found in Brock, "Christology of the Church of the East," and in the anonymous appendix (written by R. H. Connolly) to J. F. Bethune-Baker, *Nestorius and his Teaching: A Fresh Examination of the Evidence* (Cambridge, 1908), pp. 212–32.

76 This was a traditional correspondence that was also found in Ephrem and Aphrahat, but in Syrian Orthodox usage where translation technique had been heavily refined from the fifth century on, *ousia* and *physis* were distinguished, and *physis* was more closely associated with *prosopon*.

77 There were of course some dissident voices within the Church of the East – as within all churches – most notably Sahdona (known in Chalcedonian circles, where his spiritual writings were widely read, by the Greek form of this name, Martyrius), who was condemned by his church around 630 for arguing that Christ had not two but one *qnoma*, and that only this emphasis on one *prospon* and one *qnoma* guaranteed the union and involved a real appropriation of the being and activity of humanity by the divine Word, and of divinity by humanity. Cf. A. de Halleux, "La Christologie de Martyrios-Sahdona dans l'évolution du nestorianisme," OCP 23 (1957), pp. 5–32.

78 Cf. *Sobornost/Eastern Churches Review* 17:1 (1995), pp. 52–4.

79 For the text of the monument and other Chinese Christian texts, cf. P. Y. Saeki, *The Nestorian Documents and Relics in China* (2nd edn., Tokyo, 1951); A. C. Moule, *Christians in China before the year 1550* (London, 1930); J. Foster, *The Church of the T'ang Dynasty* (London, 1939). For recent overviews of the history of Syriac missionary activity in China, cf. I. Gillman and H.-J. Klimkeit, *Christians in Asia before 1500* (Richmond, 1998), and S. H. Moffett, *A History of Christianity in Asia: I, Beginnings to 1500* (New York, 1992).

80 I.e. the Old Testament.

81 The Beatitudes.

82 The three great commandments of Matt. 7:12, 22:37–40?

83 A Buddhist concept.

84 Cf. D. G. K. Taylor, "Basil of Caesarea's Contacts with Syriac-speaking Christians," in E. A. Livingstone, ed., *Studia patristica* XXXII (Leuven, 1997), pp. 204–10.

85 In the subsequent centuries of controversy over the Chalcedonian definition, during which each side sought to portray its opponents in the worst possible light, the Syrian Miaphysites were frequently condemned as Eutychians, despite their condemnation of this Christology, and it is a sad comment on many modern handbooks that the charge that they denied the humanity of Christ is still to be found.

86 Cf. A. Grillmeier and T. Hainthaler, *Christ in Christian Tradition*, vol. 2: *From the Council of Chalcedon (451) to Gregory the Great (590–604)*, pt. 2: *The Church of Constantinople in the Sixth Century* (London, 1995); J. Lebon, *Le Monophysisme sévérien: étude historique, littéraire et théologique sur la résistance monophysite au Concile de Chalcédoine jusqu'à la constitution de l'église jacobite* (Louvain, 1909); J. Lebon, "La Christologie du monophysisme syrien," in A. Grillmeier and H. Bacht, eds., *Das Konzil von Chalkedon: Geschichte und Gegenwart* (I.425–580; Würzburg, 1951); R. C. Chesnut, *Three Monophysite Christologies: Severus of Antioch, Philoxenus of Mabbug and Jacob of Sarug*

(London, 1976). For the history of the larger Miaphysite movement, and the creation of an independent hierarchy, cf. W. H. C. Frend, *The Rise of the Monophysite Movement* (Cambridge, 1972), which is heavily reliant on Greek sources, and W. A. Wigram, *The Separation of the Monophysites* (London, 1923), which makes fuller use of Syriac texts.

87 Letter X, cited by Chesnut, *Three Monophysite Christologies*, p. 16.

88 Both Chalcedonians and the powerful "Phantasiast" faction within their own community who argued that Christ's body was not subject to corruption or passions. Cf. R. Draguet, *Julien d'Halicarnasse et sa controverse avec Sévère d'Antioche sur l'incorruptibilité du corps du Christ* (Louvain, 1924); A. Grillmeier and T. Hainthaler, *Christ in Christian Tradition*, vol. 2: *From the Council of Chalcedon (451) to Gregory the Great (590–604)*, pt. 2: *The Church of Constantinople in the Sixth Century* (London, 1995), esp. p. 25, pp. 79–111.

89 Cf. A. de Halleux, *Philoxène de Mabbog: sa vie, ses écrits, sa théologie* (Louvain, 1963), and R. Chesnut, *Three Monophysite Christologies*.

90 Some differences are, however, highlighted in Chesnut.

91 Cf. A. de Halleux, ed., *Philoxène de Mabbog. Commentaire du Prologue johannique* (CSCO 380; Leuven, 1977), p. 53.

92 A. de Halleux, ed., *Lettre aux moines de Senoun* (CSCO 231–2; Louvain, 1963), pp. 51ff.

93 Cf. D. G. K. Taylor, "The Christology of the Syriac Psalm Commentary (AD541/2) of Daniel of Salah and the Phantasiast Controversy," in E. J. Yarnold, ed., *Studia patristica* XXXV (Leuven, 2001), pp. 516–23.

94 Only in the 1960s was his miaphysitism demonstrated beyond doubt, and that from some of his letters where he was being specifically questioned by his correspondents about his attitude to Chalcedon. R. Chesnut's discussion of Jacob's Christology is a good example of what can go wrong when a scholar tries to fit a Syriac thinker into a Greek mold, and it should be used with great caution. Far more satisfactory are T. Bou Mansour, *La Théologie de Jacques de Saroug* (Kaslik, 1993, 2000), and T. Kollamparampil, *Select Aspects of the Economy of Salvation in Christ according to Jacob of Serugh* (Rome, 1997).

Ambrose

ch a p ter 19

Boniface Ramsey

The ordination of Ambrose as bishop of Milan on 7 December 374 – an event remarkable on several counts, mostly because the new bishop had not even been baptized when he was elected to his post by popular acclaim several weeks previously – marks the emergence of the first Latin personality to capture the Western Christian world's attention, and to hold it, since the death of Cyprian of Carthage in 258. Among those who lived and worked between the dates of Cyprian's martyrdom and Ambrose's ordination there were major figures such as Arnobius of Sicca, Lactantius, Ossius of Cordova, Hilary of Poitiers, and Eusebius of Vercelli, but none of them had the stature that Ambrose did. He was not only bishop of the capital of the West, which Milan had become at the time, thanks to the presence there of the imperial household; he was also a politician to be reckoned with, a poet and mystic, a preacher of note, and a man of learning whose familiarity with Greek theology helped substantially to make that theology a part of the Latin heritage.

Ambrose was born in Trier, a Roman settlement in what is now Germany, in 339. Although it is not entirely reliable, we are fortunate to have a biography of our subject in the form of *The Life of Saint Ambrose* by a certain Paulinus of Milan, who tells us that Ambrose was the son of the pretorian prefect of the Gauls, a high official who was responsible for administering much of the north-west portion of the Roman Empire. Aurelius Ambrosius, as he was called, already had two other children, Marcellina and Satyrus. Not long after Ambrose's birth his father died, whereupon the family moved to Rome. There is no satisfactory explanation as to why neither Ambrose nor Satyrus were baptized at infancy, but they must have had some significant exposure to Christianity at home, since in early 353 their sister dedicated herself to a life of virginity in the presence of Pope Liberius in the Roman basilica of Saint Peter.

Due to the solid if conventional education that he acquired in Rome and to the connections that he had as the son of a distinguished father, Ambrose seemed to have no difficulty in beginning a suitable career for himself. Both he and Satyrus found employment as advocates at the court of the pretorian prefect of Italy, located at Sirmium, near Belgrade in present-day Serbia. The prefect who hired the brothers soon died and was succeeded by another, the fabulously wealthy Sextus Petronius Probus, who evidently recognized their talents because he promoted each of them within two or three years of his accession to office. Each received a governorship: Satyrus' we do not know, but Ambrose was appointed to Aemilia-Liguria, whose chief city, and the one with which his destiny would thenceforth be inextricably linked, was Milan.

It was as governor of Aemilia-Liguria that Ambrose intervened in the unrest that occurred in Milan following the death of Bishop Auxentius in the fall of 374. Auxentius had been an Arian, which meant that, in keeping with the doctrine of the early fourth-century Alexandrian priest Arius, he denied the full divinity of Christ. Although Auxentius, during his nearly twenty years as bishop, seems to have been largely successful in maintaining the peace between Arians and Catholic Christians, who insisted that Christ was both completely human and completely divine, the modus vivendi collapsed with his passing. Milan was now openly divided between two factions, Arian and Catholic, neither of which was disposed to concede the newly available episcopal office to the other. It fell, then, to Ambrose to prevent an ecclesiastical disagreement from degenerating into civil chaos. The story of what occurred, which is one of the great legends of Christian antiquity, is memorably recounted in Paulinus' biography:

> Now that Auxentius was dead . . . and the people were on the brink of causing a riot in their demand for a bishop, it was incumbent upon [Ambrose] to prevent a riot, lest the people imperil the city. So he came to the church [where the crowd had gathered] and there, as he was addressing the throng, the voice of a child is said to have sounded suddenly in the midst of the people: "Ambrose for bishop!" At the sound of this voice the shouts of the people turned into cries of acclamation for Ambrose as their bishop. Thus those who had previously been in violent discord among themselves, because Arians and Catholics each wanted to overcome the other and have their own bishop ordained, all at once agreed upon this one man in a remarkable and incredible display of harmony.[1]

Paulinus continues by telling his readers that Ambrose was at first unwilling to accept the episcopate and tried in various ways to change the minds of those who had come out in his favor. But their choice was approved by Emperor Valentinian I, and shortly thereafter Ambrose was baptized a Catholic; then, a week later, after having presumably passed through the necessary preliminary stages, he was ordained a bishop.

With his election the new bishop was placed in a position that he would make incalculably more influential than the governorship of Aemilia-Liguria. In this new position he fashioned a moral and political counterweight to the emperor and his court, which through most of Ambrose's episcopal career was situated in Milan, and as the bishop of Milan he often proved himself morally superior to and politically more astute than the imperial household.

Ambrose dealt with six emperors in the little more than two decades that he spent in Milan: Valentinian I (364–75), Gratian (367–83), Valentinian II (375–92), the usurper Magnus Maximus (383–8), Eugenius (392–4), and Theodosius (379–95). Of Ambrose's relationship with Valentinian I there is little to tell apart from the fact that, as the emperor who ruled the western portion of the Roman Empire, he gave his consent to his governor's election as bishop. Both Maximus and Eugenius, the latter a somewhat hapless former professor of rhetoric, were objects of Ambrose's political attentions but also rather distant figures. Gratian, Valentinian II and Theodosius were the ones who loomed the largest in Ambrose's life, if only because these three, unlike the others, maintained a residence in Milan.

Gratian, Valentinian I's son by a previous marriage, was in his mid-teens when Ambrose first knew him as bishop, while Valentinian II, Gratian's half-brother, was only twelve years old and ruled through his mother, the formidable Empress Justina. Gratian was twenty-four when he died at the hands of an assassin, and Valentinian was twenty-one when he perished in what was probably an assassination. Virtual nonentities from the perspective of secular history, the two young emperors are of much greater significance in Church history.

Gratian, who was a committed Catholic Christian, eventually fell under the tutelage of his bishop, who seems to have regarded him almost as a son. It may have been entirely his own doing, or it may have been at the instigation of Ambrose, when in 375 Gratian refused the pagan priestly title of Pontifex Maximus that all the emperors since the time of Augustus, including Christian ones, had willingly accepted. Gratian countenanced an edict published by Theodosius, Gratian's coemperor, in 380, which forbade the practise of any form of Christianity but Catholicism, and in 381 he returned a basilica in Milan to Catholic use that for two years previously had been occupied by Arians; it seems reasonable to assume that Ambrose was at least consulted on these matters. And it is likely that Ambrose's influence was responsible for two important actions that Gratian took against paganism in 382 – the stripping of the pagan cult's revenues and the removal of the Altar of Victory, a shrine to the goddess of victory, from the Senate House in Rome.

If Ambrose's relationship with Gratian was to a great degree marked by a sense of common religious purpose, this was hardly the case in regard to his relationship with Valentinian II, who in his short life was never baptized. The young emperor's mother Justina was powerful and ambitious, and she vied with Ambrose for sway over her son; moreover, reflecting a significant portion of the imperial court itself, she was an Arian. As it turned out, however, in Ambrose's two most important adversarial encounters with the court it was he who carried the day. The first, which did not involve Justina, concerned a plea on the part of the pagan senators, written in 384 by Symmachus, the prefect of Rome and a senator himself, for the restoration of the Altar of Victory that Gratian had removed in 382. Symmachus' plea called for universal toleration and famously asked, "What difference does it make by what method a person searches for the truth? There is no one single path that leads to so great a mystery."[2] The prefect's words made a profound impression at the court. But Ambrose, on learning of this, hastily wrote to Valentinian, threatening him with ignominy and repudiation should he restore the pagan shrine to the Senate House, and the bishop's threats had the desired effect: the young emperor rejected the senatorial petition.

The second encounter was more complicated and drawn out, and in it Justina played a leading role. It was certainly she who, early in 385, persuaded the imperial council to demand of Ambrose a church in which her Arian co-religionists could worship. Ambrose not unexpectedly refused, and by Easter of that same year, after various maneuvers on the part of both the bishop and the emperor, which brought Milan to the verge of civil disorder, Valentinian bitterly backed down. In January of 386, however, Justina saw to it that an edict was published which in effect allowed Arians to worship publicly and made it a capital offense to hinder such worship. Ambrose, against whom this edict clearly was directed, ignored it. When ordered to appear before the imperial court to debate the Arian bishop Auxentius, he refused; nor would he quit Milan when the court told him that he must. Instead he blockaded himself, with a large number of his faithful, in a church, which was promptly surrounded by soldiers who refused to allow anyone to leave. But Ambrose's endurance was greater than that of Valentinian and Justina; rather than risk a disaster, Valentinian again backed down.

In June of 386, soon after Valentinian's second surrender, Ambrose discovered the skeletons of two men in a Milanese church. These were understood to be the bones of Gervasius and Protasius, martyrs who supposedly suffered during the reign of Nero in the first century. Their discovery, and a spectacular miracle of healing that followed a few days later, seemed to bestow upon the recently embattled bishop a sign of divine approbation. Modern scholarship regularly questions whether these skeletons actually were what they were claimed to be and how it was that they were found at such an opportune time, but in Ambrose's less sceptical age doubt of this kind would have been much rarer.

With the death of Valentinian in 392, Theodosius, who had been coemperor in the East with him, now ruled the Empire alone. Even before Valentinian's death, however, Theodosius had been exercising a wider authority than would ordinarily have been the case, for the young emperor had proved himself incapable of ruling. Hence Theodosius was in Milan in December of 388 when word came to him that Christian monks had burned down a synagogue in the town of Callinicum on the Euphrates, at the eastern end of the Empire. The emperor ordered that the bishop of Callinicum pay for rebuilding the synagogue, since he had apparently urged on the monks, and that the monks themselves be punished for their deed. When Ambrose, who was temporarily absent from Milan, heard of Theodosius' decision, he wrote him a letter saying that he must neither expect the bishop to rebuild the synagogue nor punish the monks who had set fire to it.[3] In Ambrose's view this would have represented an unacceptable victory for Jews at the expense of Christians, and his letter to the emperor was full of what we would now recognize as the grossest anti-Semitism. By the time Theodosius received this letter he had already modified his demands, having realized that in the circumstances they were unrealistic; so he ignored the inflammatory document. But Ambrose was relentless. Soon after his return to Milan he found himself preaching in the cathedral in the presence of the emperor and his entourage. Without warning he turned from the topic at hand and began to admonish Theodosius. When he had concluded he approached the emperor and threatened to discontinue the service unless Theodosius dropped all his demands touching both the bishop and the monks of Callinicum. The emperor, feeling himself embarrassed before Ambrose and a congregation that almost undoubtedly shared its bishop's beliefs, promised to rescind his orders entirely. Thereupon Ambrose resumed the celebration of the eucharist, greatly satisfied at what he had accomplished, in his view, on behalf of the Church.

A second confrontation with Theodosius places Ambrose in a much more attractive light. In the summer of 390 a riot occurred in the Greek city of Thessalonika, and the commander of the local garrison, a barbarian named Botheric, was murdered by the mob. Theodosius, on receiving word of this at Milan, considered it a grave affront to himself and determined to punish the Thessalonians by ordering the massacre of a substantial number of them. After sending out the order, however, he had second thoughts about the harshness of the punishment and he canceled it. But the countermanding order arrived too late. The people of Thessalonika had already been invited to the city circus for what they believed would be a spectacle of some sort when, we are told, soldiers rushed in and slew at least 7,000 persons. Ambrose's reaction to this was one of horror, and he decided that the emperor would have to be excommunicated. In a sensitive and respectful letter to Theodosius, the bishop told his sovereign that he would not celebrate the eucharist in his presence, and he concluded by expressing his love and affection for the emperor, while declaring that his love for God was greater still.[4] We do not know the details of Theodosius' excommunication, although legend has portrayed him coming to church to pray and Ambrose refusing him entrance. Whatever may have transpired in the course of a few months, by Christmas of 390 Theodosius' excommunication was lifted.

Despite these exceedingly tense moments, Theodosius and Ambrose seem to have considered each another friends. The emperor was, for one thing, a deeply committed Catholic Christian who, in a famous decree of June 391, effectively outlawed the pagan cult and, in so doing, cleared the way for the complete triumph of Christianity in the Empire. For another, he was a leader of genius and a man of basic integrity to whom posterity would grant the title of "the Great." When he died and Ambrose preached in his memory (as he also did for Gratian and Valentinian II), the bishop lamented his passing as a personal blow.

From these experiences with the men who represented the full authority of the Empire, and indeed embodied it, and also from other experiences, Ambrose worked out what was probably his most important contribution to Western culture – namely, the beginnings of a theory of the relationship between the Church and the State. According to this inchoate theory, which is perhaps most succinctly exposed in Ambrose's 21st letter[5] and in the *Sermon against Auxentius*,[6] the State had been given by God an arena within which to exercise its influence. So long as it acted morally within this arena its activities were legitimate, although much of what might have passed for moral behavior in Ambrose's day – e.g. torture, the broad practise of capital punishment, the acceptance of slavery, the disallowance of religious freedom – would not be considered such in our day. The influence of the Church, however, was not restricted to a specific arena: it was, rather, universal. In this respect the Church was superior to the State, and hence the Church could judge the State, commending it if it acted morally and condemning it if it did not. It would certainly be imprudent if the Church were to vaunt its superiority or interfere with the legitimate activities of the State: its role, instead, was to serve as something like the conscience of the State. And, in complementary fashion, the role of the State in relation to the Church was to serve as its facilitator and protector. It must be noted here that, for this theory to work, the State would have to be Christian; ideally, for Ambrose, it would have to be, like the Church itself, Catholic Christian. For, as far as the bishop of Milan and the vast majority of his contemporaries were concerned (Augustine of Hippo, a more searching thinker, was a notable exception to this), the Roman Empire, which during Ambrose's tenure openly embraced Catholic Christianity and rejected both non-Catholic Christianity and paganism, was the only state that they could imagine. This theory of Church-State relations continues with some accommodations to provide the framework for such relations even today in the Western world.

Given Ambrose's extensive involvement in the realm of the political, it is useful to be reminded that the scope of his activity was not defined exclusively by his dealings with the imperial court. Augustine hints at other preoccupations when, in a well-known passage in his *Confessions*, he describes Ambrose in his residence, where anyone could come and see him unannounced, absorbed in a book and reading quietly to himself.[7] Ambrose, in other words, was an intensely reflective figure as well as a towering public personage. It would be a mistake, of course, to suggest that the bishop's ideas on the relationship between Church and State were not the product of a reflective spirit, but his writings in other areas, prompted less by the exigencies of the moment, reveal more of his interiority.

There can be little doubt that Ambrose was a mystic – in the sense that he was serious about the things of the spirit and was aware of the activity of the divine in his life. His hymns, of which at least four certainly authentic ones have survived, imply this; although a few others wrote hymns before he did, he was the first great Latin hymnodist, and his works, recognized as masterpieces, continue to be used in the liturgy of the Western Church.[8] A glimpse of his mystical bent is also to be found on those frequent occasions when he speaks eloquently of Christ, as he does for example in some lines from his treatise *On the Faith*:

> Christ is the origin of our virtue. He is the origin of our chastity – he who taught virgins not to look forward to sharing a bed with a man but to dedicate the chastity of their minds and bodies to the Holy Spirit rather than to a husband. Christ is the origin of our frugality – he who became poor, although he was rich. Christ is the origin of our patience – he who, when he was cursed, did not curse in return, and when he was struck did not strike back. Christ is the origin of our humility – he who accepted the form of a slave, although he was the equal of God the Father in the majesty of his power. From him, indeed, each individual virtue has received its origin.[9]

Ambrose's promotion of virginity, which is evident from the passage just cited, can likewise be mentioned as an indication of his mysticism, although some recent scholarship has tended to view this more in political than in spiritual terms. It seems safe to say, in any event, that virginity was customary in his family: his sister Marcellina was a consecrated virgin and both he and his brother Satyrus were unmarried; among his forebears he boasted a martyred virgin named Sotheris.[10] The bishop's earliest treatise, which appears to have been inspired by Marcellina's consecration, was dedicated to the theme of virginity and entitled simply *On Virgins*.[11] It was eventually followed by three others: *On Virginity*,[12] *On the Training of a Virgin*[13] and *An*

Exhortation to Virginity.[14] And in his treatise *On Widows*[15] he lays more stress on a widow's chastity than he does on any other quality of hers. From Ambrose's perspective, the appeal of virginity lies primarily in its ability to gain access for the virgin to Christ, who is typically portrayed as her lover in a passage from *On Virginity*:

> It is right that our hearts should be agitated at the Lord's coming. If Mary was agitated at the coming of an angel, how much more should we be agitated at the coming of Christ! Indeed, once divine realities penetrate us, bodily feelings give way and the habits of the exterior person die out. Be agitated, then, and hasten. It is in haste that they are commanded [Exod. 12:11] to eat the lamb. Arise and open: Christ is at the door and knocks at the entry of your house. If you open he will enter, and he will enter with his Father.[16]

The bishop of Milan contributed mightily to the exaltation of virginity, both in these treatises and in other writings of his, that was so characteristic of the final quarter of the fourth century in the Latin West; in this regard perhaps only the more strident voice of Jerome came near to matching his.

It is to a large extent within the context of virginity that Ambrose speculates on the person of Mary, the mother of Jesus. She is for him the most excellent model of virginal behavior, in her humility, modesty, and diligence. But Mary also has attributes that are inimitable, for Ambrose goes so far as to affirm – for apparently the first time in patristic literature – that she was a virgin not only in conceiving her son but even in giving birth to him.[17] The cult of Mary, which had already begun to flourish by Ambrose's time, was given still greater impetus thanks to his authority.

Ambrose's mystical side is also apparent in his liturgical homilies *On the Mysteries*[18] and *On the Sacraments*[19] (whose authorship has been disputed), in which, without breaking new ground, he describes beautifully and lucidly baptism as it was practised in late fourth-century Milan. In particular, he explains its rich mystical symbolism while maintaining a strongly realistic understanding of the Eucharist as the true body and blood of Christ.[20]

The dominant theological problem of Ambrose's age, which as we have seen had also caused trouble for him in the political sphere, was Arianism. This heresy, which took on a number of different forms, in essence denied that Christ shared fully, if at all, in the divinity of God the Father. As such, in the eyes of the orthodox, it denied as well the fulness of his salvific power. In Ambrose's day Arianism had already begun its decline from the extremely threatening position that it held from the fourth to the seventh decades of the fourth century. His election as bishop of itself struck a blow against it, as did his refusal more than a decade later to cede an orthodox church in Milan to the Arians for their worship. Between these two events Ambrose masterminded – or rather manipulated – the arrangements for and the proceedings of the council of Aquileia, held in the late spring of 381, which deposed two Arian bishops and an Arian priest. This council is considered by most historians to be the Western equivalent, albeit on a smaller scale, of the council of Constantinople, which occurred in the late spring and early summer of the same year and which is generally said to mark the definitive downward turn in Arianism's fortunes.

Throughout his episcopal career, meanwhile, Ambrose wrote and preached constantly with Arianism in mind. Sometimes it is mentioned explicitly, and sometimes it is an unspoken theme, which is the case on almost every occasion when he emphasizes the divinity of Christ in what might appear to be a gratuitous manner. For all his preoccupation with Arianism as a theological concept, however, Ambrose's contribution to its eclipse was in the domain of the practical rather than the conceptual. He succeeded in defeating Arianism by combining the reiteration of theological commonplaces with the application of political pressure where it would do the most good.

Indeed, when it is a question of illuminating the great historical issues of theology, as they are commonly understood today, Ambrose is a disappointment. For such enlightening insights we must go to his contemporaries, Basil, Gregory Nazianzen, Gregory of Nyssa, and Augustine. Although a distinction of this sort would have been unheard of in the patristic era, Ambrose was not a theological master but a spiritual one.

Nonetheless Ambrose possessed a theological tool, or gift, that few other theologians in the Latin West shared with him. Thanks to his evidently having mastered Greek when he was a child, the bishop of Milan had at his disposal the theological resources in that language. Those with which he was familiar he called upon with relative frequency, and his treatises and sermons are full of references to, citations of, and wholesale borrowings from Philo, Origen, Didymus, Athanasius, and Basil, to name the most important. It was from these writers that he learned what he himself would, if asked, undoutedly have claimed as his major theological skill – the interpretation of Scripture. Especially from Origen and his disciples he discovered that the spiritual or allegorical interpretation of the Bible, and particularly of the Old Testament, was the key to comprehending it, and from them he acquired the techniques of exegesis that made his scriptural commentaries and his sermons possible. We know the effect that Ambrose's sermons had on at least one of his hearers. Augustine tells us in his *Confessions* that, on listening to Ambrose preach, which he initially did simply out of admiration for the bishop as an acclaimed public speaker, he became aware for the first time that the Old Testament was not a repulsive and barbaric document but a work of great spiritual depth.[21] This awareness was in turn a decisive step for him along the path to embracing the Christian religion and eventually, as a priest and bishop, to preaching on the text of Scripture in the same way as his mentor had done.[22]

When Ambrose died on 4 April 397 after more than 22 years as a Christian and a bishop, these were the main elements of the legacy that he bequeathed to the Latin Church and, in some cases, to that even broader entity known as Western civilization: a framework upon which to build a relationship between the Church and the State; a mystique of Christ that achieved one of its sublimest expressions in virginity embraced for his sake; the development of the cult of Mary; the suppression of Arianism by political means; the transmission of Greek theological thought, and especially of Greek scriptural exegesis, to the Latin West; and an influence exercised upon Augustine that marked one of the most important stages on the path to conversion of this greatest of all Latin theologians. With this legacy and thanks to a personality whose forcefulness and fearlessness on behalf of the Church can, in the fourth century, only be compared with that of Athanasius, Ambrose earned his place among the giants of early Christianity.

Notes

1   *Life of Saint Ambrose*, 6 (PL 14.28–9).
2   *Plea* 10 (PL 16.969).
3   *Letter* 40 (PL 16.1101–13).
4   *Letter* 51 (PL 16.1160–4).
5   PL 16.1003–7.
6   PL 16.1007–18.
7   *Confessions* VI.iii.3.3 (PL 32.720–1).
8   See Jacques Fontaine (ed.), *Ambroise de Milan: Hymnes* (Paris, 1992).
9   *On the Faith* 3.7.52 (PL 16.600).
10 *On Virgins* 3.7.38–9 (PL 16.232); *An Exhortation to Virginity* 12.82 (PL 16.360).
11 PL 16.187–232.
12 PL 16.265–302.
13 PL 16.305–34.
14 PL 16.335–64.
15 PL 16.233–62.
16 *On Virginity* 11.60 (PL 16.60).
17 *An Exposition of the Gospel according to Luke* 2.43 (PL 15.156–89).
18 PL 16.389–410.
19 PL 16.417–62.
20 See esp. *On the Mysteries* 9.53–4 (PL 16.407).
21 *Confessions* VI.iii–VI.iv (PL 32.720–2).
22 In his three books entitled *De officiis* (*On Duties*) (PL 16.23–184) Ambrose also allowed himself to be inspired by the great pagan Latin writer Cicero, whose work of the same name he reoriented by giving it a Christian slant, thus providing the Latin West with its first comprehensive treatise on the virtues from a Christian perspective.

Bibliography

Pierre Courcelle, *Recherches sur Saint Ambroise: "vie" anciennes, culture, iconographie* (Paris, 1973).

F. Homes Dudden, *The Life and Times of St. Ambrose*, in 2 vols (Oxford, 1935).

Goulven Madec, *Saint Ambroise et la philosophie* (Paris, 1974).

Neil McLynn, B. *Ambrose of Milan: Church and Court in a Christian Capital* (Berkeley, CA, 1994).

Jean-Rémy Palanque, *Saint Ambroise et l'Empire romain: contribution à l'histoire de l'Eglise et de l'Etat à la fin du IVe siècle* (Paris, 1933).

Angelo Paredi, *Saint Ambrose: His Life and Times*, trans. M. Joseph Costelloe (Notre Dame, 1964).

Boniface Ramsey, *Ambrose* (London, 1997).

Hans von Campenhausen, *Ambrosius von Mailand als Kirchenpolitiker* (Berlin, 1929).

Daniel H. Williams, *Ambrose of Milan and the End of the Arian-Nicene Conflicts* (Oxford, 1995).

Jerome

G. R. Evans

Jerome (c.342–420) was born near Aquileia. His ambitious family ensured that he had a good education, at Rome under the famous grammarian Donatus. He was baptized (at a relatively young age for those times), in 366. Jerome returned to Aquileia as a young man. He founded a community of ascetics but it broke up after three years, apparently as a result of a characteristic "abrasiveness" on the part of Jerome, which was to mark so much of his social intercourse. He moved to Antioch with some of his friends, but this community also failed. Jerome met an experienced and elderly hermit named Malchus and (perhaps on his advice) attempted to live in solitude. He retreated to the desert of Chalcis where a number of hermits were already living such lives. In an early letter (2.i)[1] he describes the desert as "the fairest city of all" and "places empty of inhabitants but thronged by bands of saints – a true paradise." For five years Jerome lived among them in extreme asceticism, studying the Bible.

He seems to have been an awkward, tense, self-reproving youth and young adult, drawn like many of his contemporaries, but to an unusual degree, to a life of extreme asceticism. Jerome's *Letter* 148.vi[2] says that it is the way of the Stoics to make no difference between sins and to consider a wickedness and a mistake to be the same. He urges vigilance about every act, every word, every thought, so that the mind is always armed against sin.[3]

He found himself strongly tempted both by the pleasures of the intellectual life and by the pleasures of the flesh, which he found tended to go together. He describes how he used to fast and then, in contradiction of this act of self-denial, pick up a secular "classic" for pleasure (*Letter* 22.xxx.1, written to one of the well-born Roman women he encouraged in the life of chastity, abstinence, and self-denial): "After frequent night vigils, after shedding tears which the remembrance of past sins brought forth from my inmost heart, I would take in my hands a volume of Plautus" (*Letter* 22.xxx.2). Painfully, he faced the famous challenge that he was "a Ciceronian not a Christian" (*Letter* 22.xxx.4). These notions that both kinds of pleasure were alike temptations were not confined to Jerome.

In 379 Jerome went back to Antioch. There he was ordained priest by its bishop Paulinus and seems to have stayed near him for a while. He was present at the general council at Constantinople in 381, where he met the "Cappadocian Fathers", Gregory Nazianzen and Gregory of Nyssa. He also spent time with Paulinus in Rome. Jerome found himself becoming "adviser" of Pope Damasus on questions of biblical interpretation.

In Rome Jerome met others who were drawn to the ascetic life, notably the circle of ladies who became his correspondents, Paula, and her daughters Blesilla and Eustochium, and the rather older Marcella, the senior figure of the group. She provided somewhere for him and others to meet for the study of Hebrew, prayer, and the singing of psalms. Jerome's letters to these women are important indicators of the norms of what to us appears an extreme asceticism but which was a reasonable choice of "lifestyle" for well-born women in the fourth-century West. He urged them to a moderate but not excessive self-discipline. To Marcella he wrote with warnings against the "real" extremists, the Montanists and Novatianists.

Letter 22 to Eustochium forms a treatise in its own right on the ascetic life. He tried to convey to Eustochium a sense of her own worth in the eyes of Christ, and a lively awareness of the companionship Christ offered his Bride: "Your Bridegroom is not arrogant. He is not proud. He has married an Ethiopian woman" (22.i.5); "I do not wish you to become proud but to be fearful because of your decision [to live in this way]" (22.iii.1). He urges her to fight actively against sin (22.iii.3–4). Jerome's letters had even at this early period of the development of Christian exegesis brought to a fine pitch of development the art of writing in a patchwork of biblical quotations, in almost every phrase an allusion to the Scriptures.

Among Jerome's works on the living of the good Christian life, and especially the ascetic life, should perhaps be included his works on church history and stories and lives of exemplary Christians, as well as the *De viris illustribus* (392, Bethlehem),[4] *Lives* of the hermits (379, Antioch), a translation of the *Rule* of Pachomius (404).

Pope Damasus died and his successor Siricius did not continue his predecessor's special favour towards Jerome. Jerome found himself out of favour. Blesilla died; some said of too much self-denial. Jerome left the city, in the company of Paula and Eustochium, intending to found a joint convent and monastery near Bethlehem. Financial support was provided by the wealthy Paula, and when that came to an end, Jerome used his own family's money to keep the monastery going for the 34 years until he died in 420.

Jerome's love of Scripture, now thoroughly awakened, made him above all a biblical scholar. He contributed to the debate about the forming of what is now often described as the canon.[5] Before 390 he gives, in a prologue to Samuel and Malachi, a list of Old Testament "biblical" books and "whatever is extra to those and to be placed among the apocrypha," rejecting Wisdom, Ecclesiasticus, Judith, Tobias. In a letter to Paulinus of 395 he gives a different list, including the New Testament. There is a further list in a letter of 400–2 to Laeta, but its purpose was different. There he was mainly concerned to suggest an appropriate order of reading for a growing child to follow.

Above all he was a textual critic. Jerome deplored the fact that, as he puts it, there had been almost as many forms of the biblical text in circulation in his day as there were copies. This was leading to outlandish attempts to harmonize the Gospels and the text was, as a consequence, straying still further from the original. The new standard version of the Gospels was mainly produced by Jerome from 382–5 in Rome.

It is his translation of the Bible, known as the Vulgate, which is historically perhaps Jerome's most important legacy. It became for the Middle Ages "our trans-lation" (*nostra translatio*); "our usual version" (*nostra usitata editio*). The Old Latin text (*vetus latina*) was in truth a number of different texts of mixed or inferior Latinity. Jerome had been commissioned by the Pope, during his period in favour in Rome, to work on a new Latin text for at least some parts of Scripture. He had been commissioned to tidy up the Old Latin translation. The work made him think about the role of the translator of the divinely-inspired text. He took a modest view of the translator's task. Jerome made a distinction in his preface to the Pentateuch (PL 28.151) between a "prophet" and an "interpreter." The prophet is inspired. The translator renders the text with the aid of his learning and a good vocabulary and his understanding of the meaning (*eruditio et verborum copia, ea quae intelligit, transfert*). God does not put every word of the translation into his mind.

His new version of the Gospels proved controversial at first. There was a hostile reaction – as there perhaps always is to change in familiar wording in a holy book. Jerome's version of the Old Testament from the Hebrew was disparaged by Rufinus. For the Old Testament, Jerome came to realise that the Hebrew text was a better source than the Septuagint. In Jerusalem, from 391 to 404 Jerome was working on translation from the Hebrew. Jerome's *Letter* 106 was written to Sunnia and Fretela, Goths and probably clerics living in Constantinople. They had asked about the differences between the Psalter derived from the Hebrew and the Psalter based on the Greek (Septuagint) text. Jerome seized the opportunity to write at length and in technical detail, creating a work of immense importance to later scholarship, even if it may have been rather more than his correspondents wanted or expected. He translated the Psalms from the Septuagint. Tobit and Judith he rendered from the Chaldean in about 398. Jerome also wrote commentaries on a number of books of the Bible; in fact, he died while still working on his commentary on Jeremiah.

Jerome was irascible, an active polemicist, and author of *Against Jovinian* (Bethlehem 393) and *Against Rufinus* (Bethlehem 402–4), as well as combative correspondence with Augustine. In 415 he was visited by Orosius, who had been sent to him by an exasperated Augustine, whom he had been pestering with ques-tions. He brought with him two letters from Augustine, each a treatise in its own right, in which Augustine asked Jerome's opinion. The first was on the origin of the soul and the second on the interpretation of James 2:10 (the assertion that whoever breaks one commandment is guilty of breaking them all).

He was prepared to take up cudgels on a number of topics of the day. To Mark, priest at Chalcis, he wrote (*Letter* 17) about the doctrine of the Trinity: "I am called a heretic for preaching that the Trinity is consubstantial. I am accused of the Sabellian heresy for proclaiming. . . . that there are three subsistent persons" (*Letter* 17.ii.2). He feels persecuted: "I am not allowed even a single corner of the desert. Every day I am asked about my faith as though I had been 'born again' without faith. I confess the faith as they require but they are not placated. I sign their form of words; they do not believe me" (*Letter* 17.iii.1). He complains that he is suspected not only of unorthodox belief but also of intending to lead the faithful astray: "you are evidently afraid that I may go round the churches leading people astray and bringing about a schism" (*Letter* 17.ii.4).

Notes

1 *Rule of Pachomius*, ed. P. Albers, *Florilegium Patristicum*, 16 (Bonn, 1923), CCSL 72–80.
2 CSEL 56, p. 334.
3 148.xv and xviii (CSEL 56, pp. 341 and 345).
4 *De viris illustribus*, ed. E. C. Richardson, *Nicene and Post-Nicene Christian Fathers* (New York and Oxford, 1892), pp. 359–84.
5 See chapter 1.

Bibliography

J. N. D. Kelly, *Jerome* (London, 1975); *A Monument to St. Jerome*, ed. F. X. Murphy (New York, 1952).

On Jerome's long-term influence, and his importance in the controversies about Bible translation in the sixteenth century, see Eugene F. Rice, *St. Jerome in the Renaissance* (Baltimore and London, 1985).

Augustine of Hippo

G. R. Evans

Augustine can be treated only briefly here. He has a chapter to himself in *The Medieval Theologians*. Important though he was in the world of his day, his impact was perhaps still greater in the thousand years which came after, when his writings were by far the most numerous in almost every monastic library, after the books of the Bible and liturgical texts. Nevertheless, something needs to be said in this volume about Augustine's attitude to the intellectual world in which he grew up and taught as a professor of rhetoric and his stance on the teaching of the faith.

When it came to borrowing from pagan philosophers, Augustine was prepared to be accommodating up to a point. In the eighth book of *The City of God*, Augustine explores at some length the questions Christians and philosophers have as common matters of interest. If the philosopher is by definition the lover of wisdom, and God himself is Wisdom, "the true philosopher is a lover of God" (*Civ.* VIII.i).[1] But philosophers sometimes hold *vanae opiniones*. Augustine takes his readers through a series of leading philosophers, fixing with approval on Socrates (*Civ.* VIII.iii) as the first important "moral philosopher." He shakes his head over the difference of opinion among Socrates' "followers" ("scarcely credible in the pupils of a single master") about the purpose of life, whether it is to seek virtue or pleasure as the highest good.

Plato, whom Augustine identifies as Socrates' leading disciple, he credits with the division of philosophy into three parts – moral, "natural" (which is concerned with *speculation*), and "rational" (or logic, by which truth is distinguished from falsehood) (*Civ.* VIII.iv). In Augustine's view, no philosopher came so close to the Christian position as Plato (*Civ.* VIII.v). He takes the opportunity to dismiss briskly those who seek to make philosophy out of theatre or politics or the bribing of inferior supernatural beings. The distinguishing feature which wins Augustine's approval is the Platonists' realization that it is essential not to confuse what the senses perceive (*quae sensibus adtinguntur*) with what the mind beholds (*quae mente conspiciuntur* (*Civ.* VIII.vii). The Platonists are especially admirable in their understanding of ethical principles (*Civ.* VIII.viii) for there they see that the objective is to seek the supreme good. Nevertheless, Platonists are not Christians. Augustine refers his readers (*Civ.* VIII.x) to Colossians 2:8, where St. Paul warns them not to be deceived by philosophers' vain deceits about the material world. At the same time, he points out, there is the acceptance in Romans 1:19–20 that God has revealed a good deal to those who have only their reason to guide them, and Acts 17:28 makes it plain that some of the pagans' own writers (*sicut et vestri quidam dixerunt*) have understood something of man's relation to God.

Augustine's careful balancing of scriptural evidences for the respectability of some pagan thought also takes him back to the Old Testament. He discusses the famous question of the possible encounter between Plato and Egyptian thought, the "despoiling of the Egyptians." Plato could not have met the prophet Jeremiah and Augustine does not think he could have read and understood the Hebrew Scriptures, but he believes he could have known something of their contents as a result of his travels. There is evidence for this belief, he suggests, in the interest Plato shows in his *Timaeus*[2] in the question of the origin of the world which is dealt with in Genesis (*Civ.* VIII.xi).

Similarly, he was inclined to take in and use the skills in rhetoric in which he himself had an outstanding professional authority. The education of the late antique world concentrated on making citizens fluent, persuasive. The boy began with grammar and went on to his teacher of oratory. "Rhetoric" teaching posts could carry a certain status. Some became state appointments with salaries funded by a benefactor (who was seen to be acting for the public good); appointments might be made by the local civic authorities.[3] Surprisingly little evidence survives of the methodology of this teaching of rhetoric, clear though its spirit is. The anonymous *Rhetorica ad Herennium* may owe its survival to the fact that it was for many centuries attributed to Cicero.[4] Cicero's own juvenile *On Invention* deals with the "finding" of arguments and ways of deploying them.[5] Quintilian may have been the first teacher of rhetoric to hold a state post. His immense *Institutes of Oratory* of the first century AD is comprehensive but it is hard to know how far it was typical.[6] Quintilian tells us that he went to great trouble to research the authorities on rhetoric and its teaching (Preface to Book I.1–2), conscious as he was that many distinguished authors in both Greek and Latin had had something to say on the subject.

Quintilian himself includes all the stages of a rhetorician's education. The "grammarian's" exercises, in which boys practised telling stories, relating fables, constructing maxims or *sententiae*, giving instructions, developed into elementary rhetorical practice sessions. The young men learned to amplify these miniatures into passages of praise and denunciation; full-scale descriptions; arguing a case for and against as in a court of law; making speeches in character (impersonating a mythical or historical figure.)[7]

For, above all, the study of rhetoric was the study of oratory. It involved the practical application of skills of composition in a way which would enable someone to be a good public speaker. Traditionally, this had three practical uses in late Rome. It made it possible for the citizen who found himself in a political office or arguing on a matter of public interest, to make powerful speeches (political rhetoric); it made all educated citizens competent orators in the law-courts where they might well find themselves as advocates for the "clients" for whom they were responsible as members of their households (forensic rhetoric); it was also intended to be used in the writing of encomiums to flatter emperors (panegyric).

Christianity had a new use for the rhetorician's skills, in the preaching of sermons, and here the gulf between the educated and the uneducated could be crossed. We know that Augustine was exceptionally good at this. He drew large congregations, and they showed their appreciation in the late Roman way, by applause in church. Some of the congregation were undoubtedly merely interested bystanders or enquirers, as Augustine himself had been when he went to listen to Ambrose preach in Milan. And beyond question he hoped to win to the faith just such arrogant unbelievers as he himself had been.

A good many of Augustine's sermons survive, especially the long series he preached on St. John's Gospel and the Psalms. They were not, of course, "published" in the modern sense, for there was no printing yet. But they were copied and circulated and Augustine kept track of his writings with some care. In old age he went through them all and took stock in his *Retractationes* of what he had written and considered whether revisions were needed. (On the whole he thought not.) The sermons of Augustine underline the central purpose of preaching at this date, especially preaching by bishops, which was to teach the faith. That was the function of the bishop's *cathedra* or throne in the principal church of a diocese. The sermons on the Bible were a means of interpreting Scripture for ordinary Christians, and showing the merely curious why they should become believers.

In their composition, these early Christian sermons reflect the good practice of late antique rhetoric. This is not necessarily modern "good practice." The train of thought can be digressive, allusive; examples are piled one upon another to make a cumulative point, in ways which can sometimes test the patience of the modern reader. There is play on words which loses its effect for the reader who does not have the Latin in front of him or her. On the other hand, the combination of figures of diction with figures of thought is as powerful now as it was in Augustine's day. He will draw a parallel, and give his phrases similar patterns of sound; he will create a paradox or an antithesis or a climax, and make the words appear to echo the thoughts. The effect is half lost in translation because it depends on the making of auditory patterns which disappear outside the Latin original, but something of the impact can be felt by the non-Latinist by exploring any good translation of the passages of prayer to God which run throughout the *Confessions*.

There are deeper questions, too, concerning the philosophy of language. In *On Christian Doctrine*, which he began in the late 390s and completed in 426, Augustine wrote a handbook on the uses to which an educated man could put his existing skills when he was interpreting Scripture and preaching. He was prompted perhaps in the first instance partly by his own youthful uncertainties about the apparent lack of sophistication of the text of Scripture when it was set beside the stylish classics he was studying at school. Furthermore, there was the question, which also greatly exercised Jerome, the author of the Vulgate translation of the Bible, whether a Christian ought to continue to study and enjoy secular writings.

Augustine begins his book *On Christian Doctrine* by asking the profoundly important question which underlies much of the medieval philosophy of language, how language conveys meaning; what is the relation between words and signs and the things they signify (*res* and *verbum*). He goes on to look at the ways in which Christians may legitimately use the devices of rhetoricians, either in their own compositions or in the critical analysis of the text of the Bible. The fact that he came back to this subject over so long a period suggests that it continued to be difficult for him to be sure how the balance should be struck. It was a matter of great and lasting interest to Augustine how human beings "know." He contemplated with interest the inner workings of his own mind, and asked himself what theory of knowledge he could derive from his own experience. In the same spirit, towards the end of the *Confessions* he gives space to the discussion of the nature of memory and the way it works. In the *Confessions* (X.viii.15), he describes the great power of memory (*magna vis*), how deep and large, even infinite, is its capacity. In his book on the Trinity he suggests that an "image" of the Trinity is to be found in human "memory, will and understanding"; or in human "mind, knowledge and love."

These all form, or derive, from applications of the knowledge and skills of a classically-educated rhetor to the needs of Christian teaching and apologetic. And as long as the "educated classes" were being taught in secular schools, Christian teachers would continue to have an uphill task in converting them and satisfying them intellectually, for their minds were furnished in the course of their education with a literature and a set of religious attitudes and the habit of disputing and selecting. It is these educated classes with whom this book is chiefly concerned, for it was in conversation with them that the first Christian theologians refined their ideas. But it is important not to lose sight of the need for educational provision for those who had not had an advanced pagan education; the adult converts to the faith of the early centuries needed teaching aids of a considerable range of sophistication.

Augustine provides useful clues in the *De catechizandis rudibus* to his own sensitivity on this point. He describes there how he proceeds to teach enquirers, sometimes surrounded by a curious crowd, and how important it is to make sure that the teaching is matched to the needs and the level of knowledge and understanding of the individual. After Augustine's day, in the West at least, the catechetical task was altered by the introduction of infant baptism as the norm. The West then began to create a different kind of catechetical instrument, designed to meet the needs of children already baptized but standing in need of instruction in the faith rather than the needs of mature adults who sought instruction in the faith before offering themselves for baptism.

Others were less self-consciously aware than Augustine that they had produced an oeuvre, a corpus of writings intended to stand in a succession of Christian thought. But Augustine's own awareness of the importance of what he had done makes him an appropriate figure to stand near the end of this volume as he stands at the beginning of the next one in the series, gazing into the eternal distance with his teacher's instinct to maintain and transmit the faith, adding something of his own by way of clarification and encouragement.

Notes

1 *De Civitate Dei*, CCSL 47 (1955).
2 Ed. R. G. Bury (LCL, 1961).
3 Stanley F. Bower, *Education in Ancient Rome; From the Elder Cato to the Younger Pliny* (London, 1977), pp. 155, 158.
4 Ed. F. Marx (Leipzig, 1964).
5 Ed. H. M. Hubbell (LCL, 1976).
6 Ed. L. Radermacher (Leipzig, 1965).
7 Bower, *Education in Ancient Rome*, p. 253.

Bibliography

G. Bonner, *Augustine of Hippo, Life and Controversies* (London, 1963).

J. Burnaby, *Amor Dei* (London, 1938).

Henry Chadwick, *Augustine* (Oxford, 1986).

Mary T. Clark, *Augustine* (London, 1994).

E. R. Dodds, *Pagan and Christian in an Age of Anxiety* (Oxford, 1965).

G. R. Evans, *Augustine on Evil* (Cambridge, 1983).

A. Fitzgerald, ed., *Augustine through the Ages: An Encyclopaedia* (Grand Rapids, MI, 1999).

Robert J. Forman, *Augustine and the Making of a Christian Literature* (Lewiston, NY, 1996).

Carol Harrison, *Beauty and Revelation in the Thought of St. Augustine* (Oxford, 1992).

—— *Augustine, Christian Truth and Fractured Humanity* (Oxford, 2000).

Edward B. King and Jacqueline T. Schaefer, eds., *Saint Augustine and his Influence on the Middle Ages* (Sewanee, TN, 1988).

Christopher Kirwan, *Augustine* (London, 1989, repr. 1999).

George Lawless, *Augustine of Hippo and his Monastic Rule* (Oxford, 1987).

Robert Markus, *Saeculum: History and Society in the Theology of St. Augustine* (Cambridge, 1970, repr. 1988).

—— *Sacred and Secular: Studies on Augustine and Latin Christianity* (Aldershot, 1994).

A. Momigliani, ed., *The Conflict between Paganism and Christianity in the Fourth Century* (London, 1963).

Eutyches, Nestorius, and Chalcedon

G. R. Evans

"The whole world groaned and was amazed to find that it was Arian," wrote Jerome.[1] When Rome fell there were tribes of Arian persuasion, mainly Teutonic, who came down on the lands of the Western Empire and occupied them, compromising the Christian position politically if not theologically speaking for many generations. The Nicene Creed, claiming as it did to be the work of an ecumenical council, was not immediately automatically "received" in the West. Hilary, bishop of Poitiers, did not get to know about the council of Nicaea of 325 and the decisions it had taken in creating its creed until the middle of the century, as he explains in the book he wrote "on the faith of the East," and addressed to the bishops of Germany and the West. He reminds them of his consistent practise of trying to make them aware of what their episcopal brothers in the East were agreeing.[2] It was a quarter of a century or more before the Nicene Creed had the impact or acceptability in the West that it had in the Greek East.[3]

The issues being debated in the East and in Greek looked different in the West and in Latin, partly because of the difference of the two languages in their respective capacity to convey nuances which, as we shall see, could lead to condemnation, excommunication, deposition. Hilary of Poitiers could speak relatively straightforwardly of the way the two natures (*naturae*) of Christ were united in a single Person (*persona*).

The figure most often credited with pulling the Nicene rabbit out of the hat in · the West and putting the Arians there to flight is Ambrose of Milan.[4] There remained work for him to do in the West, for the council of Aquileia of 381 did not do for the Latin world what the council of Constantinople achieved for the East in the same year, and, to all intents and purposes, put an end to the Arian controversy. North Italy had for some time been the geographical focus of an anti-Arian literature whose authors were prompted to write by the fact that the presence of Arians made it a pressing concern to rebut them. Zeno bishop of Verona, Filastrius of Brescia, Eusebius of Vercelli are prominent examples. Marius Victorinus should be added to their number.[5] A considerable number of Latin "Arian" texts by less celebrated authors was also in existence in the fourth century, of which it has been suggested that some perhaps survived to the present day because the librarian in question failed to perceive their heretical bent.[6] The *Opus imperfectum in Mattheum*,[7] probably written by a Latin-speaking Arian priest in the mid-fifth century, was influential during the Middle Ages, despite its (from the Nicene point of view) questionable theology.[8] Indeed, the line of texts indicating continuing controversy goes on well into the fifth century,[9] so Ambrose's achievement should not be overstated. Such disputes can linger, infecting the consciousness of an age, dividing Christendom.

In 428 Nestorius was enthroned as patriarch of Constantinople. He was much influenced by Theodore of Mopsuestia. He seems to have been dangerously tactless in giving a ruling on the question of whether the Blessed Virgin could properly be described as "God-bearer." Without the utmost precision and refinement of language, it was easy to be seen to hint at heresy – the Arian view that the Son was a mere creature or the Apollinarian argument that he was God but not really man. Cyril of Alexandria, fellow patriarch and increasingly a rival to Nestorius, seized his opportunity to define a new "Nestorian" heresy, claiming that Nestorius was saying that Christ was not one Person in two natures, but two Persons. It is by no means clear that Nestorius himself would have "owned" this heresy, but it has become inseparable from his name. It seems that he did hold quite strongly that the two natures must have remained distinct in the incarnate Christ, so as to preserve the divine from any taint of mutability, while the human was truly able to grow and develop. "Nature," in the intellectual world of this time, connoted the essence of a thing, its substance, its very being. Cyril and those of the "Alexandrian" school also spoke in terms of the preservation of the distinction of the divinity and the humanity in the incarnate Christ, but Cyril thought of this as a "hypostatic" union, which could be compared to the union of soul and body. But soul and body are not complete without one another, whereas the Word and the human nature he "took" in becoming man are complete natures. So this analogy was unacceptable to Nestorius and the "Antiochene" school of thought because it seemed to sacrifice the voluntary character of the union. The debate between these two rival accounts brought new subtleties into the debate of the Arian period and after. Most importantly, perhaps, Nestorius crystallized the idea that the *Prosopon* or Person of Christ was not identical with the Word. The incarnate Word was something other than the Word.

Cyril of Alexandria, too, was exploring the implications of this line of thought. His own view was that before the Incarnation was the Word, while after the Incarnation the Word was "in the body" or "embodied." This "human body" or "flesh" was human nature, which included the rational soul. So the incarnate Christ lived on earth as truly man.

The two patriarchs clashed energetically. Cyril, as Patriarch of Alexandria, made Nestorius' "heresy" the subject of his pastoral letter for Easter 429 (*Hom.* 17). There was correspondence between Cyril and Nestorius. Cyril, an astute politician, set about isolating Nestorius. He wrote *De recta fide*[10] for the emperor Theodosius II (408–50) and his family, with the intention of turning them against Nestorius. He sent the Pope, Celestine, a package of extracts from Nestorius and from Christian writings which favoured Cyril's view. Nestorius also wrote to the Pope. By 430 Celestine had held a synod in Rome and decided against Nestorius, whose rejection of the title *Theotokos* for the Virgin was, he said, a "denial of the birth of God."

Celestine sent a letter to Nestorius in which he warned him that unless he began to teach about Christianity as "Rome, Alexandria and the whole Catholic Church" does and "as the Church of Constantinople has done until now" and condemned what he had been teaching publicly and in writing, within ten days Nestorius would be excommunicated.[11]

Cyril was asked to carry out the sentence, which he did by holding a synod at Alexandria and then sending Nestorius a letter containing 12 anathemas to which he was to subscribe. The first required him to assert that Mary is *Theotokos*, the second that the Word was united to the flesh in the incarnate Christ "hypostatically."

But Cyril went too far. His anathemas were drafted in extreme language and alienated the moderate in his own "party." Nestorius appealed to the emperor and in November 430 Theodosius called a general council to meet at Ephesus in June 431. There a series of rival meetings of parties struggled to establish itself as "the council." The "Antiochene" bishops were late in arriving, so Cyril presided over a meeting of sixty or so bishops of his own persuasion in the absence of Nestorius, who refused to come, although he himself had already reached Ephesus. John of Antioch and the other "Antiochene" bishops arrived a few days later and held their own rival "council," repudiating the 12 anathemas and deposing Cyril. The papal legates did not arrive until July. They "endorsed" Cyril's meeting as the "true" council. Nestorius ended his days in exile and Cyril's second letter to Nestorius acquired the status of an authoritative Christological document, though the anathemas which went with it did not.

The death of Pope Celestine in 432 and the succession of Sixtus III made a degree of peacemaking possible. The condemnation of Nestorius and the list of anathemas were stumbling blocks, but Cyril was brought to explain himself in terms acceptable to the Antiochenes and a letter was sent to Cyril by John of Antioch containing a "creed of union" (433). Cyril accepted it, although on a superficial reading it contained much that he was opposing in the teaching of Nestorius. Nevertheless, he embraced it in the letter *Laetuntur coeli* (Cyril, Letter 39). He had won the political victory.

But others were less content with the theological position now reached and, after the death of Cyril in 444, partisan positions began to reemerge with some fierceness. Attacks were made on the teaching of the Antiochene leader Theodoret. Dioscorus succeeded Cyril and set about reasserting the doctrine of a single Nature in the incarnate Christ. Eutyches now entered the picture. He had influence at court and that made him a natural focus for the discontent over the creed of union of 433. At the synod of Constantinople in 448, Eusebius of Dorylaeum denounced him as a heretic.

This was a development not without its importance. The Patriarch proposed a profession of faith containing the formula "of two natures" (*ek duo physeon*) in one *hupostasis* and one *prosopon*. Eutyches at first refused to present himself at this synod, and when he eventually did so, he was sentenced and deposed. He has gone down in history as a Monophysite of an extreme kind, even a Docetist, maintaining that the humanity of Christ was virtually swallowed up in his divinity, though it is far from easy to establish what he actually thought. He made an attempt to return to the fold, by writing to the Pope. But Pope Leo had also heard from the patriarch of

Constantinople and he was not receptive to Eutyches' overture. Eutyches had more success by appealing to Dioscurus and he was rehabilitated in a synod at Ephesus in 449, known as the "robber" council.

Leo sent the patriarch of Constantinople a *Tome* (Letter 28), in which he set out his concerns about the "*scandalum contra integritatem fidei.*" The *Tome* says that the person of Christ was identical with the Word: "He who in the form of God created man is the same as he who became man in the form of a servant." "Preserving the property of each nature and substance and coming together into one Person, majesty took humility, strength weakness and eternity mortality."[12] In Christ, the Word does what is appropriate to the Word and the flesh does what is appropriate to the flesh, the two acting in harmony. These things are able to be said less subtly and therefore less controversially in Latin, and Leo's clear and relatively simple exposition provided the foundation for the solution reached at the Council of Chalcedon. It was agreed there that "Peter [had] spoken through Leo."

The last episode of this story for our purposes was the settlement achieved at the council of Chalcedon. This council was not called at the instigation of Pope Leo but at the wish of the emperor. Leo's preference would have been for bishops simply to sign his Letter to Flavian.[13] He thought that quietly bringing individuals back into the fold was less dangerous than risking open schism by holding a council. Some five or six hundred bishops were present; the record of the numbers is not consistent. The council agreed a "definition of the faith" which accorded with Leo's Tome and mentions his letter. Chalcedon reaffirmed the Creed of Nicaea and the version of the council of Constantinople of 381; it accepted the letter of Cyril of Alexandria to Nestorius.[14] To these it "added, against false believers and for the establishment of orthodox doctrine," Leo's letter to Flavian "to put down Eutyches' evil-mindedness, because it is in agreement with great Peter's confession."

The council fathers set out their position in their own words by dismissing the various false emphases which had been current in the disputes and defined the Son as

> perfect in divinity and perfect in humanity, the same truly God and truly man, of a rational soul and a body; consubstantial with the Father as regards his divinity, and the same consubstantial with us as regards his humanity; like us in all respects except for sin; begotten before the ages from the Father as regards his divinity, and in the last days the same for us and for our salvation from Mary, the virgin God-bearer, as regards his humanity; one and the same Christ, Son, Lord, only-begotten, acknowledged in two natures which undergo no confusion, no change, no division, no separation; at no point was the difference between the natures taken away through the union, but rather the property of both natures is preserved and comes together into a single person and a single subsistent being; he is not parted or divided into two persons, but is one and the same only-begotten Son, God, Word, Lord Jesus Christ.[15]

Pope Leo's address to the people in the Basilica of St. Anastasius in December 457[16] sought to consolidate the position. This was, for the West and for much of the East, the end of the matter, but it left outside the agreement those later known as the Oriental Orthodox or Non-Chalcedonian Churches. They would not accept the doctrine of the two natures of Christ but taught that he was of a single divine

Nature. This was a revival of Eutyches' teaching, and it bred a number of variants, some, such as that of Severus of Antioch, probably not far from the teaching of Chalcedon. The questions were still alive when Boethius wrote his *Treatise against Eutyches and Nestorius*[17] in about 512, in response to the letter the Oriental bishops had written to Pope Symmachus, and which had been read aloud in Boethius' presence, causing him to think out for himself the merits of the various positions. But Boethius takes us into *The Medieval Theologians*.

Notes

1 *Dialogue against the Luciferians*, 19, PL 23.172.
2 Hilary of Poitiers, *Liber de Synodis*, 91, PL 10.545.
3 Williams, *Ambrose of Milan*, p. 7.
4 See chapter 19.
5 Marius Victorinus, *Commentarii in epistulas Pauli*, ed. A. Locher (Teubner, 1972), p. 1. See in general P. Hadot, *Marius Victorinus*, Études augustiniennes (Paris, 1971).
6 *Scripta Arriana Latina*, 1, ed. R. Gryson, CCSL 87 (Turnhout, 1982), p. vii.
7 Ed. J. van Banning, CCSL 87B (1988).
8 *Opus imperfectum in Mattheum*, ed. J. van Banning, CCSL 87B (Turnhout, 1988).
9 Williams, *Ambrose of Milan*, p. 9, n. 32.
10 PG, 68–77.
11 Letter 13.11, PL 50.483.
12 Ep. 28.3, printed in *Decrees of the Ecumenical Councils*, ed. Tanner, vol. I, pp. *77–*84.
13 Leo the Great, *Letters*, ed. E. Schwartz, Acta Conciliorum Oecumenicorum 2.4 (1932).
14 The letter to John of Antioch, printed in *Decrees of the Ecumenical Councils*, ed. Tanner, pp. 70–4.
15 *Decrees of the Ecumenical Councils*, ed. Tanner, p. *86.
16 Leo the Great, *Tractatus* 96.
17 Boethius, *Theological Tractates*, pp. 72–129.

Bibliography

Michael R Barnes, and Daniel H. Williams, *Arianism after Arius: Essays on the Development of Fourth Century Trinitatian Conflicts* (Edinburgh, 1993).
Robert C. Gregg, *Early Arianism: A View of Salvation* (London, 1981).
G. L. Prestige, "The Greek Translation of the Tome of St. Leo," *Journal of Theological Studies*, 31 (1929–30), p. 183.
Daniel H. Williams, *Ambrose of Milan and the End of the Niceno-Arian Conflicts* (Oxford, 1995).
Rowan Williams, *Arius: Heresy and Tradition* (London, 1987, 2nd edn. 2001).

Conclusion: The End of an Era?

G. R. Evans

Augustine of Hippo formed the starting point for the volume in this series on *The Medieval Theologians*, yet he could equally well have formed the concluding point for the present volume, at least for the patristic period in the West. But Boethius, in the sixth century, or Gregory the Great, whose life ran on into the seventh, would be candidates too. It would be equally difficult to draw a hard and fast line in the eastern half of the old Roman Empire, among the Greek-speaking or the Syriac "early Christian theologians." It was not until long afterwards that a "patristic" period was designated, and it became appropriate even to attempt to identify the "end" of the era of writers with a special claim to have set out the parameters of Christian theology for the first time.

In any case, the line would not be drawn at the same chronological point in the West and the East, for the "end of antiquity" did not proceed even-handedly in East and West, either politically or in terms of developments in Christian thought. One important reason for this, in addition to the political circumstances which affected the two halves of the Empire differently, was the language divide. In the East the Greek language was spoken everywhere (though at many levels of sophistication and with many local dialectical variations); and cities in which there was an advanced cultural life were numerous. Schools of philosophy were to be found not only in Athens but in Alexandria and Beirut.

The effect of the growing language division needs to be taken seriously, for it marks a cultural division which becomes increasingly evident with the end of this volume. It is possible to begin to see something of the difference this began to make by contrasting the intellectual life of Jerome and Ambrose with that of Augustine. Ambrose was comfortably able to include in his sermons on Genesis reference to Platonist and other Greek ideas in the Cappadocian Fathers. Jerome was a competent linguist, with excellent Greek and a knowledge of Hebrew, which he was taught, he says, by a member of the rabbinical school of Palestinian Jews. That interest, unusual among his contemporaries, is reflected in his writing on the subject of the Hebrew names in the Old Testament (388). In this period, he also translated Eusebius on the sites and names of Hebrew places and wrote the *Questions on Genesis*.

Rufinus, a priest from northern Italy (c.345–410), spent 20 years of his maturity in the East, in Alexandria and Jerusalem. He became important as a translator from the Greek for the increasing number in the West who could not read Greek writings in the original language. His rendering of Origen's *De principiis* became controversial because he sought to improve the orthodoxy of the original, and Jerome, who thought it proper to take fewer liberties as a translator, took issue with him. Eusebius' *Ecclesiastical History* he translated in the same free spirit, making some additions to it. He also provided Latin versions of some of the writings of the Cappadocian Fathers, notably Basil's monastic *Regula*.[1]

The gradual loss of the general command of Greek by educated people in the West led to a loss of ready access to the philosophical literature of the Greeks. That was already noticeable in Augustine, who felt his debt to the circles of Marius Victorinus if he was to understand Platonism in any depth. He describes in the *Confessions* (VIII.ii.3) how he has read "certain books of the Platonists" which Victorinus, "once an orator in Rome," had translated. Jerome had met Victorinus at that time, and had indeed been his pupil, and he referred to him in his prologue to Galatians as someone who had now taken to scriptural commentary.[2] This transmitter of Platonism became a theological controversialist, author of books against the Arians[3] as well as interpretations of the Bible. The marks of Victorinus' earlier philosophical training remained in his habits of thought when he was writing on Christian texts. For example, in the opening sentences of his own commentary on Galatians he remarks on the "bodily" or materialistic understanding (*corporalis intellectus*) with which the Galatians observed the sabbath and the practice of circumcision.[4]

The differences of language went far beyond Greek and Latin. It is possible to trace a most subtle game of linguistic putting-down by the use of choice terms with pejorative shadings.[5] It was not *merely* a question of separateness of language, but of increasing divergence of culture. The interests of the Greek-speakers continued to be close to those of the Middle and Late Platonists; they were by preference mystics. The interests of the Latin-speakers were partly determined by their increasing linguistic separation, which denied them ready access to these continuing concerns of the East and to the literature they were generating. Two faith communities which do not read one another's writings and cannot talk to one another with any ease are likely to move apart at least in their emphases and concerns and in the controversies in which they are engaged. It is remarkable how close they remained in the essentials.

So much we can now say with some confidence, since we can see from a distance of more than a millennium how things went on after the end of Empire. One Byzantine historian was prepared to speak of the end as something which had already happened, and in which Christianity did not figure well, for he blames the loss of Empire partly on the abandonment of the old God, not because that was wrong in itself, but because it constituted a change to the old ways, and the change to the old ways had been a recipe for disaster. He wrote at some time in the fourth century, certainly not later than the fall of Rome in 410, and his name was Zozimus. He compares himself with the Roman historian Polybius who had depicted the rapidly successful creation of the Roman Empire. By contrast, Zozimus is, he says, going to describe how in an equally short time, and through their own folly, the Romans lost it again.[6]

As the Empire divided into two language groups and became, in a political sense, bipolar, the trajectories of the development of Christian theology in each half of the Empire became, not entirely distinct, certainly not opposed – there continued to be one Nicene faith – but still to some degree separate in spirit and flavour. The Latins seem to have been more panic-stricken than the Greeks by this loss of communication and its implications. In the early sixth century, Boethius set about his uncompleted task of translating the whole of Aristotle and Plato in order to ensure that the Latin world which could no longer read for itself in Greek would have access to these foundation texts. Cassiodorus, in the same generation, put together a digest of knowledge in the form of an encyclopedia, and a century later (borrowing heavily from his work), Isidore of Seville did the same. The Spanish monk Valerio left an account of his own life and his endeavors to ensure that peasant children were properly taught about their faith.[7] But this is taking us into the world of *The Medieval Theologians*, whither the reader may follow these figures.

Notes

1 *Basilii regula a Rufino Latine versa*, CSEL, 86.
2 PL 26.308.
3 Marius Victorinus, *Opera theologica*, ed. A. Locher (Teubner, 1976).
4 Ibid., *Commentarii in epistulas Pauli*, ed. A. Locher (Teubner, 1972), p. 1. See in general P. Hadot, *Marius Victorinus*, Études augustiniennes (Paris, 1971).
5 Timothy D. Barnes, "Christian Language and Anti-Christian Polemic," in *Ammianus Marcel-* *linus and the Representation of Historical Reality* (Ithaca and London, 1998), pp. 79–94.
6 Zozimus, *Historia nova. The Decline of Rome*, 1.57.1, ed. J. J. Buchanan and H. T. Davis (San Antonio, 1967) and F. Paschaud (Paris, 1971).
7 C. M. Aherne, *Valerio of Bierzo, an Ascetic of the Late Visigothic Period* (Washington, 1949).

Consolidated List of Selected Sources and Translations

Note: References are included here for a number of items referred to by contributors in the individual chapters. Texts or commentaries in English are listed first, followed by those in other languages.

Collected Authors and Selections

Alexandrian Christianity, selected translations of Clement and Origen with introduction and notes by J. E. L. Oulton and H. Chadwick. (Library of Christian Classics 2.) London, 1954.

The Apostolic Fathers, trans. K. Lake. 2 vols. (Loeb Classical Library.) London and Cambridge, MA, 1913.

The Apostolic Fathers, trans. J. B. Lightfoot. 2 vols. London, 1890.

Decrees of the Ecumenical Councils, ed. N. P. Tanner. Washington, DC, 1990.

Early Christian Fathers, newly translated, ed. C. C. Richardson. (Library of Christian Classics 1.) London, 1953.

Gnosis. A Selection of Gnostic Texts, I. Patristic Evidence, ed. W. Foerster, trans. R. McL. Wilson. Oxford, 1972.

The Nag Hammadi Library in English, translated by members of the Coptic Gnostic Library Project, directed by J. M. Robinson. Leiden, 1977.

A New Eusebius. Documents Illustrating the History of the Church to AD337, ed. J. Stevenson, revised with additional documents by W. H. C. Frend. London, 1987.

Acta et symbola conciliorum quae saeculo quarto habita sunt. (Textus minores XIX.) Leiden, 1954.

Die Apostolischen Väter, ed. J. H. Fischer. Darmstadt, 1992.

Die Apostolischen Väter. Griechisch-deutsche Parallelausgabe, trans. and ed. A. Lindemann and H. Paulsen. Tübingen, 1992.

Athanasius (c.296–373)

The Letters of Saint Athanasius Concerning the Holy Spirit, trans. C. R. B. Shaplan. London, 1951.

St Athanasius: Select Works and Letters, ed. A. Robertson. (Nicene and Post-Nicene Fathers of the Christian Church IV.) London and Oxford, 1891; reprint, Grand Rapids, MI, 1978.

Williams, R., *Arius: Heresy and Tradition*, 2nd edn. London, 2001 (includes translations of most of the primary texts of the controversy).

Augustine of Hippo (354–430)

The City of God, trans. Henry Bettenson. (Penguin Classic.) London, 1984, reprint 2003.

Confessions, trans. H. Chadwick. Oxford, 1992.

The Confessions and Letters of Augustine, with a Sketch of his Life and Work, ed. P. Schaff. (Select Library of the Nicene and Post-Nicene Fathers of the Christian Church.) Peabody, MA, 1994.

On Christian Doctrine. (Nicene and Post-Nicene Fathers of the Christian Church, 1st ser., II.) Reprint, Grand Rapids, MI, 1973.

The Works of Aurelius Augustine, Bishop of Hippo. A New Translation, ed. M. Dods. Edinburgh, 1873.

The texts of Augustine's writings are edited in the series Corpus Scriptorum Ecclesiasticorum Latinorum and Corpus Christianorum Series Latina.

Basil the Great (c.330–379)

The Ascetic Works of Saint Basil, trans. W. K. L. Clarke. London, 1925.

On the Holy Spirit, On the Six Days of Creation and Letters, trans. B. Jackson. (Nicene and Post-Nicene Fathers of the Christian Church, 2nd ser., VIII.) London, 1895.

St. Basil: The Letters and Address to Young Men on Reading Greek Literature, trans. R. J. Deferrari and M. R. P. McGuire. 4 vols. (Loeb Classical Library.) London, 1926–34; reprint, 1986.

Several treatises of Basil the Great are translated into French in the series Sources chrétiennes (Paris, 1976–), including: *Against Eunomius*, 299 and 305; *On the Six Days of Creation*, 26 bis; *On Baptism*, 357; *On the Holy Spirit*, 17 bis.

Boethius (c.480–524)

Theological Tractates, ed. H. F. Stewart, E. K. Rand and S. J. Tester. (Loeb Classical Library.) London, 1973, pp. 72–129. (Includes *The Consolation of Philosophy.*)

Clement of Alexandria (c.150–c.215)

Chadwick, H., *Alexandrian Christianity*. London, 1954.

Works, trans. W. Wilson. 2 vols. Edinburgh, 1882–4.

Clemens Alexandrinus, ed. O. Stählin. 4 vols. (Die griechischen christlichen Schriftsteller der ersten drei Jahrhunderte 12, 15, 17, 52.) Leipzig, 1905–36. (Volume III, 1909, includes *Stromata VII und VIII.*)

Clément d'Alexandrie, *Le Pédagogue. Texte grec*, trans. Claude Mondésert, Chantal Matray, M. Caster and Henri-Irénée Marrou. 3 vols. (Sources chrétiennes 70, 108, 158.) Paris, 1965–70.

Clement of Rome (fl. c.96)

The Apostolic Fathers, trans. J. B. Lightfoot. 2 vols. London, 1890.

Cyprian of Carthage (d. 258)

De Lapsis and *De Ecclesiae Catholicae Unitate*, text and trans. Maurice Bévenot. (Oxford Early Christian Texts.) Oxford, 1971.

The Letters of St. Cyprian of Carthage, translated and annotated by G. W. Clarke. 4 vols. (Ancient Christian Writers 43, 44, 46, 47.) New York and Mahwah, NJ, 1984–9.

Sancti Cypriani Episcopi opera III, 1–2. Sancti Cypriani Episcopi epistularium, ed. G. R. Diercks. (Corpus Christianorum Series Latina 3B, 3C, 3D) Turnhout, 1960–99.

Didachê

The Apostolic Fathers, trans. J. B. Lightfoot. 2 vols. London, 1890.

Pseudo-Dionysius (fifth century)

The Complete Works, trans. C. Luibheid. London, 1987.

Ephrem the Syrian (c.306–378)

Beck, E., *Des Heiligen Ephraem des Syrers Hymnen de Fide*. (Corpus Scriptorum Christianorum Orientalium 154.) Louvain, 1955.

Eusebius of Caesarea (c.260–c.340)

Gnosis. A Selection of Gnostic Texts. I. Patristic Evidence, ed. W. Foerster, trans. R. McL. Wilson. Oxford, 1972.

The History of the Church, trans. G. A. Williamson, revised and edited with a new introduction by A. Louth. London, 1989.

A New Eusebius. Documents Illustrating the History of the Church to AD337, ed. James Stevenson, revised with additional documents by W. H. C. Frend. London, 1987.

des Places, E., *La Préparation évangélique: Eusèbe de Césarée*. (Sources chrétiennes 266.) Paris, 1980.

Eusebius Werke II. Die Kirchengeschichte, ed. E. Schwartz. (Die griechischen christlichen Schriftsteller der ersten drei Jahrhunderte 9, 1.). Leipzig, 1903.

Gregory of Nazianzus (329–89)

Autobiographical Poems, trans. C. White. (Cambridge Medieval Classics 6.) Cambridge, 1966.

Faith Gives Fullness to Reasoning. The Five Theological Orations of Gregory Nazianzen, trans. F. W. Norris. Leiden, 1991.

Funeral Orations by St. Gregory Nazianzen and St. Ambrose, trans. L. P. McAuley et al. (Fathers of the Church 22.) Washington, DC, 1968.

Gregory's *Orations* are translated into French in Sources chrétiennes 247, 250, 270, 284, 309, 318, 358, 384 and 405.

Gregory's theological letters and his poem *On the Suffering of Christ* are translated into French in Sources chrétiennes 208 and 384.

Gregory of Nyssa (c.330–c.395)

Against Eunomius, On the Holy Spirit against Macedonius, To Eustathius on the Holy Trinity, To Ablabius that there are not Three Gods, To Simplicius on Faith, On Virginity,

On Infants' Early Deaths, On Pilgrimages, On the Making of Man, On the Soul and the Resurrection, The Catechetical Oration, On Meletius, On the Baptism of Christ, Letters, trans. W. Moore, M. Day, H. A. Wilson, and H. C. Ogle. (Nicene and Post-Nicene Fathers, 2nd ser., V.) Edinburgh, reprint 1994.

The Easter Sermons of Gregory of Nyssa: Translation and Commentary. Proceedings of the 4th International Colloquium on Gregory of Nyssa, ed. A. Spira and C. Klock, trans. S. G. Hall. Cambridge, MA, 1981.

Gregory of Nyssa's Treatise on the Inscriptions of the Psalms, trans. R. E. Heine. Oxford, 1995.

The Life of Moses, trans. A. J. Malherbe and E. Ferguson. (Classics of Western Spirituality.) New York and Toronto, 1978.

St. Gregory of Nyssa: Ascetical Works (including *On Virginity* and *The Life of Macrina*), trans. V. Woods Callahan. (Fathers of the Church 58.) Washington, DC, 1967.

Saint Gregory of Nyssa: Commentary on the Song of Songs, trans. C. McCambley. Brookline, MA, 1987.

St. Gregory of Nyssa, The Lord's Prayer, The Beatitudes, trans. H. Graef. (Ancient Christian Writers 18.) Westminster, MD, and London, 1954.

Gregory's *Letters* and *Homilies on Ecclesiasticus* are translated into French in the series Sources chrétiennes 363 and 416.

Hermas (2nd century)

The Shepherd, in *The Apostolic Fathers*, trans. J. B. Lightfoot. 2 vols. London, 1890.

Ps.-Hermes Trismegistos and the Hermetica

Corpus hermeticum, ed. A. D. Nock and A.-J. Festugière. 4 vols. Paris, 1945.

Hermes Trismegistos, Astrologica et Divinatoria, ed. G. Bos, C. Burnett, T. Charmasson, P. Kunitzsch, F. Lelli, and P. Lucentinit. (Corpus Christianorum Continuatio Mediaevalis 144C.) Turnhout, 2001.

Hermes Trismegistos, De Triginta Sex Decanis, ed. S. Feraboli. (Corpus Christianorum Continuatio Mediaevalis 144.) Turnhout, 1994.

Hermetica, ed. and trans. W. Scott. Oxford, 1924.

Hermetica, trans. B. P. Copenhaver. Cambridge, 1991.

Liber XXIV Philosophorum, ed. F. Hudry. (Corpus Christianorum Continuatio Mediaevalis 143A.) Turnhout, 1997.

Hippolytus of Rome (c.170–c.236)

Contra Noetum, intro., ed., and trans. R. Butterworth. (Heythrop Monographs.) London, 1977.

Refutatio omnium haeresium, ed. M. Marcovich. (Patristische Texte und Studien 25.) Berlin and New York, 1986.

Irenaeus of Lyons (c.130–c.200)

Against Heresies, trans. A. Roberts and W. H. Rambaut. 2 vols. (Ante-Nicene Christian Library 5, 9.) Edinburgh, 1883–4.

The Demonstration of the Apostolic Preaching, trans. J. A. Robinson. London, 1920.

The Nag Hammadi Library in English, translated by members of the Coptic Gnostic Library Project, directed by J. M. Robinson. Leiden, 1977.

On the Apostolic Preaching, trans. John Behr. New York, 1997.

St. Irenaeus, Proof of the Apostolic Preaching, trans. J. P. Smith. New York, 1952.

Irénée de Lyon, Contre les hérésies, ed. A. Rousseau and L. Doutreleau. 6 vols. (Sources chrétiennes 152–3, 210–11, 263–4.) Paris, 1969–82.

Jerome (Eusebius Hieronymus) (c.342–420)

Hebrew Questions on Genesis, trans. C. T. R. Hayward. Oxford, 1995.

Selected Letters, ed. F. A. Wright. London, 1963.

A number of modern editions of Jerome's works can be found in Latin in Corpus Scriptorum Series Latina

Justin Martyr (c.100–c.165)

The Apologies of Justin Martyr, trans. A. W. F. Blunt. Cambridge, 1911.

The Dialogue with Trypho, ed. A. L. Williams. London, 1930.

Justin and Athenagoras, trans. M. Dods, G. Reith and B. P. Pratten. (Ante-Nicene Christian Library.) Edinburgh, 1879.

St. Justin Martyr, the First and Second Apologies ACW, ed. L. W. Barnard. New York, 1997.

Die ältesten Apologeten, ed. E. J. Goodspeed. Göttingen, 1914.

Apologie pour les chrétiens, ed. and trans. C. Munier. Fribourg, 1995.

Opera, ed. J. C. T. Otto. Jena, 1876.

Justinian (483–565)

Digest, trans. C. H. Munro. 2 vols. Cambridge, 1904–9.

Institutes, trans. J. B. Moyle. 2 vols. Oxford, 1883.

Justinian, *Corpus Iuris Civilis*, ed. R. Schoell and G. Kroll. Dublin and Zurich, 1972.

Leo the Great (c.390–461)

Tractatus 96, Contra Haeresim Eutychis, ed. A. Chavasse. (Corpus Christianorum Series Latina 138.) Turnhout, 1973.

Maximus the Confessor (c.580–662)

Nichols, A., *Byzantine Gospel: Maximus the Confessor in Modern Scholarship*. Edinburgh, 1993.

Selected Writings, trans. G. Berthold. New York, 1985.

Thunberg, L., *Microcosm and Mediator: The Theological Anthropology of Maximus the Confessor*. Chicago, 1995.

Origen (c.185–c.254)

Gospel Commentaries, in *The ante-Nicene Christian Library, additional volume . . . containing selections from the commentaries of Origen*, ed. Allen Menzies. Edinburgh, 1896. Reprinted in *The Ante-Nicene Fathers*, vol. 10. Grand Rapids, MI, 1974.

Origen: An Exhortation to Martyrdom, Prayer and Selected Works, trans. R. Greer. (Classics of Western Spirituality.) New York, 1979.

Origen: Contra Celsum, trans. E. T. H. Chadwick, with introduction and notes. Cambridge, 1953; new edn. 1965.

Origen on First Principles, trans. G. W. Butterworth. London, 1936.

Philokalia, trans. J. A. Robinson. Cambridge, 1893.

Origène Contre Celse. Introduction, ed. and trans. M. Borret. II (books III–IV), III (V–VI). (Sources chrétiennes 136, 147.) Paris, 1968.

Origenes Werke VII. Homilien zum Hexateuch in Rufinus zweiter Teil. Die Homilien zu Numeri, Josua und Judices, ed. and trans. W. A. Baehrens. (Die griechischen christlichen Schriftsteller der ersten drei Jahrhunderte 30.) Leipzig, 1921.

Origenes Werke X–XI, Origenes Matthäuserklärung, ed. E. Klostermann and E. Benz. (Die griechischen christlichen Schriftsteller der ersten drei Jahrhunderte.) I. *Die griechisch erhaltenen Tomoi.* Leipzig, 1935; II, *Die lateinische Übersetzung der Commentariorum Series,* ed. Ursula Treu, 2nd edn. Berlin, 1976.

Orosius

Contra Paganos, ed. M. Arnaud-Lindet. Paris, 1990.

Historiarum adversum paganos, ed. C. Zangemeister (Corpus Scriptorum Ecclesiasticorum Latinorum 5.) Vienna, 1882.

Papias of Hierapolis (c.60–130)

The Apostolic Fathers, trans. J. B. Lightfoot. 2 vols. London, 1890.

Philo of Alexandria (c.20BC–AD50)

The Contemplative Life, The Giants and Selections, trans. D. Winston. (Classics of Western Spirituality.) New York and Toronto, 1981.

Philo, ed. and trans. F. H. Colson, G. H. Whitaker and R. Marcus. 12 vols. (Loeb Classical Library.) London and Cambridge, MA, 1929–62.

The Works of Philo Complete and Unabridged, trans. C. D. Yonge, with a foreword by D. M. Scholer. Peabody, MA, 1993. (This 1855 translation is based on a defective text.)

Polycarp (c.69–c.155)

The Apostolic Fathers, trans. J. B. Lightfoot. 2 vols. London, 1890.

Tertullian (c.160–c.220)

Against Marcion, trans. E. Evans. 2 vols. Oxford, 1972.

Against Praxeas, ed. and trans. E. Evans. London, 1948.

Homily on Baptism, ed. and trans. E. Evans. London, 1964.

Tract on Prayer, ed. and trans. E. Evans. London, 1953.

Treatise on the Incarnation, ed. and trans. E. Evans. London, 1956.

Treatise on the Resurrection, ed. and trans. E. Evans. London, 1960.

Works, trans. P. Holmes and S. Thelwall. 4 vols. (Ante-Nicene Christian Library 7, 11, 15, 18.) Edinburgh, 1870–84.

Quinti Septimi Florentis Tertulliani opera I–II. (Corpus Christianorum Series Latina I, II.) Turnhout, 1954.

Theodosian Code (435–439)

The Theodosian Code and Novels, and the Sirmondian Constitutions, trans. Clyde Pharr, T. S. Davidson and M. B. Pharr. (Corpus of Roman Law 1.) Princeton, NJ, 1952; reprint, New York, 1969.

Theodosiani libri XVI cum Constitutionibus Sirmondianis et Leges Novellae ad Theodosianum pertinente, ed. T. Mommsen and P. M. Meyer. Berlin, 1954.

Theodotus (c.393–458)

Early Christian Fathers, newly translated, ed. C. C. Richardson et al. (Library of Christian Classics 1.) London, 1953.

Clément d'Alexandrie, Extraits de Théodote, Greek text, introduction, and notes by F. Sagnard. (Sources chrétiennes 23.) Paris, 1970.

Index of References

General Index

*Index compiled by Meg Davies
(Registered Indexer, Society of
Indexers)*

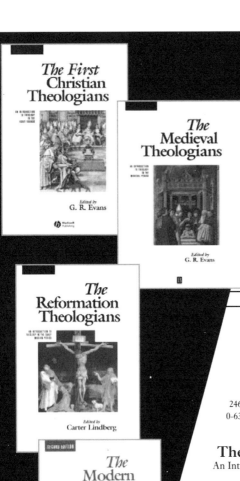

the Great theoloGians
series

Written by world-renowned scholars, The Great
Theologians series offers a comprehensive
introduction to a range of key theological periods
by focusing on the important writers of the time.

This comprehensive and lively series discusses the
major strands of each of the periods under discussion,
and explores the work of a range of influential figures.
Each volume introduces the theological context, thought,
and contributions of theologians of the time, offering
students and scholars an essential resource and insight into
the development of the history and theology of the Church.

The First Christian Theologians
An Introduction to Theology in the Early Church

edited by G. R. evans
University of Cambridge

246 x 171 mm ~ 352 pages ~ 2004
0-631-23188-9 ~ Hardcover   0-631-23187-0 ~ Paperback

The Medieval Theologians
An Introduction to Theology in the Medieval Period

edited by G. R. evans
University of Cambridge
246 x 171 mm ~ 408 pages ~ 2000
0-631-21202-7 ~ Hardcover   0-631-21203-5 ~ Paperback

The Pietist Theologians

edited by carter Lindberg
Boston University
246 x 171 mm ~ 320 pages ~ 2004
0-631-23517-5 ~ Hardcover   0-631-23520-5 ~ Paperback

The Reformation Theologians
An Introduction to Theology in the Early Modern Period

edited by carter Lindberg
Boston University
246 x 171 mm ~ 416 pages ~ 2001
0-631-21838-6 ~ Hardcover   0-631-21839-4 ~ Paperback

The Modern Theologians
An Introduction to Christian Theology in the Twentieth Century
Second Edition

edited by david f. ford
University of Cambridge
246 x 171 mm ~ 792 pages ~ 1996
0-631-19592-0 ~ Paperback

Blackwell
Publishing